The Inspiration
and
Authority of Scripture

The Inspiration and Authority of Scripture

by René Paché

Translated by
HELEN I. NEEDHAM

MOODY PRESS
CHICAGO

Moody Paperback Edition, 1980

All Scripture quotations in this book are from the
American Standard Version.

ISBN 0-8024-4091-6

Printed in the United States of America

CONTENTS

PREFACE

Let my lips utter praise;
For thou teachest me thy statutes.
Let my tongue sing of thy word.

PSALM 119:171-172

ONE OF THE MOST SIGNIFICANT of all themes to the Christian is that of
the inspiration and authority of the Bible. The truths concerning
God, Christ and salvation are surely of supreme importance. But
how can we get to know these truths if it is not by means of the Scriptures themselves? In this sense, one might say that the inspiration of
Scripture is the first dogma of all: If the Scriptures are truly of God,
clothed with His authority and put entirely within the reach of man,
all revealed religion has a solid foundation on which to stand. If, on
the other hand, inspiration is uncertain, partial, or varying according
to the experience and opinion of the reader or the preacher, everything totters.

More than at any time in the past, the question of inspiration has
today become the great theological battlefield. The very first attack
of the tempter was aimed at the Word: "Hath God said . . .?" (Gen.
3:1). Nevertheless, for a long period of time the church, along with
the synagogue, held the Bible to be what it claims to be: the Word
of God. During the past two centuries assaults against the Scriptures
have become increasingly violent. Without any doubt we are coming
up to the time of which Paul speaks: "Every scripture [is] inspired of
God. . . . Preach the word. . . . For the time will come when they will
not endure the sound doctrine; but, having itching ears, will heap to
themselves teachers after their own lusts; and will turn away their
ears from the truth, and turn aside unto fables" (II Tim. 3:16; 4:2-4).

It all comes back to the question of truth. Can we affirm with
Christ "Thy word is truth" (John 17:17), or are we rather going to
ask with Pilate: "What is truth?" (18:38).

7

The purpose of this book is, first of all, to examine what the Bible itself says about revelation and about its own inspiration; then, while enunciating the testimony given to it by Christ and by the church throughout the centuries, to sum up certain theories proposed regarding it; and, finally, to bring out the supernatural characteristics which attest the divine origin of Scripture and which establish its sovereign authority. Some repetitions occur because certain texts or arguments have a bearing on more than one part of the study. We also conceived of each chapter as more or less forming a whole, since this concept facilitates study, whether personal or group.

May the marvelous truth of the Scriptures so fully captivate the readers of this work that it can be said of them what Paul of old wrote of the Thessalonians: "We . . . thank God without ceasing, that, when ye received from us the word of the message, even the word of God, ye accepted it not as the word of men, but, as it is in truth, the word of God, which also worketh in you that believe" (I Thess. 2:13).

Part One

THE REVELATION

1

REVELATION FROM GOD

Why Is a Revelation Necessary?

MAN ON EARTH is placed in a paradoxical situation. Endowed with intelligence and logic, he seems intended to know the reason for his existence and the meaning of it, as well as the origin of the universe and the person of his Creator.

Actually, however, he finds himself surrounded by mysteries. Left to his own devices, he is incapable of answering the questions which press in on him so closely: From whence has he come? Why is he the victim of suffering and death? Will he ever find happiness and peace? What will occur after death: annihilation, judgment or eternal life? And above all towers this question: Does God exist? Then, if He does, why is He so far from us; and how can we manage to have an encounter with Him?

All religions and theologies testify to man's indefatigable efforts to ferret out the truth and to find out about God. It must, however, be acknowledged that the results of this search have been deceptive and even tragic. How many imperfect gods, created in the image of man, and how many complicated systems, often absurd, have come into being as a result, each in turn setting aside the others! Modern science itself, of which we are so proud, does not help us solve the enigma behind the universe; and certain astronauts who have gone into outer space have naïvely protested that they did not "find anybody" there.

In order for man to come to any true understanding, he must have a revelation from above, chiefly for the following two reasons.

1. *God is, by definition, inaccessible to the creature.* His omnipotence, eternality and absolute perfection are by their very essence inconceivable to our limited minds. Has He Himself not said, "As the heavens are higher than the earth, so are my ways higher than your ways, and my thoughts than your thoughts" (Isa. 55:9)? "The

blessed and only Potentate, the King of kings, and Lord of lords . . .
dwelling in light unapproachable; whom no man hath seen, nor can
see" (I Tim. 6:15-16). Thus the prophet cries out: "Thou art a God
that hidest thyself, O God of Israel, the Saviour" (Isa. 45:15). It is
evident, moreover, that for man to conceive of the Supreme Being in
His absolute nature, he would have to be God Himself!

But the Lord takes pleasure in revealing Himself. He made man
in His image, so as to have creatures who could respond to Him,
beings who could love and glorify Him. In Eden Adam enjoyed the
immediate presence of God and lived in happy fellowship with Him.
Since God's "delight was with the sons of men" (Prov. 8:31), this
marvelous state could have simply continued on into the realm of
eternal perfection.

2. *By the fall, man broke the contact with God.* After he was driven
out of paradise, his condition thenceforth was one of spiritual death
(Gen. 2:17; 3:24; Eph. 2:1, 5) and of blindness. He "receiveth not
the things of the Spirit of God: for they are foolishness unto him; and
he cannot know them, because they are spiritually judged" (I Cor.
2:14). "The god of this world hath blinded the minds of the unbelieving, that the light of the gospel of the glory of Christ . . . should
not dawn upon them" (II Cor. 4:4). The sinner, the unregenerate
man, cannot see the kingdom of God or enter into it. To enter the
kingdom, one must be born again, appropriating truths revealed
from above. Indeed, these are the "things which eye saw not, and
ear heard not, and which entered not into the heart of man, whatsoever things God prepared for them that love him. But unto us God
revealed them through the Spirit" (I Cor. 2:9-10).

CAN GOD REVEAL HIMSELF TO MAN, OR DOES HE EVEN WISH TO DO SO?

Does the possibility of a revelation from God exist? Some philosophers have denied such a possibility, saying, "How could the Infinite communicate with the finite, the Creator with the creature? Is
absolute truth expressible in the relative terms of human language?"

But do we not see, as an everyday occurrence, a father instructing
his son word by word, adapting his thought and vocabulary to the
child's comprehension? Likewise, a traveler describes the unknown
by beginning in terms of the known. God acts thus when He con-

descends to where we are in order to communicate His truth to us in an intelligible manner. "The opening of thy words giveth light; it giveth understanding unto the simple" (Ps. 119:130).

Let us emphasize one very important fact: revelation is of necessity an act of God. The intimate thoughts of a man can be disclosed only by the man himself (I Cor. 2:11). Even so, and in a far deeper sense, no one but the Spirit of God can make us understand the mysteries of the Deity. We have just observed that if man could sound out these mysteries all by himself and explain them, he would be equal with God. The thoughts of the Lord infinitely surpass ours. Irenaeus rightly said, "The Lord taught us that no one can know God unless God Himself be the teacher; that is, without God, God cannot be known."[1] In claiming to doubt the possibility of revelation, the agnostic holds up to question two things: the capacity of God to reveal Himself and the capacity of man to know God.

The first of these suggestions amounts practically to the denial of God, for the idea of a divine revelation is tied in with that of the very existence of the Lord. Indeed, if He exists, it is to be expected that He would reveal Himself—and this even in a supernatural and infallible way. Any man wants to communicate with his child. So would not God desire to come into contact with the beings He created in His image, beings capable of communing with Him on a moral, an intellectual, and a spiritual plane? And if He speaks, what will He get across to them unless it is the message of truth and of love which emanates from His very nature? The faraway god of the deists, silent and indifferent to his creatures, is no perfect god: in him the greatest of perfections is missing—that of love; thus in no way does he merit the name of God.

What can we say about man's inability to perceive the voice of God? To admit such inability would be the same as to deny God Himself. After having given man an ear to hear the subtle or the discordant noises of earth, and after having also put into his heart the thought of eternity and a longing for it, would He have failed to make him recognize the voice from heaven? Such a powerless god as this would not even be able to capture our attention. The whole Bible demonstrates, on the contrary, that the Lord does address Himself to us and that our greatest felicity is to hear Him: "Hear, O heavens, and give ear, O earth; for Jehovah hath spoken" (Isa. 1:2).

Humanity cannot live apart from the work of its Creator, and fallen man is saved only by a revelation from the Almighty: "This is life eternal, that they should know thee the only true God, and him whom thou didst send, even Jesus Christ" (John 17:3).

WHAT UNIVERSAL REVELATIONS DO MEN RECEIVE?

The God of power and love desires to make Himself known and to be loved by His creatures. So He manifests Himself to them and descends to the level of their comprehension. Even before the fall, He gave two particularly eloquent revelations of His person and His attributes.

1. *The revelation of God in nature.* According to Paul, "that which is known of God is manifest in them [men, including the idolatrous heathen]; for God manifested it unto them. For the invisible things of him since the creation of the world are clearly seen, being perceived through the things that are made, even his everlasting power and divinity; that they may be without excuse: because that, knowing God, they glorified him not as God, neither gave thanks" (Rom. 1:19-21). The psalmist cries out: "The heavens declare the glory of God; and the firmament showeth his handiwork" (Ps. 19:1).

Such a striking natural revelation as this leads every sincere man to feel his own littleness in view of the creation and its Author: "When I consider the heavens, the work of thy fingers, . . . what is man, that thou art mindful of him?" (Ps. 8:3-4). "Who hath measured the waters in the hollow of his hand, and meted out heaven with the span? . . . Behold, the nations are as a drop of a bucket, and are accounted as the small dust of the balance" (Isa. 40:12-15).

At the same time we perceive the omnipotence, wisdom, providential love and eternality of the Creator of all things. "A living God, who made the heaven and the earth and the sea, and all that in them is: who in the generations gone by suffered all the nations to walk in their own ways. And yet he left not himself without witness, in that he did good and gave you from heaven rains and fruitful seasons, filling your hearts with food and gladness" (Acts 14:15-17). This same God has determined that all men "should seek God, if haply they might feel after him and find him, though he is not far from each one of us: for in him we live, and move, and have our being" (17:27-28). One would have to be blind or would have to blind himself voluntarily to deny evidence like this. "The fool hath said in his heart, There is no God" (Ps. 14:1). Indeed it is only a fool who can claim that the world came into being all by itself. Even Voltaire said, "The world poses a problem for me, and I cannot suppose that this clock exists without there having been a clock-maker."

The following summarizes what P. E. Hughes has to say on this subject:

The scientist proceeds from the a priori position that the universe and nature are coherent and that the discovery of one "law" will logically lead to another. Science cannot be science unless nature is a coordinated whole, a universe, not a chaotic set of facts isolated, independent and meaningless. The scholar knows that established facts will lead him somewhere. Such knowledge is inherent in the heart of man. He knows that he himself was created and that the world follows a plan and a purpose determined by God. To reject that interior, innate conviction is for him to refuse to know himself. To acknowledge that the world is the handiwork of God is normal for the one who has been created in His image.

We have just observed that the revelation of these great truths is clearly seen in creation (Ps. 19:1-4) and that everything around speaks to us of it. Still, it is this same ever-present revelation which fallen men refuse to accept. Blinded by sin, they refuse truth. "Knowing God, they glorified him not as God . . . but became vain in their reasonings. . . . Professing themselves to be wise, they became fools" (Rom. 1:21-22). Obsessed by human wisdom and philosophy, men devote their intellectual and spiritual energy to an interminable "search for truth," regardless of the fact that it has always been right in front of their eyes, as plain as day. Man has literally "exchanged the truth of God for a lie, and worshipped and served the creature rather than the Creator" (v. 25). This attitude characterizes not only the idolatry of primitive paganism, but also every humanistic culture.

The fundamental contradiction at the heart of all the thinking of unregenerate man is basically this: next to the rational principle indispensable to any logical reasoning, man has introduced an irrational principle. He knows the truth regarding the eternal power of the divine Creator and regarding the order in creation established according to His will—a truth which alone makes possible any rational, scientific understanding of the world. But at the same time he irrationally suppresses this truth. Not willing for God to govern him, he prefers to interpret the facts of the universe in terms of an egocentric philosophy rather than a theocentric one, glorifying man rather than God. Because of this false logic in the depths of his being, his highest faculties are, as it were, paralyzed. From this comes the failure of all human systems of philosophy, however impressive they may appear. "Based on a contradiction, they are destined to fragility; and they destroy one another."[2]

Let us, however, bring out the fact that, especially since the fall, the revelation given in nature is insufficient. It does allow us a glimpse of the power, providence and eternality of God; but it fails to present clearly His person, His holiness, His righteousness and— above all—His redeeming love and everlasting purposes for us. One recognizes this in looking at the confused and contradictory conclusions arrived at from the revelation in nature by the ancient Babylonians, Egyptians and Romans, as well as by Muslims, Hindus, Buddhists and even the western humanists and rationalists. It is indispensable then that humanity be given some entirely different kinds of illumination.

2. *The voice of God in conscience.* To nature, outside of mankind, God adds another way of speaking, by addressing Himself to the conscience. Paul says, " (When Gentiles that have not the law [written by God] do by nature the things of the law, these, not having the law, are the law unto themselves; in that they show the work of the law written in their hearts, their conscience bearing witness therewith, and their thoughts one with another accusing or else excusing them) ; in the day when God shall judge the secrets of men, according to my gospel, by Jesus Christ" (Rom. 2:14-16).

In creating man in His image, God endowed him with a moral and a spiritual sense. The great principles of the divine law are imprinted on his heart: appreciation for the excellence of that which is good, and joy in accomplishing it; also knowledge of the evil that is opposed to the divine will, and a feeling of guilt, desire for justification, and responsibility before the Creator. Obviously one can distort and silence his conscience. An individual, or a people, can stray far away from these great principles. However, even involuntarily, some trace of them always makes itself felt. The conscience of a child not hardened by life reacts in the most lively way. He will quite naturally have the feeling of sin, even if it is only a question of minor disobedience, thefts or lies of relative importance. It is for this same reason that people the world over are haunted by the need of expiation. In one way or another, human religions express the guilt of man who has offended divinity. Very rare are those which do not set forth the bleeding sacrifice of a victim slain in the place of the guilty one. We believe, moreover, that the universal concept that "without shedding of blood there is no forgiveness" did not simply surge up out of the conscience of man. It was the object of a primitive revelation, which was granted to the first men after the fall: the nakedness of Adam and Eve was covered by skins of animals, which doubtless were put to death expressly for this (cf. Gen. 3:21; 1:29). Abel was justified by the sacrifice of the firstborn of his flock and of the fat of it (Gen. 4:4; Heb. 11:4). Noah, after going out from the ark, offered sacrifices to God (Gen. 8:20-21).

Ideally, any man instructed by the twin revelations of nature and of conscience ought to be ready to receive salvation. Realizing his littleness and the marvelous grandeur of the universe, he worships the invisible Creator. At the same time, he trembles before Him, for his conscience accuses him, since no one on earth has ever obeyed all its injunctions. More or less directly he seeks for a redemption. If he wants to accomplish it himself, he will become adept at one of the innumerable human religions, all of which propose a salvation of man by man. If, convicted by the Spirit of God, he recognizes his absolute inability to get rid of the evil he has committed and to accomplish the good required, he will accept with comfort and gratitude the announcement of the Saviour that fills the whole Bible, which is God's written revelation. We have the example of this attitude on the part of heathen, such as the Ethiopian eunuch (Acts 8:27-28) and the centurion Cornelius (10:1-48). On every mission field there have sometimes been such reactions on the part of choice souls after they have heard the gospel for the first time. Unfortunately such cases have been only very rare exceptions. The immense majority of men do not pay the attention that they should to the two great voices of nature and conscience. The so-called primitive heathen turn away from the Creator to worship false gods, idols, fetishes and even animals. Modern, civilized pagans worship themselves and proudly exalt man, in every aspect, preparing for the acclamation of the superman, who will be the Antichrist (Rom. 1:21-25; II Thess. 2:3-4). Having lost their good conscience, they are afraid of the true God; and they have become shipwrecked concerning the faith (I Tim. 1:19). This is why the Apostle Paul declares them inexcusable (Rom. 1:20); they are lost and are subject to the terrible judgment of the Lord. Still He loves them and sent His Son into the world on purpose to snatch them from such a perdition. To make us know His redeeming love, God had to give us a third revelation, that of the Scriptures, which revelation makes the theme of the study before us.

Can a heathen who has received only the revelations of nature and of conscience come to salvation?[3] Paul expressly declares that everyone will be judged according to the light which he has received: "As many as have sinned without the law shall also perish without the law: and as many as have sinned under the law shall be judged by the law" (Rom. 2:12). We have seen that the revelations of nature and of conscience are sufficient to produce, on the part of the heathen, both worship and repentance and the full responsibility for both. However, God, who is just and omniscient, knows perfectly whether a sincere yet ignorant man, given a chance to accept salvation, would take it or not. Christ died for the sins of the whole world, those committed before His coming as well as those in times and places not yet reached by the gospel (cf. Rom. 3:25). The Lord, then, will know how to treat every sinner according to His love and His righteousness.

This does not exempt us, who are the recipients of all this divine light, from making it known to every creature. As a matter of fact, in view of the horrible darkness with which their lives are surrounded, how many "sincere heathen" are there? Their bodies are defiled, their consciences perverted, and their hearts captivated by evil spirits. Let us have pity on their sufferings and their spiritual abandonment; and let us hasten to take to them the Bible, the marvelous message of the Saviour. How shall we escape if we neglect to transmit to them this so-great salvation?

Can Reason Be an Independent Means of Arriving at the Knowledge of God?

Is not reason a wonderful gift granted to man, this faculty that permits him to judge everything—to put a correct value on everything? Having nature all around him and the voice of conscience within him, can he not, without any other revelation, arrive by reason at a complete understanding? Many do esteem man perfectly capable of perceiving all the truths essential to his life, both earthly and heavenly, without any supernatural help. On the other hand, in our country it is difficult to dissociate reason entirely from revelation, for elements of revelation have penetrated right to the marrow of our so-called "Christian" civilization. In reality, if one were to disregard the universal revelations already cited (creation and conscience), a glance at the peoples and individuals limited to the light from them would suffice for a deplorable demonstration of the limitations of both human nature and human perception.

As just noted, man, separated from God by the fall, is wholly contaminated by evil. No longer is he that perfect creature made in the image of God. His heart is capable of harboring shocking feelings, his will is weak and rebellious, and his defiled body is every day steadily approaching the grave. Likewise his mind, still capable of fine reasoning, is at once twisted and fallible. Paul said of the very refined pagans of his day what is also true of those in our day: They "became vain in their reasonings, and their senseless heart was darkened. Professing themselves to be wise, they became fools" (Rom. 1:21-22). The natural man (*animal*, that is, unregenerate) "receiveth not the things of the Spirit of God; for they are foolishness unto him; and he cannot know them, because they are spiritually judged." The spiritual man, on the other hand, receives by revelation the very thought of Christ (I Cor. 2:14-15). The apostle, therefore, is not much impressed by human wisdom, which he charges with foolishness (1:19-20). He goes so far as to say: "Casting down imaginations, and every high thing that is exalted against the knowledge of God, and bringing every thought into captivity to the obedience of Christ" (II Cor. 10:5). "Take heed lest there shall be any one that maketh spoil of you through his philosophy and vain deceit, after the tradition of men, after the rudiments of the world, and not after Christ" (Col. 2:8). Does not such a declaration oblige us to rethink, from a biblical point of view, the so-called Christian theology which is mingled with such a multitude of philosophical and intellectualistic elements?

It is clear, at any rate, that in view of the insufficiency of nature, conscience and reason, the only way to a personal and true knowledge of God is the revelation which He by His Spirit freely grants us.

What Have Been the Methods and Stages of the Revelation Since the Fall?

Immediately after the disobedience of our first parents, the Lord set in motion the realization of His plan of salvation. According to the Bible, man is not seeking the true God (Rom. 3:11). All the initiative comes from the Lord, who is indefatigably seeking His lost sheep. Since "this is life eternal, that they should know thee the only true God, and him whom thou didst send, even Jesus Christ" (John 17:3), He availed Himself of every means to communicate to man. He gave man not only His blessings, but also His very person. "His divine power hath granted unto us all things that pertain unto life and godliness, through the knowledge of him" (II Peter 1:3). Such a great undertaking, of course, had to be accomplished in a progressive and varied way. These are the principal stages of it:

1. *The theophanies* (appearances of the Deity) occur frequently in the early books of the Bible. God appeared directly, or in the guise of the Angel of the Lord, for example:

> to Abraham (Gen. 17:1, 22; 18:1, etc.)
> to Isaac (Gen. 26:2)
> to Jacob (Gen. 32:30)
> to Moses (Exodus 3:2-6; 33:11)
> to Gideon (Judges 6:12, 14-18, etc.)

One might ask oneself whether this Angel of the Lord, identified with God, was not the anticipated but temporary manifestation of Jesus Christ Himself. No one but the only begotten Son can make God known (John 1:18). According to Exodus 23:21, the Lord said of that Angel, different from all the others: "My name is in him." It was the same One who spoke with Moses on Sinai (Acts 7:38) and who saved Israel from all her distresses (Isa. 63:9).

2. *Dreams and visions* (Num. 12:6) granted, for example,

> to Jacob (Gen. 28:12-16)
> to Solomon (I Kings 3:5-15)
> to Daniel (Dan. 2:19, 28; 7:1; 10:7-8)
> to Joseph, the "husband" of Mary (Matt. 1:20; 2:13), etc.

3. *Direct contacts* established without mention of a particular appearance. God came to Balaam (or went before Balaam, Num. 22:9; 23:4). The Lord spoke with Moses face to face, as a man speaks to his friend (Exodus 33:11).

4. *Miracles and signs* drew man's attention and demonstrated to him the power, the holiness, the presence and the acts of the sovereign God in

> the judgment of the flood and the salvation of Noah (Gen. 6—9)
> the destruction of Sodom and the preservation of Lot (Gen. 19)
> the burning bush, the plagues of Egypt, the column of cloud, the deliverance of Israel (Exodus 3—15)
> the miracles of the desert (Numbers) and the entrance into Palestine (Joshua), etc.

The farther one goes in the Old Testament, the more the revelation becomes spiritual and inner. (We find the same progression as we pass from the period of the Gospels and the beginning of the Acts into that of the Epistles.)

5. *The prophets.* God, having revealed Himself to individuals chosen for His service, sends them to make known to the people what they have heard. He does not, therefore, speak so much *to* the prophet as *by* the prophet. In the Hebrew, moreover, the word *nabhi* (prophet) means a "forth-teller."

The first of these great messengers was Moses, the revealer of the law. In the beginning he declared that he was unworthy and unable to accomplish such a task; but God answered him: "Who hath made man's mouth? or who maketh a man? . . . is it not I, Jehovah? Now therefore go, and I will be with thy mouth and teach thee what thou shalt speak" (Exodus 4:11-12).

Visions and words are often confused. The book of Amos begins like this: "The words of Amos, . . . which he saw concerning Israel" (1:1). A prophet was formerly called a seer (I Sam. 9:9); and the distinguishing mark of false (foolish) prophets was precisely this: they "have seen nothing!" (Ezek. 13:3).

The prophets were obviously under the control of the Spirit of God. It is solely by His enabling that any man can prophesy (Num. 11:25, 29; I Sam. 10:6, 10). Speaking of God's appeals to Israel, Nehemiah said: "Yet many years didst thou bear with them, and testifiedst against them by thy Spirit through thy prophets: yet would they not give ear" (9:30; cf. Zech. 7:12). Ezekiel declared that the hand of the Lord was upon him, that it was "strong" upon him, that the Spirit lifted him up and took him away, that He entered into him and set him upon his feet (1:3; 3:14, 22, 24). Micah said that he was filled with power by the Spirit of the Lord, to deliver his redoubtable message (3:8). Peter affirmed that the prophets spoke from God, being moved by the Holy Spirit (II Peter 1:21).

The office of these men took on even more importance in Israel after the rejection of the theocracy and the institution of the kingdom (I Sam. 9:17). God never leaves Himself without a witness, and by means of such a ministry He unceasingly spoke to His people. According to the words of Amos, "the Lord Jehovah will do nothing, except he reveal his secret unto his servants the prophets" (3:7). The role of these men was also to lay the foundation for the next stage of the revelation: the incarnation and the redemptive work of the Messiah.

6. *The revelation of God in Jesus Christ.* All of the preceding communications were only indirect and fragmentary. They did indeed speak of the true God, but they pictured Him as far away and invisible; rather, they afforded only a quick glance, a glimpse, a communication that was meaningful, even overwhelming, but necessarily incomplete. Isaiah, the most spiritual of the prophets, felt this insufficiency so keenly that he cried out: "Verily thou art a God that hidest thyself, O God of Israel, the Saviour. O Jehovah, why dost thou make us to err from thy way? Oh that thou wouldest rend the heavens, that thou wouldest come down!" (45:15; 63:17; 64:1). And the same prophet voiced as follows the response to this heartrending cry on the part of a lost humanity: "Be strong, fear not: behold, your God . . . he will come and save you" (35:4).

Jesus Christ is God incarnate, the eternal Word made flesh. He does not simply bring us a new revelation; He is Himself this revelation. "No man hath seen God at any time; the only begotten Son, who is in the bosom of the Father, he hath declared him" (John 1:18). "Neither doth any know the Father, save the Son, and he to whomsoever the Son willeth to reveal him" (Matt. 11:27). And Christ Himself adds: "He that hath seen me hath seen the Father" (John 14:9). He embodies the sum total of all the divine attributes: omnipotence, absolute holiness, perfect love, omnipresence and omniscience (except as in Matthew 24:36, a case in line no doubt with His voluntary humiliation). He is for us "wisdom . . . , and righteousness and sanctification, and redemption" (I Cor. 1:30), for "in him dwelleth all the fulness of the Godhead bodily" (Col. 2:9). The theophanies are only a flash of lightning in the night in comparison to the incarnation of the One who is the light of the world.

The prophets gathered up and transcribed one by one the hints of the mysteries which the Lord willed to make known to them. But the Father has no secrets from the Son. The Son is Himself "the mystery of God, . . . in whom are all the treasures of wisdom and knowledge hidden" (Col. 2:3). This is why the epistle to the Hebrews sums up thus the history of the revelation: "God, having of old time spoken unto the fathers *in the prophets* by divers portions and in divers manners, hath at the end of these days spoken unto us *in His Son*" (1:1). And more than ever before, in Jesus Christ God's words have been acts: by the sacrifice of the cross, He gave a dazzling demonstration of His love and righteousness by providing there the full expiation of our sins. Then, He kept His promises of eternal life by raising up His Son from among the dead.

Christ, God fully manifested, is therefore not only the end of the law (Rom. 10:4), but also the consummation of the revelation. And He is the very heart of it, since it was His Spirit who inspired all prophecy (I Peter 1:11; Rev. 19:10) and since throughout eternity's day we shall find ourselves in the presence of the "apocalypse": the revelation of Jesus Christ (Rev. 1:1).

7. *The Scriptures.* All the revelations discussed above were accorded to individuals or to generations now passed away. What could we know of the illumination granted, the realities experienced, and the redemption accomplished, had these not been given substantial form by their incorporation into an inspired Book? First of all, the law was drawn up for a people called to receive the oracles

of God. Then the prophets put in writing these words of light and fire. Finally came the message of Christ and of the apostles. We shall subsequently consider the means employed for the reception, preservation and transmission of this divine communication.

Part Two

THE WORD

2

THE DIVINE WORD

BEFORE COMING TO THE INSPIRATION of the written Word, let us first consider the role played by the Word itself.

THE GOD OF THE BIBLE IS A GOD WHO SPEAKS

From the creation on through the entire history of His people, He reveals Himself by speaking. He spoke, and out of nothing the universe sprang forth (Gen. 1:3, 6, 9, etc.). John declared of Christ, who became incarnate for our salvation, revealing to us the Father: "In the beginning was the Word, and the Word was with God, and the Word was God. And the Word became flesh" (1:1, 14). The Lord, who is both light and love (I John 1:5; 4:8), takes pleasure in making Himself known to His creatures. He expresses His nature, His thoughts, His will and His plans. He explains His work, past and present; and He announces His future acts and His ultimate triumph.

Our God does not remain silent like the idols of the heathen, both ancient and modern (I Cor. 12:2). The Bible is full of irony on this point:

> "Such as lavish gold out of the bag, and weigh silver in the balance,
> They hire a goldsmith, and he maketh it a god;
> They fall down, yea, they worship.
> They bear it upon the shoulder,
> They carry it, and set it in its place, and it standeth;
> From its place shall it not remove:
> Yea, one may cry unto it, yet can it not answer, nor save him out of his trouble" (Isa. 46:6-7).

He neither answers nor saves! This is descriptive of the false god. On Mount Carmel, the prophets of Baal had been challenged by Elijah to obtain an answer from their god. They "called on the name of Baal from morning even until noon, saying, O Baal, hear us. But there was no voice, nor any that answered. . . . At noon . . . Elijah mocked them, and said, Cry aloud; for he is a god: either he is musing, or he is gone aside, or he is on a journey, or peradventure he sleepeth and must be awaked. . . . But there was neither voice, nor any to answer, nor any that regarded" (I Kings 18:26-29).

Neither has the Lord anything in common with the cold and absent god of the philosophers, who would have left us in the dark without any message on his part. He does not keep silent in indifference, malevolence or powerlessness, since it is His very nature to express Himself. Rather, if He does remain silent, it is because very grave reasons constrain Him to do so. In such a case, His very silence is a terrible judgment.

When Saul, rejected because of repeated disobedience, "inquired of Jehovah, Jehovah answered him not, neither by dreams, nor by Urim, nor by prophets" (I Sam. 28:6). In regard to Israel, God said to Jeremiah: "Pray not for this people for their good. When they fast, I will not hear their cry" (14:11-12). And He says further: "When ye make many prayers, I will not hear: your hands are full of blood" (Isa. 1:15). To the unbelieving, who mock Him, the Lord declares: "Turn you at my reproof . . . I will make known my words unto you. Because I have called, and ye have refused . . . I also will laugh in the day of your calamity. . . . Then will they call upon me, but I will not answer; they will seek me diligently, but they shall not find me" (Prov. 1:23-28).

MAN, GIFTED WITH THE POWER OF SPEECH, CAN COMMUNICATE WITH GOD

Man, created in the image of God, is, like Him, endowed with the ability to express himself. His word is a reply to the divine Word and an echo of it. It is this one factor—language—which establishes a fundamental distinction between man and beast. Of an intelligent and affectionate dog, do we not say "All he lacks is the ability to speak"? Speech is by far the best means of communication between two individuals. By means of the sense of touch, I can caress a person, or I can strike him; but what does that mean in comparison to speech? And how handicapped are they who are deprived of it!

Speech can convey the most subtle shades of thought and feeling. And it does so with a variety which makes bodily sensations seem primitive and uniform. It is speech which permits the most complete expression of the personality. Thus throughout the world it exerts an incomparably strong influence. Nations are governed by men firm in will and irresistible in word.

In a certain sense speech has more effect than acts themselves; rather, speech is that which provides the true source of conduct. Our thoughts, expressed, communicated by language, are the spring of our behavior. For it is from the heart of man, the inner life, that come good or evil works (Mark 7:21).

One can therefore speak—and this not only concerning God—of the creative power of the Word. "In the beginning was the Word. . . . All things were made through him" (John 1:1-3). This means that God, before anything existed, simply expressed in a word His thought and His will. By speaking, He acted and made Himself known. As for man, he reveals himself also whenever he opens his mouth. This is why "every idle word that men shall speak, they shall give account thereof in the day of judgment. For by thy words thou shalt be justified, and by thy words thou shalt be condemned" (Matt. 12:36-37). God could, therefore, not have chosen any better means than this to communicate with us.

THE DIVINE USE OF THE WORD IS VARIED

The eternal Word. The Word, being the expression of God revealing Himself, is eternal in heaven. "In the beginning was the Word" (John 1:1). "For ever, O Jehovah, thy word is settled in heaven" (Ps. 119:89). In similar vein Jesus, thinking of the ages yet to come, declared: "Heaven and earth shall pass away, but my words shall not pass away" (Matt. 24:35). "The word of the Lord abideth forever" (I Peter 1:25).

The Word as a creative agent. "God said, Let there be light: and there was light" (Gen. 1:3; the word "said" is repeated eleven times in this chapter). "By faith we understand that the worlds have been framed by the word of God, so that what is seen hath not been made out of things which appear" (Heb. 11:3).

The Word of God in the Old Testament. God spoke constantly to the patriarchs (Gen. 12:1, etc.). At Sinai He simply let the sound of His words be heard; it was only a voice (Deut. 4:12), so that His revelation would remain completely spiritual. The epistle to the

Hebrews sums up like this the entire old covenant: *"God, having of old time spoken unto the fathers in the prophets by divers portions and in divers manners . . ."* (1:1). He has certainly wrought many startling works, but the most essential thing is that He has spoken!

The Word incarnate. The whole new covenant, on the other hand, is summed up as follows: *"God . . . hath* at the end of these days *spoken* unto us *in his Son"* (Heb. 1:1-2). "The Word became flesh, and dwelt among us" (John 1:14). Jesus Himself, at the close of His ministry among His disciples, emphasized the main thrust of it this way: "The words which thou gavest me I have given unto them; and they received them" (John 17:8).

The Word of the Holy Spirit. Again, this Word is that which taught the disciples after Pentecost: "The Spirit of truth . . . shall guide you into all the truth: for he shall not speak from himself; but what things soever he shall hear, these shall he speak: and he shall declare unto you the things that are to come" (John 16:13). In reality, throughout the book of Acts, the Spirit did speak to the church: "The Spirit said to Philip, Go near" (8:29). "The Holy Spirit said, Separate me Barnabas and Saul for the work whereunto I have called them" (13:2). Even the apostles' word is attributed to the Holy Spirit, as had been that of the prophets of old (I Peter 1:12; II Peter 1:21).

CHRISTIANITY IS A RELIGION OF THE WORD

The biblical revelation is essentially a piece of good news, the proclamation of a message. Christianity is presented above all as a religion of the Word, concentrated on the manifestation of the divine presence and of the truth concerning it. Thus Christianity rests on a purely spiritual plane. As for human religions, they are based on things to do, on rites to observe, on statues to worship and to carry in processions, and on ecclesiastical framework.

It is with wonderful simplicity that Christ declares to us: "Verily, verily, I say unto you, He that heareth my word, and believeth him that sent me, hath eternal life, and cometh not into judgment, but hath passed out of death into life" (John 5:24). "The words that I have spoken unto you are spirit, and are life" (6:63). And we have this promise from God: "My word . . . that goeth forth out of my mouth . . . shall not return unto me void, but it shall accomplish that which I please, and it shall prosper in the thing whereto I sent it" (Isa. 55:11).

"Lord, to whom shall we go? thou hast the words of eternal life" (John 6:68).

3

THE WRITTEN WORD

IF THE GOSPEL is a religion of the Word, it is also a religion of a Book.

THE NECESSITY FOR THE WRITTEN WORD

A written revelation is necessary. An oral communication given to a man of God, to one generation or to a chosen people is not sufficient. It is indispensable that the message be put into writing. In the whole history of humanity, no such thing has ever been found as a people possessed of a true culture or of any coherent development of thought apart from writing. The first thing that a savage tribe has to learn in order to come out from barbarism is to put its language—the words of it—on paper. Likewise, a lasting divine revelation must rest on a written base.

WRITING IS INDISPENSABLE FOR ESTABLISHING THE MESSAGE

After revelation takes on a definite form, it is preserved from the variations, additions and errors of oral transmission. It cannot be corrupted or become untrustworthy. The book of the law was laid next to the ark of the covenant as a testimony against Israel (Deut. 31:26). The immutable norm for the divine will, it would serve throughout the centuries as a measuring stick for the disobedience of men. Thus invested with precision, the revelation takes on a permanent value: "For verily I say unto you, Till heaven and earth pass away, one jot or one tittle shall in no wise pass away from the law, till all things be accomplished" (Matt. 5:18).

THE BENEFITS OF THE WRITTEN WORD

The written text calls to mind the original message. After the great events at Rephidim, God commanded Moses: "Write this for a memorial in a book" (Exodus 17:14). This passage makes us think of the same expression as used by Malachi: "Then they that feared Jehovah spake one with another; and Jehovah hearkened, and heard, and a book of remembrance was written before him" (3:16).

A book groups together all the messages received. By this means one can affix one message to another, accumulate the revelations of the past, and transmit them all as one entity to future generations. "These things happened unto them [the Israelites] by way of example; and they were written for our admonition, upon whom the ends of the ages are come" (I Cor. 10:11).

The written message works independently of orator and writer. Jeremiah furnishes a striking example of this fact. After his many years of ministry and of preaching, God commanded him to write down in a book all the words which he had received from Him (Jer. 36:2). The prophet dictated to his secretary, Baruch, these successive messages (v. 4). But as he himself was in prison, he sent Baruch to read the text before the people and their leaders (vv. 5-13). The hearers were so moved that they saw to it that the king heard the reading (vv. 14-21). The king, furious at such words, cut the book and threw it into the fire; whereupon the message came to the prophet simply to write another book, more nearly complete even than the first one (vv. 28, 32). Thus the written message is superior because of its mobility. In spite of the imprisonment of its editor, the book sped past gates and iron curtains, reaching in course of time the most diverse circles; further, it proved itself capable of easy reproduction. The prophet may disappear; God continues to speak by the inspired text.

The written message becomes universal, indestructible and almost omnipresent. The first revelation was given to the prophet himself. Orally, he was able to get a small hearing. But as soon as the text was written down, it could be copied without any limitation. The copying, translating, and reproducing of Scripture in edition after edition was a relatively easy process. It has now become possible for nearly everyone to have his own copy of the Word of God. Persecutions come, and missionaries disappear; the Scriptures remain. Sometimes one single page stays buried like a seed for a long period of time. If someday it germinates, it will have lost nothing of its freshness or its vigor. To reach the billions in our day we must at any cost keep disseminating this wonder-working seed.

The written revelation makes its readers forever afterward re-

sponsible. "They have Moses and the prophets; let them hear them" (Luke 16:29)! The brothers of the wicked rich man assuredly did have all they needed: God would not grant them any superfluous intervention or miracle. And this is even more the case with men of our generation, who so easily can possess the entire Scripture record.

4

THE INCARNATE WORD AND THE INSPIRED WORD

CHRIST AND THE SCRIPTURES

IT IS FASHIONABLE TO CLAIM that only Christ is the Word of God and that the Bible is not that Word but merely "contains" it (see chap. 6, subhead "The Bible 'contains'—but 'is not'—the Word of God"). One glance at the Bible is enough to show the absurdity of such a statement. Christ Himself enunciated the Word of God in His preaching (Luke 5:1). Philip preached Christ in Samaria, and the apostles discovered that the Word of God had been received there (Acts 8:5, 14). Paul affirmed that his preaching was not the word of men, but truly the Word of God (I Thess. 2:13). Thus, the teachings of Christ and of the apostles (like those of the earlier prophets), as deposited in the Scriptures, are really for us the Word of God.

A comparison between Christ, the Word of God made flesh, and the Bible, the Word of God made a book, can be enormously instructive, as much by the contrasts it reveals as by the similarities.

Of His coming into the world, Christ said: "A body didst thou prepare for me; . . . Lo, I am come (in the roll of the book it is written of me)" (Heb. 10:5-7). "What book? What Person?" asked Luther in regard to this passage. One Book, the Bible; one Person, Jesus Christ, must be the answer. We shall see to what extent the two are inseparable.

Christ	*The Scriptures*
1. The divine and eternal Word (John 1:1), second Person of the Trinity, Christ is—with the Father and the Spirit—the real Author of the Holy Scriptures (I Peter 1:11; Rev. 19:10).	The thoughts of God stored up in the Scriptures are themselves eternal: "For ever, O Jehovah, thy word is settled in heaven" (Ps. 119:89). Paul sets forth the mystery of Christ and of the church, which

His Name is the Word of God (Rev. 19:13).

"for ages hath been hid in God" (Eph. 3:9; Col. 1:26-27).

2. Christ was conceived by the Holy Spirit (Luke 1:35).

"Every Scripture [is] inspired of God" (II Tim. 3:16). "Men spake from God, being moved by the Holy Spirit" (II Peter 1:21).

3. "The Word became flesh, and dwelt among us" (John 1:14). The divine and eternal Christ became human, visible and accessible to men. They were enabled to know Him, to hear Him speak and to love Him. He put Himself within reach of the humblest, having appeared as a simple man, a servant, a workingman (Phil. 2:7). "Having never learned," He spoke spontaneously the language of plain people (John 7:15; Luke 10:21).

The unsearchable thoughts of the Ruler of the universe (Isa. 55:8-9) have been expressed in our earthly language: the Word of God became the human word. In this sense, it was written for men and by men of flesh and blood, in their own time and country. Truly incarnate, it does not take us into some unreal world, but it goes right into the midst of sinners. It makes the divine message readable, comprehensible and translatable into the language of all. Setting aside the wisdom and philosophy of men, it deliberately addresses itself to the humble, to reveal to them the glories of the Lord (I Cor. 2:4-10).

4. Christ, in becoming incarnate, voluntarily humbled Himself (Phil. 2:5-8). He took a body, was born and grew up gradually. He limited His presence to a small number of people and to a little country. Still, this "Son of Joseph" is at the same time the divine Saviour of the world.

The written Word of God also accommodates itself to the comprehension of man. It reveals to us only a part of the divine mysteries (I Cor. 13:12). The revelation is characterized by a slow development, from Genesis to Revelation; and some of the pages are hard to understand. The Bible is primarily a Jewish book, out of a very small country. Still it is the most universal of books, the Word of God for all humanity.

5. Christ incarnate, in all respects like us, was at the same time perfect, without sin (John 8:46; Heb. 2:17; 4:15), omniscient (John 4:16-19), true (14:6) and omnipotent (11: 44).

Jesus declares: "Thy word is truth" (John 17:17). The psalmist adds: "The precepts of Jehovah are right. Thy law is truth. The sum of thy word is truth" (Ps. 19:8; 119:142, 160). The author of the epistle to the Hebrews, after quoting at length from the Old Testament, concludes: "For the word of God is living, and active, and sharper than any two-edged sword . . . and quick to discern the thoughts and intents of the heart" (Heb. 4:12). The Scriptures in their original autographs, at once human and divinely inspired, have been kept free of error (see chap. 13).

6. Jesus Christ had unique authority. "He taught as having authority, and not as the scribes" (Mark 1:22). "Never man so spake" (John 7:46).

Neither has any other book ever spoken like this one. It has the audacity to say: "Hear, O heavens, and give ear, O earth; for Jehovah hath spoken" (Isa. 1:2). The Old Testament alone affirms 3,808 times that it is transmitting the very words of God.

7. Christ was betrayed and rejected. His own did not receive Him (John 1:11-12; 7:5). The religious leaders did not believe in Him (7:48). Men loved their own darkness more than His divine light, because their works were evil (3:19; 7:7). They crucified Him because He affirmed that He was the Son of God (19:7). The testimony that Jesus gave of Himself was clear and true, but right to the end they accused Him of ambiguity and

More than any other, the Book of books has been detested and rebelled against. It has undergone fierce opposition on the part of sinners, who have felt themselves condemned by its pages. It has been torn to pieces, burned (cf. Jer. 36:23) and forbidden. It has been ridiculed and criticized even by those who ought to have been reverencing and distributing it. Men cannot endure its claim to be the Word of God, having authority to govern their lives. In spite of the innumerable declarations of of lying: "If thou art the Christ, tell us plainly" (10:24). "Thy witness is not true" (8:13).

8. Christ is gloriously manifested as the victorious Saviour. He is the light of the world and the living bread which came down out of heaven (John 8:12; 6:51). He regenerates and gives eternal life (5:24; 10:28). From His mouth proceeds the sharp two-edged sword of His sovereign word (Rev. 1:16; 19:15). It is He who will be the Judge of the world and the Saviour of them that believe (Acts 10:42; I Tim. 4:10).

9. Christ reveals Himself to faith: "If thou believedst, thou shouldest see the glory of God" (John 11:40). "Be not faithless, but believing. Thomas answered and said unto him, My Lord and my God" (20:27-28).

10. Christ unreservedly bears witness to the Scriptures: to their inspiration, their authority and their final character (Matt. 4:4; 5:17-18; John 10:35, etc.; cf. chap. 18).

Scripture, there still are those today who claim that they do not know whether or not it really is the Word of God. And men also declare unacceptable the testimony which it gives of itself.

The Bible at all times triumphs over its enemies. It is always living and relevant. The Scriptures are a light on our path (Ps. 119:105). Man does not live by bread alone, but by every word that proceeds out of the mouth of God (Matt. 4:4). The living, permanent Word of God regenerates and saves the sinner (I Peter 1:23; James 1:21). It is the two-edged sword which penetrates and reaches to the depths of our lives (Heb. 4:12). The Word of God will judge the unbeliever in the last day (John 12:48).

The Scriptures are useful and accessible only to believers (Heb. 4:12). They open themselves up only to those who believe in Jesus (II Cor. 3:14-16).

The Scriptures, in turn, constantly bear witness to Christ, who embodies the great theme of their revelation (I Peter 1:10-12; Luke 24: 27, 44). The two Words, then, are indissolubly bound together: If one does not believe in the Scriptures, how could he believe in the One whom they reveal? And if one does not accept Jesus, the living Word, how could he trust in the written Word, the foundation of all His teaching?

11. Christ alone makes known the Father (John 1:18). He that has seen Him has seen the Father, and no one comes to the Father but by Him (14:9, 6). Thus, when Christ speaks, it is God who speaks, requiring our absolute faith and obedience (8:28, 24).

Only the Bible brings us the full revelation of the Father and of the Son. What could we know, outside the Scriptures, about the true God and about Jesus Christ (John 5:39)? Thus the written revelation demands of us unreserved faith and obedience (cf. Rev. 1:3; 22:18-19).

OUR ATTITUDE IN REGARD TO THE WRITTEN WORD DETERMINED BY OUR ATTITUDE CONCERNING THE LIVING WORD

By hardening their hearts and shutting out Jesus Christ: men can neither see nor understand the revelation (John 12:37-41). The Word does not penetrate into them (8:37, 43); and the Bible remains a sealed Book, which condemns them (Isa. 29:11; Jer. 6:10).

It is impossible to refuse to believe in Christ and at the same time to claim to believe in the Scriptures, for they bear witness of Him (John 5:39-40).

Inversely, one who doubts the Scriptures could not maintain his faith in Christ, who constantly attested to them (John 5:46-47).

On the other hand:

When we listen to the message of Christ, the Scriptures convince us of their truth (Acts 17:2-3, 11; 18:28).

When hearts are converted to the Lord Jesus Christ, the Old Testament and the whole Bible shine forth, as the veil is taken away (II Cor. 3:15-16).

When we obey Christ and keep His teachings, the Word of truth sanctifies us (John 17:6, 17).

If we preach Christ,	it is the Scriptures which are our authority (Acts 2:17, 25, 31, 34-35; 3:18; I Cor. 15:3-4, etc.)
If we love Christ,	His Word, deposited in the Scriptures, fills us with joy, strength and comfort (John 14:23; 15:9-11; cf. Jer. 15:16).

In concluding this parallel, let us emphasize that we in no wise make the Scriptures an object of worship. The great contrast between Christ and the Bible stands: the Lord alone is the divine Saviour, whereas the Scriptures are only a divinely inspired means of revealing Him and of leading us to Him. We hold in reverence the holy Book and accept its words without reservation, but we adore only the Father, the Son and the Holy Spirit.

THE MYSTERY OF THE TWO NATURES OF CHRIST AND OF THE SCRIPTURES

We have just seen that by the incarnation Christ is at once perfect God (John 1:1, 14; 20:28; Rom. 9:5) and perfect man (Heb. 2:14, 17). The Scriptures also, by the miracle of inspiration, are at the same time a divine word and a human word. We do not claim that we can explain the one miracle or the other—we who cannot even explain the birth of man or the new birth of a believer. We are born, it is true, with a body and a spirit—and no scholar can tell us where the one begins and the other ends, or where and how the one is attached to the other. That the divine nature is communicated to the believer by the Holy Spirit (Titus 3:5; II Peter 1:4) is an equally glorious certainty for us, even though it remains entirely beyond our comprehension. We quote Adolphe Monod on this point:

> When the Scriptures speak, it is God who speaks. . . . There is no limit to the confidence and the submission that we owe to the Scriptures—no more limit than to the truth and the faithfulness of God. . . . But in closer examination of it, I find it full of man. . . . I recognize indeed in the writers of this book an individuality both of style and of character. . . . We thus see the place that the spirit of man has in the composition of the Word of God. It was evidently intended by God that, at every page of this book which we call the Word of God, we should recognize

at the same time the word of man. . . . But it is the more divine as it is the more human; that is to say, that the power and the presence of the Spirit of God and its influence upon our souls are the more felt because God used instruments to write it, to whom His Spirit alone could impart that power and supernatural light which made of them "chosen vessels" to carry the truth to the ends of the world.

The Word sometimes gives the same name to Jesus Christ and to the Holy Scriptures; it calls both the Word of God. The one, *Jesus Christ*, is the living Word of God, the personal manifestation of His perfections among men; the other, *the Scripture*, is the written Word of God, or a verbal manifestation in language of these same invisible perfections. They are inseparable for us; for Jesus Christ is revealed to us only by the Scriptures, and the Scriptures are given to us in order only to reveal Jesus Christ. Thus Scripture is the written Word of God, as Jesus Christ is the living Word of God. Those who find in the human character of Scripture a pretext for denying its divinity reason like those who find in the human personality of Jesus Christ a pretext for refusing Him the title of God. . . . It is not more surprising that Scripture, though the Word of God, should at the same time bear so many traces of humanity than it is that Jesus Christ, though God, should be man. As to the manner in which the two natures in one case, and the two voices in the other, are blended— this is the very foundation on which faith rests concerning this subject; a profound mystery, no doubt, but, as St. Paul says, a "mystery of godliness," which fills our soul with joy and hope.[1]

Finally, this is the conviction of Louis Gaussen on this subject:

The dogma of inspiration is like that of the incarnation. In both there is one fact fully revealed; and this fact I fully believe. But before both these dogmas I rest attentive and submissive; I explain nothing. . . . In the one, it is God Himself speaking in the Scriptures; it is the ineffable work of the Holy Spirit, causing His divine oracles to be written by man and for man. . . . And *"all this Scripture,"* said St. Paul, "is theopneustical," i.e. inspired by God. What an adorable mystery! In the other, it is the Word "which was in the beginning with God, and which became flesh." . . . "Without controversy," said the same apostle, "great is the mystery of godliness: God was manifested in the flesh. . . ." Do not say then "If Jesus Christ is God, how is it that

He is a man?" Or "If Jesus Christ is a man, how is He God?" And do not say either: "If the Scriptures are the Word of God, how are they the word of man?" Or "If the Scriptures are the word of man, how are they the Word of God?" No, let us simply read and study, believe, and adore![2]

Part Three

INSPIRATION

5

DEFINITIONS AND GENERALITIES

DEFINITIONS

Revelation is the act by which God makes Himself known to His creatures.

Inspiration (in the limited sense of the word, as used in this work) is the determining influence exercised by the Holy Spirit on the writers of the Old and New Testaments in order that they might proclaim and set down in an exact and authentic way the message as received from God. This influence guided them even to the extent of their use of words, that they might be kept from all error and omission. (The question of inexactitudes introduced into the text by copyists is discussed in chap. 16.) A like inspiration was granted to the sacred writers in regard to events or facts already known by them without special revelation, that their accounts of them might be that which God willed.

> Biblical inspiration . . . is that . . . activity of the Holy Spirit through which He mysteriously filled the human spirit of the biblical writers and guided and overruled them, so that there arose an infallible, Spirit-wrought writing, a sacred record, a Book of God, with which the Spirit of God evermore organically unites Himself.[1]

THE CLASSIC TEXT, II TIMOTHY 3:16-17, AND ITS TEACHINGS

All Scripture is inspired by God—in the Greek *theopneustos*, literally: breathed out from God (not "breathed in," in-breathed) — produced by the life-giving breath of God, proceeding from Him, spoken by Him. B. B. Warfield goes so far as to say that the term *inspiration* as such is not found in the Bible. The sacred authors were laid hold on by the initiative of the Lord and borne along by His irresistible power, which was not breathing the Scriptures into something or somebody, but was, rather, causing them to emanate directly from His own mouth.

The creation, that other great "book" of God, came about in the same way: "By the word of Jehovah were the heavens made, and all the host of them by the breath of his mouth" (Ps. 33:6). Josephus, Jewish historian and contemporary of Paul, said in his first book, *Against Apion,* that the prophets responsible for the twenty-two sacred books (of the Old Testament)* wrote "according to the 'pneustia': that which originates in God" (I, 7). Thus, all the Scripture is from God, everywhere and in everything from God, although it is written by man for him.

How ought II Timothy 3:16 to be translated? Should it be "Every Scripture is inspired of God and profitable . . ." or "Every Scripture inspired of God is profitable . . ."?

One should realize that the word *is* belongs here in the Greek and that we ought to put it in somewhere. It is part of the genius of the original language to place this verb as it appears each time in the following New Testament verses, which are all constructed in exactly the same way:

Romans 7:12: "The law is holy, and the commandment holy, and righteous, and good" (not "The holy commandment is also righteous and good").

II Corinthians 10:10: "His letters . . . are weighty and strong" (not "His weighty letters are also strong").

I Timothy 1:15: "Faithful is the saying, and worthy of all acceptation" (not "The faithful saying is also worthy of all acceptation").

I Timothy 2:3: "This is good and acceptable in the sight of God our Saviour" (not "This good is also acceptable in the sight of God our Saviour").

Hebrews 4:13: "All things are naked and laid open" (not "All naked things are also laid open").

*Translator's note: Gleason L. Archer, Jr., *A Survey of Old Testament Introduction,* p. 60, observes: "The earlier division [of the Old Testament books] consisted of the same content as the thirty-nine books [which we have], but arranged in only twenty-four books. This meant that I and II Samuel were counted as one book; likewise I and II Kings and I and II Chronicles. The twelve Minor Prophets were also counted as one book, and Ezra and Nehemiah formed a single unit. Josephus . . . gives evidence of a twenty-two book Canon. . . . This apparently involved the inclusion of Ruth with Judges and of Lamentations with Jeremiah." (See also chap. 15 of this book.)

(See also in the Greek I Cor. 11:30; I Tim. 4:4, 9.) Thus the following translation is certainly the correct one:

II Timothy 3:16: "Every scripture is inspired of God and profitable. . . ." This being said, let us make it clear that the translation "Every scripture inspired of God is also profitable" would not, as a matter of fact, say anything different, for it is clear that:

1. *It is "every Scripture," or "all the Scripture," which is inspired;* this means, in other words, according to the context, all the Old Testament, "the sacred writings" of which Paul speaks in verse 15. That which is affirmed here of the Old Testament with no restrictions whatsoever is obviously valid also for every scripture of the New Testament (see chap. 9).

2. *It is the Scripture, the text itself, which, according to Paul, is inspired.* This is vital for us, for what use would the divine revelation received by the sacred writers be to us if those writers had not been enabled to draw them up in an absolutely sure and authentic way? We know that Balaam, David and Peter, for instance, were not at all infallible, either in words or conduct, when they were not being inspired (Num. 22-24; II Sam. 11; 24:1-11; Gal. 2:11-14). Then, if God had inspired only the thoughts in the minds of the writers, there would be nothing left of the message today, for the men have been dead for a long time.

3. *Every scripture is "profitable."* This is evident. It is profitable because inspired, and inspired so as to be profitable. Even the least-read pages and books in the Bible have their place, and we are to add nothing to them or to take nothing away from them (Deut. 4:2; Rev. 22:18-19). Our tendency is just to content ourselves with a few favorite passages, with certain verses found here and there. Still, it all has value, as placed in context: the genealogies and the lists of names, invaluable from the point of view of history; the ritualistic laws of Exodus and of Leviticus, which teach in pictured form how a sinner can enter into communion with a holy God (which explains the epistle to the Hebrews); the book of Ecclesiastes, to show the total inadequacy of mere earthly wisdom and goods; the prophets, to set forth the development of the plan of God; the dark pages of the historical books, to show the gravity of sin, the judgment of God, and the absolute necessity of salvation; and the epistles, indispensable to

the establishment of the relevancy of Christian doctrine to the life of the church and to that of the believer, etc.

According to II Timothy 3:16-17, the whole of Scripture is profitable "for teaching," that is, for the laying of a foundation for the divine truth. "The study and meditation of its pages is the best course in theology and religion" (A. Monod). "Out of heaven he made thee to hear his voice, that he might instruct thee" (Deut. 4:36). "Blessed is the man whom thou . . . teachest out of thy law" (Ps. 94:12). "Whatsoever things were written aforetime were written for our learning" (Rom. 15:4).

"for reproof" (the same word as in John 16:8): to produce conviction, to refute and to dispel error, which is more serious than ignorance. Man's understanding is darkened and his heart hardened (Eph. 4:18); it takes the power of the divine Word to open his eyes and to persuade him of the truth (Jer. 23:29; Heb. 4:12).

"for correction": to lead a wandering child of God back to the right path and to warn and censure him with the love and authority of the Lord Himself. Man so readily turns away in the matter of morals as well as in doctrine; like a young tree, he needs a strong support to hold him straight. "Wherewith shall a young man cleanse his way? By taking heed thereto according to thy word. Thy word have I laid up in my heart, that I might not sin against thee" (Ps. 119:9, 11).

"for instruction . . . in righteousness": that is, for building up and establishing the believer by that spiritual instruction which molds both thought and character; this instruction provides a deep significance to life, a philosophy for one's whole being. "Thy commandments make me wiser than mine enemies. . . . I have more understanding than all my teachers, for thy testimonies are my meditation. The opening of thy words giveth light; it giveth understanding unto the simple" (Ps. 119:98-99, 130). "The sacred writings . . . are able to make thee wise unto salvation" (II Tim. 3:15).

"that the man of God may be complete, furnished completely unto every good work." This is the purpose of the Scriptures: to bring us to salvation by the knowledge of the Lord, to make out of every one of us a man of God, a complete and responsible personality (cf. James 1:4), manifesting by his life and works the divine character of the revelation which he has received.

THE UNEXPLAINED AND INEXPLICABLE MIRACLE OF INSPIRATION

How much can we know, at the minimum, of the process of inspiration?

1. *The origin of inspiration, according to I Cor. 1 and 2:*

   a. There is a mind of the Lord, a mysterious, hidden and eternal wisdom of God (2:7, 16).

   b. The natural man, blinded by his sin, can neither know nor receive it. For him the gospel is both foolishness and a stumbling block (2:14, 9; 1:18, 23).

   c. God, of His own initiative, reveals to us through the Holy Spirit His person and His salvation. He has prepared this revelation for them who love Him (2:9-12).

   d. Having received His marvelous grace, we can tell of it and can make it known. Paul did this orally, when he preached the very Word of God (I Thess. 2:13); he also put the message in writing (4:8, 15; I Cor. 14:37). The apostles, clearly, were guided in this ministry (even more explicitly in what they wrote than in what they spoke), their discourse (*logoi* Greek, literally, "their words, their mode of expression"), having been taught by the Spirit of God (I Cor. 2:13).

   e. *The spiritual man,* that is, the one who is regenerated and submissive to the Spirit of God, can take in this inspired language. He appreciates it and knows how to examine it with discernment: thus he has the mind of Christ (vv. 14-16).

2. *The declarations of the Apostle Peter.* In like manner Peter speaks of the way in which the writers of the Old Testament were inspired (I Peter 1:10-12; II Peter 1:19-21; the word "prophet" here has the broad meaning of "forth-teller" of the revelation).

   a. Christ, the Lamb of God, was predestined before the foundation of the world to become the Author of our salvation (I Peter 1:10, 19-20).

   b. The Holy Spirit communicated with the prophets (He "was in them"), revealing to them the time and the circumstances of the coming of the Messiah, as well as His "sufferings" and "the glories that should follow them" (v. 11); for herein is the central and essential message of the Scriptures.

c. The revelation went beyond the prophets: realizing that others would see the fulfillment of this salvation, they sought and searched diligently these things beforehand (vv. 10, 12).

d. The announcement of the work of Christ stirs the angels, along with all the other inhabitants of the heavenly places, with astonishment and admiration (v. 12; Eph. 3:10).

e. Moved by the Holy Spirit, the prophets spoke in a manner authorized by God Himself (II Peter 1:21); they became for us the ministers of these things (I Peter 1:12); that is, they announced them to us by means of their writings.

f. The message of the earlier prophets (in the Old Testament) is identical in essence with the gospel (in the New Testament), its proclamation being with the same power of the Holy Spirit (v. 12; I Thess. 1:5).

We cannot but admire the prudence and sobriety of the Scriptures. At all times they affirmed the miracle of inspiration; but never did Paul, Peter or anyone else disclose just how it took place, or the exact manner and extent of the divine influence brought to bear on the sacred writers. So we have no authority, either, to try to sound the depths of this mystery, any more than we do that of the incarnation of Jesus Christ, the regeneration of the believer, or the creation of the universe. However, an examination of a few concrete facts from the Bible will help us to comprehend certain aspects of the divine action.

HOW GOD SPOKE TO HIS PROPHETS

"God, having of old time spoken unto the fathers in the prophets by divers portions and in divers manners, hath at the end of these days spoken unto us in his Son" (Heb. 1:1-2). It is still the same God speaking in both the Old Testament and the Gospels. Let us see in what different ways He did it.

A decisive meeting with God normally marks the beginning of a prophet's career. This meeting proves that it is the Lord who takes the initiative, choosing and preparing His instrument before He communicates His message to him.

Moses claimed at the burning bush that he did not know how to speak. God said to him: "Who hath made man's mouth? . . . Go, and I will be with thy mouth, and teach thee what thou shalt speak. . . . Aaron . . . shall be thy spokesman unto the people; . . . he shall be to thee a mouth, and thou shalt be to him as God" (Exodus 4:11-16).

Samuel wrote: "The word of Jehovah was precious [rare] in those days; there was no frequent vision. . . . Samuel did not yet know Jehovah, neither was the word of Jehovah yet revealed unto him." Three times God called Samuel, who answered Him, "Speak; for thy servant heareth. . . . Samuel . . . did let none of his words fall to the ground. . . . Jehovah revealed himself to Samuel in Shiloh" (I Sam. 3).

Isaiah saw the Lord in His holiness. A seraph purified his lips with a live coal from off the altar. The prophet wrote: "I heard the voice of the Lord saying, Whom shall I send, and who will go for us? Then I said, Here am I; send me. And he said: Go and tell this people . . ." (Isa. 6:1-9).

Jeremiah wrote: "The word of Jehovah came unto me, saying, Before I formed thee in the belly I knew thee . . . I sanctified thee; I have appointed thee a prophet unto the nations. . . . Whatsoever I shall command thee thou shalt speak. . . . Behold, I have put my words in thy mouth" (Jer. 1:4-9). "I will make my words in thy mouth fire, and this people wood, and it shall devour them" (5:14). The prophet replied: "Know that for thy sake I have suffered reproach. Thy words were found, and I did eat them; and thy words were unto me a joy and the rejoicing of my heart" (15:15-16). Then he was given this promise by the Lord: "If thou take forth the precious from the vile, thou shalt be as my mouth" (v. 19).

Ezekiel wrote: "He said unto me, Son of man, I send thee to the children of Israel. . . . All my words that I shall speak unto thee receive in thy heart, and hear with thine ears. And go . . . speak unto them . . . whether they will hear or whether they will forbear. . . . Tell them: Thus saith the Lord Jehovah. . . ." The Lord had him eat, symbolically, the scroll on which was written the message, at once sweet and bitter, which he was to deliver (Ezek. 2:3—3:11).

Amos declared: "I was no prophet, neither was I a prophet's son; but I was a herdsman, and a dresser of sycomore-trees. And Jehovah took me from following the flock, and Jehovah said unto me, Go, prophesy unto my people Israel" (7:14-15).

Paul was told by Ananias: "The God of our fathers hath appointed thee to know his will, and to see the Righteous One, and to hear a voice from his mouth. For thou shalt be a witness for him unto all men of what thou hast seen and heard" (Acts 22:14-15). The apostle himself added: "When it was the good pleasure of God, who separated me, even from my mother's womb, and called me through his grace, to reveal his Son in me, that I might preach him among the Gentiles; straightway I conferred not with flesh and blood" (Gal. 1:15-16).

John wrote: "I was in the Spirit on the Lord's day, and I heard behind me a great voice . . . saying, What thou seest, write in a book, and send it to the seven churches. Write therefore the things which thou sawest, and the things which are, and the things which shall come to pass hereafter" (Rev. 1:10-11, 19). John also had to "eat" a book; then he was told: "Thou must prophesy again over many peoples and nations and tongues and kings" (10:8-11).

Christ Himself, the Word made flesh, received His message from His Father. Isaiah said of Him: "Jehovah . . . hath made my mouth like a sharp sword" (49:1-2). "The Lord Jehovah hath given me the tongue of them that are taught, that I may know how to sustain with words him that is weary: he wakeneth morning by morning, he wakeneth mine ear to hear as they that are taught" (50:4-5). Farther on we see where God said this to His Servant: "I have put my words in thy mouth . . . that I may plant the heavens, and lay the foundations of the earth" (51:16). Jesus declared specifically: "I do nothing of myself, but as the Father taught me, I speak these things" (John 8:28). Then He said to His Father: "The words which thou gavest me I have given unto them; and they received them, . . . and they have kept thy word" (17:8, 6).

Inspiration was granted by God in an absolutely sovereign way. In any case, it was not continuous, for the Spirit speaks and causes an individual to write when and as it pleases Him. We read, for example, the following:

The word of Jehovah was addressed to Jeremiah in the time of Josiah,

> in the thirteenth year of his reign (Jer. 1:2),
> on the occasion of the drought (14:1),

in the fourth year of Jehoiakim (25:1),
at the beginning of the reign of Jehoiakim (26:1) and, in the
  same year, at the beginning of the reign of Zedekiah (28:11),
after the attack of Nebuchadnezzar (34:1),
in the prison court (39:15), etc.

Habakkuk expressed himself like this: "I will stand upon my watch, and set me upon the tower, and will look forth to see what he will speak with me, and what I shall answer concerning my complaint. And Jehovah answered me, and said, Write the vision" (2:1-2).

The prophets, then, did not speak as or when they wished. They waited until a message was communicated to them from on high. God spoke directly with Moses, "mouth to mouth" (Num. 12:6-8). But He could also reveal Himself in a dream, as He did to Daniel (7:1); in a vision (8:1); by sending an angel (9:21-22; 10:5-11); or, on an exceptional occasion, in an ecstatic experience (II Cor. 12:2-4; Rev. 1:10).

As a general rule, the sacred writer retained complete lucidity, even to the point of entering into a dialogue with the Lord, asking Him questions and acquainting Him with his reactions (Isa. 6:11; Jer. 14:13; 15:15; Ezek. 9:8; 11:13, etc.). Daniel was terror-stricken at his visions; but the explanations were given him immediately (Dan. 7:15-16, 19, 28; 8:15-16, 26), unless he was given the order to seal the message for the time being (8:26; 12:4, 9).

It also often happened that, whether or not the writer was aware of it, his message surpassed his comprehension. We have just seen this in the case of Daniel (e.g., 12:8-9). At any rate, God's hidden wisdom "entered not into the heart of man" (I Cor. 2:9); the revelation of His plans for the present, and still more of those for the future, can indeed stun even the most spiritual man. The prophets realized that it would be others who would see the fulfillment of their message, and they would naturally have liked to know more about it themselves (I Peter 1:10-12). This is why Jesus said to His disciples: "Blessed are the eyes which see the things that ye see: for I say unto you, that many prophets and kings desired to see the things which ye see, and saw them not" (Luke 10:23-24). In Psalm 22 David described in detail something which he could not understand: the anguish of the crucifixion (vv. 1-3, 7-9, 15-19), a form of punishment unknown among the Jews, introduced into Palestine by the Romans only a short while before our era. Did he grasp all the Messianic implications of his words in Psalm 16:8-10? It was manifestly easier for Peter and Paul than for him to discern in this passage a prophecy of the resurrection of Christ (Acts 2:24-31; 13:35-37).

Daniel received and wrote words which obviously were not for himself or for his time. He said, "I heard, but I understood not." In reply he was given this instruction: "Go thy way, Daniel; for the words are shut up and sealed till the time of the end" (12:8-9).

The same is true, and to an even greater extent, of those who, without suspecting it, were themselves to be considered as types of Christ and of His work: Adam, the figure of Him who was to come (Rom. 5:14); Hagar and Sarah, representing the two covenants (Gal. 4:22-26); Aaron, the type of Christ Jesus, our High Priest (Heb. 7–10). These people were, each in his own way, instruments of a revelation the import of which they could not understand.

All of this shows us that although the human instrument plays a part in the transmission of the message, the One who counts above all is the Author of the revelation.

Inspiration was given at times in a wholly compulsive way. The Lord, for example, imposed on Jeremiah a terrible message, which he tried in vain to resist: "O Jehovah, thou hast persuaded me, and I was persuaded; thou art stronger than I, and hast prevailed: I am become a laughingstock all the day. . . . For as often as I speak, I cry out . . . Violence and destruction! because the word of Jehovah is made a reproach unto me, and a derision, all the day. And if I say, I will not make mention of him, nor speak any more in his name, then there is in my heart as it were a burning fire . . . I am weary with forbearing, and I cannot contain" (Jer. 20:7-9). From the moment that He called him, God had warned the prophet: "Whatsoever I shall command thee thou shalt speak. Behold, I have put my words in thy mouth" (1:7, 9).

Balaam, having come to curse the people, was literally forced to bless them. The angel said to him, "Go . . . but only the word that I shall speak unto thee, that thou shalt speak." When Balak's anger was kindled against him, Balaam replied: "I cannot go beyond the word of Jehovah, to do either good or bad of mine own mind; what Jehovah speaketh, that will I speak" (Num. 22:35; 24:13).

Neither did Caiaphas speak of his own volition when he prophesied that Jesus was to die for the nation. Under those circumstances, God had expressly willed that such a declaration be made by the high priest, even though that one was an unbeliever (John 11:51).

It is, indeed, not by the will of man that any prophecy has ever come (II Peter 1:21).

At times the author did not even suspect the divine action brought to bear on him. When the faithful historian Luke gathered together his documents and interrogated the eyewitnesses, did he realize that his account would be included in the Holy Scriptures? Usually he simply put down in writing facts which he had known apart from any supernatural revelation. But it was inspiration which guided him in both the choice of these facts and their interpretation and even in the omission of matters not chosen by the Holy Spirit. A similar remark could be made in regard to the narrators of the other historical books of the Bible. In summary, let us say that prophetic inspiration could lay hold on a man without his anticipation of it, as with the old prophet of I Kings 13:20; without his knowledge of it, as with Caiaphas (John 11:51); without his desire for it, as with Balaam (Num. 23 and 24); without his comprehension of it, as with Daniel (Dan. 12:8-9).

In essence, divine inspiration knows no degrees. It is always perfect and complete. As we have just seen, Balaam, when he pronounced his oracles, was as much under the control of the Spirit as was David when he cried out: "The Spirit of Jehovah spake by me, and his word was upon my tongue" (II Sam. 23:2). The prophecy of Caiaphas, the high priest (John 11:51), was just as exact and as supernatural in origin as were the revelations of the Apostle Paul (Eph. 3:3, 5).

> Illumination is susceptible of degrees; inspiration does not admit of them. A prophet is more or less enlightened by God; but what he says is not more or less inspired. It is so, or it is not so; it is from God, or it is not from God; here there is neither measure nor degree, neither increase nor diminution. David was enlightened by God; John Baptist more than David; a simple Christian possibly more than John Baptist; an apostle was more enlightened than that Christian, and Jesus Christ more than that apostle. But the inspired word of David, what do I

say? the inspired word of Balaam himself is that of God, as was that of John Baptist, as was that of St. Paul, as was that of Jesus Christ! *It is the Word of God.*[3]

The prophets fully believed that they were transmitting the very words of God. Moses repeated over fifty times in the book of Leviticus alone some such expression as this: "Jehovah called unto Moses"; "Jehovah spake unto Moses, saying: Speak unto the children of Israel, saying. . . ." Except for about a dozen verses in chapters 10 and 24, it is therefore declared of the book of Leviticus that it contains nothing but the words of God put into writing by Moses for his people.

David, as we have just seen, cried out: "The Spirit of Jehovah spake by me, and his word was upon my tongue" (II Sam. 23:2).

Jeremiah constantly employed an expression like this: "The word of Jehovah came unto me, saying. . . ." "Then said Jehovah unto me. . . ." "Thus saith Jehovah. . . ."

Paul did not hesitate to say: "The word of the message, even the word of God, ye accepted it not as the word of men, but, as it is in truth, the word of God" (I Thess. 2:13).

John solemnly declared: "The Revelation of Jesus Christ . . . unto his servant John; who bare witness of the word of God. These things saith the Son of God. He that hath an ear, let him hear what the Spirit saith to the churches. These are true words of God" (Rev. 1:1-2; 2:18, 29; 19:9).

Later on we shall take up in more detail this all-important question: Is the Bible the Word of God? (See chap. 8.)

6

THEORIES OF INSPIRATION

ONE MIGHT CONCEIVABLY REGARD the Holy Bible in four different ways:

1. It is only a remarkable human book without divine inspiration.
2. It is partially inspired by God.
3. It is only divine, devoid of any human adjunction.
4. It is at the same time divine and human, God having fully inspired the sacred authors who spoke in His name.

The first three of these concepts appear in the present chapter, and the fourth in a subsequent chapter.

THE BIBLE IS ONLY A REMARKABLE HUMAN BOOK WITHOUT DIVINE INSPIRATION

Religious geniuses could have indited the Scriptures in just the same way as gifted artists, writers, poets and musicians have created unique masterpieces. Endowed with the exceptional intuitive sensibilities of the great visionaries, they could have produced literature on the same plane as Homer's *Odyssey*, Muhammad's *Koran*, Dante's *Divine Comedy*, Shakespeare's tragedies or the sacred books of the Hindus. The Bible is possibly the greatest of all works, a marvelous document out of antiquity, the most universal book known to man. But it is fallible, as are all other human productions; and it is not the direct result of a divine intervention.

The above theory, that of "natural inspiration," is in reality a denial of true inspiration. Exalting human authorship to the exclusion of the divine, it is actually the expression of unbelief. This position is clearly untenable in the light of the following facts. The radiant personality of Christ surpasses in its purity, love, righteousness and perfection anything ever to be found in universal human literature. Where then did the authors of the Gospels find the model for such a figure, one which has never existed anywhere in the world? As Rousseau put it: "This is not the way a thing is invented!" To "create" such a personage the writers would need to have been superior to Him, for the artist is always greater than his work. Now the disciples knew themselves, and showed themselves, to be far from any such perfection. On the other hand, if the sacred authors could have conceived by themselves of the sublime pages of Scripture, they would have been capable of writing others like them. How then is it that, left to themselves, they produced absolutely nothing similar to the canonical books?

There are countless other manifestations of the divine character of the Scriptures that we shall present later (see chap. 22) ; all these would be incomprehensible apart from supernatural intervention. To cite only one more in this chapter: How were the biblical writers able to make so many detailed predictions, confirmed by history, if they had had no revelation from above? If the Scriptures were only the product of the human brain, inherently fallible as it is, the Bible would have failed completely in its purpose, which is to give us a sure knowledge of truth.

THE BIBLE IS ONLY PARTIALLY INSPIRED BY GOD

The great number of partisans of this theory present it in very different ways:

Inspiration had to do only with the author's thoughts, not with the words used. God suggested the ideas and the general trend of the revelation, then left the man free to express them in his own language, as he liked.

In reality, it is plain that ideas can be conceived of and transmitted only by means of words. If the thought communicated to man is divine and of the nature of a revelation, the form in which it is expressed is of prime significance. It is impossible to dissociate the one from the other. In a legal document, everything may depend on a single expression. In the case of the promises and the solemn declarations of the Bible, these may derive their strength and value from one particular word. The exegetical study of the Scriptures in the original languages is a minute consideration of the words. If these expressions are not inspired, the study loses its meaning. The Bible itself insists on the revelation of the words; we shall come back to this point when we take up verbal inspiration. As for Paul, he said of the things revealed by the Spirit of God: "We speak, not in *words* which man's wisdom teacheth, but which the Spirit teacheth" (I Cor. 2:13; the Greek here is *logoi*, correctly translated "words").

Beneath this distinction between inspired *thoughts* and *words* left to the free choice of man is hidden, in reality, a refusal to give credence to the authority of the sacred text. Those who make such a distinction seem to admit that God spoke to the prophets, but they consider themselves entirely free to reject or to make changes in the written message. They suppose that in this way they can eliminate certain difficult or obscure points in the text. Actually, if the expressions are inexact or uncertain, any assurance as to the thought of God vanishes. Moreover, this irrational and unwarranted hypothesis solves nothing. If some people find it difficult to imagine how God guided the authors in the choice of the words of the Scriptures, is it any easier for them to explain how He inspired the thoughts?

> When Moses recounted the creation of the world;
> when David put down a thousand years beforehand the prayers of the Son of God on the cross;
> when Solomon personified the Eternal Wisdom;
> when Daniel reported in detail, and without understanding them very well himself, distant events involving the world and the people of God;
> when ignorant fishermen of Galilee drew up the sublime pages of the Gospels;
> when Paul expounded the deepest truths of salvation;
> and, finally, when John painted in bold outlines the fresco of eternity,

was it not necessary that every little word be given them by God?[1] The believers at Pentecost even began suddenly to speak in some fifteen different languages the wonders of God "as the Spirit gave them utterance" (Acts 2:4-11).

In conclusion, let us sum up a few more remarks of Louis Gaussen. Any who say that the thoughts are of God but the words only those of men begin at once to attribute to the words all kinds of contradictions, misunderstandings and mistakes. These supposed errors, therefore, are in the men's thoughts much more than in the words. We cannot separate the two, for a revelation of the thoughts of God always requires the inspiration of the Word of God.

If the Scripture is inspired, God unfailingly watched over the expressions of the text, even though He did not always inspire the other thoughts of the writer. Paul before the high priest was wrong, but not when he wrote the Word of God or when Jesus Christ was speaking in him (Acts 23:5; I Thess. 4:15; II Cor. 13:3). Peter was mistaken before Christ and at Antioch (Matt. 16:22-23; Gal. 2:11-14), but not when he wrote the oracles of God. The same also applies to Balaam when his wicked thoughts were changed into words of blessing (Num. 22:6, 38; 23:5). In summary, inspiration of the thoughts may be granted to a believer, inspiration of the words makes a prophet, inspiration of the writings makes a sacred author. The most profound discourses of Cyprian, Augustine, Luther and Calvin are only men's words about the truths of God: words venerable, precious and powerful; nevertheless, words which, lacking the inspiration of which we have been speaking, must remain in the category of mere sermons.

In extreme cases it is possible for one to declare the words of God without even comprehending them: Daniel wrote things that were still "sealed" (12:8-9); Caiaphas prophesied without realizing the import of his declaration (John 11:51); the old prophet spoke without having either willed or anticipated what he spoke (I Kings 13:21). This therefore means that men matter much less than the message, whether spoken or written. The Lord was able to combine the individuality of the authors—their conscience, memory and emotions—with the material He was causing them to produce. However, the essential truth is that "no prophecy ever came by the will of man: but men spake from God, being moved by the Holy Spirit" (II Peter 1:21).

Whether the vehicle was mighty like Moses, wise like Daniel, impure like Balaam, an enemy of God like Caiaphas, holy like John, without bodily form like the voice from Sinai, insensible like the hand that wrote on the wall in Babylon—except for the necessity of Christ's incarnation to make the message accessible to us, the essential thing is the thought and the very Word of God.[2]

Only the moral and spiritual teachings of the Bible were inspired. Some say that God did reveal supernatural things, things otherwise beyond the grasp of man; but, performing no useless miracle, He let the sacred writers set down as they chose the material which they already knew, especially matters pertaining to the history and concepts of their time. Thus there were brought into the Bible many inexactitudes, legends and notions considered false from our modern point of view.

To this we reply that if a witness employs double-talk and misleading language on one point, it is difficult to grant the truth of the rest of what he has to say.

Was it really necessary for the historical accounts to be inspired? It is important to emphasize that the Judeo-Christian religion was incarnated in history. The great facts of the revelation and of redemption actually took place here on earth and at exact points in time. If we know of these facts only by imprecise or legendary records ("myths," to use the word most in vogue today), what spiritual certainties can we base on them?

The Bible itself affirms the veracity and the spiritual value of its historical accounts. Jesus Christ with absolutely no reservation subscribed to the great events detailed in the Old Testament (see chap. 18). Paul declared that these were written for our instruction and that in type they contained the spiritual truths of the gospel (I Cor. 10:4, 6, 11). The authors of the historical books had all the more need to be inspired, since with the account of the facts as God saw them they mingled in an inextricable way revelations, exhortations, prophecies and laws of an indisputably supernatural origin.

Thus it is that a simple recital of the past often presented, quite unknown to the writers but by the express will of the Lord, a detailed prefiguration of the Messiah—His personality, sufferings, death and glory. Adam was the "figure of him that was to come" (Rom. 5:14); the water of the deluge was "a true likeness" of baptism (I Peter 3:21); Hagar and Sarah symbolized, respectively, the covenants of the law and of grace (Gal. 4:24); the Jewish Passover, with its sacrificed lamb, represented Christ, our passover (I Cor. 5:7); the rock struck at Horeb "was Christ" (10:4), etc.

Finally, the sacred historians needed to be guided step by step in choosing from the materials at their disposal. According to John 21:25, the world could not contain the entire recital of the "things which Jesus did." What divine inspiration it took to produce the inimitable sobriety, brevity and diversity of the Gospels (to say nothing of the other historical books) !

This is so true that the more one goes on to know of the Scriptures, the more he finds of spiritual teaching on every page. This is to be expected, since "whatsoever things were written aforetime were written for our learning" (Rom. 15:4). We shall doubtless see even more clearly someday the perfection with which history, revelation and inspiration blend together in the Bible.

The Bible "contains"—but "is not"—the Word of God. This is the expression in vogue today. In the minds of a large number of theologians, the Scriptures include many myths, legends and errors, which fact, they say, in no wise hinders their way of discerning in them the Word of God. According to these men, no cultured, honest individual can admit its total inspiration any more. Modern science has thoroughly swept away such a naïve concept. (See, farther on, chap. 13.)

For Roland de Pury, "to confound Scripture and the Word of God" is as serious as the Roman error; the difference is essential, and unless Protestantism retains this sharp distinction, it will "run the risk of slipping into paganism." The Bible is only "a witness to revelation," a revelation shot through with textual contradictions. From the critics' viewpoint, fundamentalism, with its "book fallen from the sky," is a biblical fetishism which, brushing away difficult problems, is well adapted to a primitive mentality.[3]

One of the most influential of contemporary theologians, Rudolf Bultmann, has done his best to separate all the "myths" from the biblical text, so as to conserve the essence of the gospel, the *kerygma* (Greek, proclamation) ; that is, the truth to be proclaimed. Here are a few of the elements of the New Testament which, according to Bultmann, should be eliminated, because their mythological character makes them unacceptable to the modern mind. It amounts, in fact, to taking out all that is miraculous or supernatural:

> The preexistence of Christ
> His virgin birth
> His Deity
> His miracles
> His substitutionary death on the cross

His resurrection and that of believers
His ascension
His return in glory
The final judgment of the world
The existence of spirits, both good and evil
The personality and power of the Holy Spirit
The doctrine of the Trinity
Death as the result of sin
The doctrine of original sin[4]

After this "demythologizing" of the biblical text, there is no need to ask oneself what remains of "the essence of the gospel" or what proclamation (kerygma) may still be drawn from it! Since this dissection is applied in an even more radical way to the Old Testament, one can readily see that if the Bible does contain some elements of the Word of God along with the myths and legends, these latter have a strong tendency to invade the whole. If Bultmann wanted to carry this idea through to its logical conclusion, what would keep him from ending up with a declaration that God Himself is the last myth to be eliminated?

If the Scripture really does abound in doubtful and undependable things, one cannot regard it as being, in itself, the revelation of God. This is why these same authors claim that it is only a human echo of the revelation, a fallible witness to it. We find here again the idea that after God spoke to the sacred writers, He then left them to their own devices, so that among their memories were mingled inexactitudes, "embellishments" and legends. One is forcibly struck with the fact that in this case it would be completely impossible for anyone today to sort the truth out of the error in the mixture.

In their attempt to extricate themselves from this difficulty, the great theologians have arrived at this reasoning: the Bible is only a human word; but God can *make it become* His Word when He addresses some message to us by means of it. In that moment of "personal encounter," God communicates some fragment of His truth; however, this transmission does not change the fact that the biblical page under consideration remains a legend, simply the recording of an uncertainty or the indication of a distorted tendency. Theodore Engelder says in his *Scripture Cannot Be Broken* that such men "refuse to believe that God performed the miracle of giving us by inspiration an infallible Bible, but are ready to believe that God daily performs the greater miracle of enabling men to find and see in the fallible word of man the infallible Word of God."[5] We confess that we find it very difficult to understand why God would make use of error to teach us the truth.

Even more perplexing is the question If the biblical text is erroneous, by what criterion could we control the experience of the believer for whom this page suddenly were to "become" the Word of God? Such a theory could only lead to the most subjective and irrational mysticism. Let us pause a moment at this point to think of the confusion of the simple believer whose faith in all the Scripture is thus shaken. He has been told to sort it out and to keep what is good. But then, what enables him to distinguish the false from the true, the human from the divine? How will he go about classifying the pages of the Bible as inspired, partially inspired or not inspired? By what authority can he say this is, or is not, the mind of God? An extremely grave matter confronts us here, since our eternal salvation depends on it. Moreover, who would have the audacity to claim of a human word It is God who said it, or of a divine word It is only man who is speaking?[6] To attempt to decide what is inspired in the Bible and what is not is to put oneself above the Scriptures and to lose the divine message.

In practice, since nobody can do the sorting, questions of inspiration and authority are kept in a foggy half-light. You are left to decide whether or not such and such a commandment should be taken seriously, whether a given promise is credible or fallacious, whether this or that author is an imposter or a reliable witness. Question marks throng in from first to last. Preaching itself becomes paralyzed, since the speaker is compelled to talk about doctrines that he is not sure of and accounts which he considers only legendary. He generally will not dare to say from the pulpit that creation, the fall of man and the deluge are only myths and the Pentateuch a collection of counterfeit documents. What can men preach, furthermore, who find mythological the miraculous birth of Christ, the cross, the resurrection and the glorious second coming? One man declared recently in a very conspicuous place: "When I was a student of theology, my friend and I used to spend a good deal of time arguing about whether the tomb of Christ was empty or not. But I have come to see that it really doesn't make any difference." At a Christmas service recently, another preacher, after reading the gospel record, added: "This is what Luke and Matthew say, but we know now that it is just a legend." A theological student, assigned to prepare a message for the same occasion, exclaimed: "What is there for me to preach about a myth?"

If a great many of the pages of the Bible are unauthentic and mythical, what remains that is sure? Jesus Himself was mistaken, then, as well as the prophets and the apostles, for they believed without reservation in the sacred text. On the other hand, whom can we trust? We wouldn't risk our lives and our eternal destiny on a book so open to question as this one. Are we to put our confidence in these great theologians, with their ever changing theories? In the church, which down through history has so often proved fallible and untrustworthy? Or will it be our "religious conscience," which constantly plays tricks on us?

Christ alone is the "Word of God." To provide a little reassurance, there are those who say We believe without reservation in the Word of God, but it is Jesus Christ alone who is this Word; as for the Bible, it is simply an "echo." These concepts cannot be reconciled. Such a declaration seems at first to be very devout, but it is nonetheless inexact and incomplete. Certainly Christ is par excellence the Word, divine, eternal and creative, who was made flesh to save us (John 1:1-3, 14). However, we know exactly nothing about Him—His person or His redemptive work—apart from the written Word.

If Jesus alone is the Word of God, independent of Holy Scripture, which Christ is really meant? If the Christ of Matthew, John and Paul is subject to question, are we to look to the Christ of Bultmann or Robinson or some other of the celebrated theologians who are constantly revising and correcting the sacred text?

As for the Bible itself, it reiterates throughout that it *is* the Word of God. The Old Testament repeats 3,808 times such synonymous expressions as "Jehovah saith," "thus saith Jehovah," and "the word of God came saying. . . ." The psalmist, as did Jesus Himself, called the Law (the Old Testament Scriptures) "the word of God" (Ps. 119:9; Matt. 15:6). The same expression is used in the New Testament of the word preached by Christ and His apostles (Luke 5:1;

Acts 13:44; and, especially, I Thess. 2:13. We shall continue this line of argument in chap. 21).

THE BIBLE IS A BOOK WHICH IS ONLY DIVINE, HAVING BEEN DICTATED MECHANICALLY TO MEN

The sacred author was wholly passive, registering and transmitting the revelation the way a tape recorder would work today. His personality was completely set aside, so that the text might be free from any fallible human aspects. It would, therefore, be like the claims of the Muslims for the Koran: already fully spelled out in Arabic in heaven, it supposedly came down to earth with no change whatsoever. For this reason, also, Muslims have been slow to give permission for any translation of the Koran at all, since no other form is admissible but the flawless one given to Muhammad. According to those who deny the plenary inspiration of the Scriptures, our theopneustic convictions would inevitably lead us to an attitude comparable to the above.

Let us hasten to say that we have absolutely no such conception, even though it is constantly being attributed to us. We declare, on the contrary, that God did not at all annihilate the personalities of Moses, David, John and Paul. Their style, temperament and personal feelings are everywhere apparent (see Rom. 9:1-5). Their writings bear the imprint of their times and reproduce the local color of the places where they were drawn up. This is why a minute study of the context of the sacred writings—historical, cultural and linguistic—contributes so much to the understanding of their spiritual import. A mechanical dictation would have produced a complete uniformity on all the pages of the Bible, a condition which is very far from the truth.

F. E. Gaebelein puts the matter like this:

> Unfortunately, there is a persistent tendency to caricature the intellectual position of those who accept the Bible as a fully inspired book. . . . Almost always there is the insistence upon equating plenary inspiration with the dictation theory: "The authors of the Bible were little better than human dictaphones, recording mechanically the words of the divine writer. The individuality of the writer was lost, his function being but that of parrot-like reproduction. As for the Bible which we now have,

it is entirely free from error, even the punctuation having been translated unchanged." Such a view is then said to be intellectually impossible and fit to be held by only the most ignorant.[7]

Why do they persist in attributing to evangelical believers such a false theory, which to our knowledge nobody holds today? It is because we recognize the twofold nature of the Scriptures: the divine inspiration of every page of it, along with its admittedly human character. Such a supernatural view does not seem acceptable to modern unbelievers, even "religious" ones. For them, to affirm divine inspiration for the whole Bible is to set aside any participation on the part of the sacred writers; it is to deify Scripture as having been received "all of a piece, as if fallen out of the sky." This creates the possibility of interpreting it in the most literal fashion and consequently of practicing "Bible-worship."

Actually, these critics simply refuse to believe in the miraculous. For them there are only two possibilities: if the text was entirely from God, it would inevitably have had to be dictated mechanically (which idea is absurd) ; or if man enters into it throughout, the Scriptures are inevitably fallible, full of legends, exaggerations and "pious" frauds (which notion makes its testimony unacceptable).

Did not the Jews and the docetists in the early centuries adopt the same attitude toward Christ? For them, the Messiah would have had to be only God, with His humanity merely apparent, or only man and therefore fallible, capable of lying and even of imposture. The Gospels expressly state that Christ in His perfection is at the same time God and man, just as the fully inspired Bible is at once of God and of men.

It has often been claimed that "mechanical dictation" was taught by the Reformers and again by Lutheran theologians of the seventeenth century. However, such scholars as Robert Preus[8] and James I. Packer[9] affirm that those men never did conceive of the word "dictated" in the sense attributed to them. Packer writes:

> Because Evangelicals hold that the biblical writers were completely controlled by the Holy Spirit, it is often supposed . . . that they maintain what is called the "dictation" or "typewriter" theory of inspiration. . . . But it is not so. This "dictation theory" is a man of straw. It is safe to say that no Protestant theologian, from the Reformation till now, has ever held it;

> and certainly modern Evangelicals do not hold it. . . . It is true
> that many sixteenth and seventeenth-century theologians spoke
> of Scripture as "dictated by the Holy Ghost." But all they meant
> was that the authors wrote word for word what God intended.
> . . . The use of the term "dictation" was always figurative. . . .
> The proof of this lies in the fact that, when these theologians
> addressed themselves to the question, What was the Spirit's
> mode of operating in the writers' minds? they all gave their
> answer in terms not of dictation, but of *accommodation*, and
> rightly maintained that God completely adapted His inspiring
> activity to the cast of mind, outlook, temperament, interests,
> literary habits, and stylistic idiosyncrasies of each writer.[10]

Not only was a mechanical notion of inspiration foreign to the
mind of these dogmaticians, but they openly and expressly condemned it. They declared absurd the idea that the authors were like
inanimate objects. If God "dictated," He inspired and suggested
(these same theologians readily used the word *Eingebung*, an inner
communication). On their part, the sacred authors set about to
write voluntarily, consciously, from conviction and experience, and
spontaneously. If these two statements seem paradoxical, even contradictory, these same theologians made no attempt whatsoever to
bring them into harmony, as they did not in reference to the many
other paradoxes in the Scriptures.[11]

Professor B. B. Warfield is no less categorical on the subject of the
reformed churches: "It is by no means to be imagined that it [the
doctrine of plenary inspiration] is meant to proclaim a mechanical
theory of inspiration. The Reformed Churches have never held such
a theory: though dishonest, careless, ignorant or over-eager contro-
verters of its doctrine have often brought the charge. . . . The Reformed Churches hold, indeed, that every word of the Scriptures,
without exception, is the word of God; but, alongside of that, they
hold equally explicitly that every word is the word of man." Indeed
one can recognize "the fervid impetuosity of a Paul, the tender saint-
liness of a John, the practical genius of a James, in the writings which
through them the Holy Ghost has given for our guidance."[12]

What is the position here of the Genevan Revival, to which evangelical groups of the French language owe so much? Louis Gaussen,
author of the classic book *Theopneustia* (now known as *The Inspira-*

ration of the Holy Scriptures) repudiated in these words the "dictation" theory which some have attempted to foist upon him:

> There is gratuitously attributed to me an idea which I have never entertained for a single moment, one for which I have always felt the greatest repugnance. I wish here to loudly disavow this theory, for of all conceivable systems there is none more contrary than this one to the large place which I give the individuality of the sacred writers in the composition of the Scriptures.[13]

As representative of the evangelical theologians of the close of the nineteenth century, J. I. Packer quotes fourteen, all of whom forthrightly repudiated the theory of mechanical dictation. In 1893 B. B. Warfield wrote: "It ought to be unnecessary to protest again against the habit of representing the advocates of 'verbal inspiration' as teaching that the mode of inspiration was by dictation."[14] Packer adds: "Still less ought it to be necessary in 1958—but hoary error dies hard!" The well-known compendium of the faith entitled *The Fundamentals* (from which was derived the epithet "fundamentalist") also vigorously refutes this theory, declaring that the theologians made it up out of whole cloth, and adding: "It never existed at any time during the past century save in certain people's imagination."[15]

For Adolph Saphir, "mechanical dictation" is nonsense. Indeed, if a man is preserved from error and sin, that does not at all signify that he has lost his individuality or his originality, he explains. When the Holy Spirit fills his mind with light and his heart with love, He sets him free before God; he is then in his normal state. In heaven the saints will have the most marked individuality. Can we fail to perceive the admirable variety among the sacred writers, arising out of the differences in their profession, language, time, and country? Would it not be absurd to suppose

> that Isaiah did not feel awe and reverence when he wrote the sixth chapter of his prophecy; that Jeremiah, in writing the book of Lamentations, was a mere amanuensis, who, without sympathy in his heart and tears in his eyes, obeyed a higher voice; that David's heart was not filled with joy and gratitude when he sang the 23rd or the 103rd Psalm; that Paul, in writing to his congre-

gations, did not pour out the rich treasure of his own experience and love.[16]

As for Erich Sauer, he wrote only a few years ago:

> Let us not be mistaken. We do not speak of a stiff, mechanical, dictated inspiration of the Word. This would be completely unworthy of a divine revelation. A mechanical inspiration [automatic dictation] is found in occultism, spiritism, and therefore demonism, where the evil inspiring spirit works by setting aside [substitution] and excluding the human individuality. Divine revelation, however, has nothing to do with such suppression of the human personality. It will not sanction the annulling of the God-given laws of human consciousness, nor transforming the man into an automaton; it causes rather the intensifying and heightening than the excluding of the human faculties. "Light cannot produce darkness, but rather acuter sight." The divine revelation desires fellowship between the human spirit and the Divine Spirit. It seeks the sanctifying and transfiguring of the personality and setting it to serve. It desires not passive "mediums," but active *men* of God, not dead tools, but living, sanctified co-workers with God, not slaves, but friends (John 15:15). Therefore its inspiration is not mechanical but organic, not magical but divinely natural, not lifeless dictation but a living word wrought by the Spirit. Only so can God's word be man's word and man's word God's word.[17]

Dr. André Lamorte also rejects strongly the theory which makes purely passive organs out of the sacred writers.[18]

In spite of all the preceding, the following notation by Edward J. Young is only too true concerning most of the modern theologians. They seem to be agreed in saying: "There is one thing . . . that we cannot do. . . . We cannot, whatever else we may do, return to the old orthodox view of a mechanically dictated Scripture. We want no static conception of inspiration."[19] As far as we are concerned, we also have no need to return to such an imaginary view; we never professed anything of the kind in the first place.

7

PLENARY AND VERBAL INSPIRATION
OF THE SCRIPTURES

HAVING EXAMINED VARIOUS THEORIES OF INSPIRATION—all of them inadequate—let us see what the Bible seems to teach about it.

DEFINITIONS

What do we mean by *plenary* and *verbal* inspiration?

We believe that in the composition of the original manuscripts, the Holy Spirit guided the authors even in their choice of expressions—and this throughout all the pages of the Scriptures—still without effacing the personalities of the different men.

Scholars have expressed themselves on this subject as follows:

> The Church has held from the beginning that the Bible is the Word of God in such a sense that its words, though written by men and bearing indelibly impressed upon them the marks of their human origin, were written, nevertheless, under such an influence of the Holy Ghost as to be also the words of God, the adequate expression of His mind and will. It has always recognized that this conception of co-authorship implies that the Spirit's superintendence extends to the choice of the words by the human authors [verbal inspiration, but not a mechanical dictation!] and preserves its product from everything inconsistent with a divine authorship—thus securing, among other things, that entire truthfulness which is everywhere presupposed in and asserted for Scripture by the biblical writers' [inerrancy].[1]

> The doctrine of plenary inspiration holds that the original documents of the Bible were written by men, who, though permitted the exercise of their own personalities and literary talents, yet wrote under the control and guidance of the Spirit of God, the result being in every word of the original documents a perfect and errorless recording of the exact message which God desired to give to man.[2]

71

According to Gaussen, the theopneustia (in II Tim. 3:16 *theop-neustos*, breathed by God) is the mysterious power which the divine Spirit put forth on the authors of the Scriptures of the Old and New Testaments, to enable them to compose them as they have been received by the church of God at their hands, a guidance extending to the very words employed and preserving the writings in this way from all error.[3]

Let us now see what positive implications the above definitions contain, leaving for later chapters the answers to common objections.

AS USED OF THE BIBLE, WHAT IS THE MEANING OF THE EXPRESSION "PLENARY INSPIRATION"?

It signifies that the inspiration is entire and without restriction. This is what the sacred authors everywhere affirm: "Every scripture [is] inspired of God" (II Tim. 3:16) ; the prophets and apostles have transmitted to us, not the word of man, but truly the Word of God (I Thess. 2:13). The written revelation is complete, so that none can add to it or take away from it (Rev. 22:18-19) ; there shall not pass away from the Law (the Old Testament Scriptures) one jot or one tittle till all things be accomplished (Matt. 5:18).

One could not emphasize too much the importance that the Scriptures attach to the exact reception and communication of the divine expressions.

Moses well knew that he was transmitting the very words of God in the book of the law, just as he did in the case of the tables of stone which contained the Ten Commandments (Exodus 24:4, 7, 12). Indeed, "Jehovah said unto Moses, Write thou these words: for after the tenor of these words I have made a covenant with thee and with Israel" (34:27).

Balaam knew himself to be inspired, even to the extent of feeling constrained by the message: "The word that God putteth in my mouth, that shall I speak. I cannot go beyond the word of Jehovah, to do either good or bad of mine own mind; what Jehovah speaketh, that will I speak" (Num. 22:38; 24:13). Now that which God did for a vile and hostile man, a false prophet, could He not also do for His true disciples, for those who joyously submitted to His will?

David said to Solomon, in speaking of the construction of the temple: "All this . . . have I been made to understand in writing from the hand of Jehovah, even all the works of this pattern" (I Chron. 28:19). Doubtless this was a question of a revelation faithfully transcribed by one of the prophets. David considered it as having been written by the very hand of God. He cried out again: "The Spirit of God spake by me, and his word was upon my tongue" (not merely "the divine thought was in my mind") (II Sam. 23:2).

The psalmist considered the Law, the Jewish Scriptures, to be the very truth of God: "I trust in thy word . . . the word of truth. . . . All thy commandments are faithful. . . . For ever, O Jehovah, thy word is settled in heaven. . . . Thy commandment is exceeding broad. Oh, how love I thy law! . . . Thy law is truth. . . . The sum of thy word is truth" (Ps. 119:42-43, 86, 89, 96-97, 142, 160).

Jeremiah received from God these instructions: "Behold, I have put my words in thy mouth. Speak unto them all that I command thee. He that hath my word, let him speak my word faithfully. Speak . . . all the words that I command thee to speak. . . ; diminish not a word. Take thee a roll of a book, and write therein all the words that I have spoken unto thee" (Jer. 1:9, 17; 23:28; 26:2; 36:2; see also Isa. 6:7, 9; 51:16; Ezek. 2:7-8; 3:10-11, 17; Deut. 18:18).

Jesus Christ declared in regard to His words which are conserved for us in the New Testament: "Heaven and earth shall pass away, but my words shall not pass away" (Matt. 24:35).

Paul described thus his own attitude toward all the Scripture: "So serve I the God of our fathers, believing all things which are according to the law, and which are written in the prophets . . . saying nothing but what the prophets and Moses did say should come" (Acts 24:14; 26:22). He reiterated, "Whatsoever things were written aforetime were written for our learning" (Rom. 15:4).

As for John, he confidently repeated all through the last book of the Bible: "These are true words of God. . . . These words are faithful and true: and the Lord, the God of the spirits of the prophets, sent his angel to show unto his servants the things which must shortly come to pass" (Rev. 19:9; 21:5; 22:6).

WHY IS A "VERBAL" INSPIRATION SPECIFIED?

A plenary inspiration of necessity extends to the words (Latin, verbum, word). We have already stated this (chap. 6): the words are inseparable from the message. The sense of the divine revelation is inextricably tied in with the language of the Scriptures; their content cannot be expressed apart from words. So then, if we cannot say that the words of Scripture are given by God, we cannot affirm that the Scripture is inspired either, for it consists of words. We shall never feel certain of what the Spirit of God means in the Scripture unless we can be sure that the words of the text were expressly given by Him.[4]

Hammond comments:

> The only method of communication of ideas which we can understand as rational beings is that which achieves its purpose by the awakening of similar ideas in the object to whom the communication is made. The most universal form of such communication is by means of language. While language in its primitive form does not exclude other signs, it has gradually confined itself to sounds and their visual symbolic expression in written characters. If the story of the Incarnation and the voice of the prophet convey any true message from God, then God has employed the media of spoken and written words, the universal characteristic of language, to reveal His will to man. . . . The success of any communication, moreover, depends upon the adequacy of the expression. Where the mode of expression is defective, the apprehension of the original idea or thought is imperfect.[5]

Regarding the expression "verbal inspiration," Hodge says that for many theologians this implies the idea of a mechanical dictation. He declares:

> This view we repudiate as earnestly as any of those who object to the language in question. At the present time the advocates of the strictest doctrine of inspiration, in insisting that it is verbal, do not mean that, in any way, the thoughts were inspired by means of the words, but simply that the divine superintendence which we call inspiration extended to the verbal expression of the thoughts of the sacred writers, as well as to the thoughts themselves, and that, hence, the Bible considered as a record, an utterance in words of a divine revelation, is the Word of God to us.[6]

Let us summarize the opinion of Erich Sauer:

> We believe in full inspiration because of the inner connection

of thought and word. For the unmistakable expressing of thought there is necessary a careful choice of corresponding words. . . . The thinking of man arises from indistinct notions, sensations, and conceptions. But this does not contradict the fact that everything spiritual, if it is to attain to *clear* unfolding of a real thought or "idea," reveals itself in *words*. A thought only becomes properly a conscious thought if out of the subconscious realm of sensation and the indeterminate impression of will and feeling a word is born. . . . The word may be regarded as the body of the thought, giving the spirit "visibility" and form. Therefore if the word is blurred, the thought is blurred; and all becomes foggy and indistinct.[7]

If then the thoughts are inspired, the words must also be so. Luther justly said: "Christ did not say of His thoughts, but of His words, that they are spirit and life." (Cf. John 6:63.) J. A. Bengel declares, speaking of the prophets: "With the ideas God at the same time gave them the words." Spurgeon, that prince of preachers, said: "We contend for every word of the Bible and believe in the verbal, literal inspiration of Holy Scripture. Indeed, we believe there can be no other kind of inspiration. If the words are taken from us, the exact meaning is of itself lost."[8]

In the case of the men in Bible days—for example, Jeremiah—none of these matters aroused the slightest doubt. Had not God declared: "Whatsoever I shall command thee thou shalt speak. Behold, I have put my words in thy mouth. Thou shalt be as my mouth. Speak . . . all the words that I command thee to speak unto them; *diminish not a word*. Take thee a roll of a book, and write therein all the words that I have spoken . . ., even unto this day" (Jer. 1:7, 9; 15:19; 26:2; 36:2).

The Lord had Ezekiel eat, symbolically, the scroll of His revelation. Then He said to him: "When I speak with thee, I will open *thy mouth* [not merely "thy thought" or "thy mind"], and thou shalt say unto them, Thus saith the Lord Jehovah" (Ezek. 2:9—3:3, 27).

According to St. Paul, the Holy Spirit taught God's spokesmen a spiritual language, the words of which (Greek, *logoi:* discourse, words in their proper sequence in quick succession in the sentences) corresponded to the supernatural message to be transmitted, the very thought of Christ (I Cor. 2:13, 16). Thus we constantly see some revelation burst forth from a particular expression, or we find some author basing his whole argument on a single word.

Matthew 22:32—Exodus 3:6: In saying "I am the God of Abraham," the Lord affirmed that the patriarchs are still alive, thus demonstrating both survival and the resurrection. (See also Luke 20:37-38.)

Matthew 22:45—Psalm 110:1: If David, inspired by the Spirit, gave to the Messiah the title of *Lord* as well as that of *God,* it was for the reason that he saw in Him much more than his descendant according to the flesh. This declaration both attests to the deity of Jesus and silences His adversaries.

John 8:58—Exodus 3:14: In crying out "Before Abraham was, *I am,*" Jesus affirmed His preexistence and His divinity, for He took to Himself the ineffable name of God which had been revealed to Moses. He said "I am"—against the rules of syntax (not *I was*). He emphasized also His ever-present eternity, before which time flees away. The Jews caught His meaning perfectly and for this one word wanted to stone Him.

John 10:33-36—Psalm 82:6: The Scriptures, which cannot be broken, had called "gods" (and "sons of the Most High") those to whom the word of the Lord had been given. Christ laid hold on that audacious expression in order to show how He Himself, having come down from heaven, could much more be called the Son of God.

Galatians 3:16—Genesis 12:7: God said to Abraham: "Unto *thy seed* will I give this land," not "seeds" (descendants). Paul, utilizing this singular noun, sets forth a specific prophecy concerning the unique person of Christ, from the line of Abraham.

The multiplication of such examples could lead us far afield. Let us limit ourselves then to a consideration of the way the author of the epistle to the Hebrews based his apologetic on just one word of Scripture:

Hebrews 1:5-6—Psalm 2:7; II Samuel 7:14: God calls the Messiah His *Son.*

Hebrews 1:9—Psalm 45:7: The repetition of the word *God,* applied to the Son and to the Father.

Hebrews 2:6-8—Psalm 8:4-6: *"all things* in subjection under his feet" (in subjection to the "Son of man"). Three times the author repeats this expression, to point out its import and its relevance in time.

Hebrews 2:11-12—Psalm 22:22: again, the word *brethren*.

Hebrews 3:7-11—Psalm 95:8-11: here the two words emphasized are *today* and *rest*.

Hebrews 6:13-17—Genesis 22:16: God said to Abraham: "By myself have I sworn," an expression taken up and developed by the author of the epistle.

Hebrews 7:3—Genesis 14:18-20: the silence of the Scriptures is also inspired. The omission of any indication of the origin and genealogy of Melchizedek is compared to the eternal being of the Son of God.

Hebrews 12:26—Haggai 2:6: the words "yet once more" give to the sentence a very special implication.

We may say in résumé that very often the meaning of a whole passage rests entirely on one word, a singular or a plural number, the tense of a verb, the details of a prophecy, the precision of a promise and the silence of the text on a certain point.

The prophets of old often found that their message went beyond them. Still, the Holy Spirit who was in them helped them predict with astonishing accuracy the time of the coming of Christ (Dan. 9:22-27), the circumstances of His birth (the indications in Matthew 1 and 2), His sufferings (Ps. 22; Isa. 53) and the glory of the risen Lord (Ps. 2; 110).

They would have been mistaken in so minute a description if God had not guided them even in the choice of their language. Were they not to speak of things they knew nothing about, things even unperceived by angels, things reserved for future generations? And how could Daniel have drawn up all by himself messages which he did not understand and which were destined to remain secret and sealed until "the time of the end" (Dan. 12:8-9)?

Likewise, the compilation of the promises regarding salvation could not have been left to the imagination of a human author, however devout. Take John 5:24. Every expression in this verse is important: the words, the tenses of the verbs, the designation of actions and the divine assurances. Jesus indeed was treating here the most solemn of all questions, namely: What must we do to be saved? "He that *heareth my word* [the word of Christ], and *believeth him* [the Father] that sent me, *hath eternal life,* and *cometh not into judg-*

ment, but *hath passed* out of death into life." Thus we have revealed to us: the conditions of salvation, its divine Author, its gratuitousness, its present possibility, its eternal significance and the role of the Word and that of faith. What could we change in a declaration like the above?

Let us take as another illustration I John 5:13. On what does our assurance of salvation rest? *John* (the Lord's beloved disciple) said: "These things have I *written* [not just said] . . . that ye might *know* [not hope, feel, suppose] that ye *have* [now, not later, or in heaven] *eternal life* [the only reason for our existence], even unto you that *believe* [the only condition for receiving grace] on the name of *the Son of God* [the only name given among men]." What assurance, what certitude could we have if every time we read such marvelous texts we had to wonder: Was the author exaggerating here? Wasn't he going beyond the divine thought? Wouldn't it be better to substitute another wording for the one given? If the biblical text were actually uncertain, would we not have to cry out with Jeremiah: "Wilt thou indeed be unto me as a deceitful brook, as waters that fail?" (15:18).

What despair, then, would creep into our hearts before a revelation which claims to be divine, since we have no other light to guide us on the way everlasting! To doubt the Word of God—what a tragedy! Not to know where it is to be found, to have nothing of it available except little hints from the pens of authors wholly open to error—this would certainly keep us mourning in the dark.

As Erich Sauer says, full inspiration is necessary because of the fall of man. Were the Bible a mixture of truth and error, we would have to try to decide by ourselves what should be acknowledged as of divine origin or rejected as containing the alloy of human error. If man has not received from on high an exact standard, how can he distinguish between what is divine and what is human? How could we have the audacity to analyze, or even to dissect, God's Book, for the most part simply on the basis of impressions, subjective feelings or insufficient historical knowledge? What fallen man thinks about God is largely erroneous and generally untrustworthy; it is only "religion." Man must, on the contrary, find out what the Most High thinks about him and what He testifies concerning Himself and His plan of redemption. This essential objective really is a Person, not a book. Jesus Christ incarnate, crucified and raised again is the truth and the light, and the source of all knowledge. The revelation of Him to men, and this through the intermediary of men of darkened intellect (Eph. 4:18; I Cor. 2:14), required a supernatural inspiration, fully adequate and worthy of confidence. Even as we need *grace* because of our moral incapacity, we need *inspiration* because of our intellectual and spiritual incapacity.[9]

8

THE BIBLE–THE WORD OF GOD

EVANGELICAL BELIEVERS have always used interchangeably the two terms "Bible" and "Word of God." But one school of contemporary theology claims to find in the Scriptures only the experiences of men seeking after God. Since such attempts are viewed as having succeeded to a certain extent, these men seem somewhat above other religious geniuses. But they are far from infallible, as we have seen. The most that can be said of liberal theologians is that to them "the Bible *contains* but *is not* the Word of God." According to another slogan much in vogue, "There is only *one* Word of God, Jesus Christ."

One great theologian expresses himself in a quite different manner: Man cannot set himself to seeking the infinite God, totally "Other" in His transcendence. On the contrary, the sovereign God approaches man, coming to him in Jesus Christ. However, no one but the prophets and apostles really perceived this revelation. These transcribed their impressions for us; and their testimony (albeit human and fallible) is still superior to that of all other writers, even to that of Christians. But it remains true that this testimony, contained in the biblical text, is only an "echo" of the revelation; it could not be the revelation itself. However difficult it may be to admit it, this faulty and uncertain text *"becomes" the Word of God* for me when the Lord grants me a personal encounter, addressing Himself to me, here and now.

Who is right; and—above all—what does the Bible have to say on this subject? Since we deliberately take our stand on the terrain of revelation, have we scriptural and spiritual grounds for believing that the Bible is truly the Word of God?

THE BIBLE CONSTANTLY AFFIRMS THAT IT IS THE VERY WORD OF THE LORD

We have already mentioned the fact that in various expressions the Old Testament declares 3,808 times that it conveys the express words of God. Here are some particularly striking examples.

The Pentateuch makes this point 420 times; for instance, in the following terms: "Jehovah said unto Moses, Write this for a memorial in a book. These are the words which thou shalt speak unto the children of Israel. And Moses . . . set before them all these words which Jehovah commanded him. And God spake all these words. And Moses wrote all the words of Jehovah. And he took the book of the covenant, and read in the audience of the people: and they said, All that Jehovah hath spoken will we do, and be obedient. And Jehovah said unto Moses, Write thou these words: for after the tenor of these words I have made a covenant with thee and with Israel" (Exodus 17:14; 19:6-7; 20:1; 24:4, 7; 34:27).

Ezra initiated a revival when he led the people, on their return from Babylon, back to an observation of the law. "Then were assembled unto me every one that trembled at *the words of the God of Israel*. Now therefore let us make a covenant with our God . . . and let it be done according to the law" (Ezra 9:4; 10:3).

Nehemiah confirmed the fact that this revival was characterized by the public reading and the practical application of the "book of the law of God." The Scriptures exercised this influence because there was seen in them the very word of the thrice holy God: "Thou camest down also upon Mount Sinai, and spakest with them from heaven, and gavest them right ordinances and true laws, good statutes and commandments . . . and commandest them commandments, and statutes, and a law, by Moses thy servant" (Neh. 8:1-8; 9:13-14).

The psalmist in Psalm 119 calls the Scriptures "the word [or the words] of Jehovah" twenty-four times. Using ten different expressions, he mentions this fact 175 times and constantly exalts the Scriptures in these terms: "Thy word is very pure. Thy law is truth. Thou teachest me thy statutes. Let my tongue sing of thy word" (vv. 140, 142, 171-172).

The prophets, in a peculiarly exact way, identified their written message with the word of God: "Hear the word of Jehovah. The word of Jehovah was addressed to me in these words. The mouth of

Jehovah hath spoken. Jehovah spake unto me. Thus hath Jehovah said unto me," etc. We find such expressions in Isaiah 120 times, Jeremiah 430 times, Ezekiel 329 times, Amos 53 times, Haggai 27 times (in 38 verses) and Zechariah 53 times.

To entertain doubts about affirmations multiplied so many times over would pose a serious ethical problem. The Bible, beyond any controversy, presents to us the highest and purest moral principles. Its declaration repeated, not hundreds, but thousands of times, that it is the Word of God can only be either true or false. If it is false, how is it that the very highest moral principles could have come out of such a fabric of lies? Water rises no higher than its source, and a lie does not produce truth. For our part, we are thoroughly convinced that the Bible is exactly what it claims to be.

Christ and the Apostles Confirm the Testimony of the Old Testament

Two subsequent chapters expressly develop this point (chaps. 18 and 19).

1. On the one hand, the New Testament authors use the words "God said" when, in fact, it is the Scriptures that speak. On the other hand, the expression "the scriptures say" really means for them "God says." In both cases, the relationship between God and the Scriptures is such that the same direct authority is recognized as residing in both. The expressions "it is written," "the scriptures say," and "God says" are therefore synonymous.

2. "The scripture, foreseeing that God would justify the Gentiles by faith, preached the gospel beforehand unto Abraham, saying, In thee shall all the nations be blessed" (Gal. 3:8; Gen. 12:1-3).

"The scripture saith unto Pharaoh, For this very purpose did I raise thee up" (Rom. 9:17; Exodus 9:16). Actually, the Scriptures were not yet in existence at the time when God Himself addressed these words to Abraham and to Pharaoh. This kind of communicating was possible only through a complete identification of the inspired text with the God who speaks. Thus it becomes quite normal to find "the Scriptures say" in the sense of "God, in the Scriptures, says."

3. Jesus declared to the Pharisees: "God said, Honor thy father and thy mother: and, He that speaketh evil of father or mother, let

him die the death. But ye . . . have made void the word of God because of your tradition" (Matt. 15:4-6). So Christ put into the very
mouth of God the two texts Exodus 20:12 and 21:17. At another
time He asked, "Have ye not read, that he who made them from the
beginning made them male and female, and [*that He*] *said,* For this
cause shall a man leave his father and mother" (Matt. 19:4-5). Now
this is simply the text of Genesis 2:24.

4. The first disciples expressed themselves in the same way: "O
Lord, thou . . . by the Holy Spirit, by the mouth of our father David
thy servant, didst say, Why did the Gentiles rage?" (Acts 4:24-25).
Similarly, the sentence in Psalm 2:1 is attributed to God Himself.
The passage in Acts 13:34-35 also puts into His mouth the declaration of Isaiah 55:3, along with that of Psalm 16:10. (Again, cf. Heb.
1:5 and Ps. 2:7; Heb. 1:6 and Ps. 97:7; Heb. 1:7 and Ps. 104:4; Heb.
1:8 and Ps. 45:6-7; Heb. 1:10 and Ps. 102:25-28, etc.)

The two sets of passages above prove from our present point of
view that Christ and the apostles wholly identified the Scriptures
with the speaking God.[1]

EVEN CHRIST'S PREACHING AND THAT OF THE APOSTLES WAS CALLED "THE WORD OF GOD"

Of Jesus it is said: "The multitude pressed upon him and heard
the word of God" (Luke 5:1). As for Paul, he wrote to the Thessalonians, "When ye received from us the word of the message, even
the word of God, ye accepted it not as the word of men, but, as it is
in truth, the word of God, which also worketh in you that believe"
(I Thess. 2:13). This the book of Acts fully substantiates: "Samaria
had received the word of God" (8:14); "The Gentiles also had received the word of God" (11:1); "But the word of God grew and
multiplied" (12:24); "The proconsul . . . sought to hear the word
of God" (13:7); "Almost the whole city was gathered together to
hear the word of God" (v. 44); "Teaching and preaching the word
of the Lord" (15:35; see also 17:13; 18:11; 19:20).

Paul put the same idea in these words: "We give thanks to God . . .
because of the hope . . . in the word of the truth of the gospel, which
is come unto you . . . as it is also in all the world bearing fruit and
increasing, as it doth in you also, since the day ye heard and knew

the grace of God" (Col. 1:3-6). "So belief cometh of hearing, and hearing by the word of Christ" (Rom. 10:17).

If, then, the *preaching* of the apostles was called the "word of God," in spite of all that it contained which belonged merely to the current times and circumstances, how much more are their *writings* worthy of such a name! Drawn up with the greatest care, inspired even down to the very choice of words (I Cor. 2:13), they are the exact embodiment of the highest revelations of the new covenant, the grounds for faith and for the message of the church of all the ages.

Let us add that, from this perspective, every faithful proclamation of the gospel enunciates the Word of God. Did Peter not write: "If any man speaketh, speaking as it were oracles of God" (I Peter 4:11)? Whereas Paul, in his turn, declared: "We have renounced . . . handling the word of God deceitfully; but by the manifestation of the truth commending ourselves to every man's conscience in the sight of God" (II Cor. 4:2). "We waxed bold in our God to speak unto you the gospel of God. . . . For our exhortation is not of error, nor of uncleanness, nor in guile: but even as we have been approved of God to be intrusted with the gospel, so we speak. . . . We preached unto you the gospel of God" (I Thess. 2:2-4, 9).

This is exactly what every preacher needs today: to speak out faithfully and with authority, knowing that he is announcing the divine oracles. To be able to proclaim "God says" gives a different impression than does the delivering of some hesitant, questionable human word.

IN DRAWING UP THE NEW TESTAMENT, THE APOSTLES WERE
FULLY CONSCIOUS THAT THEY WERE WRITING "THE
WORD OF GOD"

Paul declared, in his letter to the Corinthians, that it was not he, but the Lord, who commanded certain things concerning marriage (I Cor. 7:10). The apostle was able to say in another place, "I received of the Lord that which also I delivered unto you" (11:23). And again: "This we say unto you by the word of the Lord" (I Thess. 4:15).

IT IS THEREFORE INEXACT TO SAY THAT "JESUS CHRIST ALONE IS THE WORD OF GOD"

Such an expression confuses several biblical ideas. Christ is certainly the Word par excellence: the Word divine, eternal, creating, who became incarnate so as to declare to us all the marvelous grace of the Father (John 1:1-3, 14-16). His very name is the Word of God (Rev. 19:13). He is here on earth the perfect manifestation of the Deity, the express revelation of the Father. Christ humbled Himself to come down to where we are. When Jesus spoke, God spoke; His word is spirit and life, carrying in itself salvation and truth. It is no less evident, as we have just seen, that the Scriptures are also the Word, though in a more limited sense; and that the preaching of the apostles—the liberating message they proclaimed— was also the very Word of God. The above is all the more true in the light of the fact that the great theme of the Scriptures and of preaching is still, and always will be, Jesus Christ.

THE ETERNAL WORD OF GOD IS ANNOUNCED TO US BY THE GOSPEL

This is what the Apostle Peter clearly affirms: "Having been begotten again . . . of incorruptible [seed], through the word of God, which liveth and abideth. . . . The word of the Lord abideth for ever. And this is the word of good tidings which was preached unto you" (I Peter 1:23, 25; see also Col. 1:3-6 already quoted).

THE BIBLE IS STILL THE EVER PRESENT WORD OF GOD

For Christ and the apostles, the Bible was not only something inspired in the past; by means of it God speaks directly to us today.

Very frequently (forty-one times, according to R. Nicole[2]), quotations from the Old Testament are introduced by a present tense verb, such as "He says," rather than by "He said":

"How then *doth* David in the Spirit call him Lord?" (Matt. 22:43).

"These [the Scriptures] *are* they which bear witness of me" (John 5:39).

"David *saith* concerning him, I beheld the Lord always before my face" (Acts 2:25).

"As *saith* the prophet, The heaven is my throne" (7:48-49).

"For what *saith* the scripture?" (Rom. 4:3).

"As he *saith* also in Hosea" (9:25).

"For the scripture *saith* . . ." (Rom. 10:11).

"Even as the Holy Spirit *saith*, To-day . . . so long as it is called To-day. . . . He [God] again *defineth* a certain day, To-day, saying in David . . ." (Heb. 3:7, 13; 4:7).

We well understand, therefore, why the author of the epistle to the Hebrews, after explaining these Bible passages, cried out in all solemnity: "See that ye refuse not him that speaketh" (12:25). The "oracles" published in the world are indeed "living oracles" (Acts 7:38), a "word" ever "living, and active, and sharper than any two-edged sword" (Heb. 4:12). The revelations pronounced of old have lost nothing of their efficacy, being forever quickened by the divine voice which gets through to our hearts here and now.

On other occasions the pronouns employed (*we, you,* etc.) indicate the person or persons whom the text is specifically addressing.

"Have ye not read that which was spoken unto *you* by God, saying, I am the God of Abraham, and the God of Isaac, and the God of Jacob?" (Matt. 22:31-32). Indeed, even as God spoke this to Moses, He still says it to us today.

"Ye hypocrites, well did Isaiah prophesy of *you*, saying, This people honoreth me with their lips" (Matt. 15:7).

"It is written in the law of Moses, Thou shalt not muzzle the ox. . . . Saith he it assuredly for *our* sake?" (I Cor. 9:9-10).

"The Holy Spirit also beareth witness to *us;* for after he hath said . . . then saith he . . ." (Heb. 10:15-16).

"Ye have forgotten the exhortation which reasoneth with *you* as with sons, My son, regard not lightly the chastening of the Lord" (12:5-6).

"He [Jesus] is the stone which was set at nought of *you* the builders" (Acts 4:11; whereas Psalm 118:22 simply says "which the builders rejected").

"Lo, we turn to the Gentiles. For so hath the Lord commanded *us,* saying, I have set thee for a light of the Gentiles" (Acts 13:46-47).

Finally, this perennial relevance of the written revelation of God is underscored forcibly by the declarations of the Apostle Paul: "It was not written for his [Abraham's] sake alone, that it was reckoned unto him; but for *our* sake" (Rom. 4:23-24). "For whatsoever things were written aforetime were written for *our* learning" (15:4). "These

things . . . were written for *our* admonition, upon whom the ends of
the ages are come" (I Cor. 10:11).

CONCLUSION

Issuing from the preceding texts is the certainty that the Bible is
indeed today the very Word of God. In delivering to us their eternally living message, its authors are in a way our contemporaries.
They address themselves to us every day, and we truly purpose to
walk with them in the way of God.

If our faith depended only on a lifeless book, a relic of a grandiose
past, we would be simply legalists, groveling in slavery to a dead
letter. But from the inspired Book there leaps up an overwhelming
dynamic, potent with judgment, life and resurrection.

In closing, we want to quote the interesting testimonies of two
contemporary theologians who are known for their unequivocal
fidelity to the Bible, the Word of God. Dr. James I. Packer, Anglican
theologian, writes:

> The biblical concept of Scripture, then, is of a single, though
> complex, God-given message, set down in writing in God-given
> words; a message which God has spoken and still speaks. On
> the analogy of scriptural usage, therefore, it is evident that to
> describe Scripture as the Word of God written is entirely accu-
> rate. Accordingly, if when we speak of "the Bible" we mean not
> just a quantity of printed paper, but a written document declar-
> ing a message—if, that is, we view the inspired volume as a lit-
> erary product, a verbal expression of thought—then . . . it will be
> correct to call the Bible the Word of God, and to affirm that
> what it says, God says.
>
> If, on the other hand, we are thinking of the Bible simply as
> a printed book, it will not be wrong to say that the Bible *con-
> tains* the Word of God, in the same sense in which any other
> book *contains* the pronouncements of the author. To speak in
> these terms, however, is to invite misunderstanding, since Lib-
> eral theologians have been in the habit of using this formula
> to insinuate that part of what the Bible contains is no part of
> the Word of God. It is worth guarding our language in order
> to avoid seeming to endorse so unbiblical a view.[3]

Professor Edward J. Young has this to say:

> A word is simply the vehicle by means of which thought is

communicated from one mind to another. And when we then speak of the Word of God, we are employing an expression to designate the means which God uses to convey to us the thoughts of His heart. God has spoken to us in order that we may know what He would have us do: through the medium of words He has revealed His will. Whatever Word He has uttered, since it has come from His mouth, is true and trustworthy. . . . Those whom God raised up to declare unto the nation His truth were inspired of Him. "I will place my words in his mouth, and he shall speak all that which I command him" (Deut. 18:18) .[4]

The pages which result from such inspiration are called "the holy Scriptures" and "the oracles of God" (Rom. 1:2; 3:2) .

The epistle to the Hebrews warns us very solemnly: "See that ye refuse not him that speaketh. For if they escaped not when they refused him that warned them on earth, much more shall not we escape who turn away from him that warneth from heaven" (12:25) . It was at Sinai that God delivered His oracles in a voice that shook the mountain (Exodus 19:18-19; Acts 7:38) . Those who disobeyed the law were caught up in judgment. God speaks now from heaven, as He promised in Haggai 2:6 that He would do. He has come down to us in the person of His Son, and the sublime revelations of the new covenant are even more compelling for us. Since God speaks to us directly through them, let us take care not to refuse to hear His living oracles!

9

THE INSPIRATION OF THE
NEW TESTAMENT

CHRIST AND THE APOSTLES continually affirmed the full inspiration of what was to them the Scriptures, namely, the Old Testament. But what can be said regarding New Testament inspiration?

THE DIVINE ORIGIN OF THE WORDS OF JESUS CHRIST

Jesus is the eternal Word, made flesh so as to bring to us in human language the whole message of God. He is the promised Messiah, into whose mouth the Lord put His own words (Deut. 18:18). His mouth (i.e., His message) is like a sharp sword (Isa. 49:2). Out of His mouth proceeds a sharp sword (Rev. 1:16; cf. 19:15, 21). He is Himself the truth and life eternal (John 14:6; I John 5:20). Moreover, He is able to say: "As the Father taught me, I speak these things" (John 8:28). "The things which I heard from him, these speak I unto the world" (v. 26). "The Father that sent me, he hath given me a commandment, what I should say, and what I should speak. . . . The things therefore which I speak, even as the Father hath said unto me, so I speak" (12:49-50; cf. 14:10).

At the close of His earthly career, Jesus said to His Father: "The words which thou gavest me I have given unto them. I have given them thy word. Thy word is truth" (17:8, 14, 17). This is why Christ solemnly affirmed: "Heaven and earth shall pass away, but my words shall not pass away" (Matt. 24:35). "He that rejecteth me, and receiveth not my sayings, hath one that judgeth him: the word that I spake, the same shall judge him in the last day" (John 12:48). As for us, we can only say with the disciples: "Lord, to whom shall we go? thou hast the words of eternal life" (6:68).

JESUS' PROMISE OF DIVINE INSPIRATION TO THE AUTHORS OF THE NEW TESTAMENT

We have already seen that the revelations of God to the prophets would have been lost had they not been transmitted to us in an inspired Book. The same can be said for the teachings of Christ—and so much the more because He left us no documents written by His hand. At the same time, when He left His apostles, He did not fail to promise them all the supernatural help they would need for the composition of the New Testament. In the famous passages of John 14:26; 15:26-27 and 16:12-15, the Lord specified the different parts of the New Testament.

> *the Gospels*: "The Holy Spirit . . . shall . . . bring to your remembrance all that I said unto you";
>
> *the Acts:* "He shall bear witness of me: and ye also bear witness" (cf. Acts 1:8);
>
> *the Epistles*: "The Spirit of truth . . . shall guide you into all the truth: for he shall not speak from himself. . . . He shall glorify me: for he shall take of mine, and shall declare it unto you . . . He shall teach you all things";
>
> *Revelation*: "He shall declare unto you the things that are to come."

It is evident that none but the Holy Spirit could meet the needs of the four evangelists in their staggering task: that of recounting the essentials in the life of Christ, of reproducing exactly His words, of choosing the most significant events for the blessing of centuries to come, of passing over numerous details (John 20:30; 21:25) and of recounting facts which were unwitnessed (such as the temptation in the desert). Moreover, the four accounts were all to harmonize in complementing one another, Matthew presenting the Messiah-King, Mark the Servant of Jehovah, Luke the Son of Man, and John the Word and the Son of God.[1]

As for the rest of the New Testament, the apostles plainly would never of themselves have been able to preach the wisdom of God, mysterious and hidden as it is (I Cor. 2:7), to unveil the mystery of Christ unknown even to the angels (Eph. 3:3-11), to exalt the excellence of the new covenant (Heb. 5:11; 8:6) or to reveal future and eternal things (Rev.).

In concluding this part, let us cite the following promises, which, although not primarily having to do with the compilation of the Scriptures, can nevertheless be applied to it also:

"As the Father hath sent me, even so send I you. . . . Receive ye the Holy Spirit" (John 20:21-22).

"Ye shall receive power . . . the Holy Spirit . . . and ye shall be my witnesses" (Acts 1:8). This testimony was clearly to be carried, not only by word, but also by pen!

"He that heareth you heareth me" (Luke 10:16).

"It shall be given you in that hour what ye shall speak. For it is not ye that speak, but the Spirit of your Father that speaketh in you" (Matt. 10:19-20).

"I will give you a mouth and wisdom, which all your adversaries shall not be able to withstand or to gainsay" (Luke 21:15).

These last two texts speak of the testimony of the disciples before the leaders of this hostile world. If in such circumstances the help of the Spirit was assured, would such help not be all the more available for bringing to the whole universe of lost humanity the message of eternal life?

THE INSPIRATION OF THE APOSTLE PAUL

Paul was a true apostle, a witness to the risen Christ. "Am I not an apostle? have I not seen Jesus our Lord?" (I Cor. 9:1). "In nothing was I behind the very chiefest apostles. . . . Truly the signs of an apostle were wrought among you" (II Cor. 12:11-12). He was, in fact, "an apostle, not from men, neither through man, but through Jesus Christ and God the Father" (Gal. 1:1).

Paul received direct and unique revelations. The Lord had announced this to him by Ananias from the time of his conversion: "The God of our fathers hath appointed thee to know his will, and to see the Righteous One, and to hear a voice from his mouth. For thou shalt be a witness for him" (Acts 22:14-15). Thus the apostle could say: "The gospel which was preached by me . . . is not after man. For neither did I receive it from man, nor was I taught it, but it came through revelation of Jesus Christ. . . . It was the good pleasure of God, who separated me, even from my mother's womb . . . to reveal his Son in me" (Gal. 1:11-12; 15-16).

"By revelation was made known unto me the mystery . . . of Christ. . . . Unto me, who am less than the least of all saints, was this grace given, to preach unto the Gentiles the unsearchable riches of

Christ" (Eph. 3:3-4, 8). This mystery "hath now been revealed unto his holy apostles and prophets" (v. 5; note here Paul's affirmation that the other New Testament writings were also inspired).

He did not hesitate to say in other places: "I received of the Lord that which also I delivered unto you. I delivered unto you first of all that which also I received. This we say unto you by the word of the Lord" (I Cor. 11:23; 15:3; I Thess. 4:15). "The Spirit saith expressly, that in later times some shall fall away from the faith" (I Tim. 4:1).

God granted to the apostle the ability to transmit faithfully to the church the revelations that he had received. Regarding divine truths communicated from on high, Paul wrote: "We speak, not in words which man's wisdom teacheth, but which the Spirit teacheth; combining spiritual things with spiritual words. But we have the mind of Christ" (I Cor. 2:13, 16).

He thus could affirm with full assurance: "We are not as the many, corrupting the Word of God: but as of sincerity, but as of God, in the sight of God, speak we in Christ . . . not . . . handling the word of God deceitfully, but by . . . manifestation of the truth" (II Cor. 2:17; 4:2). "For our exhortation is not of error, . . . nor in guile: but even as we have been approved of God to be intrusted with the gospel, so we speak . . . pleasing . . . God who proveth our hearts" (I Thess. 2:3-4). "According to the dispensation of God which was given me to you-ward, to fulfill the word of God, even the mystery which hath been hid for ages and generations: but now hath it been manifested" (Col. 1:25-26).

"God, who cannot lie, . . . in his own seasons manifested his word in the message, wherewith I was intrusted according to the commandment of God our Saviour" (Titus 1:2-3).

There is then an identification of the divine revelation and the message of the apostle, who could truly speak of it as *his* gospel: God "is able to establish you according to my gospel and the preaching of Jesus Christ, according to the revelation of the mystery which hath been kept in silence through times eternal, but now is manifested . . . by the scriptures of the prophets" (Rom. 16:25-26). For this, Paul's gospel, is the one and only true one. If an angel from heaven, or if Paul himself were to distort it by preaching something else, let that one be anathema (cf. Gal. 1:8-9).

Paul thought of his message as clothed with divine authority. He said to the Corinthians: "If any man thinketh himself to be a prophet, or spiritual, let him take knowledge of the things which I write unto you, that they are the commandment of the Lord. I give charge, yea not I, but the Lord. So ordain I in all the churches. I think that I also have the Spirit of God. If any man seemeth to be contentious, we have no such custom, neither the churches of God" (I Cor. 14:37; 7:10, 17, 40; 11:16).

Again, Paul wrote to the Thessalonians: "When ye received from us the word of the message, even the word of God, ye accepted it not as the word of men, but, as it is in truth, the word of God" (I Thess. 2:13). Consequently, "he that rejecteth, rejecteth not man, but God" (4:8). "And if any man obeyeth not our word by this epistle, note that man, that ye have no company with him, to the end that he may be ashamed" (II Thess. 3:14).

The revelations transmitted by Paul are indeed indispensable to the life of the church: "I adjure you by the Lord that this epistle be read unto all the brethren" (I Thess. 5:27). "So then, brethren, stand fast, and hold the traditions which ye were taught, whether by word, or by epistle of ours" (II Thess. 2:15). In all his relations with the Thessalonians, the apostle made it clear that his inspiration was exclusive and sufficient. What he had said to them in his first letter could not be contradicted "either by spirit, or by word, or by epistle as from us" (2:2).

Paul's letters were, during his lifetime, put into the category of Holy Scripture. Peter expressed the opinion of the primitive church about this: "Our beloved brother Paul also, according to the wisdom given to him, wrote unto you; as also in all his epistles . . . wherein are some things hard to be understood, which the ignorant and unstedfast wrest, *as they do also the other scriptures,* unto their own destruction" (II Peter 3:15-16).

It is remarkable that, for Paul himself, what had already been written of the New Testament constituted an authority. In I Timothy 5:18 he began with "the scripture saith" for a reference to Deuteronomy 25:4 ("Thou shalt not muzzle the ox"). The same principle appears in the text of Luke 10:7 ("The laborer is worthy of his hire").

If the apostle had a genuine right to be called a sacred author, his revelations concerning the new covenant superseded, in a sense, those concerning the Old Testament, by that time completed. In the epistle to the Galatians, Paul referred to himself as the defender of verbal inspiration. He quoted the Scriptures (3:11, 13), emphasized the import of a single word (*his seed,* Abraham's), singular number (v. 16), and justified the essential role of the law (vv. 21-24). But, after having presented Christ as the Emancipator, he cried out: "How turn ye back again to the weak and beggarly rudiments [the law], whereunto ye desire to be in bondage over again? Ye observe days, and months, and seasons, and years [according to Moses]. I am afraid of you, lest by any means I have bestowed labor upon you in vain" (4:9-11).

The New Testament, then, is fully inspired, just as is the Old. Let us complete our presentation of proof by two more illustrations.

THE INSPIRATION OF THE NEW TESTAMENT, ACCORDING TO THE EPISTLE TO THE HEBREWS

We shall call attention later (chap. 19, "The Testimony of the Epistle to the Hebrews") to the unreserved confirmation that the epistle to the Hebrews gives to the inspiration of the Scriptures. In fact, it attributes to the same Lord both great parts of the revelation: "God, having of old time spoken unto the fathers in the prophets by divers portions and in divers manners [this refers to the Old Testament], hath at the end of these days spoken unto us in his Son [this takes in all of the New Testament]" (1:1-2).

The theme of the whole epistle is that the new covenant is superior to the old and that, consequently, the New Testament, clothed with the authority of the same God, not only fulfilled the Old, but also went beyond it. "If the word spoken through angels [at Sinai, Acts 7:38, 53] proved stedfast, . . . how shall we escape if we neglect so great a salvation? which having at the first been spoken through the Lord, was confirmed unto us by them that heard [the apostles]" (Heb. 2:2-3).

"See that ye refuse not him that speaketh. For if they escaped not when they refused him that warned them on earth, much more shall not we escape who turn away from him that warneth from heaven" (12:25). The oracles published on earth were those of the law, whereas the gospel was given us directly from heaven by God's coming in the flesh in the person of Jesus Christ. The message of the New Testament is therefore even more marvelous and worthy of respect; and its inspiration is even more assured, if that were possible.

It is from this perspective that the law has been abolished "because of its weakness and unprofitableness," to bring in "a better hope," "a better covenant," "a ministry the more excellent," and "a better covenant . . . enacted upon better promises" (7:18-19, 22; 8:6). Levitical worship was "a copy and shadow of the heavenly things," the reality of which the New Testament brings us now (8:4-5). (Paul spoke in a similar vein in Galatians 4:9-11: Desiring to be under the law is to turn back again to the bondage "of those weak and beggarly rudiments" which would make vain all the labor bestowed by the apostle.)

THE INSPIRATION OF REVELATION

The last book of the Bible is also presented as a message divinely communicated to the Apostle John. According to Revelation 1:1-2: *God* Himself gave to *Jesus Christ* the revelation (Greek, the apocalypse) which his *angel* made known unto his servant *John* for the whole *church*.

The role of the apostle was to attest to the Word of God and to the testimony of Jesus Christ (v. 2). He was commanded to write this attestation in a book accessible to all (v. 11). Each of the seven letters to the churches has a double signature (chaps. 2 and 3). At the beginning of each is the expression "these things saith he [Jesus Christ]"; at the end of each is the warning "He that hath an ear, let him hear what the Spirit saith to the churches."

In chapter 10, after the symbolic swallowing of the little book both sweet and bitter, John was called upon to prophesy again "over [concerning] many peoples . . . and kings." This signifies that, having received the message of grace and judgment, he was to make it a very part of himself and then to proclaim it to all around him (vv. 8-11; cf. Jer. 15:16). The order to write is reiterated in 14:13. Then comes the solemn threefold repetition: "These are true words of God" (19:9). "Write, for these words are faithful and true" (21:5). "These words are faithful and true" (22:6).

This is why special blessings and curses are attached to the acceptance or the rejection of the message of Revelation: "Blessed is he that readeth, and they that hear the words of the prophecy, and keep the things that are written therein" (1:3). "Blessed is he that keepeth the words of the prophecy of this book" (22:7). "If any man shall add unto them . . . if any man shall take away from the words of the book of this prophecy, God shall take away his part from the tree of life" (vv. 18-19).

CONCLUSION

Each one of the authors of the New Testament, and Christ too, constantly affirmed that their words were identical with the Word of God as communicated to them. For the Jews, there was no doubt about the inspiration and authority of the ancient Scriptures: they were the very oracles of God. Likewise, the apostles and the primitive church say with John of the whole New Testament: "These are true words of God" (19:9).

Let no one say then that we cannot demonstrate the inspiration of the New Testament by its own declarations. This is the reproach which had already been addressed to Jesus: "Thou bearest witness of thyself; thy witness is not true. Jesus answered and said unto them: Even if I bear witness of myself, my witness is true; for I know whence I came, and whither I go" (John 8:13-14). None but God can reveal His unsearchable person and perfections. And Jesus alone can speak of what He is, with the claim: "The witness which I receive is not from man" (5:34). When we accepted Him by faith, He gave us life and convinced us of His deity.

In like manner, the Scripture touches the heart and spirit of the sincere reader. The Lord who inspired it and who gives it life makes His voice heard from heaven by means of it—that voice which the good Shepherd's true sheep instinctively know. They believe and are convinced, not through any rationalistic argument, but because they have met the living God who has saved them. (We shall come back later to the inner witness afforded the believer by the Holy Spirit [chap. 17, subhead "The Inner Witness of the Holy Spirit"], as well as to the convicting power which emanates from the supernatural quality of Scripture [chap. 22, subhead "The Power of Life Which Emerges from the Bible"]).

10

QUOTATIONS FROM THE OLD TESTAMENT IN THE NEW[1]

THE TWO TESTAMENTS, equally inspired, present a mutual testimony and are absolutely inseparable. The study of the quotations from the Old Testament found in the New leads to a double goal: on the one hand, it emphasizes the extraordinary place which Christ and the apostles gave to the ancient writings; and on the other, it elucidates certain problems arising out of the way in which the citations are made.

NUMBER AND IMPORTANCE OF THE CITATIONS

At least 295 quotations or direct references to the Old Testament have been counted in the New, a total of one verse out of every 22. If we add to this the evident allusions (613, according to C. H. Toy),[2] the proportion reaches to about 10 percent of the New Testament text. The discourses of Jesus and such books as Hebrews, Romans and Revelation are literally saturated with expressions, allusions and actual texts drawn from the Old Testament. The exact quotations number 278, coming from every book of the Jewish canon except 6 (Judges-Ruth, the Song of Solomon, Ecclesiastes, Esther, Ezra-Nehemiah and the Chronicles); whereas the allusions go back to every book in the Old Testament without exception.

It is at the same time very remarkable that in the entire New Testament there is not one explicit citation from the Old Testament Apocrypha, those books declared canonical in the sixteenth century by the Roman Church.

The apostles, as well as Christ Himself, constantly referred to Scripture—in their sermons, their histories, their letters and their prayers. They used it in addressing Jews and Gentiles, churches and individuals, friends and enemies, young believers and advanced Christians. They based their arguments and illustrations on it; and they drew from it instructions, documentation, prophecies, and warnings. Always and everywhere they were quick to show their dependence on the impregnable authority of the Holy Scriptures.[3]

DETERMINING EXACTLY WHAT A CITATION IS

Certain difficulties confront at times those who try to find in the Old Testament a text mentioned in the New. First of all it is helpful to remember that the ancient authors did not follow the same rules for writing that we do. Punctuation marks, so useful in making our modern books intelligible, were quite unknown to them. Without the aid of quotation marks, one can not always be sure of the places where a citation begins and ends. Moreover, the ancient authors did not always feel obliged to precede a citation by an introductory remark or by such a sign as a colon. A citation might also have been shorter than one would ordinarily think, with the rest of the words an explanation by the author himself. Neither were ellipsis marks used to indicate a partial citation; that is, the intentional omission of some of the words in the original. Finally, with the absence of brackets or of footnotes one cannot make distinctions where whole passages or biblical expressions are interspersed with a certain citation. Considering all these factors, we cannot find grounds for complaint against the authors of the New Testament, nor can we blame them for treating the sacred text in a way not consistent with our own procedures.

LIBERTY WITH WHICH CITATIONS ARE MADE

1. The authors of the New Testament felt free to paraphrase a quoted text or to make use of only the one word or thought in it which was suitable to their ends. Sometimes they gave a free rendition of the Hebrew text rather than translating it literally, thus particularly emphasizing a shade of meaning. They sometimes permitted themselves slight liberties, such as the change of a pronoun; the substitution of a noun for a pronoun, or vice-versa; or the modification of a verb form, etc. We do something similar when we want to give contemporaneity to a text which we are quoting. Someone has said, "A careful paraphrase that does complete justice to the source is preferable to a long quotation."

Here, for example, are various ways by which the text of Isaiah

6:9-10 is quoted, slightly altered according to the context where it is inserted:

Isaiah said, "Make the heart of this people fat, and *make their ears heavy*, and shut their eyes; lest they see with their eyes, and hear with their ears."

When Jesus quoted this passage, He changed it like this: "This people's heart is waxed gross, and *their ears are dull of hearing*, and their eyes *they have closed;* lest haply they should perceive with their eyes, and hear with their ears" (Matt. 13:15).

John expressed the same thought in a different way still: "For this cause they could not believe, for that Isaiah said again, He hath blinded their eyes, and *he hardened* their heart; lest they should see with their eyes, and perceive with their heart" (John 12:39-40).

Paul at Rome followed Jesus' paraphrase when he said: "Their ears are dull of hearing, and their eyes they have closed" (Acts 28:25-27).

From this we see that a passage is sometimes cited quite loosely, especially by the Lord Himself. The above modifications do not change the central message of the text, and the ones who did the quoting were inspired authors themselves. Each nuance is legitimate: the people hardened their hearts; next, the prophetic message—rejected by them—aggravated the hardening; and, finally, it is God Himself who hardens unbelievers. (See the identical case of Pharaoh: God said that He would harden the king's heart, Exodus 4:21; Pharaoh began by hardening his own heart, 7:13, 22; 8:15; 19; 9:7; after that, God did what He had said He would do: He, in turn, hardened the heart of the potentate, 9:12, etc.) P. Fairbairn brings out from such examples the principle of the apostles' free rendition of scriptural meaning, as over against formalism and the Jewish rabbis' superstitious insistence on "the letter." Quite an impressive number of passages do stress the exact words from the Old Testament, showing the value of the very form of the divine communication and the essential rapport between inspiration and the written record as it stands. God's words are words which, rightly interpreted, cannot be too closely held to.

But there were cases where, if nothing depended on a rigid adherence to the letter, the sacred writers did not confine themselves to it in any absolute sense: they simply set forth the substance of the revelation. This practice is fraught with an important lesson: the letter has no value except for the truth couched in it; it is to be esteemed and defended only insofar as may be required for the exhibition of the truth.[4]

2. It happened sometimes that the sacred authors, instead of referring to specific verses of Scripture, summarized the teaching on some point as found in another passage or throughout the entire canon. The "quotation" in such a case is not word for word, but is rather a condensation of a text known to the auditors or readers. Here are a few examples of these "citations of the substance," as they might be called:

Matt.   2:23—Christ called the Nazarene
        5:31—the writing of divorcement as ordered by Moses
        5:33—perjury and vows made to the Lord
        12:3-4—the episode of David's eating the showbread
        12:5 —the burnt offering by which the priests profaned the
              Sabbath in the temple
        22:24—the law of the "levirate"*
        24:15—the abomination of desolation spoken of by Daniel
        26:24—the going of the Son of Man "as it was written of
              him" (cf. vv. 54 and 56)

USE OF THE OLD TESTAMENT VERSION KNOWN AS THE SEPTUAGINT

The sacred authors, in drawing up the Greek text, had at their disposal the Greek translation called that of "the Seventy," by the Jewish rabbis of Alexandria, about 250 B.C. This version, far from perfect, was used rather freely by the authors of the New Testament:

1. When it seemed satisfactory to them, they quoted the text. It was evidently very familiar to all Hellenist Jews.
2. When necessary, they amended it, quoting according to the original Hebrew, which they retranslated themselves more correctly.
3. They sometimes paraphrased the text in question, using new expressions, so as to indicate the shade of meaning which they particularly wished to bring out.[5]

*Translator's note: "Levirate" from the Latin levir, brother-in-law.

Conclusion

The attitude of the authors of the New Testament toward the Old, in the general framework suggested above, was always one of trust and reverence. Concerning texts put into the very mouth of God, even when—according to the Old Testament—they were not spoken directly by Him, B. B. Warfield very justly says that these passages can be considered as sayings of God recorded in Scripture only on the hypothesis that all Scripture is a declaration of God.[6]

Finally, let us mention some authors not suspected of partiality on this subject, men who make exactly the same statement:

"We know, from the general tone of the New Testament, that it regards the Old Testament, as all the Jews then did, as the revealed and inspired word of God, and clothed with His authority."[7]

> Our authors view the words of the Old Testament as [the] *immediate* words of God, and introduce them explicitly as such, even those which are not in the least related as sayings of God. They see nothing in the sacred book which is merely the word of the human authors and not at the same time the very word of God Himself. In everything that stands "written," God Himself is speaking to them.[8]

> In quoting the Old Testament, the New Testament writers proceed consistently from the presupposition that they have Holy Scripture in hand. . . . The actual author is God or the Holy Spirit; and both, as also frequently the *graphe* [Scripture], are represented as speaking either directly or through the Old Testament writers.[9]

11

PROGRESSION IN THE REVELATION

PROGRESS IS APPARENT FROM GENESIS TO REVELATION

THE BIBLE DID NOT FALL FROM HEAVEN all in one piece. From Moses to John, its composition took about sixteen centuries, during which ·time the divine truth was manifested with increasing clarity.

The appearance of the sun makes an excellent illustration of this truth: dawn approaches progressively; then the sun bursts forth on the horizon, gradually but steadily mounting to its zenith, while its light steals nearer and nearer to illuminate the whole landscape.

Christ is our "sun of righteousness" (Mal. 4:2), the revelation of God, the theme of all the Scriptures. In the pages of the Old Testament, we see His coming long prepared for and minutely predicted. With the fullness of the time, the divine Word became visible by means of the incarnation, thus addressing Himself to men of good will. After the descent of the Holy Spirit, the apostles completed and explained this glorious message, Revelation carrying it through to its eternal consummation. The final step will be the cessation of present knowledge, when we shall see face to face and shall know even as we have been fully known (I Cor. 13:8, 12).

GOD, FOR INSTRUCTING US, USES A PEDAGOGIC METHOD; BUT HE DOES NOT TEACH US TRUTH BY MEANS OF ERROR

He treats humanity in its infancy like a child just starting in kindergarten. The teacher makes the needed adjustments following the mentality and development of her little pupil. She will teach him only truths, but she will present them in a simplified, visualized way. Later, going into rapid calculation and algebra, for example, she will not have to correct his early impressions of arithmetic, but will merely need to make these more specific and comprehensive.

Even so, God from the beginning taught men only the truth, but in a way adapted to their circumstances and their understanding. He

102

did not inject into His early revelations any errors or legends requiring painful removal later on. Those who maintain that He did
are back with evolution, the never proved theory that man, after
descending from a monkey, slowly emerged from his caverns, barbarism and crude patriarchal "polytheism," to arrive at last at the
more realistic image of God as seen in the prophets and in Jesus
Christ. In fact, such a concept is the farthest possible from the biblical view of revelation, even as it has been contradicted by the discoveries of archaeology and the history of early civilizations. Fallen
man seeking to create for himself an image of God is obviously only
groping in the dark, as all human religions and philosophies so tragi-
cally prove. The Bible alone brings us something else: in it, God,
inaccessible and sovereign, is shown coming down to speak to us and
to save us. Without a denial of Himself, He cannot do this except
on the basis of the strictest integrity, even if right through to the end
of the Scriptures He does continually keep completing and spir-
itualizing His revelation.

THE TWO GREAT PARTS OF THE BIBLE ARE CHARACTERIZED BY AN ANALAGOUS PROGRESS

OLD TESTAMENT

Historical books: beginning of the revelation, the theophanies, personal communications to the patriarchs; redemption of Israel, covenant accredited by signs and miracles, law given in detail to Moses
and written in part by the finger of God; the biographies of the
patriarchs and the life of the chosen people reveal the Lord of history,
even as they illustrate the struggles and victories of believers.

Poetical books: devotion, communion, prayer, temptations and
consolations of the man of God.

Prophetic books: increasingly precise announcement of the sufferings and final triumph of the Messiah, Saviour of Israel and of the
nations; message more abstract, but at the same time more spiritual;
action more personal and experiential, hidden in the heart.

NEW TESTAMENT

An analogous schema gives us the following steps:

The Gospels: in place of the theophanies, the incarnation of God
in Christ; direct revelation to the apostles; proclamation of the new

covenant based on the sacrifice of the cross and confirmed by signs and miracles. The gospel writers simply transcribed the words and works of Christ.

The Acts: historical demonstration of the intervention of God, the birth and growth of the church, salvation taken to the nations.

The Epistles: by the Holy Spirit's indwelling, the apostles expressed themselves. They revealed the pattern for the life of consecration, sanctification, unity and victory of believers.

Revelation: great prophetic fresco which depicts the definite triumph of Christ and of His own, on earth and into eternity.

THE PASSAGE FROM THE OLD TO THE NEW TESTAMENT MARKS A CONTINUOUS PROGRESS IN THE REVELATION

1. God, after having spoken by the prophets, speaks to us now in His Son (Heb. 1:1-2).

2. The promises made to Israel find their fulfillment in the gospel (Acts 13:32-33).

3. The worship, sacrifices, tabernacle and feasts of the old covenant were the copy and shadow of the heavenly things revealed in Christ (Heb. 8:4-5; Col. 2:16-17).

4. The instructions given to Israel correspond to her degree of development. The pillar of cloud and the pillar of fire led the people and indicated their halting places, as well as the way they should take (Exodus 14:19-20; Num. 9:15-23). In times of testing they consulted the Lord by means of the Urim and the Thummim (Num. 27:21; Ezra 2:63). At other times they cast lots before the Lord (Josh. 18:6; I Sam. 14:41-42; I Chron. 24:5); this custom prevailed until just before Pentecost (Acts 1:26). Such exterior means were well suited to a people whose nascent faith incessantly demanded signs and miracles (cf. John 4:48).

Since Pentecost the Lord has led His people by the inner presence of the Holy Spirit and by the conviction produced by the written Word. No longer have we a pillar of cloud, but the good Shepherd Himself goes before us. He causes each of us personally to hear His voice, as He had promised in Isaiah 30:21 (John 10:3). He does not say to us "Do this, and thou shalt live," but "If thou believedst, thou shouldest see the glory of God" (John 11:40).

5. Israel herself, in a sense, prefigured the church. The Israelite

became a member of the elect people by birth (hence, the importance of the genealogies). He promptly received this identification by means of circumcision. A hierarchy was established as follows: Aaron the high priest was admitted into the holy of holies, the Levites and priests into the holy place, and the people into the court.

In contrast, one becomes a member of the church by the new birth and the baptism of the Holy Spirit, which is the circumcision of Christ (Col. 2:11-12). And here we have the new hierarchy: Christ, sole Head of the church, entered once for all into the holiest for us (Heb. 9:12); all believers have become a royal priesthood, who serve God in the sanctuary (I Peter 2:5, 9-10); while the entire world is invited to come up to the court, where stands the cross of the expiatory sacrifice.

6. The law was the necessary preparation for grace. Written on tables of stone (the Decalogue, II Cor. 3:3), outside man, the law could only reveal the absolute requirements of God and could only condemn every ascertained transgression of it. It was a tutor to lead us to Christ, convicting of sin and convincing of the universal need for a Saviour (Gal. 3:24).

Grace, on the other hand, writes in our hearts the will of God (Heb. 8:10). Its purpose is the transformation of our very intentions, thoughts and hidden feelings (in regard to anger, facial expressions, divorce, words, revenge, etc.: Matt. 5:21-22, 27-28, 31-32, 33-34, 38-39). It changes our heart of stone into a heart of flesh and puts within us the Spirit of the living God (Ezek. 36:26-27).

7. The perspectives of the Old Testament are principally earthly; those of the New are, above all, heavenly. Abraham received the promise of a seed, a country and an earthly blessing (Gen. 12:3). By the Passover, Israel was bought out of Egypt, to find her rest in Canaan. The devout Israelite had the promise of a blessing accompanied by material prosperity (Deut. 28:1-14). The chastisements were also earthly and corporal (vv. 15-68). The concept of a life beyond this one was then only slightly perceived.

The New Testament, on the contrary, presents us with a community of the elect, all born anew by the Holy Spirit, having received eternal life as beneficiaries of the graces which are first of all spiritual and heavenly. "Our citizenship is in heaven" (Phil. 3:20). Henceforth, holy living was not to guarantee material benefits, but rather, persecutions (II Tim. 3:12). On the other hand, prospects for the future life startlingly flash gleams of terror and splendor: everlasting punishment for the impenitent, glorious resurrection and everlasting happiness for the redeemed.

8. The progression of the "kingdom of God" is gradually revealed. What is this kingdom in principle if it is not the sphere where God reigns? In the Scriptures we can trace for it seven distinct steps:

a. Paradise, where all was "very good" until the catastrophe of the fall (Gen. 1:31).

b. The *theocracy* in Israel, in which God governs by means of "judges," from Moses to Samuel.

c. The kingdom announced by the prophets: God, whose sovereignty the people rejected (I Sam. 7:8), continues to predict the reign of righteousness and peace which the Messiah would inaugurate (Isaiah 11).

d. The kingdom offered and rejected in the gospels: "The kingdom of heaven is at hand. The kingdom of God is within [in the midst of] you. The kingdom of God is come nigh unto you" (Matt. 4:17; Luke 17:21; 10:9-11). "We will not that this man reign over us. We have no king but Caesar" (Luke 19:14; John 19:15).

e. The kingdom hidden in the heart is the quality of the present kingdom, entered into by the new birth and accessible to Gentiles as well as to Jews (John 3:3, 5; Col. 1:13). In the world, even the "religious" one, good is mixed with evil (cf. the parables of the kingdom of Matthew 13; see v. 38); but the absent King will return to superintend the great separation (vv. 38-43; Luke 19:12, 15).

f. The thousand-year reign, gloriously established on earth (Rev. 20:1-10).

g. The eternal kingdom in heaven (II Peter 1:10-11; II Tim. 4:18).

It is evident that if certain revelations concern some limited period in time, others have an absolute and eternal import. Provisionary measures may fall away: bleeding sacrifices, circumcision, the feasts and the Sabbath, the portions for Jews alone among the people of God—these progressively lose their *raison d'être* as the revelation uncovers the permanent realities of which they were only the shadow and the prefiguration (Col. 2:16-17).

9. The moral conduct and holiness required of the people of God are the object of more and more precise revelations. It would be

inexact to attempt to evaluate all the pages of the Old Testament by our more perfect knowledge of the gospel of love and grace brought in by Jesus Christ. God evidently requires more of His people under the new covenant, since the Holy Spirit makes provision for the attainment of a higher plane of holiness.

Six times Jesus declares: "It was said of old time ... *but I say unto you*" (Matt. 5:21, 27, 31, 33, 38, 43). In every case His requirements far exceed those of the law of Moses, in respect to feelings, words, looks, marital fidelity, vows, nonresistance and love.

As for divorce, Christ makes it clear that although Moses permitted it for their hardness of heart, "from the beginning it hath not been so" (Matt. 19:8). In Eden the man and the woman enjoyed perfect union (Gen. 2:24). After the fall, when sin threatened the conjugal bond, there was given the temporary measure of divorce. But Jesus revoked this permission under the new covenant, because the Holy Spirit enables believing couples to remain faithful to their holy commitment.

The same thing is true of polygamy. Making its appearance (Gen. 4:19) for carnal motives, it always produced deplorable jealousies and rivalries. Consider the sad examples of the wives of Abraham, Jacob, Elkanah, Solomon, etc. Moses discouraged polygamy (Deut. 17:17) and regulated the abuse of it, without, however, abolishing it with a single blow. On the other hand, it has no place at all in the New Testament.

The revelations having to do with war have likewise become progressively conformed to the divine ideal. Let us note first of all that the commandment "Thou shalt not kill" forbids murder and that the law imposed the death penalty for offenders (Exodus 20:13; chap. 21). In ordering the destruction of the deeply corrupted Canaanites, God eliminated a gangrene which would have nullified His purpose of assuring the salvation of the world through Israel. Jesus gave the church a new commandment of love, pardon and nonresistance (Matt. 5:39, 44; cf. Rom. 12:17-21). When a religious institution influences political powers to burn heretics, it goes all the way back to the Old Testament and exhibits a complete lack of comprehension of both the Saviour's love and the progression of God's revelation. Let us note, however, that the situation in the unbelieving world has not changed: this world is still subject to the law. Paul declared that a magistrate (Roman, under Nero) was God's servant, who was to wield the sword (inflict the death penalty) for the punishment of a wrongdoer (Rom. 13:4).

THE REVELATION PAR EXCELLENCE, THAT OF JESUS CHRIST, GREW PROGRESSIVELY MORE CLEAR

To treat this subject adequately would really be to launch out into a consideration of the entire Bible. Let us limit ourselves to bringing out here a few indications apropos of the unity of the Bible as a whole.

In the Pentateuch the promise of the Messiah-Saviour became increasingly understandable (Gen. 3:15; 22:18; 49:10, etc.) :

the historical books stipulated that He would be a descendant of David (II Sam. 7:14);

the Messianic psalms are full of extraordinary prophecies (e.g., Ps. 22);

the Prophets complete the portrait with overwhelmingly dramatic strokes (e.g., Isa. 53);

the Gospels at last present in plain view the Lord who could say of Himself: "He that hath seen me hath seen the Father" (John 14:9);

the Epistles fulfill the promise made in John 16:12-13; they set forth the person and work of Christ, as well as the excellence of the new covenant;

finally, Revelation fully discloses the Lord as glorious Head of the church, inflexible Judge of the world and of Satan and sovereign Master of time and eternity.

When believers shall see face to face (I Cor. 13:12), nothing shall mar their rapturous satisfaction with the vision of the omnipotent God and the glorified Lamb (Rev. 21:23).

THE GOD WHO REVEALS HIMSELF PROGRESSIVELY REMAINS FOREVER IMMUTABLE

The sun, which little by little dissipates the shadows, does not in itself know change, as its rays, ever brightening in intensity, reach their climax in the dazzling glory of midday. Right from its opening pages the Bible describes God—sovereign, eternal, all-powerful and all-wise—as unique in His immutability.

His holiness and righteousness shine out in every line, in the attitude He maintains toward evil. Those who think the Old Testament judgments shocking associate them with a cruel tribal divinity totally "other" than the God of Jesus Christ. In reality, that which these people cannot tolerate is this very attribute of infinite holiness, capable of inflicting the most devastating punishments. People with such a bias can accept neither the deluge, the destruction of Sodom, the punishment of the Canaanites, nor the chastisements of the Israelites themselves. As for the New Testament, they want to take out eternal perdition for the impenitent: all men, these say, are already saved in Christ, though some do not know it yet. Now the Scriptures speak very differently about this matter: the earthly, physical punishments of the Old Testament were serious—but those of the New, spiritual and eternal, are infinitely more formidable (Heb. 10:26-31).

God's love and mercy form a golden thread running through the whole Bible. The books of Exodus and Numbers illustrate the providence and patience of the God who knows how to deliver His recalcitrant people, for He provides for all their needs. Deuteronomy declares twenty-four times that the law was given to assure the happiness, fulfillment and longevity of an obedient people. The psalmists, like the prophets, exalt the one God: faithful and holy, near to His creatures, omnipotent, Master of the universe, marvelous in His designs of love and salvation for all nations.

Whoever thus knows the God of the Old Testament meets Him again in the New, with no transition adjustment necessary other than the recognition that the latter gives a more personal and developed revelation of His infinite perfections. "No man hath seen God at any time; the only begotten Son, who is in the bosom of the Father, he hath declared him" (John 1:18). The gospel leads us into "the mystery of his will, according to his good pleasure which he purposed in him . . . to sum up all things in Christ" (Eph. 1:9-10); ". . . to the intent that now unto the principalities and the powers in the heavenly places might be made known through the church the manifold wisdom of God" (3:10).

What an unimaginable miracle this is: "The blessed and only

Potentate, the King of kings, and Lord of lords; who only hath immortality, dwelling in light unapproachable; whom no man hath seen nor can see: to whom be honor and power eternal" (I Tim. 6:15-16) yearns to use our stammering tongues for an endlessly multiplied communication of Himself! Little wonder that the Author of such a revelation as this devoted so many centuries and so many different human instruments to the accomplishment of His great purpose as portrayed in all sixty-six of the books of the Bible!

12

THE UNITY OF THE BIBLE

AN EXTRAORDINARY MIRACLE

THE SCRIPTURES are a veritable library, composed of sixty-six different books, written during sixteen centuries (from about 1,500 years before Jesus Christ until 100 years after Jesus Christ). This period of time would be comparable, approximately, to that from the triumph of Christianity in 313 up to now. The human authors of the sacred text (about forty-five) varied enormously: there were shepherds, kings, statesmen, scribes, priests, scholars, poets, historians, lawyers, a tax collector, a medical doctor and unlettered fishermen, along with some unnamed individuals. Still, we observe with astonishment the prodigious unity of inspiration throughout the Bible, as seen in its message and doctrine and even in its structure, yet along with all this a refreshing diversity.

PARALLELISM AND STRUCTURE OF SCRIPTURE

UNITY OF VISION IN GENESIS AND REVELATION

The first pages of the Bible agree in an extraordinary way with the last ones. The themes brought in at the beginning of the Scripture continue all the way through it, to find their completion in its closing pages.

It is interesting to establish the following comparison:

Genesis	*Revelation*
Creation of the heavens and the earth (1:1).	Creation of the new heavens and the new earth (21:1).
The first man, Adam, with his wife in an earthly paradise, called to reign over the earth (1:27-28).	Christ, the last Adam, with His bride, the church, in the paradise of God, there to reign forever (21:9; 3:21).

In the midst of the garden, the tree of life and the river to water it (2:9-10).	In this paradise, the tree of life and the river of water of life (2:7; 22:1-2).
Appearance of Satan, the tempter (chap. 3).	Final judgment of Satan (12:9; 20:10).
Beginning of sin and the fall of man; who, expelled from paradise, became subject to the first death (Gen. 3:19, 24; Rom. 5:12).	End of sin, with the restoration of man. Marriage feast of the Lamb and eternal life in paradise (19:7; 22:1-5). Second death for the impenitent (20:14-15; 14:10-11).
First universal judgment, by the flood (chaps. 6–9).	Last judgment, by fire (20:11; II Peter 3:6-12).
At Babel, God's destruction of the unity of the race, and the confusion of tongues (chap. 11).	Before the heavenly throne, unity sealed by the blood of the Lamb, gathering together of every kindred and tongue and people and nation (5:9).
Preparation by God of the redemption of humanity through His creating of Israel, the elect people, the beneficiaries of eternal promises (chap. 12).	Completion of redemption, as "the Israel of God" finds her place in the heavenly Jerusalem beside the elect of the new covenant (21:12, 14).

Only the Lord, for whom time has no meaning, can take in with a glance the destiny of all the universe. From eternity to eternity He is God (Ps. 90:2). He envisions at once the eternity behind us and that before us, so to speak. He alone, the One who inspired all of Scripture, could have given to it the singleness of perspective which it has.

PARALLELISM OF STRUCTURE

The biblical writings are not thrown together pell-mell: the structure of the Old Testament was worked out in a way analogous to that of the New, as we have already mentioned in chapter 11.

	Old Testament	*New Testament*
Revelation:	Pentateuch	The Gospels
History:	Joshua to Esther	The Acts

Devotion:	Job to the Song of Solomon	The Epistles
Prophecies:	Isaiah to Malachi	Revelation

From another point of view, we can also say that we have

in the Old Testament:	salvation prepared
in the Gospels:	salvation effected
in the Acts:	salvation propagated
in the Epistles:	salvation explained
in Revelation:	salvation fulfilled

COORDINATION OF THE VARIOUS BOOKS

The Pentateuch indicates the following progression:

Genesis:	Fall—Election
Exodus:	Redemption
Leviticus:	Communion—Sanctification
Numbers:	Walk of the believer
Deuteronomy:	Instruction

The Gospels present four complementary portraits of Christ:

Matthew:	the King
Mark:	the Servant
Luke:	the Son of Man
John:	the Son of God

Although the books in the canon are not grouped entirely in chronological order, the arrangement was not simply made by chance. And Paul's general epistles give the distinct impression that their messages follow one another with a design, to form a completed whole:

Romans:	Justification
Corinthians:	Sanctification
Galatians:	Liberation
Ephesians:	Spiritual resurrection
Philippians:	Satisfaction
Colossians:	Fullness
Thessalonians:	Glorification

THE UNITY OF SCRIPTURE ASSURED BY THE STEADY UNFOLDING
OF THE PLAN OF SALVATION

We have already touched on this point in relation to the progression of the revelation.

The eternal and sovereign God governs the world from the height of His infinitely exalted throne. From Genesis to Revelation, from the fall to the marriage supper of the Lamb, He has but one purpose for us and one message to us: the coming, the person and the work of the Saviour of the world. From this perspective it has been said of the two Testaments that

1. The New is in the Old concealed; the Old is by the New revealed.

2. One can see the link between the Old and the New Testaments, in spite of the four hundred years between them.

   > Malachi closes the first revelation with the prediction of the next anticipated event—the appearance of the Messiah and that of His forerunner, animated with the spirit and power of Elijah (Mal. 3:1; 4:5-6; Luke 1:17).

   > Matthew, in his first verse, introduces Christ as Son of David and Son of Abraham, Heir of the throne and of all the promises made to Israel since Genesis 12.

   > Luke carries the genealogy of the Lord even farther back, to the "son of Adam, the son of God" (3:38), embracing with one sweeping gesture the whole of the foregoing revelation.

3. The tie between the Old and New Testaments is strongly reaffirmed; for example, in Matthew, by the constant reminder of the ancient prophecy in the process of being fulfilled: "All this is come to pass that it might be fulfilled which was spoken by the Lord through the prophet" (1:22; 2:5, 15, 17, 23; 3:3; 4:14, etc.).

4. God's grand and glorious plan of salvation is apparent from the first page of the Bible to the last. Here are some of its stages:

   > the perfect creation (Gen. 1)
   > the happiness and innocence of the man and the woman in paradise (chap. 2)

the fall and separation from God (chap. 3)

the universality of sin (chaps. 4-11)

the calling and role of Israel (Gen. 12 to Malachi)

the giving of the law to reveal the requirements of the holy God; to show the insufficiency of works; to condemn the sinner; and, like a tutor, to lead him to Christ (Gal. 3:10, 19-24)

the incarnation, teaching, expiatory death and resurrection of the Saviour (the Gospels)

the effusion of the Holy Spirit and His role (Acts 1-2)

the church: founding and propagation (the Acts) and instruction (the Epistles)

the final combat and triumph, eternity (Revelation)

5. The experiences of Israel are an illustration of our own anticipated experiences (I Cor. 10:11). The people were

called by the sovereign grace of God

placed with the patriarchs in Canaan

cast down, driven into exile, made slaves of Pharaoh (a type of the "prince of this world")

redeemed from judgment by the death of the Passover Lamb (I Cor. 5:7-8)

buried and, as it were, raised again in the crossing of the Red Sea ("baptized," I Cor. 10:1-2)

given at Sinai the perfect law of God, the worship, the priesthood and the tabernacle

forced to wander forty years in the wilderness because of their unbelief in refusing to enter the promised land, fed nevertheless by manna from heaven and provided with thirst-quenching water from "that rock" which was Christ (I Cor. 10:3-4)

granted, on crossing the Jordan by faith, a decisive experience of spiritual death and resurrection

made conquerors of the promised land, as constantly impelled by the irresistible Joshua (whose name is equivalent to the name *Jesus*)

afforded at last the enjoyment of rest in the land, the picture and foretaste of heaven

6. The worship and priesthood of Israel also prefigured in detail: the new covenant

the Mosaic worship—the copy and shadow of the spiritual realities accomplished in Jesus Christ (Heb. 8:5; 10:1)

the bleeding sacrifices—a type of the cross, where the Lamb of God was slain for our sins (9:12-14)

the earthly tabernacle—a pattern of the heavenly sanctuary (9:11, 24)

the veil barring the entrance to the holy of holies—representation of the flesh of Christ, torn for us, to give us access to that place (9:8; 10:19-20; Matt. 27:51)

Aaron—a type of Christ, our High Priest, who enters into the very presence of God to plead on our behalf, and who will soon return to be our eternal Saviour (Heb. 9:24-28)

Unity of Doctrine

Marvelous it is to trace all the great themes of the Bible as they unfold from Genesis to Revelation, coherent and cumulative in their development:

man—his origin, his fall, his redemption, his earthly and eternal destiny

sin—its beginning, its consequences, its punishment in this world and the next

Satan—the instigator of evil, the liar and murderer from the beginning, his war against God and against believers, his final judgment

Israel—her social and political development, idolatry, preservation and final destiny

the church—her history, from her establishment to her glorification

salvation—its provision, according to the divine plan, as we have outlined it in the paragraph above

repentance, faith, the life of the believer, prayer, the service of God, etc.—subjects for infinitely rewarding study, carrying us through the entire Bible

the Holy Spirit—present at creation, pronouncing the last prayer of the Bible (Gen. 1:2; Rev. 22:17)

God—forever the same, in His sovereignty, His eternality, His spirituality, His omnipotence, His uniqueness, His omniscience,
His omnipresence, His holiness, His righteousness and His love

Jesus Christ—the theme par excellence of all the written revelation

The study of all that concerns Him throughout the Scriptures, in
the law of Moses, the Prophets, the Psalms (Luke 24:47, 44) and the
New Testament, convinces one of the unity of the Bible, in such a
way that he can never doubt it again. We strongly recommend an
approach to every book of both the Old and the New Testaments
with this question uppermost in mind: "What does this book teach
me about Jesus Christ?" Here are some of the answers which will
inevitably present themselves:

Genesis: Adam is the "figure of him that was to come" (Rom. 5:14)
    the posterity of the woman was to be Christ, who would bruise
        and crush the head of the serpent (Gen. 3:15)
    the blood of Abel, the righteous man, is compared to the blood
        shed on the cross (Heb. 12:24)
    Melchizedek is said to be like unto the Son of God (Gen. 14:18-
        20; Heb. 7:1-10)
    Isaac, the son loved of his father, was offered as a sacrifice at the
        very spot where the only-begotten Son of God was to be put
        to death (Gen. 22; II Chron. 3:1)
    Shiloh is the Sovereign from the tribe of Judah (Gen. 49:10)
Exodus: the Passover Lamb (Exodus 12; John 1:29; I Cor. 5:7)
    the manna, miraculous bread sent down from heaven (Exodus
        16; John 6:31-33)
    the smitten rock, which "was Christ" (Exodus 17:1-7; I Cor.
        10:4)
Leviticus: the bleeding sacrifices, picture of the cross (Heb. 9:12-
        14; 10:1-4, 11-14)
    Aaron, type of Christ, our High Priest (Heb. 7:11-28)
    the veil, symbol of the flesh of Jesus torn and broken on Calvary
        (Heb. 10:20)
Numbers: Aaron's rod, parable of the resurrection of the Lord
        (Num. 17:1-11)
    the red heifer, another prefiguration of the purifying sacrifice
        (Num. 19; Heb. 9:13)

the brazen serpent, representing Christ on the cross (Num. 21:4-9; John 3:14-16), etc.

Going over to the Psalms, we see the details in the portrait of the Messiah sketched in all the way through them.

Psalm	2:	Jehovah and His Anointed
	8:	the Son of Man and His humiliation
	16:	the Beloved delivered to the place of the dead
	22:	the sufferings on the cross
	69:	the insults and the gall and vinegar
	72:	the King of peace
	110:	the Lord glorified

Among the prophets, Isaiah has been called the evangelist of the Old Testament. He indeed does present to us:

Isaiah	7:14:	Immanuel, born of a virgin
	9:6:	the Son given, the Mighty God, the Prince of Peace
	11:1-10:	the shoot out of the stock of Jesse, clothed with the Spirit who "shall rest" upon Him
	40:1-10:	the God who was to come
	40:11:	the Shepherd of the sheep
	42:1-4; 49:1-7:	the Servant of Jehovah
	53:	the Man of sorrows
	61:1-2:	the Anointed of God, the Emancipator
	63:1-6:	the Judge

Let us mention, finally, the prediction of Zechariah and its extraordinary precision:

Zechariah	3:1-5:	the Angel of Jehovah, the Advocate
	3:9-10; 4:7:	the Cornerstone
	6:12-13:	the Branch of the Lord, at once Priest and King
	9:9:	the humble King, mounted on an ass
	11:7-14:	the Shepherd sold for thirty pieces of silver
	12:10:	the One whom they pierced

| 13:7: | the Shepherd smitten for the sheep |
| 14:3-4: | Jehovah triumphant |

Needless to say, Jesus Christ fills the whole New Testament: the Gospels narrate His life, death, and resurrection; the Acts show the living Christ forming the church by the Holy Spirit; the Epistles fulfill the promise of John 16:13-14 (the Comforter does not speak of Himself; He declares the things of Christ and glorifies Him) and Revelation is the total and final revelation of the Lord (1:1).

CONCLUSION

To what can one attribute this unity running through the whole Bible: unity of vision, structure, message and doctrine—in spite of the long centuries and the many individuals used as instruments for its completion? To this question there can be only one answer: in reality, Scripture has but one Author, the Holy Spirit. To Him, it is but one revelation, since it speaks throughout of the only true and proper Object of worship. There is just one salvation: announced, then effected and consummated by one only Saviour. Human nature is the same through all the ages: its needs, weaknesses and potential will always require this same divine communication. For the ever-living, omniscient God, time is as one instant; in other words, eternity means an eternal present, from the first page of Scripture to the last. Finally, truth itself is "one" and could never be contradictory.

The inexperienced reader of the Bible may perhaps be struck at first by its diversity and multiplicity. But as soon as he has laid hold on some of the connecting elements and has become aware of the sturdy structure of the revelation, he will marvel at its profound unity. He then will worship the sovereign Master of creation, the God of Abraham, Isaac and Jacob, the God of Moses and the prophets, the Father of our Lord Jesus Christ, dwelling at the heart of both Testaments, which He fuses together and authenticates—the God of the incarnation, as preached by the apostles; King of kings and Lord of lords, who is, who was, and who is to come. Thus the Scriptures bear in their unity the marks of the One who inspired it from first to last.

13

INERRANCY AND INSPIRATION

THE DEFINITION of verbal, plenary inspiration (cf. chap. 7, subhead "Definitions") implies that in drawing up the original manuscripts, the sacred authors were guided in such a way that they transmitted perfectly, without error, the exact message which God desired to communicate to men.

The terms "inerrancy" and "infallibility" seem to us practically interchangeable. There are those who think that the word "infallibility" smacks too much of the idea of papal authority, a treatment of the Bible as a piece of paper that automatically settles every question. The fact is that if Scripture is infallible, it cannot err; and if it is inerrant, this is because it contains no mistakes.

Inerrancy is the point of the theopneustia: it delineates sharply that which separates evangelical biblicists, on the one hand, from liberals and dialecticians (men who deny it) on the other. While faith rests on an ineffable and spiritual plane, the doctrine of inerrancy, on the level of observable facts, is the one more open to the attacks of unbelief (suggested by H. Blocher in a message given at Morges, Switzerland, in 1964).

We are not inventing this doctrine; it is found in the great confessions mentioned in more detail in chapter 20. Our fathers in the faith, in fact, considered the Scripture as "the criterion of all truth" (la Rochelle), "the very Word of God" (2d Helvetic Confession), and "divine and canonical" (Waldensian churches of Piedmont). The Westminster Confession adds: "Our full persuasion and assurance of the infallible truth and divine authority thereof is from the inward work of the Holy Spirit. The Old Testament in Hebrew and the New Testament in Greek, inspired by God, and by His singular care and providence kept pure in all ages, are therefore authentical."

As for Calvin, he goes so far as to say: "It obtains the same complete

120

credit and authority with believers, when they are satisfied of its divine origin, as if they heard the very words pronounced by God himself."

What is the source of the doctrine of inerrancy? It arises for us out of the nature and declarations of the Scriptures themselves. They everywhere present themselves as being the Word of God. When the Lord speaks, He cannot lie; neither can He teach truth by means of error. His veracity as well as His power is at stake. If He spoke erroneously at the beginning or mingled the true with the false, what could we think of Him? With our eternal salvation standing or falling on it, what certainty could we find in a revelation like that? Or what if God, after giving to the sacred authors a message exact in every detail, had showed Himself unable afterward to effect its transmission in a way worthy of confidence? Would this not mean that He had deceived us? And in that case, what would have been the use of His initial revelation?

THE BIBLE'S TESTIMONY TO ITS OWN INERRANCY

First of all, is it legitimate for us to base our faith in inerrancy on the Bible's own testimony? Isn't this just a vicious circle: like dispensing with debate simply on the declarations of the accused or of the interrogated witnesses? No, for here we have the Lord Himself, the only source of all true knowledge. Just as we go to Scripture for all the doctrines concerning judgment, salvation, the future, etc., we can deduce only from the revelation a sure teaching concerning the written Word. Our first question regarding any subject must be "What do the Scriptures have to say about this?" (Rom. 4:3; Gal. 4:30).

The authors of the Old Testament speak most explicitly: 3,808 times they claim to be transmitting the very words of God.

After the giving of the law, Moses declared: "Ye shall not add unto the word which I command you, neither shall ye diminish from it" (Deut. 4:2; cf. 6:1-2, 6-9; cf. 12:32).

The psalmist cries out over and over: "The law of Jehovah is perfect. . . . I trust in thy word. . . . I have seen an end of all perfection; but thy commandment is exceeding broad. . . . Thy word is very pure; therefore, thy servant loveth it. . . . Thy law is truth. . . . All thy commandments are truth. . . . The sum of thy word is truth; and every one of thy righteous ordinances endureth for ever. . . . Let my tongue sing of thy word; for all thy commandments are righteousness" (Ps. 19:7; 119:42, 96, 140, 142, 151, 160, 172).

Christ specifically confirmed the whole Old Testament. He did not find any error that needed to be eliminated, nor did He express the slightest doubt about any part of it. He consistently based His arguments and exhortations on Scripture. He declared: "One jot or one tittle shall in no wise pass away from the law, till all things be accomplished" (Matt. 5:18). Discussing a single word with the Jews, He said: "The scripture cannot be broken" (John 10:35). And He exclaimed toward the end of His days on earth: "Sanctify them in the truth; thy word is truth" (17:17).

The apostles also gave witness to the perfection of the Scriptures. Paul said of the law that it is holy—"and the commandment holy, and righteous, and good" (Rom. 7:12). The apostle's teaching is so explicit (e.g., Gal. 3:16-17) that any error in the Scriptures cited would take away the very foundation of that teaching.

For the author of the epistle to the Hebrews, the Word of God, living, effectual and penetrating, goes so far as to judge even our feelings and our innermost thoughts (Heb. 4:12). It is not our prerogative to set ourselves up as its critic.

James, describing the Word, speaks of it as "the perfect law, the law of liberty" (1:22-25). Convinced of its supreme authority, he addresses to us this solemn warning: "Think ye that the scripture speaketh in vain?" (4:5).

John brings the written revelation to a close with these words: "If any man shall add unto them [the things which are written], God shall add unto him the plagues which are written in this book: and if any man shall take away from the words of the book of this prophecy, God shall take away his part from the tree of life" (Rev. 22:18-19). If it is the Lord who has given a message from Himself, who could have the audacity to attempt to "complete" it or to despise any of it, even those parts which he might think of slight importance?

A testimony as clear and as unanimous as this is truly impressive. Nowhere does Scripture in one place declare erroneous what it gives in another place, and this holds true for even the smallest details. As it unsparingly recounts the faults and falls of men in general and of the people of God as well, its total silence about errors in the work of the sacred authors undeniably has great weight.

The Extent of Biblical Inerrancy

It is evident to anyone acquainted with the facts that the biblical text in our hands now is not without some problems. This is why, before going into the objections raised against the doctrine of inerrancy, we shall find it useful to specify what the doctrine refers to. Frank E. Gaebelein ably discusses this point:[1]

Inerrancy does not mean uniformity in all the details given in analagous accounts written by different authors. The books of Samuel, Kings and Chronicles all belong in large measure to the same historical period, but both their point of view and their expression vary sometimes. The Four Gospels all recount the life of Christ, but with different details. In the Acts, each of the three treatments of the conversion of Saul of Tarsus (chaps. 8, 22, 26) is distinguished from the others in certain definite respects.

Such differences have often been greatly exaggerated: there are even those who promptly go on to call them contradictions and errors. In reality, although the doctrine of inspiration and inerrancy of the Scriptures requires that each author write according to truth, it leaves each one free in the choice of such actual incidents as illustrate what he purposes to teach.

If four independent witnesses in court parrot syllable by syllable the same story, made up of a series of complex facts, those men would at once be charged with collusion. Their very uniformity would make them suspect. For it is a psychological fact, due to inevitable differences in point of view and in observation, that several individuals, each completely honest, will tell the very same events in quite different ways. This can also be said of the biblical authors. Inspired, they wrote nothing false. Everything they saw and reported was true, even though they did not always see and report the same details. But each had his own personality and was far from being a mere robot.

Take, for example, the accounts of the resurrection as recorded in the Gospels. The essential facts are identical: Christ arose; the tomb was empty; the Lord was seen alive by different groups of disciples in various places; His new body was not subject to the limitations of an ordinary human body; after a certain number of days, He went away from the earth again. This is the general framework on which all the Gospels agree. But they differ in certain details and in the presentation of some of the secondary facts. The accounts are nonetheless authentic for this, and the truth taught is well established.

Biblical inerrancy does not exclude the use of pictures and symbols. Although everything in the Bible is inspired, it does not follow that all of it must be taken literally. The plain meaning of many passages is clear from an historical, practical, legal and moral point of view. But there are also many pages where the language is obviously symbolical: for example, many things in Psalms, the Song of Solomon and the Prophets, as well as the parables in the Gospels and in Revelation. Besides, thousands of expressions in both the Old and New Testaments are closer to poetry than to prose. This is, moreover, why the style of the Bible always has a vital and magnetic quality. Therefore, belief in the inerrancy of Scripture in no wise requires a slavish adherence to an absolutely literal interpretation. Since when must belief in inerrancy impose a circumscribed, shackling prosaicness that shuts out those wider horizons where, in any age, picture and symbolism can strike fire to the imagination of men?

This repeated accusation of an obligatory literalness looms up partly from the false idea which critics hold about our position. They think that the concept of *verbal* inspiration forces us to consider every word by itself, irrespective of the context, as being the object of an independent inspiration. Nothing could be further from the truth. No language, no literature, could be subjected to such treatment. Words, vehicles of thought, are arranged and bound together to express one unified whole. The context will help to determine whether the interpretation is literal, spiritual or symbolical.[2]

Biblical inerrancy does not imply the use of an exact technical vocabulary, conformed to present scientific terminology. The biblical authors were all men of antiquity. They employed the language of their times, not claiming to foresee modern science. But when they did set down facts in the realm of science, they expressed themselves without error in regard to fundamental principles. For example, the biblical record of the creation touches on the following areas: geology, astronomy, biology, meteorology, zoology and physiology. The expressions used do not claim to be technical ones. Still, every page remains not only more sublime but also more logical than any other attempted explanation of the origin of the universe. Before coming back to this point (chap. 14), let us give the opinion of two contemporary scholars. The famous geologist Dana declares that the first chapter of the Bible and science are "in agreement." Another geologist, Sir William Dawson, adds that the succession of creative acts indicated in Genesis is impeccable in the light of modern science and that many details show the most remarkable harmony with the results of science.[3]

It is also clear that Scripture uses popular expressions in the fields of astronomy, geology and other scientific domains exactly the way our modern scholars do in current conversation. The preacher said, for example, that the sun rises and the sun goes down (Eccles. 1:5), precisely as we ourselves have kept on expressing the idea since the discovery of the rotation of the earth.

Apropos of inerrancy, the biblical message has to be put back into its own historical setting. Certain declarations of Scripture were true when they were made, although the circumstances are different now. When we read in the book of Joshua that the twelve stones set up in the midst of the Jordan "are there unto this day" (4:9), this obviously means that they *were* there at the time those things were written. One delicate subject is that of the chronology of the Old Testament, which has been judged as erroneous. What is certain is that the ancients did not count the way we do and had no fixed, universal calendar. The exact length of the reign of the kings is difficult to know, since the year at the end of one reign was often counted a second time as that of the beginning of the next one. At any rate, following the ancient ways of calculating and dating, one sees in Scripture a much greater precision than in the other ancient authors.[4]

The question of grammar and style is also in harmony with the historical framework. We do not have, on this point, a like statement by Muslims concerning expressions in the Koran. They think that their book came down complete from heaven, so for a long time they strongly opposed any translations being made of it. Our position for the Bible is that, according to the time or the author, the Hebrew is more or less pure and the Greek more or less correct (speaking, for example, of some of the writings of the prophets, or Revelation) ; and this concept does not signify any deviation from the integrity of the text. The style is not ceremonious or affected, as though it had been dictated. Although majestic or dramatic at times, it is often simple, varied and even completely colloquial.

It is claimed that for some who wrote in the period following the Reformation, inspiration and inerrancy included even the points added to the consonants of the Hebrew text to indicate the vowels. Suffice it to say that the vowel points were invented by the Masoretes, starting with the fifth century A.D.

Inerrancy has to do with the whole of the biblical message, within the limits specified above, and this not only for the part having to do with "faith and practice." If this were not so, would one not have to consider Scripture fallible in other respects? Take an example from history: God invaded our world. He initiated His plan of redemption in the incarnation and consummated it in specific historical facts. If the Bible is wrong about these facts, what is there for our faith to rest on? See what Paul says about the resurrection of Christ, as well as about the history of Israel (I Cor. 15:14-19; 10:11; Rom. 15:4). The historical facts are so intimately tied in with spiritual realities that we would find it very hard to separate the two. We have seen that the same is true of the account of the creation, as touching the domain of the natural sciences (geology, astronomy, biology, etc.). The creation account, and also that of paradise, the fall, the deluge, etc., we find fully confirmed by Christ and the apostles. Unless we make myths out of these records, how could we separate them from the spiritual truths which have been drawn from them? Let us make it clear, however, that for us inerrancy extends to the text itself, not to the often absurd interpretations given to it (see chap. 14, subhead "The firmament," for an example). In the realm of geography, likewise, the extraordinary exactitude of Scripture has been attested to by archaeology and by an improved understanding of antiquity.

One more word about the expression contained in a number of confessions of faith, whether ancient or recent: "Scripture is the Word of God, the only infallible rule of faith and practice." Clearly, the Bible does not claim to be a manual of science or history; its supreme domain is that of faith and life. It is the book of salvation; its aim is to lead us to God and to enable us to live with Him, first down here and then forever in heaven.

Inerrancy does not imply omniscience on the part of the biblical authors. They were not acquainted with all facets of the subjects they treated. Thus their declarations are true without always being complete. One illustration is the case of the Four Gospels. Each one has its part in filling in, adding to and putting the finishing touches on the painting. This principle explains why the Bible does not always provide a full account of a given event or the well-rounded, all-comprehensive enunciation of a truth, such as one might expect from omniscience. The Scriptures were written by men who were kept from error, but who were not endowed with the perceptive faculties which belong to God alone.

It was, moreover, not necessarily the aim of the biblical records to tell absolutely everything. For example, the Gospels give us practically nothing about Jesus from the time He was twelve until the day He was baptized by John the Baptist. Such information would certainly have a popular appeal if we may judge by the Apocryphal "gospels," but this might not be according to the purpose of either the Holy Spirit or the writers themselves.[5]

OBJECTIONS TO INERRANCY

Inerrancy is irreconcilable with the human nature of the biblical authors. Because "to err is human," everything is imperfect. And since the Bible did not fall straight down from the sky, God, in order to get it put into writing, led men whom He had at His disposal, the way an artist is limited in his expression by the materials he has available.

Now this is quite logical in view of man's fallen condition. But it does not at all take into consideration either God's omnipotence or His intervention in the providing of redemption. Just as revelation is a miracle on His part, so the inspiration which kept the sacred writer is another. If the utilization of human nature in itself necessarily implied sin, then Jesus Christ could not be the perfect Saviour; and this is exactly what unbelievers claim about Him.

We have already seen that, had the sacred writers been abandoned to their natural fallibility, this would necessarily have extended to every domain, the spiritual as well as the historical and scientific. On the other hand, if they are inerrant in regard to spiritual truths, why would they not be also in other matters?

Again, if only human fallibility were to be reckoned with in the drawing up of the biblical text, how could we discern the true from the false—we who are fallible ourselves? In that case there would be nothing left to us but skepticism.

Modern science has definitely destroyed the old idea of a perfect Bible. No cultivated person, they claim, can hold today to the inerrancy of the Scriptures. This tenet still remains subject to proof. It is true that the nineteenth century thought "science" was opposed to faith, whereas the truth is that, far from contradictory, the two are simply on different planes. A long list of great scholars could be mentioned who not only believe in God but also stoutly confess their faith in the Scriptures.

In the chapter entitled "Difficulties in the Bible," we shall see how some "errors" attributed to Scripture appear in the light of the better information which we now possess. Here is the opinion of Professor Robert Dick Wilson of Princeton, who held several doctorates and who knew forty-five languages and dialects of the Near East, including all of the Semitic languages: "I have come to the conviction that no man knows enough to attack the veracity of the Old Testament. Every time when anyone has been able to get together enough documentary 'proofs' to undertake an investigation, the biblical facts in the original text have victoriously met the test."[6]

Let us not forget, furthermore, the extent to which "science" is always relative and subject to change. It is a continuous and progressive attempt to explain the many mysteries of nature. It would be senseless, and even antiscientific, to reject everything we think of as up-to-date knowledge just because a good deal in it still needs to be clarified.

On the other hand, any scientific declaration is always open to revision and improvement. What scholars say today can be contradicted, or it can be completed, tomorrow. As for "theological knowledge," that is necessarily less controllable than the so-called natural sciences. It touches on the spiritual world; and, in that which concerns the Bible, it all too often takes its point of departure from eminently subjective philosophical and psychological suppositions. According to Lüscher, since 1850 biblical criticism has proposed more than 700 theories, all supposed to be the last word in science. By now more than 600 of these have become outmoded and dis-

carded in the light of a more enlightened and extended scholarship.[7]
We are ready to learn from what human science has to teach us, but
we are not going to do it with our eyes closed. "Prove all things; hold
fast that which is good" (I Thess. 5:21). We do not claim the ability
to explain everything; neither do we at all desire to seek a rationalistic support for our faith. Faith, based on solid facts, will always
be created and nourished by a "demonstration of the Spirit and of
power" (I Cor. 2:4).

*Mistakes made by copyists are evident from the variations in the
different manuscripts.* This is true, and we shall devote a subsequent
chapter to the consideration of it. But since these errors affect no
more than about one one-thousandth part of the biblical text, we
believe them far too insignificant to shake our faith in the inerrancy
of the original manuscripts. (For the latter expression, see our
explanation in this chap., subhead "Inerrancy of the Original Manuscript.")

*The citations from the Old Testament as found in the New, taking
liberties with the text, do not seem to consider it as inviolable.* Again,
this is a claim which we think should be closely examined. Let us at
this point merely recall that Christ and His apostles, those responsible
for the quotations, everywhere regarded the Scriptures with an attitude of total confidence and submission.

When one affirms inerrancy, he "petrifies" the biblical text. This is
the expression used by J. K. S. Reid: "God's Word is petrified in a
dead record."[8] Let us sum up S. Van Mierlo's view of the question:
The theologians opposed to plenary inspiration say that it is a profound error to believe a thing simply because it is in the Bible. This
is for two reasons: (1) There are doubtless historical and scientific
errors in the Bible, and therefore one constantly exposes himself to
controversies with science. (2) A Bible without error would be like
an idol, exercising an inadmissible authority over our minds. We
would then accept its teachings as true in a mechanical manner, without personal faith in the Lord Jesus Christ, who is the embodiment
of the true divine revelation. This would make only a collection of
doctrine and so a dead letter. We would then have to do with an
authoritative religion which says what has to be believed, a teaching
one must accept quite apart from any personal experience.[9]

Such reasoning as this seems to us untenable. Why would the

biblical text be petrified merely because it contains divine truths rather than human error? God has provided "living oracles" as gifts to us (Acts 7:38). The written Word is the Word of the Holy Spirit (Heb. 3:7); and it has always been living and active (4:12). From it there emanates that quickening power, at once human and divine.

The doctrine of inerrancy hinders the exercise of faith. "The old Protestant doctrine of verbal inspiration transforms the living word of God into a sacred text and its consequent denial of the human character of Scripture evades and fails to appreciate not only the possibility of offense, but at the same time the reality of faith."[10] We have already given quite enough, assuredly, on the human side of Scripture and the part played by the personality of its composers. As for "real faith," is it actually true that "faith cannot be properly exercised unless and until we recognize that there are fallible elements in the Scripture"?[11]

The above arguments reveal a complete lack of understanding of the role of the Holy Spirit in the illumination and regeneration of the reader. The inspired text becomes intelligible to us only as we receive by faith the Saviour which it reveals and then as, by that faith, we allow the Holy Spirit to regenerate us. For all readers of the Scriptures, "a veil lieth upon their heart. But whensoever it [a man] shall turn to the Lord, the veil is taken away. . . . Now where the Spirit of the Lord is, there is liberty" (II Cor. 3:15-17).

Further, what is this "Christ, the only true divine revelation" that the fully inspired text keeps people from knowing, unless it is a figment of the imagination born in the reader's subjective experience and, thus, different for each one, whether he be just an ordinary individual or some well-known theologian?

As for what concerns us, we should like to emphasize again what Warfield has to say. As is true for all other doctrines, our faith in verbal inspiration is based on the affirmations of Scripture itself. We do not ask: What do the confessions of faith say? What is the word of the theologians? What does the authority of the church declare? but rather: What does the Bible itself teach? We depend entirely, then, on an exegetical fact; that is to say, on a minute and reverent study of the text itself. If criticism by its discoveries should render untenable the doctrine of plenary inspiration, we would be forced to abandon not only "a particular theory of inspiration" but also the apostles and the Lord Himself, as our doctrinal teachers and guides, for plenary inspiration was plainly their teaching.[12] This would mean nothing less than an actual renunciation of the attitude of faith, in which attitude, by God's help, we are determined to persevere.

There are those, indeed, who do not hesitate to say to us: "When you insist so much on the necessity for a totally inspired text, without which no one can be sure of anything, aren't you simply following the psychological and almost pathological need for security?" Once again, we reply that we must not reverse the priorities. Man, naturally in darkness, longs to be led in the way of light and truth, even as he could not live without an earthly and an eternal hope. This principle could not suffice as the foundation of the doctrine before us; but God, who has put such an aspiration in us, responds to it by a perfect revelation of His person, adapted to us in our present state. Obviously, He might be pleased to bring conversion to Christ to someone by means of a testimony in itself imperfect—an oral one, or possibly a written one, such as a tract. But these testimonies with their limitations could not "declare the whole counsel of God." It is the Lord Himself who has indissolubly bound the message of salvation to a written revelation worthy of confidence. One automatically deprives himself of the first at the moment when he rejects the second.

The most objectionable aspect of inerrancy seems to be its limitation of the freedom of the critics. Now this objection clearly arises out of the declarations made above. People do not want to be bound by a verse, a collection of Bible doctrines, or a paternalistic and authoritarian religion. A Bible without error would squeeze our minds into an unendurable straitjacket! Professor Emil Brunner says: "The fundamentalist is in bondage to the biblical text. . . . This makes the Bible an idol and me its slave."[13]

Obviously if everyone claimed the right to appraise any part of the text he happened to want to, affixing such erroneous labels as "contradictory," "legendary" or "mythological," he would be completely "free" in regard to it. If there were nothing to affirm that a given passage expresses a truth, the criterion of evaluation would be even more personal and subjective. Finally, the "religious conscience" of the individual and his mere reason would supplant the authority of the divine revelation. Experience shows that conscience and reason are not about to capitulate to authority. As for the inner witness of the Holy Spirit, it is clear that it follows along the line of truth which He Himself has already revealed.

Inerrancy produces a paper pope. One often hears it said that if Luther liberated Christianity from the pope at Rome, orthodox Protestants have replaced him by a "paper pope." We do not believe in an infallible church; and here, they say, you are trying to impose an infallible Scripture on us! Jesus Christ is alone infallible and ought to have this supreme authority. Protestants have put the Bible in the place of Christ, and this constitutes one of their greatest weaknesses.[14]

These are nothing but sophisms. Luther and the other evangelical believers did not invent anything. They simply went back to the scriptural position of Christ and His apostles (see chap. 18), a position of unqualified submission to the fully inspired Scriptures. But this matter of authority is of supreme importance, and we shall shortly be coming back to it. Let us point out here that spiritual authority can have only three forms:

> the authority of the Lord
> and His written revelation;
> the authority of the church
> and its "infallible" pope;
> the authority of human reason,
> with its self-styled sovereignty

Did the Reformers really make the Scriptures supplant Christ? On the contrary, Christ cannot be known except through the Scriptures. Along with giving the world the open Bible, they wonderfully preached the gospel of grace in Jesus Christ. Edward J. Young says again on this subject:

> Those who are so concerned lest the Bible occupy a position which belongs to Christ have also themselves an "absolute" or "infallible" authority . . . the "infallible" mind of man. . . . This Jesus Christ whose position has supposedly been dethroned by the Bible, . . . is He the eternal Son of God, the second Person of the Holy Trinity, who for our salvation took unto Himself human nature, without sin, being born of the Virgin Mary . . . to die upon the cross in our stead and to rise from the dead? Is that the Christ about whom the modern theologian is concerned?[15]

In any case, this is not true for Brunner, Niebuhr and Bultmann.

The only way to reverence the sovereignty of Christ is to learn to know Him in that unique revelation which we have of Him and then to obey His teachings, just as we do those of the prophets and apostles, which He invested with supreme authority.

A belief in inerrancy brings a danger of "bibliolatry." Those who take the Bible to be fully inspired and inerrant are also constantly accused of bibliolatry. "The fundamentalist makes an idol out of the Bible," they say, "and himself a slave to it." In reality, nothing is more untrue of sincere evangelicals, whose only desire is to worship and to glorify the Lord whom the Bible reveals. The Book is only His mouthpiece, the instrument forged by the Holy Spirit to make Him known to us.

We shall develop in more detail this important matter of the sovereign authority of the Holy Scriptures (chaps. 18-19).

Did not Paul himself admit that he was not always inspired? He wrote to the Corinthians: "The things which I write unto you, . . . they are the commandment of the Lord" (I Cor. 14:37); "Unto the married I give charge, yea not I, but the Lord" (7:10); "To the rest say I, not the Lord" (v. 12); "So ordain I in all the churches . . ." (v. 17); "Now concerning virgins I have no commandment of the Lord: but I give my judgment, as one that hath obtained mercy of the Lord to be trustworthy" (v. 25).

Paul was touching on a very serious subject, where there was brought into the question of divorce a modification of the law of Moses. There is no doubt but that he knew himself to be fully inspired when he dared to say that some things were "the commandment of the Lord." However, he shows here that, although some rules are absolute, in other cases God lets man decide according to his conscience, his circumstances and his particular gift (vv. 6-9, 36, 39). Paul, out of his great experience and special calling, felt free to offer faithful advice, given also by the Spirit of the Lord (v. 40). There is nothing false in that which he says, nothing to mar the inerrancy of the text.

Does not the Bible report some things which are false in themselves? Most certainly, for it cites the words of the devil, as declarations of the enemies of God; and it even recounts the most enormous sins of believers, as well as some of the bad feelings of their hearts.

This obviously does not mean that the Lord takes the responsibility for those things! He purposed, however, that they be written very exactly for our instruction, under the control of the Holy Spirit.

Can one make inspiration and inerrancy applicable to truly insignificant details? Paul said to Timothy that he should take a little wine for his stomach's sake rather than to drink water (I Tim. 5:23). From Rome the elderly apostle, as a prisoner, asked that before winter came on he might be brought the coat which he had left at Troas in the home of Carpus, as well as his books and parchments (II Tim. 4:13). The passage in Romans 16:1-16 is full of friendliness and personal appreciation for the individuals whom Paul wished to greet at Rome. Some scholars have seriously called such details insignificant, trivial and unworthy of inspiration. Scripture certainly finds it hard to satisfy everybody! Do not others become all worked up at times about emphasizing its human aspects? Passages like these, it seems to us, very definitely show the perfect naturalness of biblical style, along with traces left by the personality, affections and circumstances of the authors. Such indications actually constitute proof that the Scriptures could not have been dictated mechanically.

In regard to II Timothy 4:13, let us mention an interesting comment by Erasmus: "See what the goods of the apostle consisted of: a coat for protection against the rain and a few books." And this one by Grotius: "See the poverty of the great apostle, who thought an article so slight in intrinsic worth and so far distant as a loss to himself."[16]

We could go on to find other objections to the inerrancy of Scripture, but they would only be a repetition in different forms of the same opposition in principle to the authority of the biblical revelation. Let us now bring up the other side of the subject, the positive and important one.

INERRANCY OF THE ORIGINAL MANUSCRIPT

God watched over the writing down of the message to keep it faithful to the revelation He had given. We believe that it is in keeping with Scripture on the one hand and with the nature and honor of God on the other to affirm that in inspiring each sacred author, He jealously guarded His original manuscript to preserve it from error. What would be the good of saying that it was God who spoke if the written expression of that Word did not faithfully reproduce what He had said?

We have already seen to what point such an affirmation becomes an integral part of the notion of inspiration (cf. chap. 7, subhead "Definitions"). If the whole Bible claims to be the Word of God, it certainly had to be wholly inspired; otherwise its authors either were deceived themselves or else deceived us.

It is evident, on the other hand, that in no case has the original manuscript been preserved. Our chapters on the transmission of the text and the variations and difficulties in the Bible explain in what state the text in our hands is at the present time, a text which one cannot call totally inerrant. Emil Brunner says that fundamentalism, faced with all the contradictions and non sequiturs discovered by the critics, had to resort to an infallible original, of which only two things are known: first, that it was the infallible Word of God; and second, that it was the same Bible as that which we have today—although quite different from it. Brunner condemns our explanations as "apologetical artifices." It goes without saying that his presentation of the facts is very much twisted; and we shall examine his position subsequently.

Why is it important that the original manuscript was itself free from error? Since God has not permitted us to have it, could we not get along all right without knowing what it was like? The scholars can refer to the Hebrew and Greek texts, as they were transmitted to us by the copyists. Now the ordinary reader in his own language has to content himself with a translation which is necessarily imperfect, one which is still further away from the original. But if God is blessing him anyway by means of what he has, what is the need of probing further?

First, we believe that the veracity of the Godhead is at stake, as well as His power to reveal Himself—not only to an individual, but also to the whole of humanity. If God from the start had allowed error to slip into the composition of His message, what would we have to think of Him? (The transmission of this written message down to our day is another problem, which we shall be taking up in chap. 16.)· All this keeps making us revert to the same question: If the original manuscript already had mistakes in it, who can say now how far this element of error goes, and how are we to get the errors sorted out? We would be in complete confusion.

Second, it is evident that the writer of the original text had before him a task infinitely more difficult and more crucial than was the work of any copyist or translator afterward. Following Louis Gaussen, let us first of all consider the original text in relation to the translations made of it through the centuries.

1. The sacred authors had to give a human form to the divine message, an operation mysterious, delicate and open to error (if ever there was one) ; and for this responsibility the full assistance of the Spirit was needed. The mind of the Lord having been in a sense incarnated in human language, it was no longer a question, in translating, of giving it a body, but simply of changing its clothing, so as to make it say in our own language what it had said in Hebrew and Greek—that is, to modestly replace each word by an equivalent expression. This is an operation far inferior, comparatively, to the preceding one; it could conceivably be done even by a scrupulous unbeliever if he knew perfectly the languages in question.

2. The author of the original text, without entire inspiration, would have been far more in danger of error than the translators. The translators' work was done by a great many men, of every tongue and country, who could devote all their time to it and all their care, who were disciplining themselves through the centuries, and who were instructing and correcting one another. The original text, on the other hand, had to be written at a given time, by a single man, and once for all. No one was with that man except his God to hold him to the line and to furnish him with better expressions when his were faulty. If God had not done it, then nobody could have done it.

3. Whereas all the translators of the Scriptures were cultured people and specialists in the study of languages, many of the sacred authors were ignorant men, scarcely fluent in their own language. They would have been incapable of putting the divine revelation together with impeccable artistry all by themselves.

4. God's thought flashed like lightning across the mind of the prophet. It can be discovered again in our times only in the same rapid expression he gave to it as he wrote it down. If his transmission of it was inexact, how could the divine message ever be recaptured in all its pristine purity? The fault would be irreparable, for it would

have hopelessly marred the eternal Book. The situation is quite different for the translations. Since we have today a biblical text extremely close to the original (see chap. 16), our versions can be ceaselessly corrected and recorrected, with a view to conforming them to it with ever increasing precision. This work goes on from one century to another; and one can still revise today the Vulgate of St. Jerome after 1,500 years, Luther's translation after 450 years, and the English Authorized Version after 350 years. How important it was for the original to be without error and for it to have been transmitted to us with rigorous fidelity!

Apropos of this, let us again consider a thought of Gaussen's.

> A book is from God, or it is not from God. In the latter case, it were idle for me to transcribe it a thousand times exactly—I should not thereby render it divine; and in the former case, I should in vain take a thousand incorrect copies; neither folly nor unfaithfulness on my part can undo the fact of its having been given by God. . . . If then the Book of Maccabees was a merely human book in the days of Jesus Christ, a thousand decrees of the Roman Catholic Church could not have any such effect thereafter as that, in 1560, becoming what it had never been till then, it should be transubstantiated into a divine book.[17]

5. If the original text was faulty, the streams of potential error flowing out from it would only tend to increase constantly. On the other hand, if it was inerrant, the possibility of error in the copies and in the translations would constantly diminish. The painstaking study of the innumerable copies of the Scriptures in our possession; the discovery of new manuscripts, such as those of Sinai and the Dead Sea; the progress in exegesis and philology; and the ceaseless revision of the translations—all these means have contributed in a wonderful way to confirm the basic text and to increasingly eliminate such mistakes in copying and translating as occurred through the centuries. Once again, such progress presupposes a dependable original manuscript as the source from which all the rest has proceeded, however far from it are the times in which we are living.

L. Gaussen concludes like this:

> Who now can fail to perceive the enormous distance inter-

posed by all these considerations between those two texts [that of the Bible and that of the translations], as respects the importance of verbal inspiration? Between the passing of the thoughts of God into human words and the simple turning of these words into other words, the distance is as wide as from heaven to earth. God was required for the one; man sufficed for the other. Let it no longer be said, then, What would it avail to us that we have verbal inspiration in the one case [the original manuscript] if we have not that inspiration in the other case [the subsequent translation], for between these two terms, which some would put on an equality, the difference is almost infinite.[18]

Now let us consider a very recent voice, that of Dr. J. I. Packer.

It is sometimes suggested that we can have no confidence that any text that we possess conveys to us the genuine meaning of the inspired Word. . . . But faith in the consistency of God warrants an attitude of confidence that the text is sufficiently trustworthy not to lead us astray. If God gave the Scriptures for a practical purpose—to make men wise unto salvation through faith in Christ—it is a safe inference that He never permits them to become so corrupted that they can no longer fulfill it. It is noteworthy that the New Testament men did not hesitate to trust the words of the Old Testament as they had it, as a reliable indication of the mind of God. This attitude of faith in the adequacy of the text is confirmed, as far as it can be, by the unanimous verdict of textual scholars that the biblical manuscripts are excellently preserved; and no point of doctrine depends on any of the small number of cases in which the true reading remains doubtful. Professor F. F. Bruce expresses the verdict of scholarship as well as of biblical faith when he writes: "By the singular care and providence of God the Bible text has come down to us in such substantial purity that even the most uncritical edition of the Hebrew or Greek . . . cannot effectively obscure the real message of the Bible or neutralize its saving power."[19]

Why did God not let the original manuscripts be preserved for us? Might it be to keep us from making an idol of them? The Christians in Rome, for example, privileged to handle the very text of Paul's epistle, written by his own hand, based their faith directly on the inspired message (just as we are called upon to do today). But later, as this faith became less virile, might they not have been tempted to make of the material document that came from Paul's hands a sort of relic, even a fetish? The example of the brazen serpent which became an object of worship and which was finally destroyed by Hezekiah should cause us to reflect on such a possibility (Num. 21:8-9; II Kings 18:4).

Since we are deprived of the original manuscripts, we are all the more led to study the existing documents to compare them and to keep bringing them back to the primitive text, which, after all, is not so far from us. Having been laid hold on by the powerful message of Scripture, and feeling ourselves overwhelmed by its revelation of the living God, we can do no other than to cling to it wholly by faith. It is possible for us to adopt such an attitude, even if we are not able fully to explain, demonstrate and harmonize the little which still seems obscure to us.

We are, moreover, certainly obliged to accept in this same way all the great biblical doctrines:

the Trinity: God revealed in three Persons
the incarnation: Jesus Christ, at once God and man
the fall: man incapable of doing good, yet responsible
justification: the believer at the same time a sinner and declared righteous
predestination: the eternal election of man, who yet possesses free will
resurrection: a new body—"body," but at the same time something spiritual
eternal perdition: the question of reconciling this concept with the love of God.

We accept all these things by faith in the Scriptures, being fully convinced of its witness to the truth, even if we cannot explain every detail in it. Likewise, it is possible for us to take by faith the doctrines of inspiration and inerrancy: the Word wholly of God and at the same time of man, preserved from error to reveal the truth to us in no uncertain way.

This being said, faith in inerrancy is not at all conducive to an obscurantist attitude, which would blind us to plain problems or make us disparage the light that emanates from true science. Evangelical faith knows how to distinguish between positive and negative criticism. It endeavors to examine all things so as to retain that which is good. On the other hand, the thing that seems positively anti-scientific to us is the flat rejection of the testimony to the integrity of the Scriptures which Christ Himself gave and which the apostles and an impressive number of real facts substantiate.

THE DIFFICULTIES OF THE BIBLE

A VERY COMMON OPINION TODAY is that the many "errors" and "contradictions" in the Bible give ample reason for doubting not only the infallibility of the Bible but also its inspiration. The discoveries of "science" and the "established results of higher criticism" supposedly demonstrate the small amount of confidence that one can place in a Scripture text. The most outstanding theologians declare the Bible to be only a fallible witness to revelation, given by men who were themselves fallible. We recognize, frankly, that the biblical text presents some problems. But our task is to discover which of these are valid and then to define and examine them so as to learn whether or not they can be solved.

IMAGINARY DIFFICULTIES

It is an incontrovertible fact that the supposedly unsolvable problems in the Bible have been grossly exaggerated. Warfield says that often these are only apparent and that, like phantoms, they vanish when anyone attempts to touch them.[1] Here are a few which we think ought not to trouble us at all.

The firmament. The accepted opinion of the critics is that the Hebrews thought of the sky as a solid, fixed vault with the stars fastened in it like nails. The Bible says absolutely nothing of the kind. *Firmament* is a mistake in translation from the Vulgate, and the expression in Genesis 1:6 really signifies a nebulous expanse. It was Aristotle and the ancients who pictured the sky as a solid sphere. Rare biblical passages may speak poetically about the "pillars" and "foundations" of heaven (Job 26:11; II Sam. 22:8); but we are also told elsewhere that God "stretcheth out the north over empty space, and hangeth the earth upon nothing" (Job 26:7).

Cain's wife. Where did he get her, since before Genesis 4:17 there were only the first couple and their two sons? True, but according to Genesis 5:4 Adam lived a very long time and "begat sons and daughters." In those early days of the human race, it is evident that Cain married his sister. (We might call attention here to the fact that through the centuries the crown rights of Egypt were transmitted by the women and that the new Pharaoh, in order to get the throne, married his own sister.)

The hare that chews the cud (Lev. 11:6). People have wondered whether the hare was named among the ruminants just because of a particular movement of its jaws, when actually it gnaws. But it is very possible that our translation of the Hebrew *arnebeth*, based on the equivalent given by the text of the Septuagint, is false and that this animal was not a hare. Any linguist knows how hard it is sometimes to find the true equivalent for names of flowers, plants and animals. There has also been some difficulty with the exact sense of the Hebrew *behemoth* in Job 40:15. The Authorized Version has a note "or the elephant, as some think." The Revised Standard states "or hippopotamus."

Since the use of this particular argument persists as an irrefutable proof of errors in the Bible, let us quote as documentary material a recent article by François Prévost which seems to support the present translation of Leviticus 11:6. "One thing is absolutely certain, yet unbelievable: the hare and the rabbit chew their cud! This strange fact was already discovered in antiquity, but no one actually believed it: the affirmation of it was taken as fantasy."[2] According to the author of the article, foods normally digested are expelled in the form of little green balls and are generally retrieved by the animal before they fall to the ground. The absorption of these balls would be the source of considerable nutritive benefit. This is not a question of scatophagy, as one would take it a priori, but of a special kind of rumination on the part of these animals.

So-called "doublets." It is axiomatic among critics that an event cannot be reenacted at a somewhat later time and in a slightly different way. The second account is promptly labeled a "doublet," as evident proof that another author inserted into the text a plagiarism of the first version. The fact that Abraham lied the first time about his wife (who was, in reality, his half sister) would rule out the possibility that he did the same thing a second time (Gen. 12:10-20 and 20:1-13). When Isaac, later on, fell into the same sin, the "doublet" suddenly becomes a "triplet" (Gen. 26:7-11)! This interpretation cannot in any wise be sustained; for nothing, unfortunately, except a theological prejudice keeps people from succumbing twice to the same sin; nor is there anything to prevent sons from imitating their fathers' sins.

The critics have drawn up an imposing list of such doublets. A few of them are as follows: the two rocks struck by Moses (Exodus 17:1-7; Num. 20:1-13); the double giving of the tables of the law (Exodus 31:18; 32:19, and 34:1-4, 28); and the repetition of the Lord's Prayer (Matt. 6:9-13 and Luke 11:1-4) and of the Sermon on the Mount (Matt. 5—7 and Luke 6:20-49). A close study of the four last-mentioned passages reveals from the differences in details, presentation and circumstances that Jesus must have uttered several times such important words as these. None of the above accounts say anything false, and the different texts complete one another. The two multiplications of bread (Matt. 14:15-21 and 15:32-38) present flagrant "contradictions," they say: the first time, five loaves and two fish, twelve baskets left over, and five thousand men fed; the second time, seven loaves, a few small fish, seven baskets left over, and four thousand men fed. We cannot see any reason why Jesus could not have repeated this kind of miracle under slightly different circumstances (cf. Matt. 16:9-10).

The most ridiculous example of a "doublet" is the repetition of the announcement by an angel of the birth of Jesus. The famous critic Strauss cites no fewer than five contradictions in the comparison of the visit of the angel to Joseph (Matt. 1:18-25) and the announcement made to Mary (Luke 1:26-38). Warfield comments on this point that there might well be inadmissible differences between an account of the war for the independence of Holland and another concerning the Crimean War![3]

Jonah's "whale." Everybody knows that the throat of a whale is so narrow that no man could possibly go down it. So the Bible must be wrong—that is, if it really mentions a whale! Actually, the text calls it only a *great fish* (Jonah 2:1). Now it is common knowledge that a "shark" can swallow a human body whole. Just recently an instance was cited of a man rescued alive out of a sperm whale.

The expression "three days and three nights." "So shall the Son of man be three days and three nights in the heart of the earth"

(Matt. 12:40). In fact, this meant the evening of the Sabbath, the Sabbath, and the time up to the morning of the first day of the week. The young Egyptian found by David near Ziklag, who had been left ill for three days, had eaten and drunk nothing for "three days and three nights" (I Sam. 30:12-13). Esther wanted the people to fast with her for "three days, night or day"; then, on the third day (not the fourth) she presented herself before the king (Esther 4:16; 5:1). From these texts it appears that with the Hebrews, as very often with us, from a legal point of view a fraction of a day counted for a whole day, designated by the expression "one day and one night." We underscore here a previous comment about the necessity of locating the biblical accounts and expressions in their historical and cultural context. If we fail to do so, we shall certainly conjure up contradictions existing neither in the purpose of the writers nor in the understanding of the readers.

A possible contradiction between the text in Jeremiah 7:22-23 and the law of Moses. In an explosion of indignation against formalism, solely exterior rites and the atrocity of sacrificing children to Baal (19:4-5), the Lord exclaims: "I spake not unto your fathers, nor commanded them . . . concerning burnt-offerings or sacrifices: but this thing I commanded them, saying, Hearken unto my voice, and I will be your God" (7:22-23). He is speaking here of something relative, as Jesus did when He said that we are to "hate" father and mother (Luke 14:26). The first commandment of the law was to love God and to obey His voice. Rites and sacrifices were to come afterward and would lose all their value when the first condition was not met. Jeremiah made it very plain that Israel had received the law of Moses on leaving Egypt, with the covenant and the ark of the covenant, then later the temple. However, when they despised the law, God turned away His face from the fastings, burnt sacrifices and offerings which He had Himself commanded (cf., for example, Jer. 2:18; 3:16; 5:4-5; 6:19-20; 7:4; 11:3-4; 15:1). He expresses Himself in the same way in Isaiah 1:11-15: "What unto me is the multitude of your sacrifices? . . . Incense is an abomination unto me; new moon and sabbath . . . when ye make many prayers, I will not hear: your hands are full of blood."

O. T. Allis makes a very pertinent observation about this. He shows that the expression translated "concerning" ("I spake not . . .

nor commanded them . . . concerning burnt-offerings," Jer. 7:22) is elsewhere rendered "for your sakes" or "because of" ("Jehovah was angry with me *for your sakes,*" Deut. 4:21; "Jehovah had fast closed up all the wombs of the house of Abimelech, *because of* Sarah," Gen. 20:18). Another shade of meaning would also be "for the sake of" or "on your account." This amounts to saying that God did not at all speak for the sake of the burnt offerings in themselves. The sacrifices had their place in the worship service; but unless they were offered with sincerity and devotion of heart, they were valueless. (Cf. I Sam. 15:22; Ps. 51:16-17, 19; Hosea 6:6; Ps. 50:8-14.) [4]

This sort of expression in no way justifies the use that the critics have made of the one verse—Jeremiah 7:22—to eliminate the books and the law of Moses, as if they had never existed until they were forged by quacks, mainly at the time of the return from the captivity. The unanimous testimony of the Old Testament and the historical experience of Israel demonstrate the falseness of such a supposition.

DIFFICULTIES RESOLVED THROUGH BETTER INFORMATION

Progress in the natural sciences, most especially in archaeology, has provided answers for many of the questions that have been raised. In fact, if one does not accept the biblical revelation as the truth, he quickly charges it with error the moment it seems out of line with his preconceived ideas or his present knowledge. Any such objection, of course, is dropped as soon as new light appears which substantiates the Bible; but the scholarly hypothesis which had brought it under suspicion is then quickly put out of mind. Here again, before the abundance of factual material, we must limit ourselves to the mention of only a few examples.

The number of the stars. God said to Abraham: "Look now toward heaven, and number the stars, if thou be able to number them. I will multiply thy seed as the stars of the heavens, and as the sand which is upon the seashore" (Gen. 15:5; 22:17). For a long time, at least up to the time of Pascal, it was supposed that the stars, as estimated by the astronomer Ptolemy, numbered exactly 1,022. Now who was it that rightly described the number of astral bodies as incalculable?

Geocentricism. Before Kepler, people really supposed that the Bible teaches an immobile earth as center of the universe, simply because they themselves had that false conception. In reality, although Scripture speaks from man's point of view, it clearly envisages on the one hand the smallness of the earth and on the other the infinite greatness of the Creator and His creation. The psalmist exclaims: "When I consider thy heavens, the work of thy fingers, . . . what is man, that thou art mindful of him?" (Ps. 8:3-4). "The heavens declare the glory of God; and the firmament showeth his handiwork" (19:1). Solomon proclaimed that "heaven and the heaven of heavens" cannot contain the Lord Jehovah (II Chron. 6:18). As for Isaiah, no one can measure the dimensions of the heavens; and before God the earth is like "the dust . . . in a measure . . . [and] the nations are as a drop of a bucket" (40:12-15). "Lift up your eyes on high, and see who hath created these, that bringeth out their host by number" (v. 26). When the Roman Church condemned Galileo for teaching the rotation of the earth, its own interpretation of Scripture was false, not the biblical text itself, which affirms the truth.

Life at the time of the patriarchs and of Moses. Critical science up to one hundred years ago scornfully declared false the events recorded in the opening books of the Bible. According to Kuenen, the material given in the Exodus is completely nonhistorical. Wellhausen called the expedition of the kings, as related in Genesis 14, radically impossible. Anything, moreover, that belonged to Source P (the famous "priestly code"), especially Leviticus, had no historical significance. The Pentateuch could not be dated from the time of Moses, for the people on the whole were illiterate and devoid of legal, moral and religious norms. Moses himself was unable to write and thus could not have been responsible for the books attributed to him.

Now archaeology has overturned all such opinions by revealing the refined civilization of the people of antiquity. Not only do we have proof that before the year 2000 B.C. the Babylonians and the inhabitants of Ur of the Chaldees knew how to write, but men have also found the tables of square roots and cubes which they used in their schools. A commentary written by theologians of the modern critical school says that discoveries relating to the Abrahamic period tend to demonstrate that the biblical traditions speaking of those times are not artificial constructions made by priest historians who lived later; on the contrary, they are really conformed to pre-Mosaic conditions and are extraordinarily exact, containing more really historical material than some scholars have ever believed up to the present time.[5] This acknowledgment is worth retaining. What we might wish is that the teachings based on those so-called "sources" would themselves be revised!

The famous archaeologist Albright, after fifty years of scientific discoveries and work, said that for him the historical authenticity of the Bible increasingly stands out in bold relief. He commented in particular that the Dead Sea Scrolls not only revolutionize biblical science and introduce an entirely new method of study, but that they "demolish the critical grounds" of the disciples of Wellhausen and "completely refute Bultmann." The older critics denied the exactitude of the biblical accounts; and the more recent ones (including Rudolf Bultmann) have abolished the role of history itself, claiming that it has nothing to do with faith. On this point the evangelical position is firmly established, for all the weight of historical and linguistic science is on that side.[6]

The Hittites. For a long time these great people of antiquity were never mentioned except in the Bible (forty-seven times, plus fourteen times for the word "Heth"), and all such allusions were treated with a good deal of skepticism. Then, in 1906, excavations were begun at Bogazköy (ninety miles east of Ankara, Turkey), which proved to be the capital of the Hittite empire. Work continues at this site annually, producing exciting results. It is thus very risky to accuse the Bible of error in cases where science and the history of mankind do not allude at all to the facts which it affirms.

Nineveh. Capital of Assyria, "Nineveh was an exceeding great city, of three days' journey" (Jonah 3:3). However, the immense city had so completely disappeared that Voltaire ridiculed the biblical description of that phantom metropolis. It was not until after 1842, at the time when modern archaeology was born, that research totally confirmed the scriptural statements. The city was immense, a megalopolis composed of a group of smaller units. There has also been rediscovered the palace of Ashurbanipal, having seventy-one halls and rooms, with a library, still intact, containing twenty-two thousand cuneiform texts.[7]

Sargon and Tartan. A hundred years ago people used to ridicule Isaiah 20:1, the sole mention of a king of Assyria not known about up to that time in secular history. So it was claimed that this king never lived. Now it was in 1842 again that, at Khorsabad (a suburb of Nineveh), Botta, the consul of France, discovered Sargon's own palace, with a quantity of detailed documents in it. For a long time, likewise, the sense of the word "Tartan," also used in Isaiah 20:1, was completely unknown. Once more, it is archaeology which has showed that this was not a proper noun, but the title of the top general of the Assyrian army.

Belshazzar. Daniel (chap. 5) relates the story of the king who could offer to the prophet only the third place in his kingdom and who was killed after a night of orgy at the time of the capture of Babylon. Secular history had lost all traces of this personage, whose circumstances seemed inexplicable to the critics. The Babylonian archives revealed that Belshazzar was under his father Nabonidus and consequently could offer only the third place (v. 16). The fact that it was said of this personage that Nebuchadnezzar was his "father" (v. 18) is in line with ancient custom. The same expression was sometimes used of the grandson (II Kings 9:2, 20) or even of a descendant. In the Assyrian documents Jehu is called "son of Omri" when he simply had succeeded him on the throne.

Lysanias, tetrarch of Abilene. Up to the discovery of an inscription which completely confirmed the gospel text, critics used to allude with amusement to Luke's claiming that this personage was a contemporary of Herod (3:1). Many similar examples could be given.

POSSIBLE HARMONIZATIONS

Certain difficulties are more apparent than real. It is sometimes possible, by means of close study, to show without forcing the issue that two supposedly contradictory passages are really complementary. As Warfield says:

> It is a first principle of historical science that any solution which affords a possible method of harmonizing any two statements is preferable to the assumption of inaccuracy or error— whether those statements are found in the same or different writers. To act on any other basis, it is clearly acknowledged, is to assume, not prove, error.[8]

The two creations. Chapters 1 and 2 of Genesis present, critics tell us, two opposing accounts of the creation. They claim that the text here had different authors; this furnishes the starting point for the "documentary theory," according to which various unknown authors (the "sources") wrote the Pentateuch. We confess that, the more we study this authoritative beginning of the written revelation, the fewer contradictions we find in it, in spite of the evident and natural differences in style. Chapter 1 recounts in a grandiose way the principal steps in the creation of the universe, where the Creator, Elohim, appears in all His majesty, omnipotence and infinite wisdom. Chapter 2 develops in more detail that which concerns man. In verse 4 the word translated "origins" is *toledoth* ("generation") in the Hebrew, which is repeated eleven times in Genesis (5:1; 6:9; 10:1, etc.). Here it refers to what followed the creation of the heavens and the earth and is not a record of a new creation different from the first. God is called Yahweh-Elohim, the title Yahweh having largely to do with redemption. Genesis 2 develops that which concerns man: his two natures, the ideal environment where he was placed and his relationship to the animals and to his companion. The order of the verses is not necessarily chronological. Otherwise, it would be as though God created man (v. 7) before having made a place to put him (v. 8); or else He would have had to place him in the garden at two different times (vv. 8 and 15).

To accept Genesis 1 and 2 as forming two successive and complementary pictures does not appear to us at all as an absurd attempt at harmonization (even if we cannot explain every verse). These chapters give us the proper basis for the subsequent revelation, and no one has ever been able to replace them by anything better. To reject them would be to refuse the definite testimony of Jesus Christ and the apostles. Moreover, it is clear that laying open to question the beginning of Genesis permits critics to get rid of the specific creation of man and the accounts of both paradise and the fall. The field is thrown open then to the development of a religion where human reason and efforts take the place of redemption and revelation.

The numbering by David. According to II Samuel 24:1, God incited the king to number the people, whereas, according to I Chronicles 21:1, Satan is responsible for having done it. It seems to us that both texts show an aspect of the truth. Satan also attacked Job with the express permission of God (Job 1:12; 2:6). Saul was "agitated by an evil spirit which came from the Lord" (was sent by Him, acting with His permission, I Sam. 16:14; see also I Kings 22:19-23).

The question of Saul's consulting the Lord. On the one hand we read: "Saul inquired of Jehovah, [and] Jehovah answered him not" (I Sam. 28:6); on the other hand, I Chronicles 10:13-14 says: "He asked counsel of one that had a familiar spirit, . . . and inquired not of Jehovah: . . . therefore he slew him." In the first text the word is *shä'al:* to "ask, consult." In the second, it is *därash,* which we find also in Psalm 77:2: "I sought the Lord" and in Psalm 119:10: "With my whole heart have I sought thee." Saul plainly *consulted* the Lord, as he afterward consulted the witch of Endor; but he did not *seek* Him, the way a submissive believer is to seek.

The two genealogies of Christ. The one in Matthew (1:1-17) goes from Abraham to Joseph, son of Jacob and "husband" of Mary. This legal genealogy is meant to show to the Jews that Jesus, the adopted son of Joseph, was from Solomon's line, the heir of the throne of David. Luke's genealogy (3:23-38) begins with Christ, "the son (as was supposed) of Joseph, the son of Heli," and goes back to Adam through Nathan and David. This genealogy, we believe, is that of Mary; it shows to the Gentiles that Jesus is the direct descendant of David. Luke declares categorically that Christ had no human father; thus the meaning is that He was the grandson of Heli, the father of Mary.

The blind men of Jericho. At the time of His last trip to Jericho, Jesus healed a blind man at the gates of the city (Luke 18:35) and two more when He left (Matt. 20:30; Mark 10:46). Mark mentions only the one whom he could call by name: Bartimaeus. Since we have no other information about this memorable day, we are left with suppositions. It is possible that the first cure which Jesus effected at Jericho gave two other blind men the courage to cry out to Him in the same way as He was leaving the city. It seems to us, at any rate, that not enough facts are available here for anyone to say that the gospel writers were wrong.

Archaeology moreover has shown that at the time of Christ the old city of Jericho and the new stood only about a mile apart. Thus, as the Lord went out of one, He could shortly have entered the other. According to such an explanation, Luke may have viewed the miracle as occurring as Jesus was about to enter one Jericho, whereas Matthew and Mark thought of it as taking place on Jesus' exit from the other Jericho.

The accounts of the resurrection. It is clear that each of the four evangelists gives particular details about the great events which took place on Easter. The critics have given them a hard time, especially because the various personages are not presented as immobile, set in one spot like statues. The facts are that the women saw an angel and then two angels—first seated, then, apparently, standing. The women fled, met Jesus, and informed the disciples. Peter and John ran to the sepulcher. Mary Magdalene stayed in the garden weeping, and there she saw the Lord. These facts in no way contradict one another. Their very differences show that each of the evangelists recounted what had struck him the most forcibly. Their testimonies, considered together, are far more true to life and far more convincing than a word-for-word, stereotyped recital would be. This fact, however, does not keep Professor Brunner from insisting that for anyone to find the record of the resurrection coherent, he would need to be either ignorant or else less than honest. The apostles, the unanimous voice of the early church and of all subsequent believers up to the nineteenth century—must all these, then, be classed among the ignorant or dishonest?

The death of Judas. How can the differences between the accounts in Matthew 27:5 and Acts 1:16-25 be reconciled? It appears that the events took place like this: full of remorse, Judas threw down the money in the temple and went out and hanged himself, probably with his girdle. It broke or became undone; and his body fell on the rocks, which tore it open, as Acts 1:18 tells us. Money wrongly acquired could not be put into the sacred treasury (cf. Deut. 23:18). The conscience of the high priests was uneasy about those thirty pieces of silver. Refusing this money, they pretended to consider it as from a traitor; then they used it to buy the potter's field in the traitor's name.

Gaussen gives a similar case. He tells about a man who committed suicide: placing himself on a fifth-story windowsill, he at the same time shot himself in the mouth with a pistol. From nothing but the bare facts, this man's death could be told in three ways: He blew his brains out; he jumped out of a fifth-story window; and he did both.[9]

Let us notice in closing that the word *prēnēs* used in Acts 1:18 for

Judas is a controversial expression. It can mean "fell down," but several specialists suggest the meaning "swollen" or "distended." This idea was held by Chase, Moffatt and Goodspeed, as well as by Harnack, who did not exactly claim to be a fundamentalist.[10]

REAL DIFFICULTIES

We recognize that for certain questions we have no solutions, at least not at this time, and that in its present state the biblical text does pose some incontestable difficulties; fortunately, these are few in number and of minor importance, as we shall see.

Variations among the different manuscripts. The books of the Bible were copied by so many hands and during so many centuries that slight variations crept into the manuscripts. The study of these is so interesting that we devote a separate chapter to it (chap. 16). We shall then see that such a study only confirms our faith in the inerrant original manuscripts.

Errors of the copyists. These are most often very small, having to do with only one letter; it is true that in other cases the copyist's mistake does assume a degree of significance. Acts 7:16 says that the sepulcher of Shechem, where Joseph was buried, was bought by Abraham. In comparing Joshua 24:32 with Genesis 23:2-20 and 33:19, we see that Abraham bought the cave of Machpelah, whereas the field of Shechem was purchased by Jacob. In Matthew 27:9 we read that the prophecy of the thirty pieces of silver was taken from Jeremiah, when, actually, we find it in Zechariah 11:13.

Hebrew figures. Some texts contain numbers difficult to decipher or to harmonize with those in other passages treating the same facts. According to II Samuel 8:4, David took from Hadadezer seventeen hundred horsemen and twenty thousand footmen. According to I Chronicles 18:4, these figures become "a thousand chariots, and seven thousand horsemen, and twenty thousand footmen." II Samuel 10:18 says that the king killed of the Syrians "the men of seven hundred chariots, and forty thousand horsemen." In I Chronicles 19:18 we find "seven thousand chariots, and forty thousand horsemen." First Kings 4:26 tells us that Solomon had forty thousand stalls of horses for his chariots, and twelve thousand horsemen. In II Chronicles 9:25 the numbers indicate four thousand stalls and twelve thousand horsemen. Another verse not easy to understand is I Samuel 6:19. The American Standard Version says that the Lord "smote of the men of Béth-shemesh . . . seventy men, and fifty thousand men." The Hebrew says, literally, "seventy men, fifty leaders."

Are these errors on the part of copyists or misunderstandings about how to express figures? In any case, although the differences are apparent, they are not very important; and they do not at all affect the historical events in the passages.

Terah and Abram, and their respective ages. According to Genesis, Terah, seventy years of age, begat Abram, Nahor and Haran (11:26). He left Ur with Abram and Lot to go to Haran, where he died at the age of two hundred five (vv. 31-32). Abram, commanded by God to go to Palestine, left Haran at the age of seventy-five. Now, according to Stephen, the patriarch had already become aware of that calling when he was in Ur, his true country; and he went out from Haran "when his father was dead" (Acts 7:2-4). What are we to make of this discrepancy?

First of all, we believe that Genesis 11:26 does not mean that the three sons of Terah were born the same year. On the other hand, it seems very likely that God had already called Abram at Ur (cf. Gen. 15:7; Neh. 9:7) and then had made the call definite at Haran. The departure from that city marked the patriarch's actual going out of Mesopotamia and the end of his submission to his father. Was Stephen making use of a traditional Jewish manner of speaking when he tied this in with the death of Terah, which, however, was actually to take place later? We cannot say. Professor F. F. Bruce calls to our attention the fact that, according to the Samaritan Pentateuch, Terah died at the age of one hundred forty-five; and he suggests that Acts 7:4 possibly finds its support in a similar passage of the Septuagint, as with Philo.[11] Other parts of Stephen's discourse also assume variants which no longer appear in our text of the Septuagint, even though they do in the Samaritan Pentateuch.[12]

Free citations from the Old Testament in the New, and the use of these citations in the Septuagint. (On this interesting point, already treated in detail, please see chap. 10.)

Our list of "real difficulties" is certainly very short, but we fail to discover others which would be of genuine interest.

ERRORS AVOIDED

In showing that the principal difficulties generally brought up about the Bible are not actually important, we have touched on only one aspect of the question. It is interesting to emphasize also that, strictly speaking, the fact that they are so few is a miracle. How many human errors could have found their way into the Bible had it not been for divine intervention!

Gaussen, with his customary spirit, gives a whole list of them. How many unfortunate mistakes, how many grave evidences of ignorance would necessarily have accompanied the revelation were it not for the theopneustia! Errors could have occurred in the choice of facts, in the evaluation of them, in their explanation and in their rapport with doctrines; errors of omission and of exaggeration. But, thanks to God, this is not so in our sacred books.[13]

The Bible is made up of 66 books, written by about 45 different men; it has 1,189 chapters and 31,173 verses and was written over a period of 1,600 years. Try to find in all of that even one of the thousand errors which fill the works of the ancients in their writings about the earth and the heavens; you will find none of them. Sauer comments:

> Moses was instructed in all the wisdom of the Egyptians. What preserved him so that when writing the Pentateuch he did not accept the ancient Egyptian chronology which later Manetho laid down definitely in his writings and which was supposed to start 30,000 years before Christ? What influenced Daniel, who was skilled in Chaldean science, to shut his ears to the monstrous Chaldean fables as to the creation of the world? Paul was acquainted with the best science of his time. Why do we find nothing in his speeches or letters similar to Augustine's scornful rejection of the theory of the antipodes, or to the opinion of Ambrose that the sun draws water up to itself that it may thereby cool and refresh itself from its extraordinary heat?[14]

It is worthwhile for us to consider here the theological indignation of Lactantius: "Is there any man so silly as to believe that men exist having their feet above their heads; trees with their fruit hanging up; rain, snow, and hail falling topsy-turvy!" They would answer you, he adds, "by maintaining that the earth is a globe"! Augustine also was persuaded that the theory of the antipodes was contrary to Scripture.[15]

The grossest mistakes about the material world, as well as about the divine one, are found in Homer, in Greek and Roman mythology, in the wild, disordered books of the Hindus and in the traditions of the Buddhists and the Muslims. The greatest geniuses of the ancient philosophers, such as Aristotle, Plato, Pliny, Plutarch and Lucretius, wrote absurdities one single example of which would suffice to discredit the whole doctrine of inspiration had that error been found in Holy Scripture. As for Voltaire, he blasted with irony not only the existence of Nineveh, but also the reality of a deluge and the possibility of fossil remains of the animals belonging to a now extinct primitive world.

Still, the Bible treats every subject. It describes nature, the creation, the planets, light, the atmosphere, the elements, the mountains, the animals and the plants. It touches on history—not only that of Israel, but also that of the great empires around Palestine, with their kings, their wars and their successive regimes. How simply prodigious that it does all this in a way so consistently flawless!

Finally, let us bring up the fact that the minute exactitude in the transcription of proper nouns very forcibly struck the great specialist, Dr. Robert Dick Wilson:

> The fact that proper names [of the kings of Egypt, Assyria, Babylonia, etc.] have been transmitted to us in this exact way, after such frequent copying in the course of so many centuries, is an unequalled phenomenon in the history of literature. The secretary of Ashurbanipal, when he transcribed the name of Psammetichus, the king of Egypt of his time, put a *t* for a *p* at the beginning and an *l* for a *t* in the middle. Abulfeda, the author of pre-Islamic Arabian history, reproduced the names of the kings of Persia of the line of Achaemenid in a scarcely recognizable way and put *Bactnosar* for *Nebuchadnezzar*. In the list of the campaigns of Alexander given by the Pseudo-Callisten, almost every name is modified in such a way as to be unrecognizable; and the same thing is true for most of the names of the kings of Egypt found in the lists which have come to us from Manetho, Herodotus, and Diodorus of Sicily, as are also some of the names of the kings of Assyria and of Babylon given by Africanus, Castor, and the Canon of Ptolemy.[16]

CONCLUSION

As we close this chapter, we confidently assert that although inexplicable difficulties do remain in the Bible, these do not trouble us unduly. We shall never be able to give a satisfactory solution to all the problems; neither is it by attempting to do so that we shall succeed in fully demonstrating the inerrancy of the sacred text. Such a solution would be only a rationalistic one, where no margin would be left for faith.

We believe in inerrancy on the basis of the declarations of the Scriptures, and we maintain that the apparent difficulties are not sufficient to overthrow this doctrine. Two or three little rips and an insignificant patch in an ancient royal robe could in no wise detract from the august origin and prestige of the garment. If it looked flamboyantly new, its age and authenticity might well be open to question. Those tiny imperfections actually confirm its admirable origin and its wonderful preservation.

In regard to the original manuscripts, we have already raised the question of why God did not purpose to hand down to us a text with no obscurities at all. We believe that His intent in this was to test our faith. In His perfect incarnation, Jesus Christ had "no beauty that we should desire him" and "no form nor comeliness" (Isaiah 53:2). His person, words and works alone suffice to convince anyone disposed to believing in Him that He is Lord indeed. But He never dazzled anybody by imposing His presence on people, and right to the end of His earthly life His contemporaries found a thousand reasons for doubting Him. The same is true of Scripture. For us who have come to faith in Christ by means of it, its full inspiration and authority are quite evident. As for the few problems we come across, we simply put them in with those passages difficult to harmonize or to understand; and we go on, content to maintain an attitude of faith. As Charles Hodge says, these matters have no more to do with the totality of the text than a tiny streak of sandstone appearing here and there in the marble of the Parthenon would affect the entire building.[17]

We should emphasize that it is a very small proportion of the Bible which is affected by these still unresolved problems. We shall reach the same conclusion in regard to the variants, which have to do with only one letter out of 1,580 in the Old Testament and with no more than one one-thousandth part of the New Testament text. Those who because of such a very narrow margin of doubt stubbornly adopt a suspicious attitude toward the whole of Scripture are only depriving themselves in so doing of the divine confirmation which emanates from the text. Such men can find nothing but contradictions and errors in a book which the simple child of God uses all the time by faith to wonderfully build up and brighten his life. How pathetic is the critics' proclamation of relief at no longer having to keep up desperate attempts to harmonize the Scriptures or having to look to the less-than-sincere artifices of apologetics for the dissipation of their doubts! Now, having come to what they call "liberty" and "light," they can tear to pieces, whittle down and reject whatever does not fit in with their opinions, fallible as they are. We strongly suspect that those useless efforts which they have now renounced arose simply from the fact that they were trying to see apart from the light which comes down from above. Addressing such men, Robert Watts has very well said, "While the principle of your theory is a mere inference from apparent discrepancies not as yet explained, the principle of the theory you oppose is the formally expressed utterances of prophets and apostles and of Christ Himself."[18]

In conclusion, let us listen to the testimony of several men of God as to the attitude which we should adopt in the realm we are studying.

Augustine, writing to Jerome, said:

> If, here or there, I stumble upon something which seems not to agree with the truth, I make no doubt that either the copy is faulty, or the translator did not express exactly the thought of the original, or that I do not understand the matter.

Erich Sauer, after quoting the above, adds:

> In any case, faith can wait. . . . The "difficulty" can be removed solely and only by faith's bowing to the divine Word. But thereby faith will perceive that ecclesiastical and theological science has not seldom prepared its own difficulty of conception and faith, by approaching this part of the Divine revelation with false presuppositions.[19]

Paul Rader in 1930 offered a thousand dollars to anyone who could come up with one single proof that the Bible contradicts one demonstrated scientific fact in any domain: history, geology, archaeology, astronomy, physics, chemistry, ethnology, etc. Nobody ever took him up on his offer. A. Lüscher, who cites this fact, adds that there is indeed a great difference between a hypothetical acquaintance and proved facts.[20]

Again we quote Robert Dick Wilson, who said at the end of his lifetime research:

> I have come to the conviction that no man knows enough to attack the veracity of the Old Testament. Every time when anyone has been able to get together enough documentary "proofs" to undertake an investigation, the Biblical facts in the original text have victoriously met the test.[21]

Finally, let us state that we share the opinion of J. C. Ryle, Anglican bishop of Liverpool, when he says:

> Give me the plenary, verbal theory of inspiration, with all its difficulties, rather than doubt. I accept the difficulties and humbly wait for their solution. But while I wait I am standing on the rock.[22]

15

THE CANON

Definition. Although the book at hand is not technically an "Introduction to the Old and New Testaments," it cannot cover in detail the inspiration and authority of the Bible without bringing up, however briefly, the following problems: In what way were the individual books of Scripture, as inspired by God, gathered together? According to what criteria was their authority recognized, and why were these chosen when other religious works were resolutely set aside? At what times and under what circumstances was the present list of inspired books, called the canon, drawn up?

The word "canon" (taken from the Greek) means a rule which serves as a measure; and then, by extension, that which is measured. (In the Middle Ages the word canon was used for the metal tube directing a gunpowder projectile.) In the New Testament the same expression indicated the territory apportioned to Paul for his ministry (II Cor. 10:13, 15-16) ; it also designated the rule of doctrine set forth by the apostle (Gal. 6:16) .

A book is *canonical* if the Jewish synagogue or the Christian church recognized it as the bearer of the revelation communicated by the Spirit of God.

Divine inspiration as the determinant of canonicity. Divine inspiration and canonicity are inseparably bound together. By definition, the library of the sixty-six books that make up the Scriptures must contain only inspired texts: all Scripture is inspired by God. Writings lacking this quality were to have no place in it; moreover, the Spirit of wisdom and of truth Himself guarded the proceedings to assure the inclusion of all His revelations essential to salvation. As we shall see shortly, those who doubt inspiration show by this very fact that they distrust the canon itself.

Are men capable of discerning inspiration to the point of knowing with certainty whether or not a specific book belongs in the canon? In themselves, of course, they are not. The principle is the same essentially as for the revelation itself: the natural man cannot know or receive divine truths; for they are comprehended only by means of the light which the Spirit of God supplies (I Cor. 2:9-10, 14). This is, in fact, why the Lord works according to three miracles. He grants *inspiration* to the sacred writers; *illumination* to the open-hearted individual reader, that he may understand the inspired text; and *discernment* to the body of believers, for the recognition of the books of divine origin and for the inclusion of these books in the canon.

God does not speak in vain. When He addresses Himself to man, He enables him to comprehend His message with certainty. "The sheep hear his voice [the voice of the good Shepherd]. . . . The sheep follow him, for they know his voice" (John 10:3-4, 27). It is evident that a mysterious and infallible instinct guided both Israel and the early church to those sacred writings which they were to assemble and preserve for the salvation of the world. Calvin writes regarding this:

> There has very generally prevailed a most pernicious error, that the Scriptures have only so much weight as is conceded to them by the suffrage of the Church; as though the eternal and inviolable truth of God depended on the arbitrary will of men. For thus, with great contempt of the Holy Spirit, they inquire: Who can assure us that God is the author of them? Who can with certainty affirm that they have been preserved safe and uncorrupted to the present age? Who can persuade us that this book ought to be received with reverence, and that expunged from the sacred number, unless all these things were regulated by the decisions of the Church? . . . But such cavillers are completely refuted even by one word of the Apostle. He testifies that the Church is "built upon the foundation of the apostles and prophets" [Eph. 2:20]. If the doctrine of the prophets and apostles be the foundation of the Church, it must have been certain antecedently to the existence of the Church. . . . It is a very false notion, therefore, that the power of judging of the Scripture belongs to the Church, so as to make the certainty of it dependent on the Church's will. Wherefore, when the Church receives it, and seals it with her suffrage, she does not authenticate a thing otherwise dubious or controvertible; but, knowing

it to be the truth of her God, performs a duty of piety by treating it with immediate veneration.

But, with regard to the question How shall we be persuaded of its divine origin unless we have recourse to the decree of the Church? this is just as if anyone should inquire: How shall we learn to distinguish light from darkness, white from black, sweet from bitter? For the Scripture exhibits as clear evidence of its truth as white and black things do of their colour, or sweet and bitter things do of their taste. . . . Now, if we wish to consult the true interest of our consciences, that they may not be unstable and wavering, the subjects of perpetual doubt; that they may not hesitate at the smallest scruples, this persuasion must be sought from a higher source than human reasons, or judgments, or conjectures—even from the secret testimony of the Spirit. . . . Therefore, being illuminated by him, we now believe the divine original of the Scripture, not from our own judgment or that of others; but we esteem the certainty that we have received it from God's own mouth by the ministry of men to be superior to that of any human judgment and equal to that of an intuitive perception of God himself in it.[1]

The canon as the fruit of divine inspiration, not the result of human decisions. The canon was not so much a prescribed list of inspired Jewish and Christian books as it was a number of books given by divine inspiration to both Jews and Christians. Because the writings of the apostles and prophets were canonical by virtue of their intrinsic quality, the canon, in principle, existed from the time these books were written; and it was added to with successive appearances of new inspired works. It happened that the church was a long time in expressing its unanimous acknowledgment of certain of the writings; but when it finally came to it, all it did was bow in recognition of that which already existed.

From the time that Moses gave the law to the people, it made its authority felt; and from its place in the holy of holies beside the ark of the covenant, it was to be the norm and the very life of the people (Deut. 31:24-26; 32:46-47). The psalmist was far from having the entire Old Testament. But six centuries before Malachi he exclaimed "The law of Jehovah is perfect. Thy commandment is exceeding broad. Thy law is truth" (Ps. 19:7; 119:96, 142). For Isaiah also, at the beginning of the prophetic era, the then existing sacred books were the whole revelation of God as given up to that time. He recognized only one means of salvation for faithless and unhappy Israel: "Should not a people seek unto their God? . . . To the law and to the testimony! If they speak not according to this word, surely there is no morning for them" (Isa. 8:19-20). As for the New Testament, all the elements of the canon were collected by the time the last book, Revelation, was drawn up, at the close of the first Christian century, even though a certain length of time had to elapse before all the Christian churches recognized it as such.

From this we see that the canon was not given at one stated time. Gaussen uses the illustration of a bouquet which a woman holds in her hands as she slowly walks through a garden, with its owner accompanying her. As she strolls along, he presents her with one flower after another until a whole bouquet has been gathered. The bouquet exists and is admired before it is complete—indeed, from the very moment the first blossoms in it are put together; thus the canon was in the hands of God's people from the moment that the first inspired scriptures were placed there.[2]

The Gospels and Epistles were not the product of some recognition of inspiration on the part of the church; they were the basis for such recognition. The church did not have to go into the question: "Will there be one or several gospels, or a harmony of the four? Will there be a need for additional accounts, from less authorized sources?" The gospels simply were there, as well as the epistles and Revelation, supported only by apostolic authority and by the inner witness of the Holy Spirit. Verification of the above comments appears in detail in subsequent paragraphs.

THE CANON OF THE OLD TESTAMENT

The oracles of God entrusted to the Jews (Rom. 3:2). The Lord gave to Israel a marvelous commission: she was to give to the world the knowledge of the true God and the promise of the Messiah, by means of the inspired Scriptures. The chosen people were given special discernment for their task, along with such an unfaltering love for the divine Word as would insure their faithful watchfulness over it.

From Moses to Malachi—that is, over a period of a thousand years—none of the prophets, however ready to denounce the sins of Israel, ever accused her of permitting any alteration of the Scriptures, any mutilation of them or any addition to them. The Jews did transgress, neglect and even forget their law; but not once did they question its worth; and restrained by an invisible and all-powerful hand, they consistently refrained from any sacrilegious attacks against it.

It is true, on the other hand, that they did sometimes misinterpret the text; and Jesus said of them: "Ye search the scriptures, because ye think that in them ye have eternal life. There is one that accuseth you, even Moses, on whom ye have set your hope" (John 5:39, 45). To this the Jews replied: "We are disciples of Moses. We know that God hath spoken unto Moses" (9:28-29). It is no less true that these same Israelites remained the jealous guardians of the canon of Scripture as it was given over to their care. They kept it pure, not allowing the addition of any Apocryphal writings; of these we shall speak later on.

Two famous Jews from the first century after Jesus Christ offer a particularly striking testimony to the canon of the Old Testament. The historian Josephus wrote the following in about the year 100:

> Nothing can be better attested than the writings authorized among us. In fact, they could not be subject to any discord, for only that which the prophets wrote ages ago is approved among us, as they were taught by the very inspiration of God. . . . For we have not an innumerable multitude of books among us, disagreeing from and contradicting one another, but only twenty-two books, which contain the records of all past times; which are justly believed to be divine; and of them five belong to Moses, which contain his laws and the traditions of the origin of mankind till his death. . . . The prophets . . . wrote down what was done in their times in thirteen books. The remaining four books contain hymns to God and precepts for the conduct of human life. [On the number of books in the Jewish Canon, see p. 46.] During so many ages as have already passed, no one has been so bold as either to add anything to them, to take anything from them, or to make any change in them; but it is become natural to all Jews . . . to esteem these books to contain divine doctrines, and to persist in them and, if occasion be, willingly to die for them. . . . Prophets have written the original and earliest accounts of things as they learned them of God himself by inspiration. . . . But our history . . . written since Arta-

xerxes [the Apocrypha] hath not been esteemed of the like authority.[3]

Philo of Alexandria, a contemporary of the apostles, attested thus: "The Jews would die ten thousand times rather than to permit one single word to be altered of their Scriptures."[4]

We shall see, in treating the transmission of the text (cf. chap. 16), with what unparalleled care and reverence the Masoretic and Jewish scribes watched over the smallest letter of the inspired pages, which they transmitted to us intact.

Compilation of the canon of the Old Testament. The events of Israel's history were from the beginning inscribed by Moses in the book (Exodus 17:14). The Ten Commandments, written on tables of stone, were placed in the ark of the covenant (40:20). The book of the covenant contained the first statutes drawn up by Moses (20:22—23:33; 24:4, 7). The entire law was put into the holy of holies, by the side of the ark of the covenant (Deut. 31:24-26). The king was later to have a copy of this same book made for his personal use (17:18-19).

Joshua, in his turn, wrote "in the book of the law of God" the things which had been revealed to him (Joshua 24:25-26).

Samuel "told the people the manner of the kingdom and wrote it in a book," which he laid up before Jehovah (I Sam. 10:25). An allusion is made to "the history [the book] of Samuel the seer," which recorded "the acts of David the king, first and last" (I Chron. 29:29).

David himself, "the sweet singer of Israel," had a great part in the writing of the Psalms, 73 of which are attributed to him. His hymns and those of Asaph are mentioned particularly, with their musical accompaniment, after the revival in the time of Hezekiah (II Chron. 29:30, 25-28). Psalm 119 is a marvelous book poem of 176 verses praising the perfection, truth, life-giving power and formidable judgments of God's law, found in the Word of God as men had it at that time, about 600 years before Malachi. We have just noted that the Old Testament canon was then far from complete, for two-thirds of it was lacking. Still, the authority of the books already recognized as inspired was fully established.

Solomon drew up a goodly number of the Proverbs (1:1; 10:1; 25:1).

The "chronicles of the kings of Israel," the "chronicles of the kings of Judah," the "book of the kings of Judah and Israel" (I Kings 14:19, 29; II Chron. 16:11), as well as the writings of certain prophets —Nathan, Gad, Ahijah, Iddo, Shemaiah, etc. (I Chron. 29:29; II Chron. 9:29; 12:15)—were documents preparatory to the inspired writing of our books known as Kings and Chronicles.

The prophets put in writing the revelations they had received, signing their names to them. Isaiah (1:1; 2:1; 13:1, etc.) the prophet, by his appeal "to the law and to the testimony," confirmed the presence in Israel of the collected, authoritative Scriptures. Jeremiah wrote down all the words which he had received from God. His book immediately impressed very deeply both the people and their leaders. It so troubled the king that he cut it up and threw it into the fire; but God had it replaced without delay and completed it (Jer. 36). The prophecy of Jeremiah regarding the seventy years of captivity (25:11) was promptly accepted among the inspired writings. Daniel made it clear too that it was "by the books" that he believed in the imminent fulfillment of his prophecy (Dan. 9:2). The writer of the Chronicles and of Ezra testified also to the authority attributed to Jeremiah (II Chron. 36:22; Ezra 1:1). Daniel himself, like Noah and Job, was placed by his contemporary Ezekiel among the most devout men of Israel (Ezekiel 14:14). The authenticity of his writings was attested to by Christ in person (Matt. 24:15).

Micah 4:1-3 was quoted in Isaiah 2:1-4 as a message from God. Zechariah insisted on the truth, inspiration and solemnity of the words pronounced by the earlier prophets relating to the law; and all these have been fulfilled (1:4, 6; 7:7, 12). Because his was the last voice of the prophetic era, the Jews called Malachi "the seal of the prophets." Concluding the Old Testament, he recommended the observance of the law given by Moses at Sinai (Horeb); and he announced the next step in God's plan: the coming and the ministry of the forerunner of the Messiah (4:5-6).

Attitude of the critics toward the canon of the Old Testament. This attitude is a very important issue, for it reveals how the Scriptures are regarded once their veracity, historicity and plenary inspiration are doubted. One of the most ineradicable dogmas of the critic—and one of the most untenable—is that Moses could not possibly have been the author of the Pentateuch. Over a century ago, the promoters of this theory were persuaded that man fifteen hundred years before Jesus Christ, having just emerged from caves, was not familiar with writing, civilization, legal codes or complex religious rituals. This concept was proved false when refined civilizations, much more ancient still, were unearthed; but that negative theory has nevertheless persisted. From it the critics deduce the following:

about 627 B.C., under Josiah, the "book of the law" found in the temple (II Chron. 34:15) was simply Deuteronomy, forged shortly before that time by priests desirous of enhancing their own importance;

during the fifth century, the "priestly code" was composed, the part of the Pentateuch (especially Leviticus) devoted to laws having to do with ritualistic sacrifices, genealogies and origins of sacred institutions;

about 444, Ezra, as he read the law to the people, "canonized" the Pentateuch; that is, in reading it that day he for the first time admitted its authority (Neh. 8—10);

between 300 and 200 the composition of several prophetic writings and their acceptance came about (deutero, trito-Isaiah, Daniel, etc.); that is to say, the time of the writing must have been after the great events which these men "prophesied";

after 200 B.C., under the Maccabees, appeared various "writings" of the third section of the Jewish canon;

in A.D. 90, after a synod of Jewish rabbis at Jamnia (near Jaffa), the present canon was finally recognized

Such a concept as the foregoing raises far more difficulties than it solves. It is impossible to prove that the book found in the temple at the time of Josiah was nothing but Deuteronomy, rather than the whole law of Moses (we shall discuss this in more detail later on); and that the so-called "priestly code" was nothing but a forgery, for Leviticus alone affirms fifty-one times that Moses himself received the law directly from God.

Recent critics, such as R. H. Pfeiffer of Harvard, frankly declare that three of the most important and influential books of the Old Testament are "technically fraudulent."[5] The claim that at that time there was not the same understanding of truth as there is today is wholly open to question and in no way solves the problem. Reasonings such as these put us just as ill at ease as do the use of false decrees by the papacy in the Middle Ages. How can a modern theory eliminate the unanimous testimony given by the rest of the Old Testament, the Jewish synagogue, Jesus Christ and the whole historic Christian church, in regard to Moses as author of the Pentateuch?

If the theory of the "discovery" of Deuteronomy and its position in the canonical Scriptures about 620 B.C. is accepted, how can we explain the fact that later on, without arousing objections, anyone could have added to it an even more recent and entirely spurious work? In the light of the jealous care which the Jews took of their sacred writings, this is a psychological impossibility. If these late authors sincerely believed that God had spoken to them, why did they not simply say so, as did all the other prophets, instead of resorting to fraud?

How is it that modern critics differ so much among themselves? Their arguments, including linguistic ones, depend so much on a subjective evaluation that, for example, we find the book of Proverbs dated tenth century B.C. by Eichhorn, ninth by Hitzig, and sixth by Ewald.

What, in fact, do the critics mean by the term "canonical?" Does it signify for them simply a book of ancient vintage, at least a century old, fortunate—humanly speaking—to appear so venerable? In that case, it was man who determined the contents of the canon, as influenced by exterior and historical considerations rather than the direction of God. Could a book "technically fraudulent," full of untenable errors and legends, suddenly become "divinely inspired" after a sufficient lapse of time? This concept on the part of the critics is obviously the opposite of the biblical one of inspiration and canonicity. Finally, if nothing counted but the historical aspects, can anyone explain why the Jews did not incorporate into the canon any of their other religious books of the same period?

Edward J. Young, after a study of many of these questions, says in conclusion:

> If the first five books of the Bible are not essentially the work of Moses, but are a compilation of documents composed by various unknown authors living at widely separated periods of time, the whole question of the canonicity of these books becomes an insoluble mystery, and the fact that the Jews ever regarded them as divine one of the greatest enigmas of all time.

. . . The critical theories endeavor to discuss the question of canonicity from an historical standpoint alone. They would rule out of the picture the theological question: Does God exist? Did God actually inspire the writers of the individual books of the Old Testament? Does the Holy Spirit, by his inward testimony, produce within the hearts of his people a conviction that he is the author of the Scriptures? These questions are ignored by the critics, or are pushed aside, as belonging to the realm of "faith" and not to that of historic fact. And it is precisely because of this unconsciously prejudiced attitude that the critic cannot answer the questions which have just been raised.[6]

Events occurring at the time of Josiah and Ezra. To understand these events we must go farther back into the Old Testament.

We believe that the law of Moses was really given to the people, just as the Pentateuch tells us.

The book of Joshua confirms the presence and role of this law in Israel (1:7-8; 8:31-35; 9:24; 11:15-20, 23; 13:32-33; 23:6; and 24:26, as compared with Deut. 31:26). This book does not make any sense unless it is the continuation of the work of Moses.

The Psalms, especially Psalm 119, all show the veneration with which faithful Jews regarded the law and the Word of the Lord. David himself, after a particularly bitter experience, declared that God must be "sought according to the law" (I Chron. 15:13, 2; cf. Num. 4; Deut. 10).

In 721 B.C., after the abominable reign of Ahaz, Hezekiah became God's instrument of revival: this all took place "according to the law of Moses, man of God," "according to the Word of the Lord," and "as it is written." The temple was purified, the Passover was celebrated, worship was reestablished and the priests and people were sanctified "according to the Word of the Lord . . . as it is written." Nothing like it had been seen since the time of Solomon (II Chron. 30:5, 12, 16, 18, 26). Hezekiah was praised for what he had done "in the law, and in the commandments" (31:3, 21).

At the time of Hezekiah, the Samaritans apparently had their own version of the Pentateuch, and perhaps they had it even earlier. The result of this was that before the fall of Samaria, and probably before the schism, the "law of Moses" was recognized by the twelve tribes.

The wicked kings Manasseh and Amon followed Hezekiah. In

spite of a partial return to the law of Moses, the idol of Asherah was put back into the temple, so that the judgment of God became inevitable (II Kings 21:7-13). Still, about 621, Josiah again intervened and had the idols thrown down and the temple purified. "The book of the law" which was found there, "the book of the covenant," "the law of Moses," could be none other than the same revelation, left by this great man of God, to the existence of which all the above-mentioned texts give a most clear-cut testimony.

To declare that up to that time the law of Moses did not exist and that the neglected book found in the temple was only the book of Deuteronomy, just then put together by the priests, is patently absurd.

Let us go on to the case of Ezra, who, if the critics are right, "canonized" a strange conglomeration of false documents under the name of the "law of Moses," a nomenclature deliberately misapplied for the accrediting of the inventions of ambitious priests. Now let us notice first of all the numerous allusions to the true law of Moses as found in the books of Ezra and Nehemiah:

On the reconstructed altar, sacrifices were offered according to the law of Moses (Ezra 3:2; Num. 28). The feast of tabernacles was celebrated, as it had been written (Ezra 3:4; Lev. 23:34; Num. 29:12). The priesthood was established—as it is written in the book of Moses (Num. 6:18; Num. 8:14). Ezra was a "ready scribe in the law of Moses . . . the law of Jehovah . . . statutes and ordinances" (7:6, 10). Ezra 9:10-12 alludes to Leviticus 18:27 and Deuteronomy 7:3; 23:6. Nehemiah recalled the word of God addressed to Moses (1:8-9; Lev. 26:33; Deut. 30:5). The solemn reading of chapters 8 and 9 constantly emphasized what book it was: "the book of the law of Moses, which Jehovah had commanded to Israel . . . the book of the law . . . the book, in the law of God . . . the words of the law . . . the book of the law of Jehovah their God . . . upon Mount Sinai . . . by Moses . . . neither have . . . our fathers, kept thy law" (Neh. 8:1, 3, 8-9; 9:3, 13-14, 34). They vowed that they would walk in the law of God given by Moses, as it was written in the law (10:28-29, 34, 36). "They read in the book of Moses in the audience of the people; and therein was found written. . . . When they had heard the law, . . . they separated from Israel all the mixed multitude" (13:1, 3).

It is striking to note how all the actions and thoughts of Ezra,

Nehemiah and the reestablished Jewish community were based on the fundamental law of Moses, which was already authoritative, and which they finally desired to put into practice. The very same characteristics marked the Reformation, when the rediscovery of the Bible aroused joy and enthusiasm in every devout heart. To claim that at that time Luther and Calvin forged the New Testament, falsely attributing it to the apostles, would be more than untenable. To say that Ezra and his entourage managed by some extraordinary feat to "canonize" an Apocryphal law fraudulently put down as from Moses is just as unacceptable an absurdity. Ezra and Nehemiah would have been lying imposters if Moses had written nothing of the Pentateuch and if, knowing that he had not written it, they had hypocritically affirmed the contrary on every page they produced. Fortunately we have plenty of good company in our belief in the perfect authenticity of the books of Moses, as well as in the inspiration of the whole Old Testament, along with all of the New Testament.

Order of the inspired books, according to the Jewish canon. The order of the books adopted by the Septuagint was as follows:

the Law (the Torah), that is, the five books of Moses, the Pentateuch;

the Prophets (Nebiim), which included (1) the former prophets—Joshua, Judges, Samuel and the Kings; they considered, in fact, that the authors of these books, although historians, had personally filled the office of prophet; (2) the latter prophets; that is, Isaiah, Jeremiah, Ezekiel; and the twelve minor prophets, from Hosea to Malachi;

the Writings (Kethubim), also called the Hagiographa, grouped together the rest of the canonical books; that is, Ruth, the Chronicles, Ezra, Nehemiah, Esther, Job, Psalms, Proverbs, Ecclesiastes, the Song of Solomon, Lamentations and Daniel (the last-named probably placed here because its author had occupied the position of statesman)

Josephus, whom we have already quoted, speaks of twenty-two inspired books (the number corresponding to the twenty-two letters of the Hebrew alphabet). This number is arrived at by putting together as one book each of the following: Judges and Ruth; I and II Samuel; I and II Kings; I and II Chronicles; Ezra and Nehemiah; Jeremiah and Lamentations; and the twelve minor prophets.

Christ Himself divided the Old Testament into three parts: the

Law of Moses, the Prophets and the Psalms (Luke 24:44). This last section took its name, no doubt, from its most important book.

Five rolls, called Megilloth, were read on the occasion of the five great Jewish holidays. These were portions of the Psalms and Proverbs, the Song of Solomon, Ruth, Ecclesiastes and Esther.

We cannot depend on legendary Jewish accounts to explain how the above lists were finally settled on. An Apocryphal book (II Esdras 14:19-48) claims that when all the scriptural books were destroyed in a fire, Esdras was inspired to rewrite them just as before, in forty days! According to another late, and unconfirmed, tradition, the canon was established in its final form by a group of one hundred twenty men, "the great Synagogue," presided over by Esdras. A passage in II Maccabees (2:13) says that finally "Nehemiah," to make a library, reassembled the books which recounted the history of the kings and prophets, the books of David and the royal letters concerning the offerings. (These "letters" could have come from the kings of Persia, regarding gifts presented to the temple.)

The fact is that the return from captivity marked, on the one hand, the cessation of prophetic revelations, with Haggai, Zechariah and Malachi. On the other hand, in the reconstruction of the Jewish community around its temple and its sacerdotal system, it is very probable that Ezra, Nehemiah and the other men of their generation had a part in the reassembling of the inspired writings into one single collection, from that time complete.

A group of Jewish rabbis met together at Jamnia (near Jaffa) in A.D. 90. (A recent author has wondered if it is justifiable for us to call that meeting a "council.")[7] There was a great deal of discussion about the position in the canon of several books in the third section. No one questioned their right to be in the canon. The debates had to do, rather, with their contents and with their rapport one with another. As far as we know, no formal decision was taken which would have been binding on the synagogue. The discussion remained free, doubtless contributing to precision in the matter of the Jewish tradition.

The Apocrypha.[8] The word Apocrypha is the name given to the Jewish religious books of obscure origin (*apocrypha*, meaning "secret, hidden"); these were late books (between the second century B.C. and the first, or even the second, century after Christ), which never were included in the Hebrew canon. They had no place in the

Masoretic text and were not interpreted by any Targum. According to the general opinion of the Jews, the prophetic voice died with Malachi. After that, which they called "the seal of the prophets," they estimated that no other inspired writings appeared. Josephus declared this expressly (*Against Apion I. 8*); and even the book of I Maccabees stresses it (9:27; 14:41).

Here is the list of the Apocryphal books later accepted by Rome:

I Esdras	The Song of the Three Holy
II Esdras	Children
Tobit	Susanna
Judith	Bel and the Dragon
The Rest of Esther	Prayer of Manasses
The Wisdom of Solomon	I Maccabees
Ecclesiasticus	II Maccabees[9]
Baruch	

(We might also mention The Prayer of Azariah and the Epistle of Jeremy.)

Except for certain interesting historical information (especially in I Maccabees) and a few beautiful moral thoughts (e.g., Wisdom of Solomon), these books contain absurd legends and platitudes, and historical, geographical and chronological errors, as well as manifestly heretical doctrines; they even recommend immoral acts (Judith 9:10, 13).

They seem not to have been included in the beginning in the Septuagint, but they were gradually introduced into its later editions. Neither Josephus nor Philo cites them. Christ and the apostles never referred to them, although they freely used the text of the Septuagint and were certainly acquainted with the material in question. (Jude 9 may allude to the Book of Enoch, a pseudepigraph which does not appear in the list of the Apocryphal books given above.) First century Christians did not include them in their inspired Scriptures.

In the fifth century, Jerome added the Apocryphal books to his Latin translation of the Bible, the Vulgate, calling attention to the evident difference between the inspiration of the canonical writings and the less significant spiritual value of these. He declared moreover without any circumlocution that he rejected the story of Susanna and the Song of the Three Holy Children and took the story of Bel and the Dragon to be simply a fable.

The Reformers sharply distinguished the Apocrypha from the text of the Old Testament. They did not entirely oppose the reading of certain interesting portions in the churches, but they accompanied this permission with clear-cut warnings. After the beginning of the nineteenth century, the Protestant editions of the Bible did not contain these books.

On the other hand, at the Council of Trent in 1546, the Roman Church promulgated the following decree: "If anyone receive not as sacred and canonical these said books, entire with all their parts . . . Let him be anathema!" By this decree Jerome himself was condemned, while the very firm position of the synagogue on the canon was contradicted. Now, we must remember that it was the Jews who were called upon to compile the Old Testament. As Paul said, it was to them that the oracles of God were confided (Rom. 3:1-2). We received those oracles from their hands and from no one else. Why, then, did Rome take so new and daring a position? Because, confronted by the Reformers, she lacked arguments to justify her unscriptural deviations. She declared that the Apocryphal books supported such doctrines as prayers for the dead (II Macc. 12:44); the expiatory sacrifice (eventually to become the mass, II Macc. 12:39-46); almsgiving with expiatory value, also leading to deliverance from death (Tobit 12:9; 4:10); invocation and intercession of the saints (II Macc. 15:14; Bar. 3:4); the worship of angels (Tobit 12:12); purgatory; and the redemption of souls after death (II Macc. 12:42, 46).

Let us thank God that He has so marvelously watched over the integrity of His Word and that He permitted the whole canon of the ancient Scriptures to come down to us—and nothing else but that. What was sufficient for the Jews, for our Lord Jesus Christ, for His apostles and for the Reformers is also enough for us.

THE CANON OF THE NEW TESTAMENT

Just as in the case of the Old Testament, it is very interesting for us to know how the books of the New Testament were drawn up, arranged and separated from uninspired writings.

Compilation of the New Testament. Since Christ Himself wrote nothing, it is difficult to know just when His words were first put into writing. They certainly were repeated orally very often by His disciples (cf. Acts 20:35; I Cor. 7:10; 11:23-25). Then, the Gospels were put on paper; and Luke, undertaking his task in about the year 58, alluded to his predecessors in the work (1:1-4). The compilers of the Gospels could still collect documents firsthand, which were supported by the testimony of eyewitnesses.

It seems that the epistle of James was written very early; some think around the year 45. The epistle to the Galatians dates about 49, and the letters to the Thessalonians around 50 and 51. Paul's other epistles and Peter's were written before the fall of Jerusalem, in A.D. 70, as were Acts and Hebrews (thus, practically all of the New Testament). Revelation was composed in a time of persecution, in the reign of either Nero or Domitius, at the close of the first century. The gospel and letters of John also date from that period.

First testimonies given to the writings of the evangelists and apostles. The inspired texts were very quickly recognized and appreciated by the churches.

Peter, in his second epistle (3:15-16), speaks of "all the epistles" of Paul, putting them on the same plane as "the other scriptures."

Paul, in I Timothy 5:18, introduced by the expression "the scripture saith" a quotation from Deuteronomy (25:4) and another from Luke (10:7).

Clement of Rome, around 96, quoted by name from the first epistle to the Corinthians and showed that he was also familiar with other parts of the New Testament.

The epistle of Barnabas contains the following quotation: "As it is written, many are called, but few are chosen" *(Epistle of Barnabas, 4)*.

Ignatius (martyred in either 107 or 116), one of the disciples of John, recognized, as did the last two mentioned, the inspiration and authority of the writings of the apostles *(To the Romans, IV)*.

Polycarp, in 115, called the apostolic writings "Scripture" and at the same time cited as such the Psalms and Ephesians (chap. 13; Ps. 4:5; Eph. 4:26).

Papias (about 140), a disciple of John, recounted how the word of the ancient fathers had been replaced by the authority of the written Word.

Marcion, a contemporary heretic, referred in his writings to the gospel of Luke and to ten of Paul's epistles; he was also acquainted with Revelation. Another heretic, Basilides, from the year 125, in mentioning the New Testament used the terms "Scripture" and "it is written."

Justin Martyr (about 148) in regard to the meetings of Christians, wrote: "They would read either the Memoirs of the apostles or the Gospels . . . along with the books of the prophets; and in each assembly, after the reading, the president would give an exhortation based on the reading" (*Apology* I, 67).

It is very remarkable that, fifty years after the death of the last apostle, there were found in the writings of defenders of the faith and also in those of heretics exact quotations from the whole New Testament (except for six or seven of the very shortest letters); both groups referred to it for their authority.

Commentaries and translations. As the apostolic writings spread and were read in all the churches, a growing need arose for commentaries for the use of the faithful.

Papias, around 140, wrote a commentary on the oracles of the Lord. In 165, Melito, bishop of Sardius, wrote a commentary on Revelation; and Heracleon wrote one on the Gospels. A harmony of the Four Gospels, the *Diatessaron,* was composed by Tatian, disciple of Justin Martyr (around 160-180).

Origen (at the beginning of the third century) published his famous Hexapla (six parallel columns of the text of the Old Testament in Hebrew and in Greek). He also wrote commentaries and homilies on most of the books of the New Testament, the text of which he revised himself; and he defended its inspiration. Tertullian (also about 200) coined the expression *New Testament,* in contrast with the Old, thus acknowledging the same quality of inspiration in the Jewish and in the Christian Scriptures. He repeatedly cited the latter. He cried out:

> How happy is this Church [the Christian]! . . . She blends the law and prophets with the writings of the evangelists and apostles; and it is thence she refreshes her faith. . . . Woe to them who add or retrench anything to or from *that which is written.* To wish to believe without the Scriptures of the New Testament is to wish to believe against them.[10]

All during that time the gospel kept spreading throughout the Roman empire and beyond it, winning men of all races and of very different languages. Thus very soon there was felt the need for numerous translations of the Scriptures, and these were supplementary proof of the vitality and expansion of the biblical and apostolic writings. Noteworthy toward the end of the second century are these: the Old Latin version, circulating in North Africa; the first Coptic translation for the churches of Egypt; and the Syriac version (the Aramaic of the Christians of the East).

Progressive establishment of the canon. Let us note first of all that the early church, following Christ and the apostles, accepted without difficulty the Jewish canon as such. As Athanasius so well expressed it: "The Christian Church of the New Testament receives from the Hebrew Church of the Old Testament the sacred books of that Testament, because it is to the Jews, as Paul says (Rom. 3:2) that are committed 'the oracles of God.' "[11]

As for the New Testament, these books were all written before the end of the first century; and throughout the second century believers disseminated them widely, read them, and wrote commentaries on them. A certain period of time elapsed, however, before each book was unanimously acknowledged as canonical.

The criterion of acceptance was the apostolic inspiration and origin of each: the book under consideration had to have come from the apostles or had to be authorized by them; for example, Mark, colaborer of Peter; Luke, faithful companion of Paul; and James and Jude his brother (1:1), both considered to be brothers of the Lord. The long ministry of the apostles contributed to facilitate: first, acquaintance with their "teaching" (Acts 2:42) and second, familiarity with the writings which they commended with all their apostolic authority. They also made faithful disciples, who were able to teach others also the truths which they themselves had learned.

One can say that, as early as the second century, the following books were universally and unquestionably recognized:

the Four Gospels
the Acts
the thirteen epistles of Paul
I Peter

I John

that is, 7,029 verses out of the 7,959 of the New Testament, or seven-eighths of the whole text.

Questions arose regarding two important books, as follows:

Hebrews. The fact is that, although its doctrinal and spiritual content was impressive, this book was not signed and its author was not known. About the year 95, Clement of Rome declared the epistle canonical and apostolic, but did not say who wrote it. At the close of the second century, Clement of Alexandria affirmed that Paul wrote it in Hebrew and that Luke then translated it into Greek. The style and language do indeed resemble the gospel of Luke and the Acts more than they do the Pauline epistles. Origen, at the beginning of the third century, wrote this: "I am persuaded that the thoughts are those of the apostle, but that its vocabulary and composition belong to someone else." Barnabas has been suggested, or Apollos (this by Luther), as the possible author. However that may be, the canonicity and authenticity of this epistle were finally unanimously admitted, even though all have not been in agreement as to its authorship.

Revelation. Here, likewise, we have a double problem. Among all the apostolic writings, this book is the one most often and most vigorously defended in the documents of the early church. Gaussen cites authors who say of it: "Of all the New Testament books the Apocalypse is the most frequently and powerfully attested in the monuments of the primitive church."[12] The early fathers—Justin, Irenaeus, Hippolytus, Tertullian and Origen—affirm that John wrote it toward the close of the first century. It was only later, in the third century and at the beginning of the fourth, at the time of the controversy about the millennium, that some began to wonder about its right to be in the canon. These men also questioned whether its author really was John, making a point of certain differences in style. These doubts, however, entirely disappeared by the end of the fourth century.

With the uncontested inclusion of all the above-mentioned books, one might say that thirty-five thirty-sixths of the New Testament had been put together; that is, 7,737 verses out of 7,959.

Five small epistles—James, II Peter, II and III John and Jude (222 verses, one thirty-sixth of the New Testament) were the last to be unanimously admitted. They were brief; some had been written late; their destined ministry was general ("catholic"); and James and Jude were not among the Twelve. It also seems that the dissemination of the handwritten Scriptures was not everywhere the same. Each important church (or group of churches) would naturally hold especially dear those parts of the precious manuscripts which it had managed to get hold of. This does not mean that believers generally were not already in agreement about the majority of the books. During the fourth century that last tiny segment of the New Testament was fully accepted, at which time it can be said that the canon was closed.

The successive lists of recognized works cover the same ground which we have just gone over. The Fragment of Muratori, about 170, includes the Four Gospels (attributing the third to Luke and the fourth to John), the Acts, the thirteen epistles of Paul, Jude, and two epistles and Revelation attributed to John. Lacking here, then, were only five of our present books; but since the manuscript was incomplete anyway, their absence proves nothing. Clement of Alexandria, toward the end of the second century, wrote a seven-volume commentary on the books of the New Testament, including Jude and the other epistles called catholic (general). Athanasius, at the beginning of the fourth century, made a list of the books identical to our own, attributing the epistle to the Hebrews to Paul and Revelation to John. The Third Council of Carthage, in 397, decided that nothing but the canonical books were to be read in the churches as the "divine Scriptures." From that time on, all hesitation and divergence disappeared.

CONCLUSION

The history of the canon, very instructive as it is, elicits several reflections:

The canon was not established by some authoritative measure, either for the New or for the Old Testament; this we asserted in chapter 15 (subhead "The canon as the fruit of divine inspiration"). It was not a matter of councils, either Jewish or Christian, imposing on the church books first thought of as human, which they later, by some sort of decree, lifted up to what they claimed to be a divine level.

Quite the contrary: works born out of supernatural inspiration, through the silent work of the Holy Spirit, were made acceptable to the whole Christian community. In fact, as we have pointed out elsewhere, Scripture antedated the church and furnished its foundation, framework, doctrine and spiritual strength. Practically all the apostolic writings were recognized by the great majority of believers before the Nicean Council in 325, to the point where that council did not even need to debate the canon, any more than did subsequent "ecumenical" councils (Constantinople, in 381; Chalcedon, in 451, etc.) The Council of Carthage, mentioned above, was a provincial gathering; its decision to limit public readings to the "divine Scriptures" is interesting as a test case. The Council did not create the canon, but it shows that at that time the canon was clearly enough understood so that all uninspired books were excluded.

Thus it was in an exceptional climate of liberty and mutual respect that the collecting of the inspired writings took place. There was no polemic or anathema, a fact all the more remarkable when we recall that the churches of the time were sustaining a terrible struggle against heresy and were hurling out excommunications for even the smallest errors. According to Gaussen, eighteen councils are known to have been called together in the third century against the heretics of the time, with eighty-six in the fourth century, and eighty in the fifth. It is then an admirable and manifestly providential fact that, on this point alone, one can nowhere find in the historical documents any public constraint, any group decision on the part of the bishops, any decree by the councils, or any prescribing by the emperors, although, after the fourth century, these interfered with everything in the church of God; in a word, no act of human authority imposed on the flock the acceptance of any sacred code or forced any individual conscience to receive into the canon even one of the twenty-seven books of which the New Testament is composed today.[13]

The fact is that, right from the start, the writings incontestably apostolic were considered as being themselves the Scriptures, and then were added to the already existing sacred books. The first Christians, therefore, did not first of all make a canon of "new books," of which they only gradually recognized the same divine character and the same authority which the "old books" had. They received the new books one after another in the apostolic circle as being just as much the Scriptures as were the older writings. They simply joined them to the already existing collection, until finally the new books thus affixed became numerous enough to be considered as a section of the Scriptures.[14]

A fact like this has only one explanation: the unanimous conviction produced in hearts by the inner witness of the Holy Spirit, who unremittingly continued the triple miracle for the benefit of the people of God: the production of the sacred books, the formation of the canon and the preservation of the Scripture throughout the centuries.

The churches were providentially kept from accepting any illegitimate books, throughout the whole two and a half centuries while the canon was coming into being. They examined freely and unhurriedly the books presented to them. At times certain ones hesitated for a while before coming to complete agreement. But never did the believers as a whole make a definite choice which they later had to repent of. In this we discern a new providential intervention. Otherwise, what explanation would there be for the resolute rejection of the following books:

the First Letter of Clement, written from Rome to the church at Corinth (around 96), which appears in the Codex Alexandrinus (A) and which was publicly read in Corinth in 170

the Didache (about 120), or Doctrine of the Twelve Apostles, which Clement of Alexandria and Origen considered as Scripture

the Epistle of Barnabas (around 130), joined to the Sinaiticus (Aleph)

the Shepherd of Hermas (about 140), which is also found in the Sinaiticus

These books, not without interest, are spiritually very inferior to the apostolic writings; and little by little they were definitely set aside. Others presented no sufficient marks of authenticity right from the outset: the supposed Revelation of Peter (before 150); the Acts of Paul, Apocryphal; and various Apocryphal gospels: of Peter, Matthias, James, and the Nativity.

The canon was likewise guarded from including any of the deviations which little by little crept into Christianity. Just as nothing Apocryphal was admitted into the Jewish Scriptures, the churches, including the Roman Church, never put into the new canon any book or doctrine contrary to the revelation taken as a whole. Even in the last writings to be recognized by all, there are none of the incipient deviations which were to change the face of a certain "Christianity"—the worship of Mary, the angels, saints and images; the role of bishops (these, in reality, being the elders, the overseers, according to Acts 20:17, 28) ; baptism as a saving ordinance; merits acquired by works; purgatory; or prayers for the dead, etc.

One can therefore see an astonishing fact emerge: the church definitely and firmly accepted as divine some books unfavorable to its own inclinations, and everywhere it rejected as merely human others which would favor its inclinations the most. There is only one explanation for this fact: God Himself watched over the canon. The Jews never changed a thing in the Old Testament or took away a thing from it; Rome and the other churches never took away or added anything, however powerful—faithful or unfaithful—they may have been. The text for all the Scriptures has remained just what God intended it to be.

This has obtained in spite of a universally habitual tendency of the human mind: what begins in unity too often concludes in diversity. Here it was the opposite: the churches first of all received certain parts of the New Testament as they had benefited from the ministry of different apostles. Then by the irresistible action of the Spirit, they came to a perfect unanimity about them. The whole Christian world, including the Roman, Orthodox, Coptic, Nestorian and Protestant churches, counts only the twenty-seven books of the New Testament. To them, as to the synagogue of old, "the oracles of God were entrusted." Let us emphasize this once again by quoting Erich Sauer:

> The Church itself had in no way to "complete" or even to "create" the biblical Canon, but simply to acknowledge it. . . . The Canon of Holy Scripture . . . was finished and complete from the very first moment when the last New Testament book had come into existence. . . . The decisive factor . . . was the Spirit-wrought authority of the Bible itself . . . as the result of the divine inspiration.[15]

War on the canon has resulted. As an entirely natural consequence, attacks on the inspiration and authority of the Scriptures have led to rebellion against the whole canon. The Bible, it is declared, is no longer to be considered as a volume of absolutely authentic and true books, but an anthology of writings in large part doubtful, compiled in a totally different epoch from that affirmed by the text itself or by Jewish and Christian tradition. We have seen, apropos of the Old Testament, what we are supposed to think of this conglomeration of "technically fraudulent" books. As for the New Testament, Gaussen said in his day that in one hundred years "German theological science" had attacked all the books of the New Testament with the sole exception of the epistles of Corinthians and Galatians.[16] He added that, in spite of this, his century was the one eminently known for the diffusion of the Bible and for the great impetus given to evangelical missions. He concluded from this that after so many attacks, the Scriptures have remained intact, just as Daniel walked out of the lions' den and as the three young Hebrews found deliverance from the fiery furnace.[17]

In our day, the chiseling away at the canon is at once more subtle and more generalized. Modern critics, claiming that they represent the majority of contemporary theologians, have in fact come to the conclusion that the Bible is not the Word of God. With the concept of myths and legends in the Scriptures, the idea that the historicity and veracity of a text or an event means much less than does its message, and the supposed discovery of divergent "sources" for the most essential books, these men end up by completely doubting the legitimacy of the canon, as the synagogue and the early church transmitted it to us. The only thing that counts, it seems, is that God speaks to an individual here and now in such a way that both a faulty text and a fallible collection of texts become (how?) a message communicated to that individual personally.

As the words themselves no longer have the significance that they once had, a theologian may—alas—very well claim to prove that a biblical book is not authentic, but may immediately afterward hasten to add that this "fact" takes away nothing from its value or canonicity. They claim, for example, that the epistle to the Ephesians was not really written by Paul: its author belonged to a later time than that of the apostle, and his line of thinking differs from Paul's in certain respects. But "whoever the author of the epistle to the Ephesians was, its contents remain the same; and the only question raised is regarding its theological truth."[18] Now what can be said, in short, about its truthfulness, in the light of passages as personal as Ephesians 1:1; 3:1-13; 4:1; 6:19-22! The same professor also attributes the epistle to the Colossians to someone other than Paul, probably to the same one who composed the epistle to the Ephesians in his own way.[19]

As for II Thessalonians, M. Masson rejects its authenticity, at the same time admitting that this was never questioned before the day of higher criticism. Without too much imagination, he said, one might picture a disciple of Paul at the end of the first century. Because Paul's epistles strongly affirmed the imminence of the day of the Lord, which the church was looking for, this disciple perhaps felt troubled over what the more enlightened might infer from Paul's texts regarding future events. He could therefore have deemed it necessary to get the apostle himself to explain why the day of the Lord had not yet arrived: namely, that the apostasy had to come first and that "that wicked one" had to be revealed. This quite gratuitous supposition, one which reveals a deplorable concept of inspiration, is followed by an equally surprising declaration: "Need we add that the inauthenticity of II Thessalonians in no way detracts from its value?" (nor from its place in the canon, since the church put it there).[20] What then are we to think about II Thessalonains 1:1; 2:5, 15; and 3:7-10, especially verse 17? We very emphatically deny, furthermore, that those witnesses to the God of truth had moral concepts wholly different from ours and were simply conformed to their times in literary matters. In fact, their holiness, integrity of character and divine inspiration are the guarantee of their absolute veracity.

In conclusion we quote a few lines from Professor Herman Ridderbos of Kampen, in Holland:

> In recent decades the question of the authority of the Canon has again been brought to the fore in New Testament theology. It is often said now that the authority of the Canon is to be accepted *because* and *in so far as* God speaks to us in the books of the Canon. But in this very criterion "in so far as" lies the difficulty of the problem and the danger of subjectivism. Some wish to return to the essential content of the gospel as the "Canon in the canon." They search for an incontestable objective measure within Scripture. Others protest that this is a too static interpretation of the Canon. God speaks—so they say—now

here, and then again there, in Scripture. It is in the preaching, the kerygma, they say, that Scripture again and again shows itself as Canon. This actualistic concept of the Canon is interpreted by others in a still more subjectivistic manner: Canon is only that which *here and now* [*hic et nunc*] signifies the Word of God *for me*. For one like Ernst Käsemann, for instance, the Canon, as it lies before us, is not the Word of God or identical with the gospel, but it is God's Word only in so far as it *becomes* gospel. The question, what then is the gospel, cannot be decided through exposition of Scripture, but only through the believer who "puts his ear to Scripture to listen and is convinced by the Spirit" [*Evangelische Theologie*, p. 21].

It is clear that on this approach the Canon of the New Testament as a closed collection of twenty-seven books becomes a very problematical matter. Can we still hold fast to the creed of the Reformation: We accept all these books as holy and canonical? What basis remains for the Church to believe that God not only wishes to use the books of the Bible as a medium in which he speaks to us through the Holy Spirit, but that he wishes also to bind the Church to the Canon of the New Testament?[21]

The canon is responsible for unity among believers. Despite what we have just said, there is only one canon for the whole of Christianity. The theories of the critics and the fashions of theology pass away, but the Scriptures remain impregnable. Luther was so filled with the message which had been forgotten for so many centuries and with the truth of justification by faith that he appreciated less the epistle of James than he did the epistles of Paul to the Romans and to the Galatians. Thus in his edition of the German Bible he put James at the end of the epistles, along with Hebrews, which he thought of as written by Apollos. But he took nothing out of the canon; and, after 1522, he never reprinted his unfortunate comments on the epistle of James, a book which does not at all contradict, but merely complements, the declarations of Paul. Such was the thought of all the Reformers without exception, and this point has never been questioned.

It is marvelous indeed that all the branches of Christianity, however varied on the surface, have unanimously recognized the collection of twenty-seven books of the New Testament: the churches of the first centuries and of the great councils, the Nestorians and the

Coptics; the churches both Eastern and Western; the popes of Moscow and the pope at Rome, the Hussites, the Waldensians; and the Protestants, whether Lutheran, Reformed, Anglican, etc. And if there is one basis on which true believers in Christ can still meet, it is indeed on this one: the sole authority of the whole of Scripture, with its sixty-six canonical books, inspired, grouped together and guarded by divine watch-care.

16

TRANSMISSION OF THE TEXT—
THE VARIANTS

HAVING DISCUSSED the inspiration of the biblical authors, the composition of the original inerrant manuscript, and the formation of the canon, we have yet to see how the inspired text was transmitted to us down through the centuries. This is a matter of prime importance, already touched upon in a somewhat different way in the chapter on the difficulties of the Bible. What good would it be, even though God did speak to His prophets, if their message had not reached us in a form truly worthy of our confidence? The Westminster Confession declares: "The Old Testament in Hebrew and the New Testament in Greek, being immediately inspired by God and, *by His singular care and providence, kept pure in all ages,* are therefore authentical; so in all controversies of religion, the Church is finally to appeal unto them" (I. 8). Let us see the remarkable way that this providence and special care have been demonstrated.

TRANSMISSION OF THE TEXT OF THE OLD TESTAMENT

A text copied by hand over a period of 3,000 years. The fact that the sacred books were copied by hand over a period of three thousand years, from Moses to the invention of printing, poses a great problem in itself. Did not all those scribes and copyists have thousands upon thousands of opportunities to make mistakes? The fact that the present text is in such a marvelous state of preservation (in spite of the difficulties which we are about to look at) is literally miraculous. God has plainly watched over the Word that He inspired.

The Masoretes. The transcription of the Hebrew text was rendered especially delicate by the fact that in principle that language had nothing written but the consonants. So the reader had to supply the vowels, and a normal reading was assured only by tradition. But in proportion as the Jewish people became assimilated with the nations among whom they were dispersed, the exact pronunciation of the words ran the risk of becoming more and more inexact. Around the year A.D. 100 Jewish scholars had already set themselves to establish a consonantal standard Hebrew text, which furnished the basis for the later works of the Masoretes. These were rabbis of Tiberias and of Babylon, who, from the fifth to the tenth century A.D., accomplished a remarkable task. They *established* the text, choosing the best manuscript from those at their disposal. They *copied* it with extraordinary care. We are even told that an error in one single letter could have made the manuscript useless. The Masoretes also *annotated* the text, as a precaution against any addition or omission, indicating in the margin the number of letters, the repetitions of certain expressions, the middle letter, and the word and the verse in the middle of each book or collection of books. In this copying of what we call the Old Testament, they noticed that the letter aleph occurs 42,377 times, the letter beth 38,218 times and so on. If a word seemed incorrect to them, they left it in the text (the *kethib*) ; and they put in the margin the consonants of the corrected word (the *keri*). Above all, the Masoretes invented *vowel points:* dots or little strokes added in or under consonants, to indicate the pronunciation of the word, while at the same time preserving the integrity of the traditional consonantal text. Finally, these same rabbis worked out a particular system of *accents,* designed to show the reader of the text the shades of tone as well as the rhythm inherent in the Hebrew language. Thus the Masoretes contributed very much to the transmission and preservation of the Old Testament as we have it today.

The destruction of deteriorated manuscripts. Except for a very few portions, we do not possess very old Hebrew manuscripts of the Old Testament. In general, the ones which we do have go back only to about nine hundred years after Jesus Christ. How did this happen? The Jews held their copies of the Scriptures in almost superstitious veneration. When these copies became too old and worn for further use in ordinary reading, they reverently buried them. An honorable burial was preferable to the risk of seeing profaned the name of God as it was inscribed on the old manuscripts. Before burying those out-of-use copies, they kept them in a closed place next to the synagogue, called genizah ("cachette," or "hiding place"). In the second half of the last century, the discovery in Cairo of one of these old hiding places furnished very interesting copies dating from the centuries preceding A.D. 900.

Old documents serving as a check on the Masoretic Text. Since so many of the old manuscripts have been destroyed, the possibilities of establishing a comparison with the Masoretic text are considered all the more precious. Here are a few examples.

1. The version of the Septuagint. This is the translation into Greek of the whole Old Testament, done by the Jews of Alexandria between 250 and 150 B.C. It is interesting to us because it is based on a Hebrew text one thousand years older than the Masoretic text of our manuscripts. But as a translation, it is very unequal. The Pentateuch was better translated than the rest of the Old Testament. In a few places this work helps us understand the text where otherwise it has become obscure through transmission. We shall come back later to the use of the Septuagint in the citations from the Old Testament found in the New.

2. The Samaritan Pentateuch. The Samaritans, separated from the Jews and from the temple of Jerusalem, constructed their own temple on Mount Gerazim, about 400 B.C. (cf. John 4:20). Considering nothing canonical except the Pentateuch, they kept very old copies of these books. Their text was transmitted independently of the Masoretic text, and it brings one of the very first testimonies to the primitive Pentateuch. The comparison, however, establishes the manifest superiority of the Masoretic text, as well as its essential purity. Most of the present Samaritan scrolls are not held to be older than the tenth century A.D. One or two of those which are kept at Nablus (ancient Shechem) are considered the oldest.

3. The Malabar manuscript. At the beginning of the last century, C. Buchanan discovered among the black Jews of Malabar in India an immense scroll of the Scriptures, composed of 37 skins tinged with red, 48 feet long and 22 inches wide, containing 117 columns of beautiful writing. All that are lacking are Leviticus and part of Deuteronomy. A comparison of this text word for word and letter for letter with the text of the West, each independent of the other, has revealed only about 40 slight differences, none of these significant enough to cause even the slightest change in the meaning or interpretation of our ancient text.[1]

4. The Dead Sea manuscripts. Since 1947, Hebraic texts of extraordinary value have been discovered near Jericho in several caves above the Dead Sea. One of the most important of these is an entire manuscript of Isaiah, dating from the second century B.C., in a perfect state of preservation. This discovery enabled scholars to go back a thousand years farther than was possible with the manuscripts known up to that time. There might have been a question before as to whether the Masoretes had altered even to some very small extent the original text. But now this Isaiah scroll, recently brought to light, shows practically 100 percent conformity to the Masoretic text, the variants being entirely insignificant. Moreover, it has fully confirmed the unity and integrity of Isaiah. Critics had tried to make out that the book had been written by two or even three "Isaiahs," the third section belonging to about 300 or 200 B.C. This sort of argument has been proved untenable by the discovery of this manuscript, perhaps copied right from the original, or at least from copies of the original.[2]

The comparison of the above-mentioned documents with the Masoretic text always led to the same conclusion: the unique state of preservation of the latter, thanks to the extreme care with which the Jews handled their sacred writings. Although always open to whatever we can learn from critical examination of the manuscripts, we can continue to put our full confidence in the text which has come down to us.

The variants of the Old Testament. It is to be expected that scholars would seek to compare, if possible, all the ancient documents on the Old Testament at their disposal. Herculean efforts have been expended in recent centuries to bring to light all the variations which may have crept into the manuscripts of the Scriptures: the oldest versions (the Septuagint, the Jewish Targums, the Syriac Version, the Peshitta and the Vulgate) and the innumerable biblical citations made by all the church fathers, along with the allusions in the Jewish commentaries (the Talmud).

The famous B. Kennicott based his critical edition of the Hebrew Bible on the study of 581 manuscripts. Professor Rossi examined about 680. J. H. Michaelis spent thirty years of his life making a similar study. Professor R. D. Wilson declared that in the texts studied by Kennicott there are about 280 million letters. Of this total, there are about 900,000 variants, of which 750,000 are nothing but insignificant changes of *v* and of *i*. Taking the largest figure, one arrives at one variant for 316 letters. Laying aside the unimportant changes of *v* and of *i*, one finds only one variant for 1,580 letters. Add to this the fact that most of the variants are found in only a few manuscripts or even in just one. Very few variants occur in more than one of the 200-400 manuscripts of each book of the Old Testament.[3]

We can understand why the critic Eichhorn felt that the different readings of the Hebrew manuscripts collected by Kennicott hardly offer sufficient interest to compensate for the trouble they cost. Another scholar, quoted by Gaussen, says:

> In truth, but for those precious negative conclusions that people have come to, the direct result obtained from the consumption of so many men's lives in these immense researches may seem to amount to nothing; and one may say that, in order to come to it, time, talent, and learning have all been foolishly thrown away.[4]

If the critics are disappointed, believers are enthusiastic over such a shining confirmation of the sacred text. No research of scholars and no effort is too great when such a result is arrived at.

The transcription of proper names. Let us mention, in closing, one more means of verifying the exactness of the Old Testament text: the often delicate transcription of the proper names. Professor R. D. Wilson shows by numerous examples the almost incredible precision in the spelling of the names of foreign kings mentioned in the Hebrew text. He compares this spelling with that of the monuments or documents of the kings themselves. In no case can one error be found in the Hebrew text; on the contrary, the exactness of it can be shown practically every time. In 143 cases of transcription of the Egyptian, Assyrian, Babylonian and Moabitish into Hebrew, and in 40 cases the other way around—that is, in 183 all told—it was proved that during 2,300 to 3,900 years the proper names of the Hebraic Bible had been transcribed with the greatest exactitude. The fact that the sacred authors followed so closely the rules of correct philology is a marvelous proof of their knowledge and of their extreme care. Then, the fact that the Hebrew text was reproduced thus by copyists over a period of so many centuries is a unique phenomenon in the history of literature. Since it can be demonstrated that the text of the Old Testament was accurately transmitted for the last 2,000 years, one may reasonably suppose that it had been so transmitted from the beginning.[5]

TRANSMISSION OF THE TEXT OF THE NEW TESTAMENT

The abundance of the manuscripts. We possess more than four thousand manuscripts of the Greek New Testament. Some were written a fairly short time after the original. The most ancient text, on papyrus, containing a short fragment of the gospel of John, goes back to the beginning of the second century. The Chester Beatty Papyri, from the third century, include whole books of the New Testament. Over two hundred manuscripts were written on vellum in uncials (Greek capital letters) and date from the fourth to the eighth centuries. The most famous and the best are these:

1. The Sinaitic Codex, discovered by Tischendorf in 1859 in the Convent of Saint Catherine on Mount Sinai. From the beginning of the fourth century, this manuscript contains all of the New Testament. It is in the British Museum.
2. The Vatican Codex, also from the fourth century, is in the Library of the Vatican. One hundred forty-two of the 559 pages contain almost the whole New Testament.
3. The Alexandrian Codex, from the fifth century, is also in the British Museum. It contains almost all of the Old Testament (in Greek) and almost all of the New.
4. The Ephraem Codex, from the fifth century, is in the National Library in Paris. It consists of 64 sheets for the Old Testament and 145 for the New.

More than 2,400 manuscripts, in cursive writing, date from the ninth to the sixteenth centuries. There are also more than 1,600 lectionaries, containing choice texts for the public reading of the New Testament.

Moreover, there are in existence about 1,000 old manuscripts of numerous translations of the New Testament; and besides these, there are at least 8,000 manuscripts of the Latin Vulgate alone. Finally, the church fathers furnish a considerable number of quotations from the New Testament, most of them in Greek (1,819 come from Irenaeus; 17,922 from Origen; 7,258 from Tertullian; and 5,176 from Eusebius).[6]

With access to such an abundance of documents, it is interesting to study certain comparisons made by Professor F. F. Bruce.[7] The historical books of antiquity have a documentation infinitely less solid. For the *Gallic Wars* of Julius Caesar (written between 58 and 50 B.C.), there are several manuscripts, but only nine or ten of them are valid, and the oldest is dated about 900 years after Caesar. Of the fourteen books of the *Histories* of Tacitus (around A.D. 100), only four and a half have been preserved; and of the sixteen books of his *Annals*, only ten remain in toto and two in part. All that is left of those two great works rests on just two manuscripts, one from the ninth century and the other from the eleventh. For the *History* of Thucydides (about 460-400 B.C.) we have no more than eight manuscripts, the oldest of which dates from around A.D. 900. The same is true of the *History* of Herodotus (about 480-425 B.C.). Still, no scholar would question the authenticity of Herodotus or of Thucydides merely because the only usable manuscripts of their works are 1,300 years more recent than the originals. Finally, we have also only one manuscript for all the works of Sophocles, and this was copied 1,400 years after his death.

The variants of the New Testament in general. As in the case of the Old Testament, scholars have devoted their lives to studying and comparing existing manuscripts, to establish the most sure text, the one the closest possible to the original. Gaussen[8] mentions among others the extensive studies of Griesbach: 335 manuscripts for the Gospels alone; and those of Scholtz: 674 manuscripts for the Gospels; 200 for the Acts; 256 for the letters of Paul; and 93 for Revelation. Closer to our times, scholars B. F. Westcott and F. J. A. Hort produced in 1882 a monumental work on the restitution of the original text of the New Testament Greek.

In the Greek text there are somewhat fewer than 150,000 words. In more than 4,000 Greek manuscripts, about 200,000 variants have been picked out, most of very little importance. Westcott and Hort estimate that the proportion of words accepted by virtually all and without the slightest doubt is very high; it is estimated (on the whole) to be seven-eighths of the total. The remaining eighth, mostly consisting of changes in the order of words and in other relatively minor details, constitutes the field for textual criticism. Hort adds that, in his opinion, scarcely more than a thousandth part of the text can be called, in any sense whatever, a substantial variation.[9]

Dr. Warfield sums up the question as follows: "If we compare the present state of the text of the New Testament with that of no matter what other ancient work, we must . . . declare it marvelously exact." This testifies to the care and reverence with which it was copied, also to the divine providence which kept it extraordinarily intact for the church of all time. In the opinion of Dr. E. Abbott, nineteen-twentieths of the variations among the manuscripts of the New Testament rest on so little among them that no one ought to think of them as "rival readings"; and nineteen-twentieths of the rest are of so little consequence that their adoption or rejection would mean no appreciable change in the passages under scrutiny.

Warfield goes on to say that the great bulk of the New Testament has been transmitted to us without, or almost without, any variations. It can be asserted with competence that the sacred text is exact and valid and that no article of faith and no moral precept in it has been distorted or lost. Moreover, the same author expresses his conviction that, in the New Testament of Westcott and Hort, we have "in substance the original text."[10]

Dr. Philip Schaff, editor of the *Encyclopaedia of Religious Knowledge* and president of the American Committee for the Revision of the English Bible, states that the great number of variants in the Greek text should not surprise or trouble any Christian. They are the natural result of the enormous wealth of our documentary sources, and they are a testimony to the immense significance of the New Testament. They have no slightest bearing on the integrity of the text; on the contrary, they reinforce it. The study of them is very useful and stimulating. Out of the 150,000 variants, only 400 materially alter the sense. Among these, no more than about 50 have real importance for any reason whatever; and even in the case of these 50, not one touches on any article of faith or any moral commandment not forcibly supported by other entirely clear passages, or by the teaching of the Bible as a whole. The *Textus Receptus* (Received Text) of Stephanus, Beza and Elzevir and our present version teach exactly the same Christianity as the uncial text of the Sinaiticus and the Vaticanus of the oldest manuscripts.[11]

In regard to these variants, let us mention the fact that in some places they have to do with a whole group of verses. Here are two well-known examples.

Mark 16:9-20: These closing verses of the gospel are not found in the two oldest manuscripts. Some commentators think that this passage was added very early, perhaps at the beginning of the second century. In any case, it is in harmony with the other gospels and reflects the convictions of the early churches on the points treated.

John 7:53—8:11: According to the note in the American Standard Version, and such a note in other versions, most of the ancient authorities omit this account of the woman taken in adultery; but the manuscripts that do have it differ little among themselves.

It is evident that the two above-mentioned cases are quite exceptional.

The variants in the epistle to the Romans in particular. To show in a concrete way how the variants appear, let us take as an example the epistle to the Romans. The scholar Griesbach, referred to above, has made a very special study of this.[12] In it he minutely compared 7 great uncial manuscripts (Alexandrinus, Vaticanus, Ephraemi, and Passionei at Rome; and those of St. Germain, Dresden, and Cardinal Coislin), 110 minuscule manuscripts, and 30 others, for the most part at Mount Athos.

We begin by presenting a table on the first eight verses of chapter 1.

Textus Receptus (Elzevir, 1624)	Variants from all the Greek manuscripts
1: no difference	
2: by his prophets	by the prophets (in only one manuscript, that of Paris)
3: born of the posterity (seed)	begotten . . . (in the Upsal manuscript only, and this is nothing but a change in two letters)
4: no difference	

5: Jesus Christ our Lord	Jesus Christ our God (in the Vienna manuscript only)
6: no difference	
7: that are in Rome, beloved of God, called . . .	who are in the love of God, called . . . (only one manuscript, an uncial, of Dresden); who are at Rome, called (only two manuscripts, the uncial of St. Germain and the minuscule at Rome)
from God our Father	from God the Father (only the Upsal manuscript)
8: first	first (a difference impossible to put down; it exists in only one manuscript)
for you all	in regard to you all (in twelve manuscripts) .

These nine or ten different "readings"* are actually of no importance; besides, they have to do with only one or two manuscripts out of the 150 consulted on this passage (except for the last named, which occurs in twelve manuscripts). The differences between our various translations are much more numerous and ordinarily have more influence on the sense.

Griesbach pursued his study through the whole epistle to the Romans. Here is the general result: This letter has 433 verses and contains 96 Greek words which are not found anywhere else in the New Testament. In all and for all, only four variants seem to modify the meaning of the text. They are these:

1. Romans 6:16: Instead of "whether of sin unto death . . . of obedience unto righteousness," Griesbach has it: "whether of sin . . . whether of righteousness." He indicated this rendering only as a feeble possibility, and the later editions do not retain it.

2. Romans 7:6: Instead of "Having died to that wherein . . ." Griesbach has: "Being dead to it [that law] in which. . . ." In the Greek the difference is in a change of only one letter (an *o* instead of an *e*).

3. Romans 11:6: Griesbach drops the last part of the verse: "If it is by grace, it is no more of works: otherwise grace is no more grace."

*By "readings" is meant the particular form of a text compared to another form of the same text in other copies.

Charles Hodge says in his *Commentary on the Epistle to the Romans* that several manuscripts omit these words (which, in fact, are a repetition of the sense of the first part of the verse) .

4. Romans 12:11: Instead of "serving the Lord," Griesbach has: "serving as you have the opportunity." The suggested correction hangs on only two letters in one of the Greek words. The number of manuscripts does not appear to justify this reading, and it was not kept.

Here then is all that the most critical examination could find in 433 verses! The true result is a demonstration of the admirable integrity of the epistle to the Romans. We chose this letter as an example because of its length and its importance. But the rest of the New Testament fully confirms like conclusions. According to Gaussen, scarcely 10 verses out of 7,959 contain differences of any gravity.[13]

CONCLUSION

Having spoken of the number of variants and of their relatively slight importance, we might actually wonder that there are not many more of them and that they are not of far more weight than they are. Gaussen very well brings out here all that the Scriptures have undergone throughout these thousands of years:

> When one thinks that the Bible has been copied during thirty centuries, as no book of man has ever been, or ever will be; that it was subjected to all the catastrophes and all the captivities of Israel; that it was transported seventy years to Babylon; that it has seen itself so often persecuted, or forgotten, or interdicted, or burnt, from the days of the Philistines to those of the Seleucidae; when one thinks that, since the time of Jesus Christ, it has had to traverse the first three centuries of the imperial persecutions, when persons found in possession of the holy books were thrown to the wild beasts; next the seventh, eighth, and ninth centuries, when false decretals were everywhere multiplied; the tenth century, when so few could read, even among the princes; the twelfth, thirteenth, and fourteenth centuries, when the use of the Scriptures in the vulgar tongue was punished with death, and when the books of the ancient fathers were mutilated, when so many ancient traditions were garbled and falsified, even to the very acts of the emperors and to those of the councils—then we can perceive how necessary it was that the providence of God

> should have always put forth its mighty power, in order that the
> Jews . . . and the Christian Church [especially during the Middle
> Ages] . . . should transmit to us, in all their purity, those
> Scriptures.[14]

It is indeed almost incredible that the Jews would have preserved
for us, just as it was, the book that recounts their rebelliousness; that
announces their ruin, as well as their reestablishment; and that is so
full of Jesus Christ. Nevertheless, they faithfully watched over the
Word received, without ever permitting even one alteration through
addition or subtraction. We have seen that, though the Jews had
Apocryphal books, they never allowed them to be put into the canon.

Is it not remarkable also that the churches of the Middle Ages,
especially the church at Rome, transmitted to us in full the treasury
of the New Testament? Did they not at the same time forbid the
reading of sacred books, in so many ways replacing the Word of God
by their tradition? But they kept intact those very Scriptures which
condemned their deviations; and they never dared to add to them the
Apocryphal writings of the first centuries of the Christian era, even
though these had the same bias which they themselves had. The
Roman Church waited until the Council of Trent (1546) to add the
Jewish Apocrypha to the canon of the Old Testament, the composition of which had never been delegated to her charge.

For one last word on the profit which can be derived from a study
of the variants, let us summarize Professor J. H. Skilton's interesting
remarks: We are required to make choices among the "readings." It
is incumbent on us to attempt to reconstruct from all the witnesses
available to us the text essentially preserved in all, but perfectly preserved in none. It is necessary for us, in God's providence, according
to His appointment, to strive to ascertain the true, the original, text;
to obtain by faithful study of all the pertinent materials available and
by the application of correct principles a text which is better than the
best found in any manuscript. We must, in other words, engage in
what is called textual criticism of the Bible. The conservative scholar
will be moved by his regard for the worth of the original text which
he is attempting to reconstruct. . . . Believing that every word of the
original manuscripts was breathed by the Holy Spirit, the consistent
Christian scholar will be eager to recover every word of that original.
Although recognizing that no doctrine rises or falls with a disputed

reading and that most variations are relatively unimportant, the conservative will nevertheless realize that not one jot or tittle of the law of God is actually unimportant (Matt. 5:1-8); that the Scripture itself builds an argument on the very form of a word (Gal. 3:16); and that our Lord held that even with regard to a brief statement in the Old Testament the Scripture cannot be broken (John 10:34-35).

We believe that it has been the design of God to require us to labor to know His Word in its original form. Our texts the most used in the past can still be improved upon, for new sources of information have been discovered and positive textual criticism and exegesis have made progress. We must profit from these efforts and even actively participate in them. Does not God desire that all men "feel after Him and find Him though He is not far from each one of us" (Acts 17:27) ?[15]

And here is the testimony of two scholars after long research on the value of the biblical documents:

Bengel, emboldened by all that he had studied and established, wrote to a young friend:

> Eat simply the bread of the Scriptures as it presents itself to thee; and do not distress thyself at finding here and there a small particle of sand which the millstone may have left in it. Thou mayst, then, dismiss all those doubts which at one time so horribly tormented myself. If the Holy Scriptures—which have been so often copied, and which have passed so often through the faulty hands of ever-fallible men—were absolutely without variations, the miracle would be so great that faith in them would be no longer faith. I am astonished, on the contrary, that the result of all those transcriptions has not been a much greater number of different readings.[16]

Kenyon, aware of all that the most modern science has to offer, confidently maintains: "The Christian can take the whole Bible in his hand and say without fear or hesitation that he holds in it the true Word of God, faithfully handed down from generation to generation throughout the centuries."[17]

17

ILLUMINATION

Definitions and Generalities

WE HAVE JUST SEEN how the biblical text, as we now have it, was inspired, drawn up, and put together, and was subsequently transmitted to our times and to each of us individually. But for it to become really accessible to us, another direct intervention from on high was needed: illumination. By this we mean the supernatural help granted by the Spirit of God to the reader of holy Scripture, to enable him to lay hold on the divine message. A book inspired by the Spirit can be understood only by means of an intervention of the Spirit.

What is the difference between inspiration and illumination? We have seen that *inspiration* is the determining influence that acted on the sacred authors, moving them to put into writing the revelation which they had received from God. *Illumination,* on the other hand, is, in principle, that gift granted to the child of God, from the very moment of his new birth, which permits him to *see* the kingdom of God (John 3:3). The Lord even goes so far as to promise enlightenment to every sincere person who truly seeks Him by feeling after Him: "Unto the upright there ariseth light in the darkness" (Ps. 112:4).

Illumination is normally permanent and increasing. From the time the believer submits to the Spirit of God, the Spirit leads him into all truth (John 16:13). For the converted heart, the Lord takes away the veil that obscures the reading of the Old Testament (and He does the same thing in regard to the New, II Cor. 3:14-16). In proportion as we persevere in meditating on the Word of God and in putting it into practice, our horizons widen and our comprehension of it increases. "The opening of thy words giveth light; it giveth understanding unto the simple. Oh how love I thy law! . . . Thy commandments make me wiser than all my enemies; . . . I have more understanding than all my teachers; for thy testimonies are my meditation. I understand more than the aged. Through thy precepts I get understanding" (Ps. 119:130, 97-100, 104).

Illumination, as regards a particular word of the inspired text, may be a promise for some time in the future: "The words are shut up and sealed till the time of the end. . . . They that are wise shall understand" (Dan. 12:9-10). An individual can hear or read a divine message with no discernment until he has passed through certain spiritual experiences. After quoting the prophecies from Psalm 118:26 and Zechariah 9:9, John adds: "These things understood not his disciples at the first: but when Jesus was glorified, then remembered they that these things were written of him, and that they had done these things unto him" (John 12:16).

As we continue to walk by faith rather than by sight, we shall constantly need ever increasing light. For the present we know in part, but soon we shall know even as also we are known (I Cor. 13:12). Different degrees of illumination explain the various opinions of Christians on relatively minor points at any given time. The promise, fortunately, is addressed to all: "If in anything ye are otherwise minded, this also God shall reveal unto you; only whereunto we have attained, by that same rule let us walk" (Phil. 3:15-16). It is in *Christ* alone that permanent inspiration and perfect illumination completely blend together.

THE INNER WITNESS OF THE HOLY SPIRIT

The Reformers, standing without any mental reservation for the plenary inspiration of the Scriptures (see chap. 20, subhead "The Reformers") never failed to emphasize the indispensable role of the Holy Spirit for their proper interpretation.

This inner witness concentrates on these two points: *It is an aid to faith,* by producing conviction regarding the nature, worth and authority of Scripture; *it is an aid to understanding,* by providing the illumination which enables one to seize the meaning of the text.

Luther used to say: "The Bible cannot be understood simply by study or talent; you must count only on the influence of the Holy Spirit."

Zwingli put it this way: "Even if you receive the gospel of Jesus Christ directly from an apostle, you cannot act according to it unless your heavenly Father teaches you and draws you to Himself by His Spirit."

Calvin wrote:

> The testimony of the Spirit is superior to reason. For . . . these words will not obtain full credit in the hearts of men until they are sealed by the inward testimony of the Spirit. . . . Scripture, carrying its own evidence along with it, deigns not to submit to proofs and arguments, but owes the full conviction with which we ought to receive it to the testimony of the Spirit. For though in its own majesty it has enough to command reverence, nevertheless, it then begins truly to touch us when it is sealed in our hearts by the Holy Spirit. Enlightened by him, we no longer believe, either on our own judgment or that of others, that the Scriptures are from God; but in a way superior to human judgment, feel perfectly assured . . . that it came to us from the very mouth of God. We ask not for proofs or probabilities on which to rest our judgment, but we subject our intellect and judgment to it as too transcendent for us to estimate.[1]
>
> Moses and the prophets . . . boldly and fearlessly testified what was actually true, that it was the mouth of the Lord that spake. The same Spirit . . . now also testifies to our hearts, that he has employed them as his servants to instruct us. Accordingly, we need not wonder if there are many who doubt as to the Author of the Scripture; for although the majesty of God is displayed in it, yet none but those who have been enlightened by the Holy Spirit have eyes to perceive what ought indeed to have been visible to all, and yet is visible to the elect alone.[2]

It is indeed the inner witness of the Holy Spirit to our hearts and minds (cf. Rom. 8:16) that alone lends power and vitality to inspired words which hitherto may have seemed impersonal and ineffective. Paul said of his own preaching: "Knowing . . . your election, how that our gospel came not unto you in word only, but also in power, and in the Holy Spirit, and in much assurance" (I Thess. 1:4-5). "My speech and my preaching were not in persuasive words of wisdom, but in demonstration of the Spirit and of power: that your faith should not stand in the wisdom of men, but in the power of God" (I Cor. 2:4-5). The same can be said of Scripture: it is objective truth, the very Word of God; but for our faith in it to be established, we need an inner demonstration of the Spirit and of power.

Thus God persuades us of the divine inspiration of Scripture: He demonstrates it by intimate and direct conviction which He Himself puts within us. The unbeliever, even the unregenerate religious man, cannot conceive of such a thing. Anyone who is not a musician understands little or nothing of music; a person devoid of literary insight does not appreciate poetry. In like manner, it is all the more impossible for the natural man, one not born of the Spirit, to grasp the true nature of Scripture. He can understand Hebrew, Greek, grammar, ancient history, religions, etc.—anything having to do with the "letter" of Scripture, the body. But needful above all is the spirit, that divine life which He alone communicates. For the same reason, the essentials of Scripture can be apprehended by any spiritual man, even though, humanly speaking, he possesses only a modest education. Has not the Lord hidden these things from the wise and understanding, to reveal them unto babes? (Luke 10:21). Blessed, in this sense, are the poor in spirit, for theirs is the kingdom of heaven (Matt. 5:3)!

Even difficulties in the text, the apparent contradictions and the arguments of the critics, do not turn us away from this attitude of confidence and obedience. He who has truly met God in the Bible, through all the pages of it, can only repeat with the man born blind: "One thing I know, that, whereas I was blind, now I see" (John 9:25).

We can therefore testify with assurance that the Lord addresses Himself to us. The same Spirit who convinced the early church of the authenticity of the holy books convinces the believer today. Our faith is not founded on human arguments, although we can respect and appreciate such support. The Apostle Paul, in fact, clearly draws the line between the testimony of the Holy Spirit and that of our own spirit (Rom. 8:16). With the saints of all ages, we hear the voice of the good Shepherd, and a stranger we will not follow. The sheep will not fail to recognize the voice of the Son of God or the teaching of the Holy Spirit.

Not only is it true that the Bible *was* inspired; but it still *is* inspired, for the Holy Spirit has maintained His vital union with Scripture. When we read: "Every one that thirsteth, come ye to the waters, and he that hath no money" (Isa. 55:1) or "Come unto me, all ye that labor and are heavy laden, and I will give you rest" (Matt.

11:28), it is still the Holy Spirit who murmurs the words to our waiting hearts. He makes of the sacred text a living Word. His breath can be felt in it as in no other book. Thanks to Him, these written things are become spirit and life; man lives by them; they are words which even now issue from His mouth.

Whoever has had experience with it cannot doubt the supernatural origin of the Bible, for according to his capacity he receives it straight from God Himself, as did David, Isaiah, Paul and John. It is for him a word from God. He knows that when he obeys its instructions, he is obeying his heavenly Father. Counting on the promises of Scripture, he knows with certainty that it is in the Lord his God, his Redeemer, that he is placing his confidence. And when he comes up to the hour of death, his soul keeps on clinging to the firm hope offered to him in the Word of God. It is the voice of the Saviour Himself saying to him, "Be of good cheer; it is I; be not afraid" (Matt. 14:27).[3]

Since all of Scripture is theopneustia, breathed out from the mouth of God, so it keeps on moving incessantly with dynamic energy. By the testimony which the Spirit bears to Himself, the words of the Bible act in living power to demand the mastery over our spirits. Luther exclaimed: "The heart declares: This is the truth, even though I were to suffer for it a thousand deaths!"

Erich Sauer speaks in the same vein:

> Therefore the Bible is a living book.... Here there is no mere once-upon-a-time, but a now; no simple yesterday, but a today; no mere concern with the beyond, but a God-permeated interest with this life. Here is not only a written word, but a spiritually living word; not only external letters, but speech of the Spirit, spoken inwardly and still speaking. Thus Holy Scripture in a quite incomparable degree shares in the character of the Eternal as ever present.
>
> The Spirit of God has not only inbreathed the written word and given it, but has continued with it. He accompanies it and makes it operative. He marks the bare record to be a tie with heaven. God *comes* to us now through His Word, and the Word that is centuries old remains fresh and eternally young. It is as if it had been written yesterday, as if the ink was not yet dry, never growing old, superior to time, ever present.[4]

THE LIMITS OF ILLUMINATION

Confusion between inspiration and illumination leads to a grave danger: to the claim that those who use Scripture are beneficiaries of the same supernatural help as were the sacred authors. This would soon lead to the same authority being given to man as belongs to the Word of God. Here are two examples as cited by Louis Gaussen. *The Jews* considered their rabbis and doctors endowed with an infallibility which put them on a level with Moses and the prophets if not above them. They have prohibited the explanation of its oracles otherwise than according to their traditions, the Talmud (Mishna and Gemara). *The Roman Church* has also attributed to the fathers, to the councils, and—especially—to the pope an authority which puts men on the level of Jesus, the prophets and the apostles—if not above them. By their authority alone is Scripture to be interpreted.[5] (For more detail, see chap. 23.) These two examples do not exhaust the list of those in danger of making void the Word of God by their tradition (Matt. 15:6). Let us ask ourselves very seriously if, in our particular church or school of thought, we are not liable to fall into this same serious mistake.

Illuminism tends to supplant inspiration. This, in fact, consists of claiming that the inner light given by the Spirit advantageously replaces the Scripture and makes one independent of it. Calvin alludes to the "illuminated," those that made fun of the simplicity of believers who depended on the "dead letter" of the text and who thought it absurd that the Spirit of the sovereign God could submit Himself to the Scriptures. Actually, the Spirit, the Author of the holy books, simply shows Himself to be forever conformed to Himself. Having set forth the truth, He merely keeps on speaking it with the same meaning. By its prolonged action, the Word communicates Jesus Christ to us, both converting souls and nourishing them. Why should we want to separate ourselves from our sole source of sure and controllable knowledge? Jesus Christ Himself, God incarnate, was fully conformed to the Holy Scriptures. The apostles and the faithful of the early church, so plainly inspired by the Spirit, constantly did the same thing.

On the other hand, into what strange aberrations have not those fallen who have thought themselves independent of the salutary teaching of Scripture! Calvin did not exaggerate when he said that these "fantastic boasters . . . boldly accept for the Word of God anything that presents itself to their fancy while they are snoring!"[6] As for Gaussen, he adds in regard to "illumined mystics," who, basically, are rationalists:

> They will put above the text of the Bible their own hallucinations and the Christ who [they say] is within them. They will speak with disdain of "the letter" of the literal meaning of the gospel facts, of the man Jesus, or of the outward Christ [as they call Him] of the cross of Golgotha, and of preaching, of worship, of the sacraments. They are above all these carnal helps![7]

Illuminism is still very prevalent in our day. It is still an outrage to Scripture, to which we are forbidden to add anything and from which we are warned to take nothing away (Rev. 22:18-19). It is also an offense against the Spirit of truth, since it despises the Book of which He is the Author, attributing to Him means of enlightenment contrary to His own revelations.

GOD'S SOVEREIGNTY IN HIS GRANTING OF ILLUMINATION

There is nothing automatic about illumination. The fact that one holds in his hands the wholly inspired Bible does not signify in the slightest that he is master of it, should he make use of the Word of God in any way that suits his fancy. If scripture, as we believe, is objectively that Word of God, the Lord does not make it intelligible to just anybody and in any sort of way.

Isaiah said to his people: "Jehovah hath poured out upon you the spirit of deep sleep. . . . And all vision is become unto you as the words of a book that is sealed, which men deliver to one that is learned, saying, Read this, I pray thee; and he saith, I cannot, for it is sealed: and the book is delivered to him that is not learned, saying, Read this, I pray theee; and he saith, I am not learned" (Isa. 29:10-12). God Himself has willed that men seek Him and that they force themselves to find Him by feeling after Him, though He is not far from each one of us (Acts 17:27). He takes pleasure in revealing Himself to the humble and sincere heart: "Thou didst hide these things from the wise and understanding, and didst reveal them unto babes. Neither doth any know the Father, save the Son, and he to whomsoever the Son willeth to reveal him" (Matt. 11:25, 27).

When Peter affirmed his faith in the Messiah, the Son of the living God, Jesus said to him: "Flesh and blood hath not revealed it unto thee, but my Father who is in heaven" (Matt. 16:17). Paul, in describing the unmerited illumination which rescued him from his profound darkness, said this: "When it was the good pleasure of God, who . . . called me through his grace, to reveal his Son in me, . . . straightway I conferred not with flesh and blood" (Gal. 1:15-16). How many times have the old inspired pages suddenly come alive for us, reaching down to us here and now, by some mysterious operation of the sovereign grace of God!

ILLUMINATION GRANTED IN RESPONSE TO FAITH

The natural, unregenerate man can neither conceive of nor receive the things of the Spirit of God (I Cor. 2:14). God prepared them for those who love Him, and He reveals His mind to such through His Spirit (vv. 9-10). When Peter abandoned himself to his own conception of salvation, he brought down on his head strong reproaches from Christ: "Get thee behind me, Satan: thou art a stumbling-block unto me: for thou mindest not the things of God, but the things of men" (Matt. 16:23).

On the other hand, when the sheep belonging to the good Shepherd hear His voice, they know it (John 10:3-4, 27). After speaking in parables, the meaning of which was hidden from the crowd, Jesus said to His disciples: "Unto you is given the mystery of the kingdom of God: but unto them that are without, all things are done in parables: that seeing they may see and not perceive; and hearing they may hear and not understand; lest haply they should turn again, and it [their sin] should be forgiven them" (Mark 4:11-12). "With many such parables spake he the word unto them, as they were able to hear it; and without a parable spake he not unto them: but privately to his own disciples he expounded all things" (vv. 33-34). This much is clear: Jesus explained everything to His disciples, but He darkened the minds of those who voluntarily made their ears dull and who closed their eyes, that they might not be healed (Matt. 13:13-15). Consequently, the same biblical teaching and the same page of Scripture speaks to one but has nothing to say to another. This explains the exhortation, so surprising at first sight: "He that hath ears to hear, let him hear" (Luke 14:35)!

ILLUMINATION NOT GIVEN ONCE FOR ALL

Although it is normal for a believer to be enlightened by the Holy Spirit his whole life long, everything depends, nevertheless, on that one's submission to the light already received. Man by nature is terribly slow to believe, and his progress in understanding may at times appear to be nil. It was to His own disciples that Jesus addressed, almost sharply, these seven questions: "Why reason ye . . .? do ye not yet perceive, neither understand? have ye your heart hardened? Having eyes, see ye not? and having ears, hear ye not? and do ye not remember . . . Do ye not yet understand?" (Mark 8:17-21).

When Jesus spoke plainly to the twelve of His death and resurrection, "they understood none of these things; and this saying was hid from them, and they perceived not the things that were said" (Luke 18:34). Again, after the resurrection, Jesus addressed in these words the disciples on the Emmaus road: "O foolish men, and slow of heart to believe in all that the prophets have spoken!" Then, with infinite patience He interpreted to them in all the Scriptures the things concerning Himself (Luke 24:25, 27).

Believers who permit themselves to walk "after the flesh" rather than "after the Spirit" (Rom. 8:4 ff.) become progressively less able to understand. They put themselves in the place of needing "milk," being no longer able to take "solid food." Leaving the deep things, those difficult to discern, they must have repeated to them the rudiments of the first principles of the oracles of God. This is why our churches are often nurseries for spiritual infants rather than training grounds for full-grown men, for teachers and for soldiers of Jesus Christ (Heb. 5:11-14).

It is, alas, perfectly possible for a so-called minister to be deprived of illumination from above. Paul speaks of those who desire to be teachers of the law but who do not understand what they say, even what they confidently affirm (I Tim. 1:7). "Let them alone," said Jesus; "they are blind guides. And if the blind guide the blind, both shall fall into a pit" (Matt. 15:14).

Divine Illumination Enlightening Our Hearts: Both Spirit and Mind

Nothing is more dangerous than a merely theoretical and intellectual knowledge. This leads a man to suppose that he knows; he believes that he has understood it all; and he even thinks he almost knows it by heart. A certain acquaintance with the divine law can exist where a true change of life has not been produced. The man whose conscience has been quickened, however, is haunted by his knowledge of the Scripture which he is constantly transgressing: "The good which I would I do not: but the evil which I would not, that I practise. . . . For I delight in the law of God after the inward man: but I see a different law in my members, . . . bringing me into captivity under the law of sin which is in my members. Wretched man that I am!" (Rom. 7:19-24). Such knowledge, so useful in itself, is still far from sufficient if it leads only to despair.

The most evangelical of believers, those whose doctrine is completely correct, may also be threatened by the trap of rationalism, a snare which leaves no room for true faith. So orthodoxy can be dead and belief sterile. This is, of course, not the effect produced by the illumination from the Holy Spirit. He bathes every part of our being with His light and life:

"having the eyes of your heart enlightened" (Eph. 1:18);

"that ye be renewed in the spirit of your mind" (4:23);

"that ye may be filled with the knowledge of his will in all spiritual wisdom and understanding, to walk worthily of the Lord" (Col. 1:9-10);

"unto all riches of the full assurance of understanding, that they may know the mystery of God, even Christ" (2:2);

"transformed by the renewing of your mind, that ye may prove what is the . . . will of God" (Rom. 12:2);

"the Spirit himself beareth witness with our spirit" (8:16);

"then opened he their mind, that they might understand the scriptures" (Luke 24:45);

"Lydia . . . heard . . .: whose heart the Lord opened to give heed unto the things which were spoken by Paul" (Acts 16:14)

The illumination promised is not only that of the sacred text, of the letter of Scripture But through the inspired message, it brings the one revelation above all others: the very knowledge of the person of God. Jesus said: "If a man love me, he will keep my word: and my Father will love him, and we will come unto him, and make our abode with him. I will love him and will manifest myself unto him" (John 14:23, 21).

"Ye have an anointing [the Holy Spirit] from the Holy One, and ye know all things . . . The anointing which ye received of him abideth in you, and ye need not that any one teach you; but as his anointing teacheth you concerning all things, and is true . . . even as it taught you, abide in him" (I John 2:20, 27). "The Son of God . . . hath given us an understanding, that we know him that is true . . ." (5:20).

Further, both the whole written revelation and the illumination which accompanies it have as their purpose such a transformation as will make us like the Lord Himself. The veil which hindered the reading of the Old Testament is done away in Christ. Now with unveiled face we behold in the Scriptures as in a mirror the glory of the Lord, and we are "transformed into the same image from glory to glory, even as from the Lord the Spirit" (II Cor. 3:14-18).

REFUSAL OF ILLUMINATION A SIGNAL FOR JUDGMENT FROM GOD

Isaiah expressed this truth in an especially clear way: "Go, and tell this people, Hear ye indeed, but understand not; and see ye indeed, but perceive not. Make the heart of this people fat, and make their ears heavy, and shut their eyes; lest they . . . turn again, and be healed" (6:9-10).

We have already cited the following text: "Jehovah hath poured out upon you the spirit of deep sleep. . . . And all vision is become unto you as the words of a book that is sealed." The Lord Himself explains why: "Forasmuch as this people draw nigh unto me, and with their mouth and with their lips do honor me, but have removed their heart far from me, and their fear of me is a commandment of men which hath been taught them" (Isa. 29:10-13).

We have just observed that for believers the veil which made the Scriptures obscure has been taken away. But Paul adds: "If our gospel is veiled, it is veiled in them that perish: in whom the god of this world hath blinded the minds of the unbelieving, that the light of the gospel of the glory of Christ, who is the image of God, should not dawn upon them" (II Cor. 4:3-4).

There exists, then, the opposite of illumination, that is, a blinding struck upon the hardened heart. Men have let themselves be dragged along by all the seductions of iniquity "because they received not the love of the truth, that they might be saved. And for this cause God sendeth them a working of error, that they should believe a lie: that they all might be judged who believed not the truth, but had pleasure in unrighteousness" (II Thess. 2:10-12).

Jesus said: "For judgment came I into this world, that they that see not may see; and that they that see [that claim to see, like the Pharisees] may become blind. And this is the judgment, that the light is come into the world, and men loved the darkness rather than the light; for their works were evil" (John 9:39; 3:19).

The pillar of cloud was for Israel the sign of the presence of the Lord, who was guiding and protecting them all the time from their going out of Egypt. At the most critical moment, it came between the people and their enemies. The cloud looked dark to the enemies, but on the other side it gave light in the darkness (Exodus 14:19-20). What a striking picture of the revelation: impenetrable to the unbelieving world, it illumines and safely leads the steps of the children of God!

Must it be spelled out that the sacred text remains intrinsically the Word of God, even when readers or auditors close their hearts to the illumination from on high? The same was true of the message of the prophets. God said to Moses: "I will raise them up a prophet . . . like unto thee; and I will put my words in his mouth, and he shall speak unto them all that I shall command him. And . . . whosoever will not hearken unto my words which he shall speak in my name, I will require it of him" (Deut. 18:18-19). And to Ezekiel: "Thou shalt say unto them, Thus saith the Lord Jehovah. And they, whether they will hear, or whether they will forbear (for they are a rebellious house), yet shall know that there hath been a prophet among them" (Ezek. 2:4-5). When the revelation has become for the hardened like a book that is sealed, impossible to be opened up, it remains no less the "revelation," with judgments which cannot fail to be carried out (Isa. 29:10-14). Did not Jesus Himself say: "If I had not come and spoken unto them, they had not had sin: but now they have no excuse for their sin. He that rejecteth me and receiveth not my sayings, hath one that judgeth him: the word that I spake, the same shall judge him in the last day" (John 15:22; 12:48).

It is frightening to think of those who dissect the Bible as though it were a dead book. When they decree that it is not the Word of God, they thus promptly shut themselves off from the illumination which proceeds from its divine Author. What wonder is it that they no longer see anything in it but problems and contradictions! On the other hand, the one who receives the inspired text with the humility of Christ and the apostles finds a confirmation of his faith in the very books which are most under attack today. How profoundly edifying, for example, have we found a long meditation on Leviticus, Deuteronomy, the supposed "second Isaiah" (chaps. 40-66), the gospel of John, II Peter, Revelation! Through these books God has spoken to us; through them He has opened our eyes; and He has fed our souls out of them. The above argument makes unnecessary any other (even though well-documented facts can also provide helpful confirmations).

RECEIVING OF ILLUMINATION

Since God has revealed Himself and desires nothing more than to make His Word intelligible, let us simply go to Him with the prayer of the psalmist, who was himself one of the inspired writers:

"Open thou mine eyes, that I may behold wondrous things out of thy law.
Teach me, O Jehovah, the way of thy statutes . . . .
Give me understanding, and I shall keep thy law" (Ps. 119:18, 33-34).

God will certainly answer such a prayer, provided that we do our part by fulfilling His conditions.

Meditate constantly on the Scriptures, for we shall not understand them unless we assiduously put ourselves under their instruction, as did the psalmist: "Hide not thy commandments from me. My soul breaketh for the longing that it hath unto thine ordinances at all times . . . I will delight myself in thy commandments, which I have loved . . . and I will meditate on thy statutes. Oh how love I thy law! It is my meditation all the day. Mine eyes anticipated the night-watches, that I might meditate on thy word. Let thy hand be ready to help me; for I have chosen thy precepts" (Ps. 119:19-20, 47-48, 97, 148, 173). Surely God does not refuse His light to the one who seeks it thus, and in such a place!

Let ourselves be judged by the Word. The thrice holy God is speaking: the only suitable attitude on our part is one of humility and repentance. Even for the adversaries of the faith, this promise stands: "If peradventure God may give them repentance unto the knowledge of the truth, and they may recover themselves out of the snare of the devil" (II Tim. 2:25-26). This is exactly what we need as well.

Promptly carry over into practice all the light received. Jesus declared: "If any man willeth to do his will [that of the Father who sent Him], he *shall know* of the teaching, whether it is of God" (John 7:17). The one who resists, paying no attention to teaching already given, cannot be led further into the knowledge of the truth. May we be His submissive and faithful disciples, ever finding our satisfaction in watching Him fulfill His promise: "The path of the righteous is as the dawning light, that shineth more and more unto the perfect day" (Prov. 4:18).

Part Four

TESTIMONIES TO THE INSPIRATION OF HOLY SCRIPTURE

18

JESUS CHRIST AND HOLY SCRIPTURE

JESUS, THE DIVINE, ETERNAL WORD, is inseparable from Scripture, the Word of God made a book. (See the parallel we worked out to show this, chap. 4, subhead "Christ and the Scriptures.")

The points of comparison between the two Words are so complex and so important that we ponder them once more in the chapter before us.

CHRIST AS THE CENTRAL THEME OF HOLY SCRIPTURE

The Bible, the book of salvation, reveals to us the God who redeems us and who leads us to Himself. It is then not surprising that the Messiah Saviour holds the preeminent place in every part of Scripture. Jesus Himself cries out: "Ye search the scriptures, because ye think that in them ye have eternal life; and *these are they which bear witness of me"* (John 5:39).

The Spirit of Christ animated the prophets of the Old Testament and revealed to them, for our benefit, the sufferings of the Saviour of the world and the glory that should follow (I Peter 1:10-12). "The testimony of Jesus is the spirit of prophecy" (Rev. 19:10).

Thus, in order to give to His confused disciples the key to the Scriptures, Jesus reviewed all that which concerns Himself in the Law of Moses, the Psalms and the Prophets (the three divisions of the Hebrew Bible; Luke 24:44). The epistle to the Hebrews sets forth this fact in the clearest possible way: in it Jehovah, the Lord of the Old Testament, is none other than Jesus Himself, wholly one with the Father: "Let all the angels of God worship him" (Heb. 1:6; Ps. 97:7). "Thy throne, O God, is forever and ever; . . . God, thy God, hath anointed thee" (vv. 8-9; Ps. 45:6-7). "Thou, Lord, in the beginning didst lay the foundation of the earth" (v. 10; Ps. 102:25).

What an absorbing and inexhaustible Bible study: meditation on that which each book of Scripture teaches us about the Lord![1]

Let us cite here the testimony of Erich Sauer:

> From faith in Christ we reach full faith in His Word also. In Christ, the center of God's revelation, we have also the center of a view of the Bible which is according to God. Moreover, this alone is consistent with faith. For Christ Himself is the "Logos," the original form of the word, the personal, living "word," the true and faithful Witness (John 1:1; Rev. 1:5), the mouth of the eternal truth, yea, the truth itself (John 14:6). And it was His Spirit, the Spirit of Christ, who inspired the prophets (I Peter 1:11); and the "testimony of Jesus" is the "spirit of prophecy" (Rev. 19:10).[2]

CHRIST'S COMING AS A FULFILLMENT OF THE SCRIPTURES

He declared: "Think not that I came to destroy the law or the prophets: I came not to destroy, but to *fulfil*" (Matt. 5:17). "The Son of man goeth, even as it is written of him" (26:24). Commanding Peter to put his sword back into the scabbard, at the time of His arrest, He added: "How then should the scriptures be fulfilled, that thus it must be?" (v. 54). On the evening of the resurrection, He cried out again: "All things must be fulfilled, which are written in the law of Moses, and the prophets, and the psalms, concerning me" (Luke 24:44).

Thus the evangelists lost no opportunity to show to what extent all the episodes in the life of Christ are the fulfillment of Scriptures. We shall limit ourselves to citing the examples given by Matthew:

the miraculous birth (Matt. 1:22-23; Isa. 7:14)
the location, Bethlehem (2:5-6; Micah 5:1)
the descent into Egypt (2:15; Hosea 11:1)
the massacre of the innocents (2:17-18; Jer. 31:15)
the childhood at Nazareth, in Galilee (2:23; 4:12-16; Isa. 8:23; 9:1)
the forerunner, John the Baptist (3:3; 11:10; Isa. 40:3)
the healing of the sick (8:16-17; Isa. 53:4)
the beloved Servant of Jehovah (12:16-21; Isa. 42:1-4)
the hardening of the people (13:14-15; Isa. 6:9)
the teaching by means of parables (13:35; Ps. 78:2)
the hypocrisy of the Pharisees (15:7-9; Isa. 29:13)
the coming of Elijah (17:10-11; Mal. 4:6; cf. Mark 9:12)

the entry into Jerusalem, riding upon an ass (21:4-5; Zech. 9:9)

the making of the temple into a den of robbers (21:13; Isa. 56:7; Jer. 7:11)

the perfection of praise from the mouth of babes and sucklings (21:16; Ps. 8:2)

the rejection of the head stone of the corner (21:42; Ps. 118:22)

the Messiah whom David called Lord (22:43-44; Ps. 110:1)

the thirty pieces of silver offered by the chief priests (26:15; 27:3-10; Zech. 11:12-13)

the betrayal by Judas (26:24; Ps. 41:9)

the smiting of the Shepherd and the dispersal of the sheep of the flock (26:31, 56; Zech. 13:7)

the arrest, and the numbering of Jesus' soul with the transgressors (26:54, 56; 27:38; Isa. 53:7, 9, 12)

the coming of the Son of man in the clouds (26:64; Dan. 7:13)

the insults, spitting and smiting on the face of the Messiah (26:67; 27:30; Isa. 50:6; 52:14)

the wine mingled with gall, the vinegar (27:34; John 19:29; Ps. 69:21)

the crucifixion, the piercing of the feet and the hands (27:35; Ps. 22:16)

the casting of lots for the garments (27:35; Ps. 22:14-18)

the railings during the death agony (27:39-44; Ps. 22:6-8)

"My God, why hast thou forsaken me?" (27:46; Ps. 22:1)

the burial in the tomb of the rich man (27:57-60; Isa. 53:9)

the resurrection (28:7; Isa. 53:10; Ps. 16:8-9)

the good news carried to all nations (28:19; Isa. 49:6)

Truly, the person and the work of Christ are inseparable in Holy Scripture!

THE CONSISTENT ATTITUDE OF CHRIST TOWARD SCRIPTURE

He gave a dynamic testimony to its authority and to its divine inspiration. To Him, Scripture cannot be broken (John 10:35). He compared its duration to that of the heavens and the earth, because its origin is superhuman (Matt. 5:18). God Himself speaks in the biblical text, for example, in the one set down by Moses about the burning bush: "Have ye not read that which was spoken unto you by God, saying I am the God of Abraham" (Matt. 22:31-32; cf.

15:4). The inspired text is "the commandment of God," "the Word of God," for God Himself said so (Matt. 15:3, 6). It was the Holy Spirit who animated David when, in writing Psalm 110, he called the Messiah his Lord (Matt. 22:43). The commandment of God, the written Word, is indeed above all human traditions, even religious ones (Micah 7:8-9).

He emphasized the importance of each word of it. "It is easier for heaven and earth to pass away, than for one tittle of the law to fall" (Luke 16:17). "All the things that are written through the prophets shall be accomplished unto the Son of man" (Luke 18:31; cf. 24:44).

He often based His argumentation on a single expression of the text. The name that God gives to Himself: "I am the God of Abraham" (Matt. 22:32); the word "my Lord" applied to the Son of David (vv. 43-45); the expression "gods" in Psalm 82;6 (John 10:34).

He placed the text of Scripture on the same plane as His own words, divine and infallible, which themselves will never pass away (Matt. 24:35).

He had constant recourse to the Scriptures. In His struggle against the temptations of the devil, He answered three times: "It is written!" taking His arguments from Deuteronomy (Matt. 4:4, 7, 10; Deut. 8:3; 6:16; 6:13).

In His discussions with the Jews, He constantly repeated:

"Have ye not read what David did?" (Matt. 12:3)

"have ye not read . . ." (what is written about the Sabbath, v. 5)

"have ye not read that he who made them from the beginning made them male and female?" (Matt. 19:4)

"did ye never read . . ." (from Ps. 8:2; Matt. 21:16)

"did ye never read in the scriptures?" (the stone rejected, Matt. 21:42)

"have ye not read that which was spoken unto you by God" (about the "living," whose God He is, Matt. 22:31-32)

"what did Moses command you?" (about divorce, Mark 10:2-3)

"what then is this that is written?" (in Ps. 118:22; Luke 20:17)

"in your law it is written, that the witness of two men is true" (John 8:17)

"is it not written in your law . . ." (in fact, in Ps. 82:6, for all of the Old Testament was, in a sense, "the law" to the Jews; John 10:34)

In teaching His disciples, to emphasize His authority:

He began His ministry saying of a passage in Isaiah: "Today hath this scripture been fulfilled in your ears" (Luke 4:16-21). He answered the doctor of the law: "What is written in the law? how readest thou?" (Luke 10:26). The Sermon on the Mount was wholly based on the law, confirmed and completed (Matt. 5:17 ff.).

In His submission to the commandments of the law:

It was indeed Jesus' purpose to be "born under the law" (Gal. 4:4). He was circumcised and presented at the temple, as it is written in the law of the Lord (Luke 2:21-23). He told the healed leper to present the gift that Moses commanded (Matt. 8:4). He condescended to pay the required half shekel for the temple (Matt. 17:24-27).

On the cross, Jesus recited the prayers and fulfilled the prophecies of the Messianic Psalms: "My God, my God, why hast thou forsaken me?" (Ps. 22:1; Matt. 27:46). "After this Jesus, knowing that all things are now finished, that the scripture might be accomplished, saith, I thirst" (Ps. 69:21; John 19:28). Then, in crying out "It is finished" (v. 30), He meant both that His expiatory work was consummated and that the biblical prophecy was perfectly realized. "Father, into thy hands I commend my spirit" was the very prayer of Psalm 31:5 (Luke 23:46).

After the resurrection, Jesus did not go back on the unconditional confirmation which He had given to the Scriptures in the days of His humiliation (during which time some claim He renounced His omniscience). On the contrary, He interpreted to the disciples on the Emmaus road, and then again to the assembled disciples, the things concerning Himself in all the Scriptures, beginning from Moses and from all the prophets and the Psalms (Luke 24:27, 44, 46).

Christ confirmed the accounts in Holy Scripture. In the most explicit and natural way He made detailed reference to events in the Old Testament. It is plain that He did not consider these to be myths or legends, but obvious historical facts:

the creation of the first couple (Matt. 19:4-5)
the murder of Abel (Luke 11:51)
Noah, the ark and the flood (Matt. 24:37)
the role of Abraham and his faith (John 8:56)

circumcision, given to the patriarchs and performed on the eighth
day even if it fell on the Sabbath (John 7:22-23)
the destruction of Sodom
the salvation of Lot, the loss of his wife (Luke 17:29, 32)
Isaac and Jacob, as individuals (Luke 20:37)
the calling of Moses (Mark 12:26)
the law as given by Moses, permitting divorce and commanding the
purification of a leper (John 7:19; Matt. 19:18; 8:4)
the Decalogue (Matt. 19:18)
the manna (John 6:31-51)
the brazen serpent (John 3:14)
the account of David's eating the showbread (Matt. 12:3)
the queen of Sheba (Matt. 12:42)
the wisdom and glory of Solomon (Matt. 12:42; 6:29)
Elijah and the widow of Zarephath (Luke 4:26)
the future role of Elijah (Mark 9:12)
Elisha and Naaman the leper (Luke 4:27)
Jonah and the people of Nineveh (Matt. 12:40-41)
the wickedness of Tyre and Sidon and the judgment upon them
(Matt. 11:21)
the death of Zechariah between the altar and the sanctuary (Luke
11:51)
the prophecy of Daniel (Matt. 24:15)

*Jesus, it would seem deliberately, authenticated the passages of
Scripture most attacked today.* We have just seen that He attested
the accounts of Adam and Eve, the flood, Jonah, Daniel (from whom
He took His title Son of Man), etc. He likewise confirmed the authenticity and unity of Isaiah, making no distinction between the
first and second parts of the book. He began His ministry by commenting on a prophecy from Isaiah 61:1-2 (Luke 4:17-21). He drew
attention to the threat of Isaiah 6:9 (Matt. 13:14).

He applied to the people the serious reproof of Isaiah 29:13 (Matt.
15:7-9).

The evangelists were still calling by the name of Isaiah the author
of the following passages: Isaiah 6:1-5 (John 12:39-41); Isaiah 8:23—
9:1 (Matt. 4:14-16); Isaiah 40:3 (John 1:23); Isaiah 49; 42:1-4
(Matt. 12:17); Isaiah 53:1 (John 12:38); Isaiah 53:4 (Matt. 8:17).

Christ turned to the Pentateuch, which He always attributed to Moses, for the Lord's two greatest commandments (Deut. 6:4-5; Lev. 19:18; Mark 12:29-31).

We have also seen that, in His mortal combat with the devil, the Lord brandished three times the sword of Deuteronomy (Luke 4:4, 8, 12), a book which, along with Leviticus, has undergone the most severe assaults from the critics.

Jesus established the perfect sufficiency of the Scriptures to lead men to salvation. In regard to the brothers of the wicked rich man, He declared: "They have Moses and the prophets; let them hear them" (Luke 16:29). The written revelation contains all that is needed to lead a sinner to the knowledge of God and to eternal life. A dead man raised from the dead (vv. 30-31) or even an angel (Gal. 1:8) could say nothing more and nothing better.

He showed that the source of all error comes from negligence of the Scriptures and lack of comprehension of them. "Is it not for this cause that ye err, that ye know not the scriptures, nor the power of God? Ye do greatly err" (Mark 12:24, 27).

The disciples on the Emmaus road were sad and troubled because their concept of God's plan had disintegrated. Jesus well understood the cause of their disappointment and said to them: "O foolish men, and slow of heart to believe in all that the prophets have spoken!" (Luke 24:25).

John Chrysostom was indeed right when he cried out: "The cause of all evil rests in ignorance and from imperfect acquaintance with Holy Scripture!"

Conclusion

As a summary, we can say with all reverence that Jesus Christ was practically saturated with the Scriptures, which He knew "having never learned" (John 7:15). One tenth of His words were taken from the Old Testament. In the Four Gospels 180 of 1,800 verses which report His discourses are either quotations of the written revelation or else direct allusions to it. If we are criticized for constantly quoting Scripture texts, what can be said of Christ, who had them constantly at the tip of His tongue?*

For Jesus the Bible was the arsenal in which He found His arms;

*The proportion one in ten is, moreover, also that for the rest of the New Testament; and the proportion is close to half in the discourses in the Acts.

it was the fortress of truth. Tempted by the devil, He, the Lord, called on Moses, the servant, to help Him, because Moses spoke the very words of God. When the Jews sought to stone Jesus for what they claimed was "blasphemy," He still, confronted as He was with the threat of death, had recourse again to the Scripture, which "cannot be broken" (John 10:31-36). Let us learn a lesson in exegesis in the school of Christ. He demonstrates the flawless inspiration and continuity of the biblical revelation: its unity, its coherence and its complete sufficiency. He teaches us the art of setting forth the true value of every element of any text, whether big or small.

He who is the truth, the eternal Word, submitted Himself to the inspired writings with no reservation whatsoever. It is evident that for Him every declaration in the Old Testament is the Word of God. It has been claimed that, in thus doing, the Lord let Himself be influenced by Jewish ideas. Now exactly the opposite is true. Jesus certainly used the language of His time, so as to put Himself within reach of His hearers; but He did not at all espouse their errors or their areas of ignorance. Indeed, He constantly made a frontal attack on the false conceptions of His fellowmen about tradition, ceremonies, purification, the law, the Sabbath, the political and earthly "kingdom of God," the world to come and the Messiah Himself. If Jesus had had another opinion than the Jews about the full inspiration of the Old Testament, He would not have failed to attack these writings with the same vigor with which He attacked the traditions of men. Otherwise, what would we be obliged to think about His moral integrity and veracity? On the other hand, granted that He voluntarily assumed a certain ignorance during His earthly life, ought He not to have rectified His teaching of the Scriptures after His glorious resurrection? We have seen, on the contrary, that He confirmed this teaching all along the line (Luke 24).

Christ's attitude of total confidence in the Scripture and His complete submission to it dictates my own attitude toward it. My faith in Christ, the divine Saviour, is tied in with my faith in the Scripture, which reveals Him and which He confirmed. If I acknowledge the infallible authority of the Lord, I can do no other than to believe in the facts and in the doctrines of the inspired Book. Contrariwise, that individual who accepts the testimony of the Bible is led to faith in Christ. The Jews claimed to believe in Moses, while at the same time they rejected Jesus. But He said: "If ye believed Moses, ye would believe me: for he wrote of me. But if ye believe not his writings, how shall ye believe my words?" (John 5:46-47).

The well-known Dr. H. C. G. Moule, Anglican bishop, wrote: "He [Christ] absolutely trusted the Bible; and though there are in it things inexplicable and intricate that have puzzled me so much, I am going, not in a blind sense, but reverently, to trust the Book because of *Him*."[3]

Another author expresses himself like this: "The New Testament canonizes the Old; the Incarnate Word sets His seal on the Written Word. The Incarnate Word is God; therefore, the inspiration of the Old Testament is authenticated by God Himself."[4]

Christ, the theme of Holy Scripture and the Authority for it, is also its great Teacher. After His marvelous Bible lesson, the disciples on the Emmaus road said to each other: "Was not our heart burning within us while he spake to us in the way, while he opened to us the scriptures?" And the same evening the Lord opened the minds of all the believers gathered together in the upper room, that they might understand the Scriptures (Luke 24:32, 45). We have no other aim or ambition than this: that in all our present study the risen Christ may open our mind and cause our heart to burn by means of His Word, the written one and the living One!

(This chapter, obviously, deals with the testimony given by Christ to the Old Testament. We have already seen [chap. 9, subhead "Jesus' Promise of Divine Inspiration to the Authors of New Testament"] how He authenticated the New Testament in advance.)

19

THE APOSTLES AND HOLY SCRIPTURE

AFTER CONSIDERING THE TESTIMONY of Jesus in regard to Scripture, let us now listen to that of the apostles and of the early church.

THE TESTIMONY OF THE BOOK OF ACTS

Following absolutely in the steps of their Master, the first disciples based both their faith and their practice on the inspired Book, limited at that time to the Old Testament.

The plenary inspiration of Scripture was held in no doubt at all by the early church. It is the Holy Spirit who prophesied in Scripture by means of the mouth of David (Acts 1:16). God Himself spoke by the Holy Spirit, using the mouth of David (4:25). Moses, on Mount Sinai, received the living oracles, in order that he might transmit them to us (7:38). Again, it is the Holy Spirit who speaks to us through the Prophet Isaiah (28:25).

In quotations from Scripture, the very words of the text are attributed to God Himself: "He hath spoken on this wise . . ." (Isa. 55:3; Acts 13:34). "He saith also . . ." (Ps. 16:10; Acts 13:35). "For so hath the Lord commanded us . . ." (Isa. 49:6; Acts 13:47).

(We have seen that Christ also puts into the mouth of God the sentences of Scripture: Matt. 15:4; 22:32.)

The gospel is the fulfillment of all that was announced by Moses and the prophets. First, Moses was, for the apostles, the great leader and law-giver of Israel:

Moses foretold the Messiah (Acts 3:22).

He established the customs of the Jewish nation (6:14).

Having led Israel out of Egypt, he received at Sinai the living oracles of the Lord (7:36, 38).

He set forth the law and the ordinance of circumcision (15:5).

His books were read each Sabbath in every city where there was a synagogue (15:21).

224

The expression "Moses and the prophets" refers, in fact, to all of
the Old Testament (cf. Luke 16:29).

Moses and all the prophets announced the days of the Messiah
(Acts 3:18, 21-24).

The prophets, preparing for the coming of the just One, were all
persecuted (7:52).

All the prophets promised pardon for sins through the Messiah
(10:43).

The sufferings of Christ fulfilled all the words of the prophets
which were regularly read on the Sabbath day (13:27, 29).

The judgment of unbelievers was also predicted (13:40).

The salvation granted to the Gentiles was in accord with the words
of the prophets (15:15).

The historicity of the biblical accounts was fully confirmed. This
is particularly striking in the following two discourses:

Stephen, in Acts 7:2-50, referred to the following facts: the calling
and life of Abraham; the patriarchs: Isaac, Jacob and his sons; Joseph
and Israel in Egypt; Moses, Aaron; the exodus, the Red Sea, Sinai,
the golden calf, the tabernacle; the forty years in the desert; Joshua
and the conquest of Canaan; David, Solomon, the temple.

Paul, in Acts 13:16-41, also alludes to: the choosing of Israel; the
exodus, the law of Moses; the desert, Canaan; the Judges, Samuel,
Saul; David, the promise of the Messiah, the Psalms; the prophets.

In other words, these biblical books are especially authenticated:

Genesis	Joshua	Kings
Exodus	Judges	Psalms
Numbers	Samuel	all the Prophets

At that time the story of myths and legends had not as yet been
invented. God really manifested Himself in history, and we can put
our confidence in the accounts of the Old Testament as well as in
those of the New.

Scripture was the ultimate authority for the primitive church.
About half of the great sermons in the book of Acts are composed of
verses taken from Scripture:

Peter's discourse on the day of Pentecost: twelve verses out of
twenty-three (Acts 2:14-36)

the discourse of Stephen: his forty-nine verses being nothing but an
    enumeration of facts taken from the Old Testament (7:2-50)
the discourse of Paul at Antioch of Pisidia: fifteen out of twenty-six
    verses, either facts or quotations from the Scriptures (13:16-41)
What a lesson for today's preachers!

The whole argument of Paul in the presence of the Jews rests on
the same foundation: Having come to the Jews at Thessalonica, he
"reasoned with them from the scriptures, opening and alleging that
it behooved the Christ to suffer, and to rise again from the dead"
(Acts 17:2-3). As for the Jews at Berea, they examined "the scriptures daily, whether these things were so" (v. 11). At Rome, also,
Paul sought to persuade them "concerning Jesus, both from the law
of Moses and from the prophets" (28:23). This is why the apostle
affirmed without reservation his faith in all of Scripture: "So serve I
the God of our fathers, believing all things . . . which are written in
the prophets" (24:14). "I stand unto this day testifying, . . . saying
nothing but what the prophets and Moses did say should come"
(26:22). When Festus accused him of being mad, Paul replied: "I
. . . speak forth words of truth and soberness. . . . King Agrippa, believest thou the prophets? I know that thou believest" (vv. 24-27).
As for Apollos, he was a man "mighty in the scriptures"; and he made
himself useful, "for he powerfully confuted the Jews, and that publicly, showing by the scriptures that Jesus was the Christ" (18:24,
27-28). When twentieth century Christians give the same place to
the Scriptures as did those of the first century, their spiritual power
will be comparable to that of the early church.

THE TESTIMONY OF PAUL

Let us study Paul's testimony in the epistles to the Romans and the
Galatians, since the great texts of the other letters are treated elsewhere throughout this present volume.

The epistle to the Romans alone contains thirty-seven direct quotations from the Old Testament. The expression "as it is written"
keeps recurring like a refrain (seventeen times). The law of Moses
is fully confirmed: the glory of Israel, the rule of knowledge and
truth (2:17-23), it will judge every human being, and every mouth
will be stopped before it (2:12; 3:19). An astonishing number of
historical facts reported in Scripture are confirmed by Paul (see also

his other letters) . With him, there was no doubt about their authenticity. He even says that all of them were written for our instruction, to serve as examples for us (Rom. 15:4; I Cor. 10:11) .

The apostle has a truly distinctive fashion of personifying Scripture so as to make it speak or act as though it were God Himself: "And the scripture, forseeing that God would justify the Gentiles by faith, preached the gospel beforehand unto Abraham" (Gal. 3:8) . "The scripture shut up all things under sin" (v. 22) .

As Paul saw it, the gospel accomplished the promises made before by God through His prophets in the Holy Scriptures (Rom. 1:2; see, above, the testimony of Christ and that of the book of Acts) . This same gospel is now revealed in the writings of the prophets of the New Testament (16:25-26) .

The apostle sometimes interprets the text of the Old Testament in a boldly allegorical way. He sees Sarah and Hagar as types of the two covenants (Gal. 4:21-27) . Adam is the figure of Christ (Rom. 5:14) . The rock struck at Horeb "was Christ" (I Cor. 10:4) . It is Christ, again, who is our true Passover (5:6-8) . It is not surprising that Paul exclaims: "So belief cometh of hearing, and hearing by the word of Christ" (Rom. 10:17) . For him the Old Testament was already that Word; the preaching of the apostles was that Word also (I Thess. 2:13) , as were the writings of the New Testament (Rom. 16:25-26) .

Even authors of liberal persuasion cannot keep from bringing out this Pauline conception of the nature of inspiration. Paul considered "the words of Scripture co-extensive and identical with the words of God." "He [Paul] fully shared the assumption of his opponents: the irrefragable authority of the letter as the immediately revealed Word of God." "Paul held a doctrine which made the Old Testament to him the divine Word and the term 'It is written' equivalent to 'God says.' "[1]

THE TESTIMONY OF THE EPISTLE TO THE HEBREWS

Designed to form a bridge between the Old and New Covenants, the epistle to the Hebrews is particularly interesting from our present point of view. More than any other New Testament book, it is literally filled with the Old Testament. It contains thirty-seven direct quotations, taken from eleven books of the Hebrew Scriptures. It also confirms a great number of historical facts, which give both a basis for our faith and an illustration of it: creation—God's resting on the seventh day; Abel, Enoch, Noah, Abraham, Melchisedek, Sarah, Isaac, Jacob, Esau, Moses, the Passover, the Red Sea, Sinai, the two tables of the law, Aaron, the tabernacle, worship, the sacrifices, the covenant, Kadesh-Barnea, the wilderness, the manna, Aaron's rod, Joshua, Jericho, Rahab, The Judges, Gideon, Barak, Samson, and Jephthah, Samuel, David.

The Holy Spirit attests to even the details in all these (e.g., the veil, Heb. 9:8). In the Old Testament, God spoke to the fathers in the prophets; in the New, it is still He who speaks, but now in His Son (Heb. 1:1-2).

As for the Author of Scripture, nothing could be more explicit than is the epistle to the Hebrews: it is the triune God who speaks through the human author. The quotations are introduced by one or another of the following expressions:

"He [God] saith . . ." (1:5, 6, 7, 8, 13, etc.). It is then He Himself who is speaking in the Psalms mentioned, "saying in David" (4:7).

"He [Christ] saith . . ." (2:12-13; 10:5, when they are words from the Psalms and from Isaiah).

"The Holy Spirit saith . . ." (3:7-11; here it is, in fact, a question of a passage from Ps. 95:8-11). See again "the Holy Spirit this signifying . . ." (9:8) and "the Holy Spirit also beareth witness" (10:15).

This pronounced Word of God can serve for nothing unless it is united with faith in them that hear it (4:2). But for all that, it is itself no less living and active, sharper than any two-edged sword, piercing even to the dividing of soul and spirit, quick to discern the thoughts and intents of the heart (v. 12). How many times have we not felt the overwhelming and blessed action of its cutting edge! As for the unbeliever, it is to this same judging Word that he will have to give account in the last day (John 12:48). Consequently, declares the author of the epistle: "See that ye refuse not him that speaketh. For if they escaped not when they refused him that warned them on earth, much more shall not we escape who turn away from him that warneth from heaven" (Heb. 12:25).

If we have "tasted the good word of God" (6:5) and have received "the oracles of God" (5:12), so as to draw from them *milk* suited to the babe, we desire also to turn to the same source for that *solid food,* the "word of righteousness," which is needed by full-grown men (vv. 12-14).

In conclusion, let us mention the testimony of Friedrich Tholuck:[2] "The application of the Old Testament made by the author of the Epistle to the Hebrews rests on the strictest view of inspiration, since passages where God is the speaker are cited as words of God or of the Holy Ghost" (1:6, 7, 8; 4:4, 7; 7:21; 3:7; 10:15).

THE TESTIMONY OF JAMES

He presents the same unfailing faith in Holy Scripture, the Word of God.

The prophets truly spoke in the name of the Lord (5:10).

He has given us the perfect law, the law of liberty, the royal law of love (1:25; 2:8).

One alone is Legislator and Judge. The one who judges the law, thus placing himself above the Word of God, is taking a wild and dangerous risk: like a guilty man standing before the tribunal and claiming to usurp the place of the sovereign Judge (4:11-12).

The divine law is inexorable: whoever observes it all but sins in one point becomes guilty of all. If just one transgression suffices to condemn us, are we not all lost? (2:9-11; Rom. 3:19).

Let no one take this lightly: "Think ye that the scripture speaketh in vain?" (James 4:5).

Its judgments are accomplished, but so also are its promises. God having spoken, Abraham believed on Him; and his faith was reckoned unto him for righteousness. He was saved by grace; and this live, acting faith produced works which were also alive (2:21-23).

To listen to the Word, to read the Scripture—this is good, but only on condition that one translates it into practice. What is the good of anyone's looking into a mirror at his dirty face if he does not go on then to wash it? The person who is not a forgetful hearer sets to work and perseveres, and he shall be "blessed in his doing" (1:22-25). The false reasonings spoken of in verse 22 might lead one to suppose that reading the Bible or believing in its inspiration is all that is needed to please the Lord.

God created the world by His Word. He brought us forth also to new life, of His own will and by the Word of truth, so that we should be "a kind of firstfruits of his creatures" (1:18). We therefore purpose to follow the advice of James: "Receive with meekness the implanted word, which is able to save your souls" (v. 21).

Finally, James insists on the veracity of the accounts given in Scripture. Job, Abraham, the sacrifice of Isaac, Rahab and the spies and Elijah really existed (5:11; 2:21, 25; 5:17-18).

THE TESTIMONY OF PETER

Having already examined the great texts of I Peter 1:10-12 and II Peter 1:19-21 (see chap. 5, subhead "The declarations of the Apostle Peter"), let us listen to other declarations in these same epistles.

If men, moved by the Holy Spirit, spoke from God "by the Spirit of Christ which was in them," they were enabled to transmit to us "the word of God, which liveth and abideth." This Word, preached unto us in the gospel, has the power to regenerate us, begetting us again unto new life (I Peter 1:23-25). It acts like an "incorruptible seed" (cf. Luke 8:11), forever retaining its life germ, even if for years or centuries men have rejected it. Every time that a man or a people rediscovers the Bible, there comes as the inevitable result a revival, a renewal of faith.

The pure spiritual milk which newborn babes in Christ desire—what is it but the Word of God? (cf. Heb. 5:12). This is enough to cause the young convert to grow, and the hunger he experiences for it is the sign par excellence of his good spiritual health (I Peter 2:2-3).

Peter, like all the other apostles, constantly supports his arguments by quotations from the Old Testament, which he introduces thus: "it is written" (1:16); "it is contained in scripture" (2:16); or simply: "for . . ." (followed by the appropriate text, 4:8; 5:5).

Christ, the Head of the corner, becomes for the unbelieving a stone of stumbling: "They stumble at the word, being disobedient" (2:7-8). Indeed, it is the Word alone which reveals Christ and which, by Him, leads men to God. How can anyone ever know the Lord if he rejects His Word? Does not Jesus Himself say: "Ye have not his [God's] word abiding in you: for whom he sent, him ye believe not. Ye search the scriptures, . . . and ye will not come to me, that ye may have life!" (John 5:38-40).

Once more, let us note that Peter takes it for granted that the historical accounts in the Old Testament are actual facts: Noah; the flood (a figure of baptism!) ; the eight persons saved in the ark; Abraham and Sarah (I Peter 3:20-21, 6), the creation; the fall of the angels; Noah, the eighth patriarch; Sodom and Gomorrah; Lot and Balaam and his ass (II Peter 3:5; 2:4-8, 15-16).

In a striking recapitulation, the apostle presents the three parts of the written revelation (II Peter 3:2) : the words which were spoken before by the holy prophets (Old Testament), the comandment of the Lord and Saviour (the Gospels), the word through the apostles (the rest of the New Testament).

Finally, Peter does not hesitate to place the letters of Paul among "the other scriptures," proof that the canon of the New Testament was already being formed during the lifetime of the apostles. Stamped with special wisdom, these letters of Paul contain some things hard to be understood. Let the ignorant and unstedfast beware not to wrest their meaning, or that of the other Bible texts either (II Peter 3:15-16). The wresting of the sense of the Scriptures—here is a plague from which Christendom still suffers! May God give us grace not only to receive the divinely inspired Scriptures but also to interpret them correctly and to apply them to our own lives! Then we shall be able to talk about them with authority, "speaking as it were oracles of God" (I Peter 4:11).

CONCLUSION

The New Testament, Christ, the apostles, the early church and the authors of the New Testament themselves are unanimous in their attitude toward Scripture: For them all, it is the very Word of God. They all submitted without reservation to its authority. According to modern ideas, since they belonged to a new dispensation, they could have shaken off the fetters of the former revelation; but this they took great care not to do. Their conception of biblical inspiration was identical with ours: the inspiration of the words in every part of the Bible. Their use of biblical texts was also very close to our own, for they constantly quoted them. This is a comfort to us when we are accused of "hitting people over the head with Bible verses"!

Theirs was not a Bible full of myths, legends and errors. They held out no doubts about it whatsoever. Their acquaintance with

Scripture was amazing. They knew not only the letter of it, but also its deep meaning, its spirit. They obviously were guided by the Holy Spirit in their discovery throughout the Old Testament of every slightest allusion to the Messiah.

One essential characteristic of their ministry was that they knew how to handle "the sword of the Spirit, which is the word of God" (Eph. 6:17). It is for this reason that their ministry was so fruitful, for that Word never returns to Him void. This is just what was recognized by one author, Richard Rothe, although he was himself a critic:

> The authors of the New Testament look upon the words of the Old Testament as *immediate* words of God, and adduce them expressly as such, even those of them which are not at all related as direct sayings of God. They see nothing at all in the sacred volume which is simply the word of its human author and not at the same time the very Word of God Himself. In all that stands "written" God Himself speaks to them.[3]

The careful revision of the text of the New Testament and the application of the scientific principles of historico-grammatical exegesis have established beyond the shadow of a doubt the claims to inspiration made by the sacred authors. This same R. Rothe also maintained that to say one believes in the inspiration of the subject apart from that of the words is foolishness, for thoughts and words are everywhere inseparable. He admits that the orthodox theory of inspiration in even the strictest sense is professed by the authors of the New Testament.[4]

TESTIMONY OF THE CHURCH TO THE INSPIRATION OF THE BIBLE

WE HAVE HEARD THE TESTIMONY of the Jews regarding the inspiration of Scripture (chap. 15, subhead "The Canon of the Old Testament") and then that of Christ and of the apostles. Their declarations are so plain that, as Émil Brunner says, "the doctrine of verbal inspiration was already known from pre-Christian Judaism and was likewise held by Paul and the apostles."[1]

Let us see now the traditional conviction of the church on this matter throughout the centuries. This is all the more important now that most modern thinkers are in agreement on one point: to radically reject the doctrine of the plenary inspiration of the Bible. They declare that the time has come for a new concept of Scripture, and they let it be understood that nobody but ignoramuses or sectarians can still be so naïve as to accept the authenticity and authority of all the pages of the old Book. They are, of course, free to express this opinion. But it is clear that when they do so, they are going against the unanimous testimony of believers right up to the arrival on the scene of modern criticism. As for us, we are delighted, on the contrary, to align ourselves completely with the cohort which preceded us who testified to the revelation. But let the reader judge for himself.

THE CHURCH FATHERS

These men were very explicit in the affirmation of their faith. For them, the inspiration and authority of Scripture went without saying, not only in general, but in detail, as expressed in Matthew 5:18.

Clement of Alexandria says that not one jot or tittle could disappear, because the mouth of the Lord had spoken it all (Protrepticus, IX, 82, 1).

Gregory of Nazianzus: "Even the smallest lines in Scripture are due to the minute care of the Holy Spirit, so that we must pay careful attention to every slightest shade of meaning" (Orat. 2, 105).

Augustine:

> Let us give in and yield our assent to the authority of Holy Scripture, which knows not how either to be deceived or to deceive. . . . Believe me, whatever there is in these Scriptures, it is lofty and divine: there is in them altogether truth and a system of teaching most suited to refresh and renew minds; and clearly so ordered in measure as that there is no one but may draw thence what is enough for himself, if only he approach to draw with devotion and piety.[2]

John Chrysostom: "It is a great thing, this reading of the Scriptures! For it is not possible, I say, not possible ever to exhaust the mind of the Scriptures. It is a well which has no bottom."[3]

Athanasius: "They [the Scriptures] were spoken and written by God, through men who spoke of God. . . . These [the Old and the New Testament] are the fountains of salvation, that they who thirst may be satisfied with the living words they contain. In these alone is proclaimed the doctrine of godliness. Let no man add to these, neither let him take aught from these.[4]

Origen, writing on Mark 10:50:

> Shall we say that the Evangelist wrote without any thought when he related the man's casting away his garment and leaping and coming to Jesus? and shall we dare to say that these things were inserted in the Gospels in vain? For my part, I believe that not one jot or tittle of the divine instruction is in vain. We are never to say that there is anything impertinent or superfluous in the Scriptures of the Holy Spirit, though to some they may seem obscure. But we are to turn the eyes of our mind to Him who commanded these things to be written and seek of Him the interpretation of them. The sacred Scriptures come from the fulness of the Spirit, so that there is nothing in the prophets, or the law, or the gospel, or the apostles which descends not from the fulness of the Divine Majesty.[5]

Jerome:

> You see how, carried away by my love of the Scriptures, I have exceeded the limits of a letter, yet have not fully accomplished

my object. We have heard only what it is that we ought to know and to desire, so that we too may be able to say with the psalmist: "My soul breaketh out for the very fervent desire that it hath always unto thy judgments." . . . Give ear for a moment that I may tell you how you are to walk in the Holy Scriptures. All that we read in the divine books, while glistening and shining without, is yet far sweeter within.[6]

Irenaeus: "By our Lord Jesus Christ . . . give to every reader of this book to know thee . . . and to be strengthened in thee" (*Against Heresies.* III. chap. 6).

Let us conclude the enumeration at this point. According to Gaussen, except for Theodore of Mopsuestia (condemned by the Fifth Universal Council at Constantinople in 553), not one authority could be cited throughout all the first eight centuries of Christianity who failed to acknowledge the full inspiration of the Scriptures except, of course, for the heretical enemies of the Christian faith.[7]

THE REFORMERS

Following the deviations of the Middle Ages, the Reformation's return to sources could not fail to forcefully proclaim the entire inspiration and the sufficient authority of Holy Scripture.

Luther, in the articles of Smalcald, said in regard to them: "The Word of God shall establish articles of faith, and no one else, not even an angel" (Part II, art. II, 15). The Reformer constantly identified the oral Word of God and the Word of God written in the Bible: "The preacher must preach only the Word of Holy Scripture, for the Bible is the very Scripture of the Spirit." Luther also said:

> I am conquered by the writings cited by me, and my conscience is captive to the Word of God. . . . I have learned to ascribe this honor [i.e., infallibility] only to books which are termed canonical, so that I confidently believe that not one of their authors erred; but the other authors, no matter how distinguished by great sanctity and teaching, I read in this way: that I do not regard them as true because they themselves judged in this wise, but in so far as they could convince me through the authority of the canonical writings.[8]

Elsewhere, Luther said further: "It cannot be otherwise, for the Scriptures are divine; in them God speaks, and they are his Word. . . .

To hear or to read the Scriptures is nothing else than to hear God."[9]

Zwingli constantly appealed to the divinely inspired text of both the Old and the New Testaments. In 1523 he replied to the Bishop of Constance, after the latter had proposed submitting the text to the Universities of Paris, Cologne and Louvain: "The Spirit of God on the basis of Scripture is the only judge."[10]

Calvin:

> He [God] determined that the same oracles . . . should be committed to public records. . . . It will be easy to perceive the necessity of the heavenly doctrine being thus committed to writing, that it might not be lost in oblivion, or evaporate in error . . . that the truth might remain in the world in a continual course of instruction to all ages. . . . God not only uses mute teachers, but even opens his own sacred mouth."[11]

"The Scripture is the school of the Holy Spirit, in which, as nothing necessary and useful to be known is omitted, so nothing is taught which it is not beneficial to know."[12]

> The only thing I asked was that all controversies should be decided by the Word. . . . We hold that the Word of God [Holy Scripture] alone lies beyond the sphere of our judgment and that Fathers and Councils are of authority only in so far as they accord with the rule of the Word. . . . Ours the obedience which, while it disposes us to listen to our elders and superiors, tests all obedience by the Word of God; in fine, ours the Church whose supreme care it is humbly and religiously to venerate the Word of God and submit to its authority.[13]

THE GREAT CONFESSIONS OF PROTESTANT FAITH

It is very interesting and edifying to find in these monuments of the faith of the church the same precise conviction and the same unanimity. The following texts and a number of others are put together in Philip Schaff's monumental work *The Creeds of Christendom,* III.

The French Confession of Faith (The Gallican, or La Rochelle, Confession), 1559:

> III. These Holy Scriptures are comprised in the canonical books of the Old and New Testaments. . . . IV. We know these

books to be canonical and the sure rule of our faith, not so much by the common accord and consent of the Church, as by the testimony and inward illumination of the Holy Spirit. . . . V. We believe that the Word contained in these books has proceeded from God and receives its authority from him alone, and not from men. And inasmuch as it is the rule of all truth, containing all that is necessary for the service of God and for our salvation, it is not lawful for men, nor even for angels, to add to it, or to take away from it, or to change it.[14]

The Thirty-nine Articles of the Church of England:

VI. Holy Scripture containeth all things necessary to salvation: so that whatsoever is not read therein, nor may be proved thereby, is not to be required of any man that it should be believed as an article of the faith, or be thought requisite or necessary to salvation.[15]

The Westminster Confession of Faith, 1647:

II. The books of the Old and New Testament are all given by inspiration of God, to be the rule of faith and life. . . . IV. The authority of the Holy Scripture, for which it ought to be believed and obeyed, dependeth not upon the testimony of any man or church, but wholly upon God (who is truth itself) . . . and therefore it is to be received, because it is the Word of God. V. . . . The full persuasion and assurance of the infallible truth and divine authority thereof is from the inward work of the Holy Spirit. . . . VIII. The Old Testament . . . and the New Testament . . . being immediately inspired by God and by his singular care and providence kept pure in all ages are therefore authentical; so in all controversies of religion the Church is finally to appeal unto them. X. The Supreme Judge, by which all controversies of religion are to be determined, and all decrees of councils, opinions of ancient writers, doctrines of men, and private spirits are to be examined, and in whose sentence we are to rest, can be no other but the Holy Spirit speaking in the Scripture.[16]

Second Helvetic Confession, 1566:

We believe and confess the canonical Scriptures of both Testaments to be the true Word of God and to have sufficient authority of themselves, not of men. For God himself spake to the fathers, prophets, and apostles, and still speaks to us through the Holy Scriptures. They contain all things fully expounded which belong to a saving faith and also to the framing of a life acceptable to God; and in this respect, it is expressly commanded of God that nothing be either put to or taken from the same.[17]

The Belgic Confession, the Confession of the Reformed Walloon and Flemish churches, 1561 (revised at Dort in 1619) :

> VII. We believe that these Holy Scriptures fully contain the will of God and that whatsoever man ought to believe unto salvation is sufficiently taught therein. For since it is forbidden to add unto or take away anything from the Word of God, it doth thereby evidently appear that the doctrine thereof is most perfect and complete in all respects. . . . Therefore we reject with all our hearts whatsoever doth not agree with this infallible rule.[18]

We could multiply such quotations, mentioning the Scottish Confessions of Faith, those of the Waldenses and of Piedmont, the first Helvetic Confession, etc., all of which are written in the same vein. There may be some distinctions among the different branches of the Reform movement; but on this essential point, all have only one slogan: *Scriptura sola—Scriptura tota* (Scripture alone and all of Scripture) .

MEN OF GOD AND CHRISTIAN ENTERPRISES OF OUR TIMES

We have already alluded to the very strict position of the Lutheran theologians of the seventeenth and eighteenth centuries, who without exception believed in the verbal inspiration of Scripture (see p. 67 ff.) .[19] Let us now quote the opinion of some of the spokesmen for the evangelical faith between the time of the Genevan revival and our own day.

*Adolphe Monod:**

> When the Scripture speaks, it is God who speaks. . . . What it says to us is no less true and sure than as if the heavens were to open above our heads at this moment and the voice of God were to ring out as of old at Sinai, uttering the same things. There

---

*Translator's note: Renowned French Protestant preacher (1802-56).

are no limits to the confidence and the submission which we owe to the Scriptures. . . .

The Scripture is the divine expression of truths and ideas which form the very basis of invisible things. It is eternal, like a letter which God has written from the unseen world to his children who are still detained in the visible world. . . . The Scripture is, therefore, the Word of God in the highest and at the same time the simplest and most popular sense of that word. It is the only rule of faith and life. . . . All things have no value whatever except in so far as they are subordinated and subject to the sovereign, infallible, and unchangeable authority of the Word of God. . . .

There is no other book . . . which is not more or less affected by human error; this alone is exempt from it: it is the book of God. . . . In it we hear God speaking to us by the Holy Spirit. We ought to interrogate the Scripture as we would interrogate our Lord Jesus Christ . . . for it reveals him, and on his behalf it reveals all things by his Spirit.[20]

J. H. Merle d'Aubigné:†

The divine authority of the Scriptures and their inspiration are two distinct, but inseparable, truths. The authority of the Scriptures proceeds from their inspiration, and their inspiration establishes their authority. . . .

And not only did the Holy Spirit inspire the sacred writers with doctrines and thoughts; he gave them also the proper expression, the words they should utter. There are no ideas without words. If the Holy Spirit had not given the words, it is possible that man, left to his natural influences, might have made use of words which did not express his idea. . . .

Christ honored the Scriptures, explained them, adopted them as the very Word of God, as the supreme sovereign authority; and he thus taught his Church that it ought to render the same honor, the same obedience, to the books of the New Testament, to which his Spirit should commit his definite and eternal doctrines. . . .

Moreover, the Lord establishes the perfect sufficiency of the testimony of the Scriptures to give eternal life. On their authority it is his will that faith should rest. . . .

†Translator's note: Swiss Protestant theologian (1794-1872), professor of church history in Geneva and author of *History of the Reformation in the Sixteenth Century.*

But more, the Lord declares that truth, absolute and eternal, is found in the Scriptures and that they can never lie. "The Scriptures cannot be broken" (John 10:35). On this he insists: "One jot or one tittle shall in no wise pass from the law till all be fulfilled" (Matt. 5:18). Recurring to the same point, he cries: "It is easier for heaven and earth to pass than for one tittle of the law to fail" (Luke 16:17). And he affirms this not only of the words of the Old Testament, but of those of the New Testament likewise. "Heaven and earth shall pass away, but my Words shall not pass away" (Matt. 24:35).[21]

Alexandre Vinet:‡

Do not suppose that Christianity, to place itself in harmony with the age, will complacently leave out a single idea. It is from its inflexibility that it is strong. . . . Those who dare not reject it are forced to soften it down. They divest it of its barbarisms, its "myths," as they are pleased to call them; they render it even reasonable; but, strange to say, when it is reasonable, it has no power. . . . Zeal, fervor, holiness, and love disappear with these strange doctrines; the salt has lost its savor, and none can tell how to restore it. But, on the other hand, do you not in general perceive when there is a revival of these doctrines, Christianity is inspired with new life, faith is reanimated, and zeal abounds? Do not ask upon what soil, or in what system, must grow these precious plants. You can reply in advance that it is only in the rude and rough soil of orthodoxy, under the shadow of those mysteries which confound human reason, and from which it loves to remove as far as possible.[22]

Dr. Lewis Sperry Chafer:§

Without doubt it is the supernatural element which constitutes the very warp and woof of the Bible doctrine of inspiration, that not only gives to it its distinctive and exalted character but also repels the spiritually darkened mind of the unregenerate man—a darkness which is in no way relieved by human learning. . . . Devout men . . .—some of great scholarship—have always agreed in the main as to the inerrant and supernatural qualities of the Bible.

If the truth regarding inspiration is to be given full recogni-

‡Translator's note: Swiss Protestant theologian (1797–1847), author of numerous works on French literature, on Blaise Pascal, etc.
§Founder of Dallas Theological Seminary, and its president for twenty-eight years.

tion, both the divine and human authorship must be seen and accepted in their plenitude. . . . The human side of the dual authorship is rendered exceedingly complex by the fact that upwards of forty men participate in this incomparable service. God has exerted His own power by thus working through many writers; yet He has preserved the unity of His revelation and at the same time demonstrated His control over men of varying degrees of authorship qualifications. . . .

The testimony which the Bible presents as to its own inspiration is diffused throughout all its parts. Each author witnesses to the supernatural character of his writings. But by far the most conclusive evidence that the Bible is inspired is the twofold fact: that Christ so accepted the Old Testament as a whole as well as in every separate portion, and that the New Testament was written at His direction and the human authors were promised superhuman ability to write according to the mind of God. . . .

As to how He transmitted that Word to them and secured inerrant oracles at their hand, the Scriptures are silent. A dual authorship is preserved—God used the volition and faculties without injury to the divine message. Those who are disposed to disagree with these conclusions must reckon with Christ, the apostles, and the prophets, upon whom, after all, we must depend for any knowledge of any truth whatsoever. If their testimony is broken regarding the trustworthiness of the Scriptures, it is broken regarding all else.[23]

Dr. Donald Grey Barnhouse:||

Our certainty rests upon the Word of God. . . . Only with a wrong type of Bible reading can anyone ever come to the absurd conclusion so often expressed: "You can prove anything by the Bible." When, however, the shape of the individual verse is fitted into the whole divine plan of the revelation of God, the full-rounded, eternal purpose begins to be seen; and the whole of the Word of God becomes something so stupendous, so eternal, so mightily divine, that every rising doubt is checked immediately. There comes, then, a knowledge of the finality of God's revelation which becomes as much a part of the believer as his sense of being alive.

||Translator's note: American Presbyterian pastor, radio preacher and author of numerous biblical works.

If we are going to understand the Word of God, we must have a spiritual attitude toward it. The Lord said that "the natural man receiveth not the things of the Spirit of God, for they are foolishness unto him; neither can he know them, because they are spiritually discerned" (I Cor. 2:14) . . . . One must have a spiritual attitude that comes from a spiritual life. . . .

The fact that many men of varying backgrounds, writing over a period of sixteen hundred years, could produce a work in which every part may be fitted perfectly into every other part, with not one verse too many and not one verse too few, demonstrates that behind the human authors there was God, who breathed through them the message He wished to have recorded in the time and in the manner and form that suited His purpose.

It is objected by some that the marks of human personality upon the writings of the various human authors indicate that the Bible is a human book. We would answer this with an analogy. The angel who announced to Mary that she would become the mother of the Messiah heard the Virgin ask "How shall this be, seeing that I know not a man?" The answer came: "The Holy Spirit shall come upon thee, and the power of the Highest shall overshadow thee; therefore also that holy thing which shall be born of thee shall be called the Son of God" (Luke 1:35). Just as the Holy Spirit came upon the womb of Mary, so He came upon the brain of a Moses, a David, an Isaiah, a Paul, a John, and the rest of the writers of the divine library. The power of the Highest overshadowed them; therefore, that holy thing which was born of their minds is called the Holy Bible, the Word of God.[24]

U.S. Federal District Judge W. R. Wallace:

The Bible was written by God, or it is the world's greatest fraud. From beginning to end the Bible claims to be the Word of God. It breaks upon us as a voice from heaven. Five hundred times in the first five books of the Bible it prefaces or concludes its mighty declarations with the sublime assertions "The Lord said" or "The Lord spake." The same thing is true in the books of history. More than 1200 times in the seventeen books of prophecy the same and stronger claims are made. . . . More than 3,000 times the Bible makes the direct, positive, and emphatic claim that its words are God's words. . . .

The Bible brings God down to man and lifts man up to God. In it prophets speak to man for God, and priests plead with God for man. It drives ignorance, superstition, darkness, and sin before it. Missionaries have gone with the Bible into regions where the people were cannibals; today the natives of those regions kneel and pray to the God who wrote the Bible. . . .

The accurate forecasting of future events is one of the strongest evidences of the existence of God and of the authority of the Book He has written. . . . Hundreds of fulfilled prophecies establish beyond question that He who knew all things before the beginning wrote the Bible. . . .

Who but God could draw the picture of a man not yet born? Yet that is exactly what the Bible does. Jesus Christ is the only person ever born into this world whose ancestry, forerunner, birth—time and place—infancy, manhood, teaching, character, career, preaching, reception, rejection, death, burial, resurrection, and ascension were all described in the most marvelous manner centuries before He was born. . . . God had to write the Bible because it unfolds His everlasting purpose in Jesus Christ. . . .

I believe that mounting world chaos today is the result of our neglect of God's Word. . . . Our internal troubles would vanish and the world chaos would clear up like the mists before the rising sun if we in America would but take the Word of God from Genesis 1 to Revelation 22 as the inspired, infallible, eternal Book which God has given to us, and without equivocation or subterfuge proclaim to the world that this is where we stand.[25]

Dr. William Culbertson:#

The Bible, including both the Old and New Testaments, is a divine revelation, the original autographs of which were verbally inspired by the Holy Spirit. . . .

Certainly there are problems. Infinite revelation to finite minds is going to involve problems. We are still on earth, and we still do not know perfectly and fully. But it is my conviction that there is no problem for which a believing heart sooner or later will not find the answer, and a good answer, that will satisfy both the mind and the heart. . . .

The Bible attests its inspiration, and this claim is so widely spread throughout the Bible and is so all-inclusive in its appli-

#President of The Moody Bible Institute of Chicago (1948-71).

cation to the whole Bible that on its testimony we cannot logically believe in less than plenary, verbal inspiration. Since it is God's Word, it follows that it is infallible and inerrant. . . .

The need for divine revelation, the need for the inspired, infallible, inerrant Word of God lies first of all in the darkness and the twistedness of our nature. Men need—if they are ever to know the truth—the God-breathed Book, God's final revelation. . . .

The doctrine of inspiration is basic to Christian teaching. All other doctrines stem from biblical inspiration and are supported by it. . . . It is from the Bible's sacred pages that the truth, the hope, and the dynamic of life spring. The Bible has fashioned civilization as we know it. Western civilization is far from perfect; but its features of justice, of mercy, of human dignity come from the Bible.

The doctrine of inspiration is basic to Christian morality. . . . Unbelief in the Bible was the exception in the nineteenth century. What there was, was largely outside the church. Now men of little or no faith are in the church. And we wonder why our nation is in trouble. . . .

Blessed Book . . . the revelation of the heart, the will, the plan and the provision of God for men, for you and for me! May our hearts beat faster and obey more quickly. This Book is God's loving gift, and it leads men to God.[26]

The many works that came out of the Reformation had as founders men who were all animated by the same convictions. How true it is that it is living faith which produces fruits of achievement and love! And how true it is that the Word of God is forever to be depended on: "I believed, and therefore did I speak" (II Cor. 4:13). The following are a few of these beneficent works:

Bible societies
Missionary societies
Works of evangelization
Many homes for the aged, for the blind, for the deaf and for needy children
Founding of evangelical faculties of theology
The whole Bible and missionary institute movement
Publishing houses for gospel literature (for example, the Moody Press of Chicago)

The world evangelical fellowship
The YMCA and YWCA as founded, and student unions
The Red Cross also, at its inception, etc.

We do not have room to set down the testimony of all the men of zeal and faith, and these would essentially be just a repetition of the same sort of thing. At any rate, we shall mention a few of the best known:

Hudson Taylor, founder of the China Inland Mission (now the Overseas Missionary Fellowship)
Charles Finney, great American revivalist
D. L. Moody, evangelist, whose fruitful ministry is still seen throughout the entire world
William Carey, pioneer missionary to India and often considered to be the founder of the modern missionary movement
George Mueller, who established the Bristol Orphanages in England
Charles H. Spurgeon, "the prince of preachers" and initiator of various fruitful ministries
Ira D. Sankey, D. L. Moody's golden-voiced helper and song leader, prolific writer of gospel music (evangelical faith sings!)
Billy Graham, of our own times, whose name is known to everyone

It is worth our trouble to quote his testimony:

> In August of 1949 I was so filled with doubts about everything that when I stood up to preach and made a statement, I would say to myself: "I wonder if that is the truth. I wonder if I can really say that sincerely." My ministry had gone. Then I took the Bible up into the high Sierra Nevada mountains of California. I opened it and got on my knees. "Father," I said, "I cannot understand many things in this book. I cannot come intellectually all the way; but I accept it by faith to be the authoritative, inspired Word of the living God." A month later in Los Angeles I found that this book had become a sword in my hand. Where human argument had failed, the Word of God did its work.[27]

Complete faith in the inspiration and authority of the Scriptures is indubitably the foundation for works of enormous importance throughout the entire world today. For example:

The Wycliffe Bible Translators

The Sudan Interior Mission

The Moody Bible Institute of Chicago, with a day school, an evening school, a large correspondence school, and a missionary aviation school; with radio stations, the literature outreach of Moody Press and *Moody Monthly,* and the Moody film ministry

The Overseas Missionary Fellowship (formerly China Inland Mission)

The Africa Inland Mission

The Scripture Union

The Inter-Varsity Christian Fellowship, active among students throughout the world

The International Christian Broadcasters, made up of various co-operating stations (such as HCJB, Ecuador; DZAS, the Philippine Islands; ELWA, Liberia; and Trans World Radio in both Bonaire and Monte Carlo) with powerful transmitters that reach every part of the globe with gospel programs in practically all languages

Gospel Recordings, which freely distributes millions of records

The following extraordinary fact has recently been brought to light: evangelical missions (the groups called "fundamentalists," not affiliated with the World Council of Churches) comprise at the present time about two-thirds of the Protestant missionaries in the world. This proportion has kept increasing in recent years.

CONCLUSION

God never leaves Himself without a witness. When we are tempted to think that we shall soon be the only ones to maintain a testimony to the whole Bible as the Word of God, the Lord brings to our attention the thousands of believers who have not bowed the knee to Baal (Rom. 11:2-4).

A remarkable page written by the Anglican theologian James I. Packer explains this better than we could do it:

The allegation that Evangelicalism is sectarian, schismatic, and un-catholic [not universal in its outlook] is wide of the mark. . . . In fact, Evangelicalism is the truest Catholicism; and the controversy which it maintains against Subjectivism (and Traditionalism too) is the clearest proof of this. After all, there is no other standard of catholicity save Christ Himself; and the dimensions of catholicity are first theological and then historical, and not numerical at all. The catholicity of Evangelicalism appears, first, in its uncompromising submission to the teaching of Christ and of Scripture on authority . . . and, second, in its oneness with all those who down the ages have taken this same position, bowing to the authority of Scripture, glorying in the biblical gospel of free grace, and contending earnestly for the apostolic faith. Those who are conscious of standing with Augustine, Luther, Calvin, Baxter, Owen, Wesley, Whitefield, Edwards; with the Reformers, Huguenots, Puritans, Covenanters; with the Evangelicals of the eighteenth century and the architects of the world missionary movement in the nineteenth— to mention no more—such need not fear for their catholicity. Evangelicals may seem no more than a dissentient minority in the present-day Church, but this is no new state of affairs; Luther once seemed to be in a minority of one; so did Elijah, and Jeremiah, and Paul. Indeed, there are comparatively few periods in history when Evangelicals have been more than a dissentient minority within a larger group, meeting indifference, if not unfriendliness, from fellow-members of their churches. But true catholicism is not a matter of being in the biggest party. Numerically, the unreformed Church of Rome is the biggest party; but many anti-fundamentalists would no doubt agree with four centuries of Protestant theology that the self-styled "Catholic Church" is in fact the biggest schismatic group in Christendom. It is often said that one with God is a majority, however many stand against him; and it is no less true that one with Christ is a catholic Christian, however many deny his right to the title.[28]

LIMITS OF BIBLICAL CRITICISM AND OPPOSITION TO PLENARY INSPIRATION

WE CONTINUE HERE in a more general way the discussion already begun (chap. 6). For the sake of clarity, we shall review some of the arguments cited regarding various theories of inspiration.

THE MEANING OF "BIBLICAL CRITICISM"

The word *criticism* (*krinein,* "to judge") signifies a discussion having as its aim the establishment, according to a logical examination, of the truth of certain facts or documents. Let us say at the outset that it is perfectly legitimate and even necessary to undertake a positive criticism of the ancient texts. The Word of God presents itself to us in the form of a collection of books written by various authors, in different languages, at different times, and in various countries. It is quite proper for us to use our intelligence to examine the manuscripts and their variants, to study the original languages, and to establish the meaning of the sentences and the exact import of the expressions. To this procedure, that of *lower criticism,* scholars have devoted their entire lives, examining as under a microscope the smallest details of the sacred Book. Such men as B. F. Westcott and F. J. A. Hort, in their Greek New Testament, have made a considerable contribution to the science of textual criticism. In his time, so did B. Kennicott; and, still closer to us, R. D. Wilson; these men labored indefatigably over the Old Testament.

By *higher criticism,* on the other hand, is meant the examination of the literary style, the content of the message, and its rapport with customs, the times, history and so on. Do we not read of Luke himself that he "traced the course of all things accurately from the first" (Luke 1:3)?

So criticism which leads to a better comprehension is not to be rejected, and we have nothing to fear from a scientific research made in the light and in truth. But critical examination of the Bible admittedly does pose a very special problem. In this unique Book the believer has met God; both his present life and his eternal destiny have been illuminated by the knowledge of Jesus Christ. Thus he cannot approach the Scriptures as he would an ordinary human work. For their study his Guide will always be the Lord, who inspired the pages and who Himself gives their explanation. Intellectual knowledge, then, will be completed and controlled by the living power which springs up from the inspired text.

L. Gaussen expresses himself as follows about the role of biblical criticism:

> That sacred criticism is indeed a noble science! It is so because of its object: to study the destinies of the divine text, its canon, its manuscripts, its versions, its witnesses, and the innumerable authors who have quoted it. . . . May God preserve us, then, from setting faith here against science—faith which lives on the truth against science which studies it!
>
> But critical science does not keep its place when, instead of being a scientific inquirer, it would be a judge; when, not content with collecting together the oracles of God, it sets about composing them, decomposing them, canonizing them, decanonizing them; and when it gives forth oracles itself! . . . If, from this Scripture, which calls itself inspired, and which declares that it is, at the last day, to judge you yourself, that wisdom of yours dares to take away anything; if, seating itself like the angels of the last judgment (Matt. 13:48, 49), it drag the book of God to the seashore of science, in order to collect in its vessels what it sees in it to be good, and to throw out what it finds in it to be bad, if it pretend to separate there the thought of God from the thought of man . . . then, it is necessary that it should be reproved. . . . It too often happens that a prolonged course of study devoted to the extrinsic parts of the sacred book (its history, its manuscripts, its versions, its language), by entirely absorbing the attention of the men who give themselves to it, leaves them inattentive to . . . its meaning, its object, the moral power which displays itself there, the beauties that reveal themselves there, the life that diffuses itself there. . . . [Such a man] stifles

his spiritual life. . . . How can a man be acquainted with the temple when he has seen but the stones and knows nothing of the Shekinah [the glory of Jehovah, Exodus 40:35]? Can the types be understood when he has not even a suspicion of their antitype: he has seen but altars, sheep, . . . blood, fire, incense, costumes, and ceremonies; he has not beheld the world's redemption, futurity, heaven, the glory of Jesus Christ![1]

Negative criticism. It is indeed evident, unfortunately, that a certain sort of criticism, the negative kind, has overplayed its role. Too often originating in preconceived theological and philosophical notions and in unproved theories, it has taken upon itself the right to dissect Scripture as though the text were dead. We shall now examine some of the problems which have arisen out of this type of criticism and shall see where this criticism leads.

APPEARANCE AND TRIUMPH OF MODERN CRITICISM

It is universally conceded that up to about the eighteenth century (see the preceding chapter) the Jews, Christ, the apostles, the primitive church, the church fathers and the Reformers, with their successors, affirmed in a general way the plenary inspiration of the Scriptures.

Not only the rationalism of the eighteenth century, but even more the religious liberalism of the nineteenth opened up a breach in the orthodox position. Under the influence of the theory of evolution, critics came to the point of denying the biblical account of the creation and of the fall. After coming out of the caves, man supposedly made for himself gods in his own image (polytheism) ; then, emerging little by little from barbarism, he later stumbled onto the idea of only one god (monotheism). Before the development of modern archaeology, a hundred years ago, it was believed that sure historical information about antiquity could be traced to a point no earlier than the sixth century before Christ. Consequently, the whole history of the patriarchs and of Israel was declared mythical and legendary. Moses certainly did not know how to read and write, and he was incapable of instituting the complicated laws and the ritual bearing his name. The description of the Egyptians, of the Canaanites and of the kings of Israel—especially of Solomon—all that was nothing but a fable. Thus (observe the sequence of the deductions!) the supposed books of Moses could not be historical. They were, of necessity, written much later, by various authors and at wholly different times. An understanding of criticism, thousands of years later, led to an exact determining of what those multiple "sources" were, of which the following are the most important (even though scholars are far from agreed among themselves on many of these points) :

The author known as J (Jahvist, because he calls God Jahveh) probably lived in Judah about 950-850 B.C. Some critics divide this "source" again into J1 and J2. The author E (Elohist, since he calls God Elohim) is supposed to have lived around 750 B.C. After the fall of Samaria, an "editor" by the name of JE was thought to have combined J and E, adding on his own to these two sources. Document D would comprise the greater part of Deuteronomy, making this the book of the law "found" in the temple under Josiah in 621 (II Kings 22–23). H (Holiness) would be "the Code of Holiness" (Lev. 17–26), having to do with ceremonial purity; the critics differ as to whether it should be placed before or after Ezekiel. P (from the word "priest") is known as "the Priestly Code"; drawn up by the priests during the Exile, it was said to have been presented to the masses (in the name of Moses) by Ezra around 398 B.C. Finally, several compilers (editors) were thought to have blended together a great many heterogeneous elements to make the present Pentateuch. Thus, according to Oesterley and Robinson: "Early in the second century B.C. the Law was regarded as a single whole with, apparently, no suspicion of its composite origin. We have not greatly erred, then, if we assign its final completion to a date not later than 300 B.C."[2] Needless to say, there are plenty of arguments to show the fragility and the ephemeral quality of this succession of hypotheses, at once so complicated and so devoid of factual substance.

Examination of Oesterley and Robinson's book reveals extravagant examples of this slicing up of the biblical text according to the supposed theory of sources:

Genesis 2:4b–4:26 is attributed to J; 1:1–2:4a belongs to P;
Genesis 5:29, J; 5:1-28 and 30-32, P;
Genesis 6:1-8, J; 6:9-22, P;
Genesis 7:1-5; 7, 10, 12, 16b, 17b, 22a-23a; 8:2b-3a, 6-12, 13b, 20-22; 9:18-27, J;

Numbers 15:1*b*, JE; 14:3-4, J; 14:8, 9, 11-25, JE; 14:1*a*, 2, 5-7, 10, 26-30, 33-38, P;

Deuteronomy 34:1*b*-6, E; 32:48-52, P; 34:1*a*-7-12, P;

Deuteronomy 7:6, 8-9, 11, 13-16*a*, 17*a*, 18-21, 23*b*-24, 8:1-2*a*, 3*b*-5, 13*a*, 14-19, 9:1-17, 28-29, P.

There are pages and pages of such absurdities; and theological students of our acquaintance, after conscientiously underlining the "sources" with different colored pencils, have referred to what they call their "Bible rainbow." Along these same lines we have, for instance, in French, the *Dictionnaire Encyclopédique de la Bible,* published by A. Westphal in 1932, which has just been reprinted without change; and the Jerusalem Bible, the English translation having come out in 1966. (In fact, Catholics today go just as far as Protestants and Jews in textual criticism.) Such critics really remind us of the Roman soothsayers of whom Cicero wrote, commenting that he wondered how they could look at one another without laughing. To reduce the biblical text to a puzzle like this (according to some, Genesis 37 is subdivided into twenty-six fragments, three of which appear in one verse!) is to completely destroy the historical truth, and consequently the spiritual message, of the entire Old Testament.

Pursuing the treatment of the Bible as though it were an ordinary book, liberalism has also attacked the New Testament. If man did not experience a fall, but rather is evolving toward the good, he has no need of a divine Redeemer. The supernatural elements having been eliminated, the gospel accounts are simply legends. Jesus was not born miraculously, and His death could not take away sin. There is nothing to the concept of His glorious return, and an eternal hell does not exist. The fourth gospel, some of the epistles, and Revelation are certainly not authentic.

"Biblical Renewal"

Better-informed scholarship has now replied to many of the arguments of the old liberalism. The theory of materialistic evolution has been combatted by a great many scholars. The discovery of Ur of the Chaldees and of the oldest civilizations (Sumer, Babylon, Nineveh, Mari, Ugarit, Jericho, Crete, Egypt, etc.) has demonstrated the exactitude of the biblical description of the times of the patriarchs, of

Moses and of Israel. Since the discovery of the Code of Hammurabi, who would dare to say that Moses was incapable of writing something similar? Such developments have rejoiced evangelicals, although these confirmations cannot be said to have given the Scriptures back to them, since they never lost them in the first place.

A recent theology has expressed its desire to reaffirm the honor of the Word of God and to bring us back to the Bible. But the question is what Word and what Bible are meant. There has certainly been quite a considerable revival of Bible study and of publications about the text of Scripture. All the same, one thing is clear about most contemporary theologians: they are not going back to what they consider a "non-scientific" concept, that is, that the Bible is the Word of God. In their opinion, just as in that of the older liberals, Scripture has many errors, legends and contradictions. It is not the Word of God, but merely a testimony to that Word made by men who themselves were fallible.

Karl Barth writes:

> The prophets and apostles, even in their office, even in their function as witnesses, even in the act of writing down their witness, were, as we are, capable and actually guilty of error in their spoken and written word.[3]
>
> If God was not ashamed of the fallibility of all the human words of the Bible, of their historical and scientific inaccuracies, their theological contradictions, the uncertainty of their tradition, and, above all, their Judaism, but adopted and made use of these expressions in all their fallibility, we do not need to be ashamed when He wills to renew it to us in all its fallibility as witness; and it is mere self-will and disobedience to try to find some infallible elements in the Bible.[4]

> The men whom we hear as witnesses speak as fallible, erring men like ourselves. . . . We can read and try to assess their word as a purely human word. It can be subjected to all kinds of immanent criticism, not only in respect of its philosophical, historical, and ethical content, but even of its religious and theological content. . . . Each in his own way and degree, they shared the culture of their age and environment. . . . The vulnerability of the Bible, i.e., its capacity for error, also extends to its religious or theological content. There are obvious over-

lappings and contradictions. . . . Therefore, whether we like it or not, they did not speak a special language of revelation radically different from that of their time. . . . It seems to be weakened, and therefore robbed of its character as witnesses to revelation, by the fact that it has so many "parallels."[5]

In regard to this "non-scripture" doctrine of Scripture, French pastor Pierre Courthial writes with much discernment:

> On this fundamental point Barth has not been able, has not known how, and has not wanted to exorcise the demons of the already old critical tradition which he had been taught and which—alas—is still being taught in too many Protestant and Roman Catholic schools of theology and seminaries. If the amending of Protestant theology, and then of the preaching and life of the churches of the Reformation, did not bear the fruit that it promised in the thirties and forties, if a number of those churches have today been driven back into certain blind alleys (particularly regarding ecumenism), a situation which we can see all about us, it is for the reason that the biblical "basic incentives," after having been magnificently followed for awhile in the theological and ecclesiastical renewal of the Twentieth Century, have been shut out and despised through the extra-biblical and anti-biblical "basic incentives" which were already asserting themselves at the outset, in the Barthian doctrine of Scripture.
>
> . . . It is clear that for Barth the *real* humanity of the Bible implies its no less real fallibility. It is also clear that for Barth the real humanity of the Bible becomes the foundation for the legitimacy of the critical tradition.[6]

On this point Pierre Courthial very rightly replies that, for all that, the Bible is not fallible: "But, just as the Word of God incarnate was without sin, even so, the Word of God 'inscripturated' is without error. . . . The humanity of Jesus is like our own in all things *sin apart*. The humanity of the Bible is like that of every human book *except for error*."[7]

According to popular dialectics, Barth does not stop there: all that Barth has to say about the humanity and the fallibility of the Bible makes up only his first assertions regarding it. From then on (and we emphasize this) he tries to maintain with all his might that Scripture is the Word of God: "We believe in and with the Church that Holy Scripture as the original and only legitimate witness of divine revelation is itself the Word of God."[8] "But," adds M. Courthial, "we must really grasp what Barth means by this affirmation, since he *strongly rejects the inspiration of the Bible* as it was set forth by the fathers of the Early Church (by Augustine, for one) and by the Reformers of the sixteenth century (such as Calvin) and as it is affirmed by the Reformed Confessions of faith."[9]

Emil Brunner, another celebrated theologian, does not hesitate to say: "I myself am an adherent of a rather radical school of biblical criticism, which, for example, does not accept the Gospel of John as an historical source and which finds legends in many parts of the Synoptic Gospels."[10] "Whoever asserts that the New Testament gives us a definite consistent account of the resurrection is either ignorant or unconscientious."[11] Scripture then is not in itself revelation, for, claims dialectical theology, the very nature of revelation prohibits it from being put into writing. That which is "inscripturated" is given over to the control of man, to use Brunner's verbiage; and it is as though the Spirit of God "were imprisoned between the two covers of the written Word." For this reason, whatever may be our doctrine of inspiration, the biblical documents cannot be considered as "inspired."[12] Professor Brunner also rejects the doctrines of the supernatural birth and the substitutionary atonement. He believes, further, in regard to the synoptic gospels, that they record many things which are not historical; that they put into the mouth of Jesus words which He did not utter Himself; and that they declare various things about Him that never took place as they are reported to have taken place. As for the fourth gospel, according to Brunner, it is possible that Jesus did not really pronounce any of the words which John attributes to Him. "At some points, the variety of the Apostolic doctrine, regarded purely from the theological and intellectual point of view, is an irreconcilable contradiction."[13] Notice carefully this extremely serious matter: if the Bible is fallible and erroneous in theology and in moral principles, as well as in history and in science, what does it have to offer us? Does even the possibility of knowing God objectively remain? Are we not tempted to say with Mary: "They have taken away my Lord, and I know not where they have laid him"?

If the greatest theologians express themselves like this about the true value of the biblical texts, how can they establish on such a foundation a "theology of the Word of God"? In reality, this expression is given today a totally different meaning from the traditional one. God does indeed speak to us by means of the Bible, but it is not the written text which is His Word. The Word is the message which comes through to us from the Scripture, but we would be grossly in error should we believe that the message of God is tied in with this or that particular verse. Finally, M. Courthial goes on to say that for many neo-Protestant and "Barthian" theologians, such as G. S. Hendry, E. Brunner, and J. A. Mackay, since the revelation of God is the revelation of someone, some person, it can provide us with no "teachings," "truths," "doctrines" or "information." The "act," or the "acts," of God are set over against the "teachings" and "propositions" of the Bible. This, of course, is untenable; and one never ceases to marvel at the fertility of the human (or diabolical) spirit in respect to endlessly conjuring up new forms for old suspicions regarding the Word of God. Pierre Courthial very accurately sums it all up in these words: "Neo-protestantism, in its various forms, constantly speaks of a 'theology of the Word' and of a 'biblical theology,' while it at the same time always and everywhere attacks what the Bible claims for itself; that is, that its 'teachings,' 'doctrines,' 'information,' and 'propositions' constitute the written Word of God, the Word inspired by God."[14]

Contemporary theology begins with the hypothesis that Scripture in itself is not revealed truth. William Temple, Anglican Archbishop of Canterbury and in his time president of the World Council of Churches, wrote: "There is no such thing as 'revealed truth.' There are truths of revelation, that is to say, propositions which express the results of correct thinking concerning revelation; but they are not themselves directly revealed."[15] This would make Scripture the human response and the testimony to revelation; it would be the echo of it, but in no way the revelation itself. Professor D. D. Williams affirms that nearly all present-day theologians have this concept. "What it means," he writes, "is that Christian thought can be set free from the intolerable dogmatism which results from claiming that God's truth is identical with some human formulation of it [the formulation in Scripture, doubtless, no less than that, later on, in some historic creed]."[16]

Again, Mr. Temple writes: "It is of supreme importance that He [Christ] wrote no book. It is even of greater importance that there is no single deed or saying of His of which we can be perfectly sure that He said or did precisely this or that." In regard to the Bible as a whole, Temple adds: "No single sentence can be quoted as having the authority of a distinct utterance of the All-Holy God."[17] R. A. Finlayson concludes:

> This indicates how far neo-liberalism has had to go in its attempt to divorce revelation from Scripture and to denigrate the Bible as the source of any adequate and reliable knowledge of God. Presumably, what makes it "of supreme importance" to Dr. Temple that we have no certainty regarding any "single deed or saying" of Christ is the allegation that this gives greater scope for the exercise of faith. To us faith based on such uncertainties is mere presumption.[18]

The Impossibility That a Fallible Message Could "Become the Word of God"

If the biblical text is so uncertain, its authors in all points fallible, and its pages replete with legends and errors, in what way is a believer to know the truth? This happens, they tell us, when God makes use of the text, such as it is, to reach him directly, here and now. Then it is that this message becomes "God's Word"; and the revelation is granted to a man in this personal encounter with the Lord. John Murray sums up as follows the current modern position, one which, we may add, is not his own:

> Scripture is authoritative because it witnesses to the Word of God; it is the vessel or vehicle of the Word of God to us. In that respect Scripture is said to be unique. . . . But what makes Scripture really authoritative, on this view, is the ever-recurring act of God, the divine decision, whereby, through the mediacy of Scripture, the witness of Scripture to the Word of God is borne home to us with ruling and compelling power. The Scripture is not authoritative antecedently and objectively. It is only authoritative as here and now, to this man and to no other, in a concrete crisis and confrontation, God reveals himself through the medium of Scripture. Only as there is the ever-recurring human crisis and divine decision does the Bible become the Word of God.[19]

Let us quote the remark which Theodore Engelder made about these theologians: "They refuse to believe that God performed the miracle of giving us by inspiration an infallible Bible, but are ready to believe that God daily performs the greater miracle of enabling men to find and see in the fallible word of man the infallible Word of God."[20]

If it is true that the Bible transmits the Word of God to me only in the moment when I meet God by means of its truth or when its message touches me personally, this is the same as saying that the authority of Scripture resides in the one who receives its message. This concept is, in fact, a confusion between the inspiration of the Bible and the inner witness of the Holy Spirit.[21]

Furthermore, what is this text which "becomes the Word of God"? asks Robert Preus.

> It is the Word of God. It does not, and in the nature of the case cannot, *become* the Word of God. It does not become the Word of God when the Church recognizes it as such or when God acts upon a person to accept it as such. Just as the letter of a friend expresses his views, so the Scriptures present at all times God's plan concerning our salvation. . . . No matter how the Word of God is viewed, it is the same, one identical Word of God. It may be viewed as the mind of God, as in the minds of the prophets, as written by these men, or as received into our hearts; but it always remains the same Word of God.[22]

CRITERIA FOR DISCERNING THE "WORD OF GOD"

When it is claimed that the Bible merely "contains" the Word of God at the moment when a believer "discovers" it, an insoluble difficulty is actually raised. J. I. Packer clearly spells out the dilemma which contemporary theologians run into. How can we

> affirm the accessibility of revelation in Scripture without committing ourselves to belief in the absolute trustworthiness of the biblical record? How can we assert the divine authority of biblical revelation without foreclosing the possibility—indeed, it would be said, the proved reality—of human error in Scripture? . . . The aim proposed is, not to withdraw the Bible from the acid-bath of rationalistic criticism, but to find something to add to the bath to neutralize its corrosive effects. The problem

is how to enthrone the Bible once more as judge of the errors of man while leaving man enthroned as judge of the errors of the Bible; how to commend the Bible as a true witness while continuing to charge it with falsehood. One cannot help thinking that it would be something of a "tour de force" to give a convincing solution of a problem like this. However, such is the task attempted by modern theology. It is proposed . . . so to refashion the doctrine of revelation that the orthodox subjection of heart and mind to biblical authority and the liberal subjection of Scripture to the authority of rationalistic criticism appear, not as contradictory, but as complementary, principles, each presupposing and vindicating the other.[23]

Further, J. I. Packer inquires what the criterion for the revelation will be then:

If there is no revealed truth, and the Bible is no more than human witness to revelation, fallible and faulty, as all things human are, what guarantee can we have that our apprehensions of revelation correspond to the reality of revelation itself? We are sinful men and have no reason to doubt that our own thoughts about revelation are as fallible and faulty as any; by what standard, then, are we to test and correct them? . . . Historic Christianity said that the biblical presentation of, and pattern of thinking about, revelation-facts is such a standard. Modern theology, however, cannot say this; for the characteristic modern position really boils down to saying that the only standard we have for testing our own fallible judgments is our own fallible judgment. . . .

The effect of following the modern approach has naturally been to encourage a kind of biblical double-talk, in which great play is made with biblical terms, and biblical categories are insisted on as the proper medium for voicing Christian faith, but these are then subjected to a rationalistic principle of interpretation which eliminates from them their basic biblical meaning (e.g., a story such as that of the Fall is treated as *mythical*, significant and true as a symbol revealing the actual state of men today, but false if treated as the record of an objective historical happening). Thus theological currency has been debased, and a cloud of ambiguity now broods over much modern "biblicism." This, at least, is to the credit of Bultmann that, having pursued this approach so radically as to categorize the whole

New Testament doctrine of redemption as mythical, he has seen, with a clear-headedness denied to many, that the most sensible thing to do next is to drop the mythology entirely and preach simply that brand of existentialism which, in his view, represents the New Testament's real "meaning."[24]

In regard to the story of Elijah (I Kings 17 and 18), in spite of the confirmations given by Jesus (Luke 4:25-26) and by James (5:16-18), a professor in one of our faculties of theology declared not long ago: "We might say that this account is historically false, but spiritually true." What will this professor's students think; and, especially, what will they preach about it to a naïve public which "believes" that the Bible tells the truth?

ESCAPING THE TRAP OF SUBJECTIVISM

If the Bible is not itself the revelation, if it is fallible and erroneous in theology and in morality as well as in history and science, the so-called "Word of God" which I receive by means of it will be eminently subjective; that is, it will depend on my experience and my appreciation of it. In fact, who is to decide what is true and what is of value in the text before me? How am I to know if the events it relates are authentic, or if they are embellished, or even invented? How can I distinguish between facts and doctrine and between the essential message and the background, which, I am told, is not to be depended on? In fact, it turns out that human reason is what inevitably makes the decision, on the basis of certain criteria inherent in our own thinking. The knowledge and understanding of man is, therefore, the supreme judge as to what the Word of God is.[25]

Again, how can we discern any such Word of God? How identify it or recognize it? This burning question haunts E. J. Young too.[26] One keeps coming back to subjectivism, according to which man himself is the one to make the judgments.

For all practical purposes, everyone who makes a distinction between Scripture and the Word of God accepts biblical criticism, often in its most radical form. With this, every word of the text can be, and is indeed, subjected to question. All the knowledge which modern theologians have of God, the Trinity, Jesus Christ, the Holy Spirit, the resurrection and that which they call "the Word of God"—

all of this comes from the very words of the Bible. But if those words are not sure or are not worthy of confidence, must one then keep searching in his own mind for certainty? How can anything definite be made out of this nebulous communication, seeing it is not the words themselves which speak to us? Moreover, the Word perceived will be variable from one person to another, even from one great theologian to another. Just think of the fundamental differences which sometimes obtain among Barth, Brunner, Bultmann, Tillich and Robinson. Where then is the truth?

We have just been speaking about what we have called subjectivism, but we could also use the terms "illuminism" or "mysticism." In *illuminism* the believer claims that he receives a special light directly from God, some communication from the Spirit which makes him independent of the written revelation. We do indeed believe that the Lord can address Himself directly to each individual among us. But in order to keep us from extravagance, He has given us the indispensable touchstone of His infallible Word. Modern theologians are without this norm, and the whole history of the church shows us the dangers inherent in such a situation.

Mysticism is a communication of the soul with God, which in its essence remains inexpressible. This, for example, is what Brunner has in mind when he speaks of the "personal encounter," in which God speaks to the individual. The communication He effects by means of it is ineffable, and it cannot be expressed by any articulated word. Once again, with no reference to Scripture, the authoritative norm, what is this but an uncontrolled mysticism?

In the eighteenth and nineteenth centuries man was convinced of the infallibility of human reason, which he did not hold to be at all tainted by sin. Our contemporaries have been disillusioned on this point. They have seen the collapse of many philosophies and ideologies; they are aware of the influence of nonrational factors on thought; they have established the power of propaganda and of brainwashing; and they see to what lengths the uncontrolled use of human science and intelligence can lead. They are close to giving up on the hope of acquiring objective knowledge of anything at all. Where are they going to discover the certainties which their lives so much need? They are not going to find them through men who, although confessing the failure of rationalism, at the same time question divine truth put down in writing. Apart from revelation, as a standard by which to evaluate and correct our fallible human notions, sinners such as we are will be forever cast upon the shore of an ocean of doubts and speculations. And when modern theology tells us that we cannot trust either the Bible or ourselves, it turns us over to an uncertain fate with no hope or respite. All this, taken literally, leads straight to dogmatic skepticism. The situation at this point is only obscured the more if we speak of paradox, or of dialectical tension. In reality, in the attempt to reconcile two contradictory positions, modern theology simply condemns itself to an indefinite succession of arbitrary oscillations between the affirmation or negation of the trustworthiness of human speculations and the biblical dictums. The closest it can come to any fixed principle is the guarded conclusion that we can have no certain knowledge of God whatsoever. The only way to avoid such a conclusion is by a return to the traditional position concerning Scripture, identical with that of the Bible itself; namely, that it is the written and infallible revelation of God.[27]

MYTH-HUNTING

It is quite in style to talk about the myths of the Bible. A myth is not a legend or a fable, but "a story by which the events in the spiritual world are described in terms of earthly occurrences, or earthly events are shown in relation to their spiritual roots."[28] Professor Rudolf Bultmann of Marbourg has obtained a great deal of notoriety and an immense influence through his attempts to "demythologize" the Bible, especially the New Testament. Let us sum up the evaluation which P. Hughes makes of this in his *Scripture and Myth:* Bultmann's idea is that if we purge every element of myth from the biblical text, the irreducible core of the gospel—the kerygma (the proclamation, the truth to be preached)—will remain. We have already mentioned, on pp. 62-63, some "mythical" elements which, according to him should be eliminated. Whatever is miraculous is synonymous with the mythological and thus is foreign to modern man, whose mind is overwhelmingly "technological."*

According to Bultmann, Jesus of Nazareth was an ordinary man whose person and work are divested of any supernatural character.

*One book often mentioned in regard to "demythologizing" is *Kerygma and Myth*, edited by Hans Werner Bartsch.

He was, however, a concrete figure in history; and His crucifixion did really take place. As for the rest, Bultmann declares that the miraculous birth, empty tomb and ascension are stories and the resurrection a nonhistorical event that ought not to be taken literally. The doctrine which makes of Jesus Christ, the Son of God, a preexistent Being is simply mythological. Those elements of the New Testament, and others with them, are rapidly (and conveniently) dispensed with as being most certainly ulterior embellishments of the primitive tradition.[29] As for the expiatory death of Christ, that mythological interpretation is a pile of sacrificial and juridical analogies which have ceased to be tenable today. Death as punishment for sin, Bultmann goes on to say, is revolting to naturalism and also to idealism, since death, as seen by both, is simply a normal process beyond which there is nothing at all. Thus the Christian hope is pointless.

> All our thinking today is shaped by modern science. Now that the forces and laws of nature have been discovered, the miracles of the New Testament world of demons and spirits; the mythical eschatology is untenable; we can no longer look for the return of the Son of Man on the clouds of heaven, or hope that the faithful will meet in the air; and, thanks to modern man's understanding of himself, it can now be asserted that human nature is a self-subsistent unity immune from the interference of supernatural powers.[30]

P. E. Hughes concludes: Bultmann poses the principle that the knowledge of "modern man" and "modern science" is determinative of what is and what is not possible in our world. Thus he attributes authority to this knowledge of man and so pronounces against the knowledge and the authority of God. "Can he not see that the logic of his own position cries out for him to take the one last step of declaring 'God' to be the ultimate myth to be eliminated?"[31] The whole brochure is well worth pondering.

God Without God—God Is Dead—Man Is God

This step has, in fact, been taken. The book *Honest to God*, written by the Anglican bishop John A. T. Robinson, became an instant best seller throughout the whole world. Translated into nine languages, by the beginning of 1966 it had sold more than a million copies. According to the author, twentieth century man has become of age. He can no longer believe in a God outside himself, "up there," "out there," or "on the other side," to whom one might address himself as one would an "old grandfather in the sky," presiding over the world like a "heavenly dictator." Robinson calls up Dietrich Bonhoeffer as his authority and even more Paul Tillich, well-known professor at Union Theological Seminary in New York. According to Tillich: "God is not a projection 'out there,' outside ourselves and our created world, 'an Other' beyond the skies, of whose existence we have to convince ourselves, but *the Ground of our very being.*"[32] Tillich speaks here of "this infinite and inexhaustible depth and ground of all being," for, adds Robinson, the word *God* signifies "ultimate depth of all our being, the creative ground and meaning of all our existence." Martin Buber, very popular Jewish philosopher today, has expressed the idea like this: "When he who abhors the name [of God] and believes himself to be godless gives his whole being to addressing the 'Thou' of his life as a 'Thou' that cannot be limited by another, he addresses God."[33]

Does not this way of thinking signify "the end of theism" (according to Webster: "belief in the existence of one God, transcending, yet immanent in, the universe")? Robinson replies:

> It [this way of thinking] would not naturally use the phrase "a personal God," for this in itself belongs to an understanding of theology and of what theological statements are about which is alien to it. . . . To say that "God is personal" is to say that "reality at its very deepest level is personal." . . . If this is true, theological statements are not a description of "the highest Being," but an analysis of the depths of personal relationships—or, rather, an analysis of the depths of all experience "interpreted by love."[34]

It follows that Feuerbach (German philosopher) was definitely right when he wanted to transform "theology" into "anthropology" (what Bultmann, answering Karl Barth, declared he also was trying to do!).

As for Jesus Christ, Robinson goes on to say that the traditional way of presenting Him is also mythical:

> A God in the form of a man. . . . He looked like a man . . . but underneath he was God dressed up—like Father Christmas.

> . . . I am aware that this is a parody, . . . and probably an offensive one; but I think it is perilously near the truth. . . . The whole notion of "a God" who "visits" the earth in the person of "his Son" is as mythical as the prince in the fairy story. . . . The belief that we are at this point and in this person in touch with God has increasingly been left to the religious minority that can still accept the old mythology as physically or metaphysically true.[36]

The New Testament interpreted like this, he says, has never claimed that Jesus Christ is God, and nobody knows whether He affirmed Himself to be the Son of God. The doctrine of redemption is not, as viewed by the supernaturalists (those who believe in the supernatural) a highly mythological and somewhat nebulous transaction between "God" on the one hand and "man" on the other. In particular, the notion that the Father punished His Son in our place is in any case a perversion of what the New Testament teaches. Even if its content is Christian (?), the whole scheme of a supernatural Being coming down from heaven to "save" humanity from sin, as one puts his finger into a glass of water to rescue a struggling insect, is frankly incredible to man "come of age," who no longer believes in such a deus ex machina. The same is true of the myths of Christmas and the resurrection.[36]

Let us bring to a close the analysis of all this gibberish. It shows most painfully that a man can be a bishop of a church which has its membership in the World Council of Churches, or be a famous theologian in Europe or in America and yet completely deny the message and authority of the Holy Scriptures. When the Scriptures have ceased to be the infallible expression of revealed truth, man, even if he claims to be religious and a doctor of divinity, is apt to be carried away by every wind of doctrine and finally into apostasy.

God is dead. The myth of a "God in the sky" having been exploded, one group of American professors of theology and laymen has made itself famous by declaring *dead* the God of the Bible, of creation and of history.

A century ago Nietzsche, just before becoming entirely mad, uttered this cry of despair: "God is dead!" Even leaders of some denominations traditionally regarded as sound now label themselves "Christian atheists." We must recognize the death of God, they say, as a historical fact. God is dead in our times, our history and our existence. In *Look* magazine for February 22, 1966, an Episcopal bishop declared that for his part he had rejected the incarnation and the supernatural birth of Christ. He had, moreover, abandoned the idea of God as a Supreme Being and the concepts of prayer, the miracles, and the divinity of Christ. Yet he remained a bishop! Billy Graham comments on all this as follows:

> Men are not saying that we are dead toward God; they are actually saying that God *himself* is dead. These radical and ridiculous statements are only symptoms of what is happening in many of our Christian colleges and seminaries today. . . . I want to assure you that these radical views do not represent the majority view of the church. They represent only a small, vocal group that is being given publicity because their views are so far-out and so radical.[37]

Man is God. The above-mentioned tendency cannot be denied or ridiculed. It underlies the whole vast movement which, ever since the fall, had been leading man farther and farther away from the knowledge and the adoration of God, toward the exaltation and adoration of the creature (Rom. 1:18-25). The insidious promise of the tempter is always the same: "Ye shall be as gods!" (Gen. 3:1, 5). Man, as Buffon said, is "a religious animal." It is his capacity to believe and to worship which differentiates him from the beast. If he abandons the Creator and His Word, he will keep forging false gods for himself until he ends up worshiping himself in the person of the Antichrist. Nietzsche's superman, man "divine in the depth of his being," is only a prefiguration of the super-dictator who shortly will get himself worshiped by all that dwell on the earth (II Thess. 2:3-12; Rev. 13:8). In the political sphere, the exaltation of man has brought to such individuals as Hitler, Stalin and Mao Tse-tung homages strikingly akin to worship, if not the equivalent of it. On the religious and theological plane, except for the unshakable rock of the fully inspired Scriptures, there reigns nothing but the most alarming confusion. We would not be surprised now to see an immense final syncretism develop, ending up in the Great Babylon: the establishment of the *religion of man* over the whole earth, just as the prophets so clearly foretold.

WHAT FINALLY REMAINS

If all the criticism of the critics were to be added together, there would be left very few "authentic" verses in the Scriptures, few trustworthy books and few acceptable doctrines. There is, furthermore, nothing new under the sun. Over a hundred years ago now, Gaussen summed up as follows the attitude of the rationalists, those who put their own reasoning above the Bible:

> There is a mixture, they will tell you, in the Word of God. They sift it, they correct it, and it is with the Bible in their hand that they come to tell you: There is no divinity in Christ, no resurrection of the body, no Holy Ghost, no devil, no demons, no hell, no expiation in the death of Jesus Christ, no native corruption in man, no eternity in punishments, no miracles in facts (what do I say, even?), no reality in Jesus Christ.[38]

Is this not a summary of all of the doubts set forth today, an amplified echo of the old question of the tempter in Eden: "Yea, hath God said?" (Gen. 3:1).

This is certainly the opinion of Professor Finlayson when he writes that the present theological position has abandoned the historic faith of the church. It leaves the Christian religion deprived of "the divinely mediated record" and the believer with no intelligent foundation for his faith. One characteristic of this movement is the setting aside of the authority of Scripture for human experience and illumination.

> This divorce of faith and factual reality lands us only in the cloud-land of make-believe, and the Christian faith is as unsubstantial as a day-dream. It can be seen that in reality this is an attempt to recover a basis of confidence in certain of the spiritual facts and ideas of the Bible without accepting its divine authority or even its historical trustworthiness. . . . All this does not explain how, if the Bible record is untrustworthy, we can accept the trustworthiness of a spiritual experience that is based on it. . . . In no other department of human thought or research is truth based on subjective experience that lacks objective reality; yet this is what is offered us as the basis of religion.[39]

ILLOGICALNESS

In practice, many of the critical theologians are far from being logical. Having decreed that so many pages of Scripture are mythical and erroneous, they often do not hesitate to make it the object of an assiduous and profound Bible study. These men seem to have a watertight partition in the brain which permits negations to cohabit with the most beautiful affirmations. This is part of the dialectic and the existential tension so much in vogue today. Professor Brunner says it is generally admitted that the accounts in Genesis 1 and 2 are not historical, but mythical. But he insists that this in no wise hinders our perceiving in them "the Word and the revelation of God." Professor Jacques Ellul published a study of about one hundred pages on the Prophet Jonah. Throughout the first part, he points out the nonhistoricity of the account: Jonah is a legendary figure, the big fish did not exist, everything given about Nineveh is certainly inexact, the city did not repent, God never intervened like that; to believe in the miracle of Jonah is (in spite of the Lord's confirmation of it, Matt. 12:39-41) to believe in a piece of paper more than in Jesus Christ! Then, abandoning the critical problem, Mr. Ellul devotes the rest of the booklet to an edifying, positive Bible study of the four chapters of the book.[40]

Modern theologians, especially Barth, it seems, can make this sort of turnabout without the slightest difficulty. They call up words and passages of Scripture which "are not the Word of God" and which should not be used as "proof texts." We must not be surprised at this: in fact, distinctions are impossible, and nothing definite can be made out of this nebulous Word of God. Fortunately, the text of Scripture remains, which Barth, for example, often uses in the same way that a defender of verbal inspiration would use it.

By a singular turning of the tables, those who seem so lacking in logic accuse us of rationalizing. A hundred years ago the opposite was true. Liberalism boasted about infallible human reason and ridiculed evangelicals for refusing to think and for mistrusting science. Now they take pleasure in the dialectical and the irrational. Those who, because of their faith, are not willing to sacrifice accurate logic and balanced reasoning are accused of rationalizing. This is confusion. God never intended to annihilate the reason which He Himself gave us. But this reason must be regenerated and submitted to His Spirit, even as to His Word: "Whereas ye were servants to sin, ye became obedient from the heart to that form of teaching whereunto ye were delivered" (Rom. 6:17). God in fact does want us to love Him "with all our mind" (Matt. 22:37). We are to offer to Him a worship that is reasonable (logical, as the Greek puts it; Rom. 12:1); He does indeed want us to be filled with spiritual wisdom and understanding (Col. 1:9; II Tim. 2:7), and with truth and soberness (II Thess. 2:2; Acts 26:25). It is thus that we acquire good understanding (Prov. 3:4). We know the limits of the reason that is ours, and we purpose to submit it entirely to revelation. The divine wisdom is perfect; it illumines, it imparts understanding, and it leads into all truth. This wisdom is in Christ and in the Bible, which is the "yea" of God. It could not be at the same time both "yea" and "nay" (II Cor. 1:19-20).

EVANGELICALS SUPPOSEDLY NONSCIENTIFIC IN REGARD TO THE BIBLE

The accusation that Evangelicals set out from a nonscientific a priori in regard to the Bible is another ground for complaint made by modern theologians against us. They say to us: "You go around in a vicious circle. First you put up your dogma of the inspiration and infallibility of the Scriptures; then you pull out of that inspired Bible texts to prove inspiration. A scientist first examines the facts without preconceived ideas; then from these he deduces a law if he can. Likewise, we must submit the Bible to scientific examination and then honestly admit the results of the experiment."

Once more, it is easy to return the compliment. We think that S. Van Mierlo does this very well in *La Révélation Divine*.[41] This is substantially what he has to say: It is true that the scientist takes a critical attitude when he seeks for truth by the examination of natural phenomena. But he does not apply this method to nature in its ensemble. For him *nature, which is a priori true, forms an intelligible unity.* One can even speak of the profound faith of scholars in the unity of the creation. The physicist does not criticize nature when he runs up against an apparent error or a contradiction. He examines, compares, tries to understand and forces himself to find the truth which he assumes exists. Faced with phenomena which he finds incredible or in conflict with others, he concludes that it is he who is wrong. He corrects his initial appraisal, revises his theory and, if necessary, sacrifices his own thinking. He takes a humble attitude toward truth. He does not subject to question either the veracity or the unity of nature; what he criticizes is human opinion relative to nature.

Even so, the believer bows before the authority, unity and trustworthiness of Scripture. It is not that he imposes these on Scripture in any authoritative way. If he approaches it with an open and a humble heart, he gets the greatest shock of his life: he finds God in it; his eyes are opened; he receives new life from it. From there on, convinced that he has before him God's Book, he will respect its contents and will apply his critical mind to evaluating the interpretations which men, including himself, have put on it.

As for science, let us note that it is risky for theologians to be pulled along by it, as, for example, Brunner and Bultmann have been. The first declares that science has rendered faith in the Genesis account impossible; for the second, the technological discoveries of the twentieth century have once and for all demolished and put an end to belief in the supernatural. But, strangely, "modern science" does not utter a consistent voice. The scientific treatises of one generation are very quickly discarded by the next. A short time ago liberal theologians solemnly assured us that modern science made "impossible" acceptance of a catastrophic end of the world as announced by the Bible. Now they naïvely declare that atomic science permits us to come back to the belief condemned yesterday as absurdly antiscientific. Consequently theologians slavishly devoted to the science of the day have had to make a complete about-face. Brunner puts it like this: "What until recently seemed to be only the apocalyptic fantasies of the Christian faith has today entered the sphere of the soberest scientific calculations: the sudden end of human history. . . . This thought has ceased to be absurd, i.e. to be such that a man educated in modern scientific knowledge would have to give it up."[42]

Search for a "scientific respectability." Theological liberalism has been greatly influenced—if not created—by the wave of scientific rationalism that swept over the whole nineteenth century. The most recent theologians, formulating a new theory of revelation, have thought they could not abandon "the results of criticism." They have wanted in this way to stay "à la page," so as to maintain a scientific respectability, assuring them contact with the world of intellectuals. But they have shown themselves very little aware of the progress of positive biblical research. Moreover, they have been led to stand aloof from the biblical text and to take refuge in an illuminism and a mysticism that are situated entirely outside the reach and the interest of modern science.

This, among others, is one reason why we cannot but consider illusory the snobbishness which impels some Evangelicals to seek that same "scientific respectability." Since criticism is in vogue, since one practically has to adopt it to obtain certain diplomas, they sometimes do not hesitate to put in jeopardy their biblical faith and their spiritual power, exposing these to the corrosive effects of negative theories. Fortunately there is, we believe, another way to keep one's faith in the whole of Scripture and to acquire at the same time all the useful information obtainable through modern scholarship. This is through Bible schools and evangelical faculties of theology and truly up-to-date positive literature, of which there is much more in English than in either French or German.

THE BASIS OF PREACHING

If the Bible is not the Word of God, it is hard to imagine what can be preached about with any assurance. We have seen that the apostles, everywhere preaching "the Word of God," did not hesitate to fill their messages with quotations from the Bible (e.g., Acts 13:16-41, 44, 46, 48-49). But the man to whom whole books of Scripture are "pious frauds" and who considers the most essential historical facts legends or "embellishments"—what is he going to say? As for myths, he may be hard put to it to give the flock a simple explanation of their meaning.

We mentioned (p. 65) sermons that called the Christmas scriptures "legendary" and labeled "unimportant" the affirmation or negation of the bodily resurrection of Christ. Without mentioning the absence of faith on the part of such orators as these, what are we to make of the confusion into which they plunge their hearers? And what can a pastor say when the Christian public expects a sermon from him on something he no longer believes? *Either* he will resort to an "as if . . ." so as not to shock simple souls, and will use traditional evangelical language, only with a double meaning, *or*, with complicated expressions, he will develop the religious philosophy which in his mind has taken the place of pure and simple biblical theology. The reason why this philosophy ceases to be the gospel is that the gospel, hidden from the wise and the understanding, is revealed unto babes (Luke 10:21). This is why so many modern preachers are tiresome and talk over the heads of their hearers. Still, as Spurgeon paraphrased it, what Jesus said to Peter was "Feed My lambs," not "Feed My giraffes"! *Or else,* the speaker, in an effort to be frank, will suppose that the time has come to "free" his audience from old, outworn beliefs. The result will probably be that he will scandalize some devout souls and will destroy the naïve faith of many others. It can well be also that the latter will thank him for this, if we may judge by the smashing world-wide success of Bishop Robinson's *Honest to God,* summarized above.

EXPLAINING SUCCESSIVE THEOLOGICAL FASHIONS

We have just seen the embarrassing position of the preacher imbued with critical ideas. If only modern teaching were clear—and, especially, if it were stable! But, unfortunately, criticism is constantly changing in its conclusions, if not in its methods, so that it may well put up on a pedestal today what it threw into the ash can yesterday.

We have seen that criticism has fallen into subjectivism: its authority is no longer that of the Bible, but that of man, who thinks he can discern the Word of God in his experience and by his own illumination. Obviously, the great will be considered particularly illuminated; thus the tendency will rapidly develop to bow before their experience and doctrine. All such teaching will inevitably be fallible and partial, and its influence will generally not last much longer than its author. It is, moreover, grievous to us to see the critics contradict one another and the leaders differ among themselves. So each generation will see a new theology come sweeping in and will become infatuated with some mentor or other. We have seen them, one after the other:

Liberalism, which has triumphed during the past century, identified with the great names of Schleiermacher and Wellhausen (the latter so much "old hat" by now that in 1948 one theologian, after alluding to him, added: "Forgive me that I quote this old condemned dragon"![43]).

Dialectical theology, represented particularly by Barth, Brunner and Niebuhr. It seemed that this was going to endure, especially the reaction introduced by Barth. But everyone knows now that his influence has sharply declined in favor of a more negative theology.

The theology of Bultmann, E. Käsemann and Paul Tillich in Germany and in America and of Robinson in England, etc.

In view of the fact that this last-mentioned tendency is by far the most negative, one wonders with considerable trepidation what the next wave of opinion will be like. The American movement claiming that God is dead shows us that today we can expect practically anything. It is really significant here that Paul Tillich entitled one of his books *The Shaking of the Foundations.*

In the light of all this theological shift and uncertainty, it is reassuring for evangelical believers and for preachers to rely on the immutable authority of Scripture, the Word of God. Evangelicals are not disciples of any popular theologians—not even of Calvin, Luther, Wesley or Darby—but of Jesus Christ and His apostles. For them, faith has been "once for all delivered" (Jude 3). They are ready to fight and to suffer for such a glorious heritage.

The Moral and Spiritual Point of View

The terrain for the attack against the integrity of the biblical text and its plenary inspiration is purportedly a scientific one. All sorts of historical, philosophical, linguistic and literary reasons are advanced for the claim that the Bible in itself cannot be the Word of God. (See, in regard to this, chap. 14, "The Difficulties of the Bible.") But it seems to us that much more important moral and spiritual considerations are being put to one side. Here are some of them.

1. It is unthinkable that the spiritual value of a great portion of the Bible books is not altered if, as we are told, these parts are false. The fact that some sections of Scripture are anonymous (many of the Psalms) or were written by several authors, some of them unknown (the Proverbs), poses no problems and changes nothing in regard to inspiration. It is, however, quite different with the supposed "sources" of the Pentateuch, a document which, we are told, was written by various authors who contradicted one another and whose identity, actually, is unknown—authors whose literary efforts were fabricated over the centuries and then fraudulently attributed to Moses. We have, for example, brought up the fact that Leviticus affirms fifty-one times that Moses himself set down the words of God in it for the

people. Now, according to the critics, this whole "priestly code" was invented by priests at the time of Ezra and was attributed to Israel's great law-giver so it would be more easily accepted. Essentially the same thing is said about Deuteronomy, which, they say, was "discovered" for the first time in the temple in the days of Josiah (II Kings 22:8).

The prophecies of Daniel, II Timothy and II Peter, full of details about the authors and the circumstances of their lives, were likewise the result of "pious frauds," written by impostors long after the death of those men of God (or, in some cases, after the predicted events). They try to make us believe that men in those days did not possess our sense of literary propriety and that they could have done all this with a perfectly clear conscience. Now in the case of the Israelites, at least, we are convinced of just the opposite. From their very law, they had a much higher concept than our contemporaries do of truth, holiness, morality, social obligations, propriety and the rights of the individual; and, above all, of the absolute reverence due to the person and the Word of God. A prophet who falsely claimed to have received a message from the Lord was subject to death (Deut. 18:20). To suppose, moreover, that Israel, attached for centuries to Moses and her sacred books, would have adopted such fraud without the shadow of a reaction is a total impossibility from either the psychological or the ethical point of view, to say nothing of the historical. To claim that Jesus endorsed with all His authority an Old Testament full of such falsehoods is, at least, an insult to His moral sense, if not a complete denial of His deity. One can think as much of the veracity and spiritual discernment of the apostles and of the primitive church.

2. We have spoken of the difficulties of the preacher who is obliged to preach on texts which he believes to be not genuine. But what can be said about the shock experienced by the young theological student when he finds certain professors starting right off to ridicule his naïve faith and to try to persuade him that "the Bible is not the Word of God"? This type of young man often comes from an evangelical milieu or family, where it is still common for a call to the ministry to originate. Every year we have known cases where doubt thus sown has produced veritable crises. And how many young pastors, coming to grips with the realities of the ministry have again

found faith—and the Bible—by resolutely rejecting the negative criticism they have been taught!

3. If the biblical text has no authority and each one simply finds in it his own "Word of God," the invariable result is an attitude favoring relative values. All interpretations are good, and no one person can say that he has the truth. (But Paul exclaimed: "We have the mind of Christ"; and "Though we, or an angel from heaven, should preach unto you any gospel other than that which we preached unto you, let him be anathema"! I Cor. 2:16; Gal. 1:8.) Dogmas, they tell us, are not important; and they may even be dangerous. Have they not engendered all the ecclesiastical harshness, the violent polemics, and the persecutions of the past? The ecumenical trend is toward dialogue, where the most biblical matters and the least biblical matters confront each other in an amicable spirit. A typical example is the foundation laid down for the World Council of Churches. Because any agreement about the credo (the Apostles' Creed) proved impossible, there was adopted a brief formula which declares Jesus Christ God and Saviour according to the Scriptures, to the glory of the Trinity. It is understood, however, that each may interpret this formula in any way he pleases. The largest churches of France and Switzerland frankly said at New Delhi that in accepting such a statement they were maintaining their theological "pluralism" while keeping all their doctrinal liberty.

The abandonment of the great historic confessions of faith has basically been for the same reason. These confessions were very exact (too exact to suit some people) on all the essentials of the faith. (See chap. 20, subhead "The Great Confessions of Protestant Faith," what some were saying about the inspiration of the Bible.) The churches of Switzerland now declare that they no longer have any declaration of faith. Elsewhere, the theoretical conservation of the thirty-nine Anglican articles does not at all stand in the way of the greatest theological liberty. One very influential movement in the religious world acknowledges that it has freed itself of an ancient evangelical confession of faith because it had become a veritable straitjacket.

In the face of such latitude as this, one cannot help feeling very uneasy about the future. Diametrically opposite points of view already coexist in the same ecclesiastical organizations. If the biblical revelation no longer serves either as a norm or as a restraint, what will hinder an amalgamating of all these groups—even a uniting of these with other religions entirely?

4. We see that negativistic liberalism has, in general, had nothing but sterile results. But just what kind of faith could we expect to see produced by a purely human and fallible Christ, one incapable of getting Himself out of the grave so as to insure the salvation of the world (which, moreover, is not considered lost in the first place)? And what can be said for the kind of criticism which emasculates the authority and import of the Holy Scriptures? In all humility we are convinced that nothing but total faith in the inspiration of the Scriptures can produce integrity in spiritual power and life. We seek to demonstrate this in chapter 20 and in chapter 22.

5. In conclusion, we align ourselves with the opinion of Professor Finlayson on the subject of modern hostility to inspiration:

> It has severed the Christian faith from its roots in history, bringing it down to the level of mystical experience; it has emptied Christian faith of its revealed doctrinal content and obliterated the distinction between truth and error, between orthodoxy and heresy, between faith based on knowledge and mere credulity. Most serious of all, it has impugned the trustworthiness of the historical Christ and changed the heart-throbbing words of his message to the world into the mere echoes of other men's experience. Under its solvent the Person of Christ becomes elusive and illusionary, a mere intruder into history, who has troubled men with his message but left no sure word for posterity. For it must be clearly understood that the battle being waged against the inspiration of the Bible is, in the last resort, an assault upon historic Christianity and its foundation, Jesus Christ. This is an impressive acknowledgment of the fact that Scripture is recognized to be the supreme bulwark of the historic Christian faith.[44]

Part Five

THE AUTHORITY OF SCRIPTURE

22

THE SUPERNATURAL CHARACTERISTICS OF SCRIPTURE

FROM BEGINNING TO END, Scripture proclaims its divine inspiration. The prophets, Christ and His apostles confirmed it without any reservation. The synagogue and the early church also believed in it absolutely. But has the Bible internal qualities to confirm its supernatural origin? It has, beyond any doubt; and God has willed that it provide in itself its own credentials. He has not permitted the all-important question of the authority of Scripture to depend on minute research, for which study none but scholars have leisure and capacity; or on abstract metaphysics beyond the reach of ordinary mortals. There must stand out from the very pages of the Scriptures an evident demonstration of their authority and origin. To this, of course, is added the inner witness of the Holy Spirit, without which there can be no true, living faith in the Word of God.[1]

SUBLIME REVELATION OF GOD AND OF JESUS CHRIST

Scripture, which claims to be God's Word, paints a unique portrait of Him, one that exceeds any human representation of divinity. "Great is Jehovah, and greatly to be praised; he is to be feared above all gods" (Ps. 96:4-5). Apart from a few rare vestiges of a primitive revelation, the Babylonian, Egyptian, Grecian, Roman, Germanic, Celtic, Hindu, Chinese and other mythologies demonstrate an enormous shipwreck of all notions of truth, holiness and certainty. The God of the Bible is the only true God: Spirit, Creator and sovereign Master of the universe—glorious, eternal, holy, absolute in wisdom, incomprehensible in essence and perfect in justice—He is the source of unfathomable love, perpetually springing up from the depths of His Father heart. He is also the Redeemer, who suffered in identification with His fallen creatures, and who drew near to them by revelation and incarnation, so as to effect—and at what a price—the tremendous plan for God's salvation of humanity.

The person of Jesus Christ, likewise, surpasses any earthly depiction. "Not thus do men invent." No human author could ever have imagined among the sons of men a figure pure and radiant as He. "Never man so spake" (John 7:46). None other ever lived, suffered or loved like Him. Risen from the dead, He alone is able to regenerate us by His own life. Jesus Christ, the Word made flesh, is proof par excellence of the divine inspiration of the Word made Book. He is, indeed, its only really necessary proof. He who, by faith and the illumination of the Holy Spirit, has met in Jesus Christ the living God through the pages of the sacred Book—that one has need of no further demonstration. He cries out: "One thing I know, that, whereas I was blind, now I see" (John 9:25). This God-Man—and this Book—bestowed on me with one swift touch both sight and life! "I had heard of thee by the hearing of the ear; but now [that I have *read* it] mine eye seeth thee" (Job 42:5).

UNIQUE REVELATION OF MAN

In the fallen state where he finds himself, man cannot comprehend unaided the essential elements of either his nature or his destiny. From whence has he come? What is the purpose of his existence, his sufferings and his death? What is his final destiny? "Who will answer?" All of earth's religions and philosophies, curiously canceling one another out by their maze of contradictions, only leave man, before every human contingency, groping in the dark in a panic of uncertainty.

Nothing but the Bible, the Creator's own Word, provides a response to all these questions. It reveals to him his origin, inconceivably sublime, created in the image of God. It provides the story of his fall and explains the contradictory state in which he finds himself, torn between good and evil, happiness and suffering, death and life. Before this mirror, man, astonished, beholds his heart laid bare. He feels himself found out, reproved and condemned; but at the same time called, loved, valued and restored. The Author of the Bible is omniscient. He made man: He needs no one to tell Him what is in His creature. The Bible compresses, as it were, the whole of a human personality into a capsule and shows up as though by an X ray his deep springs and secret passions, and the unsuspected potential of his being (cf. I Cor. 14:25). Never did book speak like this Book; and man, by a mysterious instinct (John 10:4), recognizes in its voice that of the Father, who is conducting him along the path to everlasting life.

From the moment of that recognition he begins to see where he is going; he perceives the meaning of history, even as he does that of his own destiny; he keeps reorienting his life in view of the coming kingdom; he lives already in terms of eternity. Truly, with Paul we realize that these things have not at all entered into the heart of natural man; on the very face of them they bear the proof of their supernatural origin (I Cor. 2:9-10).

THE PLAN OF SALVATION, INCONCEIVABLE TO THE HUMAN MIND

When we compare other religions with the biblical faith, several facts become clear. Human systems can offer no true salvation because they do not know the thrice holy God, His absolute requirements and His condemnation of every disobedience to His law. They have neither a real sense of sin nor a solution to the problem of sin. Man, so they think, is not irremediably lost; and he can redeem himself by his own efforts, by his "good works." Thus he becomes his own savior. No indeed! Man in no wise succeeds in saving himself; and his conscience, troubled in spite of all, never finds the certitude of forgiveness.

The Bible, on the contrary, soundly denounces, as only God can do, our guilt and helplessness and declares our consequent eternal perdition. Then it shows the Lord Himself paying by love all our debt at the cross and freely offering us His incomprehensible grace, and total assurance of salvation along with it. All our future, both earthly and heavenly, is henceforth concentrated on the person of Him who is coming to reign forever and ever.

What human author, what religious genius, could ever have invented a message at once so humiliating for the proud sinner and so marvelous for the repentant believer? Well might Paul cry out: "God hath shut up all unto disobedience, that he might have mercy upon all. O the depth of the riches both of the wisdom and the knowledge of God! how unsearchable are his judgments, and his ways past tracing out! For who hath known the mind of the Lord? . . . To him be the glory for ever" (Rom. 11:32-36).

THE PROPHECIES, PROOF OF DIVINE INSPIRATION

God alone omniscient, therefore able to predict the future. He is eternal; time has no significance to Him; and both tomorrow and eternity itself are before His eyes even as is today. No false god, no other religion on earth has ever brought forth prophecies comparable to those of the Bible. "Who hath declared it from the beginning . . . and beforetime, that we may say, He is right? . . . There is no man; even among them there is no counsellor. . . . I have declared, and I have saved, and I have showed; and there was no strange god among you . . . that performeth the counsel of his messengers" (Isa. 41:26, 28; 43:12; 44:26).

Divination and magic, however, were very prevalent in the ancient world (as they are in our modern world). There abounded everywhere oracles, pythonesses, Delphic pythons, astrologers, augurers and diviners. False prophets can be recognized by the fact that their predictions do not come true (Deut. 18:20-22) or that their ambiguous pronouncements lend themselves to any interpretation (Delphic oracles, Nostradamus, etc.). Without divine inspiration, prophecy is so risky a business that the so-called sacred books of human religions contain practically nothing of it.

Prominence of prophecy in Scripture. In the Old Testament, seventeen out of the thirty-nine books are prophetic books, without counting the very numerous predictions contained, for example, in the writings of Moses and in the Psalms. In the New Testament, entire chapters of the gospels, many passages in the Epistles, and also the whole of Revelation are devoted to prophecy. It is therefore not a question of a few sibylline sentences from which a person draws whatever he wants to, but of significant events announced a long time in advance, minute details realized to the very letter, and a great many verifiable circumstances which God alone could thus predict. Whereas, in the case of that many human prophecies, a thousand among them could easily turn out to be false, it is very remarkable that facts have not proved one biblical prophecy false.[2]

Great prophetic themes. Let us consider some domains where the predicted fulfillment finds irrefutable verification.

Israel

Sojourn in Egypt of Abraham's descendants to last four hundred years (Gen. 15:13-16)

The royal family and the King of kings to come out of Judah (Gen. 49:10)

Israel to be forever a separated people (Num. 23:9)

Infidelity, captivity and dispersion of the people to take place (Deut. 28:20-66; Lev. 26:14-39)

The ten tribes warned sixty-five years in advance that they were to be despoiled by the king of Assyria (Ezra 7:8-20)

Judah to be carried away into Babylon for seventy years (Jer. 25:11; 29:10)

After the rejection of the Messiah, Jerusalem and the temple to be destroyed (Dan. 9:25-26; Matt. 24:1-2, 34)

Israel to undergo worldwide dispersion and suffering (Luke 21:20-24; Deut. 28:64-67)

The Jewish race to survive in spite of all, until the end of time (Jer. 31:35-36) even after the extinction of all the other great peoples of antiquity

Israel to be brought back into her fatherland, a desolate wilderness, and she—along with it—to blossom again like a rose (Ezek. 36—37)

The people of the promised Messiah to be finally converted (Zech. 12:10; Rom. 11:25-29). This prophecy is for a time yet future, but its fulfillment is certain, just as in the case of all those which have preceded it.

The Messiah. We have cited (chap. 18, subhead "Christ's Coming as a Fulfillment of the Scriptures") the fulfillment of such Messianic prophecies as are mentioned in the gospel of Matthew alone. Now, it is affirmed that 333 of the prophecies concerning Christ have been fulfilled! According to the law of probabilities, there would be one chance out of 83 billion that so many predictions would come true in the case of one single individual.[3] Needless to say, such a "chance" does not exist, and no one but the omniscient God could predict and act like this.

The nations. Outside Israel, many historical events have likewise entered into the prophetic field:

the total destruction of Nineveh, proud capital of Assyria (Zeph. 2:13-15; Nahum)

the dramatic fall of Babylon (Isa. 13; 21:1-10)

the judgment of Egypt and the final loss of her supremacy (Ezek. 29, especially vv. 15-16)

the course and decline of the empires succeeding the Babylonian, the empires of the Medes and Persians, Greece (with Alexander and his successors), and, finally, Rome, without her being named (Dan. 2:7-8, etc.)

the famous prophecy of the seventy weeks of Daniel 9, specifying the length of time before the appearance of the Messiah and the role of the nations in respect to His coming

the taking of Tyre by Nebuchadnezzar after a thirteen-year siege and the fate which Alexander finally inflicted on her (Ezek. 26; Jer. 27:1-11)

The end time. Christ, as well as the prophets of both the Old Testament and the New, sketched in detail the denouement of history, devastatingly relevant in general to what we can now see coming to pass before our eyes:

The earth will one day be completely filled with men, in accordance with the command stated in Genesis 1:28 (in twenty-five years, there will be over 6 billion people).

The gospel of Christ will be preached to all nations; then will come the end (Matt. 24:14). What an audacious declaration on the part of the humble Carpenter of Nazareth! Yet the Bible, wholly or in part, has been translated and preached in thousands of languages in the form of the spoken word, the printed page, records, radio and television, so that all can hear its message (see p. 296).

By way of contrast, most men harden their hearts in unbelief and in their repudiation of moral and spiritual values (Matt. 24:10-12). This statement needs no comment.

Wars will become increasingly violent and more widespread (Matt. 24:6-7; Rev. 6:4, 8). Peace will be taken from the earth: an appalling proportion of mankind will be annihilated: these things are all too possible in our atomic age.

Religious persecutions will grow worse and worse (Matt. 24:8-10). In the light of the destruction of 5 or 6 million Jews in this twentieth century, who could argue that this is overdrawn (cf. Dan. 12:7; Zech. 13:8-9) .

Humanity is rushing on toward a universal government and the dictatorship of the Antichrist announced by the prophets (Dan. 7:24-26; II Thess. 2:3-12; Rev. 13:1-8) .

All this will coincide with most extraordinary events in Palestine, the Jews having gone back to their land in unbelief (Ezek. 37; Matt. 24:15-16) .

Jesus Christ solemnly warned us: "When these things begin to come to pass, look up, and lift up your heads; because your redemption draweth nigh" (Luke 21:28) .

Once again, do not such prophecies, tied together, form a bundle of irrefutable proofs of the divine inspiration of Scripture?*

Spiritual value of biblical prophecies. Divination has as its goal merely the satisfaction of the curiosity and interest of man. Biblical prophecy, on the contrary, always contains an element of solemn warning and encouragement in line with the accomplishment of God's plan. In disclosing the future, the Lord reveals something of Himself and prepares man for meeting Him. Thus He makes His wisdom, omniscience, sovereignty and eternality shine out in a most convincing manner. The prophecies concerning Israel have a pedagogic value. The prophetic figure of the Messiah surpasses all the understanding and even all the expectation of the chosen people: the prophecies are meant to prepare the hearts of these people to receive Him. The predictions about the nations are not in line with the ordinary laws of human politics, but with the kingdom of God. The tableau of the end of time must govern all our life and its activities. The vision of the triumph of the Lord brings into a right perspective our view of the world, and thereafter we know ourselves marked out for eternity. Only a divine message can produce such an effect as this. None but God can reveal secrets (Dan. 2:20-23) . What He has foretold of His message strengthens our faith when we see its fulfillment (John 13:19; 14:29) .

THE POWER OF LIFE WHICH EMERGES FROM THE BIBLE

The Word of God is living and active. The eternal Word, with a word, created the world (Heb. 11:3) . From the written Word, the

---

*Those interested in the great subject of biblical prophecy will find it treated in detail in our work *The Return of Jesus Christ.*

living oracle of the Lord, there emanates a supernatural power. "Is not my word like fire? saith Jehovah; and like a hammer that breaketh the rock in pieces? Behold, I will make my words in thy mouth fire, and this people wood, and it shall devour them" (Jer. 23:29; 5:14).

After having spoken of the message given to the people in the desert and confirmed in the Psalms by the Holy Spirit, the author of the epistle to the Hebrews concludes: "For the word of God is living, and active, and sharper than any two-edged sword, and piercing even to the dividing of soul and spirit, of both joints and marrow, and quick to discern the thoughts and intents of the heart. . . . All things are naked and laid open before the eyes of him with whom we have to do" (3:7; 4:12-13).

Scripture convicts of sin and awakens consciences. Expressing the law of God and His will, it makes our disobediences stand out sharply, and it pronounces on us the judgment we merit. Like a mirror, it reveals to our eyes our natural face, which others see so easily, but which we ourselves do not see (James 1:23). If we are sincere, this discovery plunges us into great confusion. The Holy Spirit likewise confirms in us the gravity of the judgments of Scripture. The very Word of the Lord will judge us at the last day (John 12:48). And it is Moses who will accuse his impenitent readers before God (5:45).

It is easy to show that every revival in Israel came about through a rediscovery of Scripture and the conviction of sin immediately produced in the heart by means of it. One day there was brought to Josiah the book of the law that had lain forgotten in the temple. "When the king had heard the words of the law, . . . he rent his clothes. And the king commanded . . ., Go ye, inquire of Jehovah . . . concerning the words of the book that is found; for great is the wrath of Jehovah that is poured out upon us, because our fathers have not kept the word of Jehovah, to do according to all that is written in this book" (II Chron. 34:14-21). At the time of Jeremiah, all the princes of the people asked Baruch to read to them the message written by the prophet. "When they had heard all the words [of the Lord contained in the book], they turned in fear one toward another, and said unto Baruch: We will surely tell the king of all these words." But the king, quite undismayed, cut the book with a penknife and cast it into the fire. Because of that very thing, the Lord pronounced a terrible chastisement on him, his nation and his people (Jer. 36:1-

31). After the captivity, Ezra and Nehemiah, along with the people, solemnly renewed their consecration to God. This obviously came about through a public reading of holy Scripture. The effect was such that the leaders said to the crowd: "Mourn not, nor weep. For all the people wept, when they heard the words of the law." Then a fast was celebrated: "They ... read in the book of the law of Jehovah ... a fourth part of the day; and another fourth part they confessed and worshipped Jehovah their God" (Neh. 8:1-9; 9:3).

Who among God's children did not, through the holy Book, become so convinced of his lost condition in the sight of the sovereign Judge, as to cry out in the presence of Jesus like the Samaritan woman: "He told me all things that ever I did" (John 4:39)? And in all the history of the church, as in the history of Israel, every spiritual renewal has without exception been produced by a return to the Bible. Note, for example, the Waldensians of Lyons and of the Piedmont; Wycliffe and the Lollards in England; John Huss and the Bohemian brethren; the great Reformers—Luther, Calvin, Zwingli and Knox; the Pietists and the Moravians of the eighteenth century; Haldane and the others in the nineteenth century Genevan revival, etc. In every age the declaration of Isaiah stands true: "To the law and to the testimony! if they speak not according to this word, surely there is no morning for them" (Isa. 8:20).

The Word of life regenerates the sinner. Human books, even the most devotional ones, have no life in themselves. They can at best be simply an echo of the heavenly message. Holy Scripture, the living and permanent Word of God, acts like an incorruptible seed to regenerate us, that is, to resurrect us spiritually (I Peter 1:23-25). Preached or written, its message is the Word of life, which gives light to the world (Phil. 2:15). It works effectually in those who believe (I Thess. 2:13), for it is Spirit and life. The law apart from the Spirit (the "letter") condemns and kills, but the Spirit who quickens the Word transmits eternal life to us by means of it (John 6:63; II Cor. 3:3, 6). "The gospel ... is the power of God unto salvation to every one that believeth" (Rom. 1:16). "Belief cometh of hearing, and hearing by the word of Christ" (10:17). Paul said to the Corinthians: "In Christ Jesus I begat you through the gospel" (I Cor. 4:15). Finally, Jesus cried out: "He that heareth my word, and believeth him that sent me, hath eternal life, and cometh not into judgment, but hath passed out of death into life" (John 5:24).

Such affirmations are not just idle talk. Of thousands, even millions, of men it can be said that contact with the Scriptures literally has regenerated their lives. Let us cite three famous examples:

Augustine for thirty-one years led a tumultuous existence, alternating between efforts of self-reformation and repeated defeats and misery. Writhing one day in wretched humiliation in the garden, he heard the voice of a child from the neighborhood chanting: "Take and read! Take and read!" He went to get the scroll containing the epistles of Paul, and his eyes fell on Romans 13:14. All was decided by a word, in an instant: Jesus had overcome! Augustine made no attempt to inquire further; he closed the book. With the end of that sentence "a stream of light and security was poured into his soul; and all the night of his doubts had vanished."[4]

Luther, crushed by the burden of his sin and exhausted from his useless mortification, crawled on his knees up Pilate's fabulous staircase at Rome. One simple word from Scripture suddenly seized him with superhuman power: "The righteous shall live by faith" (Rom. 1:17). That word sufficed; the Reformation came into existence, giving to mankind the Bible, the Saviour, the liberty of the children of God and assurance of eternal life.

Wesley had been seeking to lead a *methodical* life of devotion (origin of the word "Methodist"). After studying theology at Oxford, he set out to do missionary work in America, although he had not yet come to any assurance of his own salvation. But on May 24, 1738, God spoke to him two different times through verses from the Bible (II Peter 1:4 and Psalm 130). He said that that evening he went very unwillingly to a meeting on Aldersgate Street, where someone was reading Luther's preface to the epistle to the Romans. "About a quarter before nine," he wrote, "while he was describing the change which God works in the heart through faith in Christ, I felt my heart strangely warmed. I felt I did trust in Christ, Christ alone, for salvation; and an assurance was given me that He had taken away *my* sins, even *mine,* and saved *me* from the law of sin and death."[5]

It is because our lives have been transformed in this same way, thanks to the Bible, that we testify to its regenerating power. All the arguments brought up against it could not keep us from replying: "I know him whom I have believed" (II Tim. 1:12); and "I believed, and therefore did I speak" (II Cor. 4:13).

Scripture sanctifies the believer. "Man shall not live by bread alone, but by every word that proceedeth out of the mouth of God" (Matt. 4:4). After communicating life to the child of God, that Word nourishes it and makes it grow. "As newborn babes, long for the spiritual milk which is without guile, that ye may grow thereby unto salvation; if ye have tasted that the Lord is gracious" (I Peter 2:2-3). The psalmist exclaims: "My soul breaketh for the longing that it hath unto thine ordinances at all times. I delight in thy law. How sweet are thy words unto my taste! Yea, sweeter than honey to my mouth! I opened wide my mouth, and panted; for I longed for thy commandments" (Ps. 119:20, 70, 103, 131).

This daily appetite for holy Scripture on the part of the newly converted is an indisputable fact. Every time that he meditates on the Word, he is strengthened, comforted and warned by it. So here again Scripture gives a pragmatic demonstration of its supernatural character.

Jesus Himself prayed: "Sanctify them in the truth" (John 17:17). He added: "If ye abide in my word, then are ye truly my disciples; and ye shall know the truth, and the truth shall make you free. Already ye are clean because of the word which I have spoken unto you" (John 8:31-32; 15:3). Christ gave Himself up for the church "that he might sanctify it . . . with the word" (Eph. 5:26). "Young men, . . . ye are strong, . . . the word of God abideth in you, and ye have overcome the evil one" (I John 2:14).

The pure and radiant lives of genuine Christians are also, in our corrupt world, one of the greatest proofs of the divine origin of Scripture. None but the Word, the Creator, could turn a selfish, sin-stained individual—sometimes even a derelict—into a victorious personality overflowing with love. Such believers are true "letters of Christ," living Bibles, known and read of all men (II Cor. 3:2-3). "That ye may become blameless," says Paul, "children of God without blemish in the midst of a crooked and perverse generation, among whom ye are seen as lights in the world, holding forth the word of life" (Phil. 2:15-16).

By God's grace, the world has not lacked living witnesses for Christ, people who have changed the course of their times, bettered the world, or revived the church. After the slumber of the Middle Ages, the Reformers caused the breath of the Spirit of God to pass over Europe. Pascal, although physically a sufferer, expressed in brilliant language some of the deepest, as well as some of the simplest, truths of the gospel. Wesley and Whitefield literally rescued England from a moral, social and spiritual situation which was dragging the country down to ruin. Elizabeth Fry in the prisons, Josephine Butler with prostitutes, William and Catherine Booth in the slums, Hudson Taylor in the heart of China and Billy Graham in his world-wide evangelistic outreach—all these and many more have demonstrated that the message of the gospel still works miracles everywhere it goes.

The Word of God puts to flight the adversary. It is the sword of the Spirit, the perfect piece of offensive armor (Eph. 6:17). Adolphe Monod in these words reminds us of the way Christ used it to triumph over Satan:

> Scripture simply quoted, without explanation or comment— this is all that Jesus used to oppose the great adversary, that mysterious and terrible day in which the whole work of our redemption hung in the balances.
> "It is written!" and the tempter stops in his tracks.
> "It is written!" and he slinks back.
> "It is written!" and he has taken to his heels.
> "It is written," and by whom? By Moses, the messenger, the servant, the creature of the One whom that word delivers in the hour of combat and distress![6]

How could such a thing be possible were it not for the fact that this word is divinely inspired?

The fact that the enemy cringes before the power of Scripture is demonstrated by the incessant attacks which he launches against it. He shudders before this Book, in which the Saviour is announced and in which he himself is completely unmasked. He hates the Bible, which shows him up as defeated and as one to be punished for all eternity, this certainty repeated from Genesis 3:15 all the way to Revelation 20:10. From the outset he has asked the wily question: "Hath God said?" (Gen. 3:1). In every age he has found doubters who have supposed they could know freedom by following him. But the most disconcerting characteristic of our times of apostasy is the adversary's planned attack the last two hundred years on the Scriptures and on their authority. One third of the population of the world is subjugated under an openly atheistic regime. We in the Western world have come into an era that has been called post-Christian, in which only about 10 percent of the people take "religion" seriously. An even more disconcerting fact, one which explains many others, is that a very great proportion of "Christianity" today are joining together in a chorus to repeat the famous question "Hath God said?" and to reject the idea that the Bible is the Word of God.

Scripture withstands every assault. The Huguenots pictured the Bible and the Christian faith as an anvil surrounded by three vigorous blacksmiths, beneath which they put this inscription:
"The more they pound and the more they shout,
The more they wear their hammers out!"
Is it not a divine irony that the nineteenth century, with its exceptionally critical spirit in theology, in literature and in politics, witnessed at the same time the greatest triumphs for the Bible? The British and Foreign Bible Society alone in 150 years (from 1804 to 1954) printed more than 600 million Bibles and Scripture portions. Counting in the other societies, the total production during that same period goes up to 1,300 million copies. Still, for so many centuries, men have been making the most determined efforts to destroy the Scriptures, to prohibit them, to refute them and to ridicule them; and all this came about since the persecutions of Antiochus Epiphanes, Domitian and the Inquisition, down to the attacks of the philosophers, the mockery of the enemies of the faith and the impressive arguments of so-called science, itself in a state of perpetual evolution.

> This is still more wonderful when we consider by whom these writings were preserved. The Jews were the conscientious guardians of the book of the Kingdom. Rome preserved the book of the Church. The Jews, who themselves rejected the Messiah of whom Moses and the prophets testify, preserve the very books which prove their unbelief and convince the world of the divine authority and mission of Jesus.[7]
> Where is there a nation preserving carefully a record which so repeatedly and emphatically declares that they are obstinate,

ungrateful, and perverse; and which attributes all their victories and excellencies, not to their natural disposition and qualities, but exclusively to the mercy and power of God? Look again at the Church of Rome, preserving the writings of evangelists and apostles: that Church preserving writings which declare that Christ hath perfected by one sacrifice them that are sanctified; that salvation is by grace, through faith, and that not of ourselves, it is the gift of God; that all believers are kings and priests unto God; that there is no Mediator between God and men but the Man Christ Jesus; that men forbidding to marry and commanding to abstain from meats are the expected false teachers; that Mary is told by the Son Himself not to interfere in the concerns of His kingdom [she had no role in the Church after the time of Acts 1:14]; that Peter savored the things that are of man [and was severely reprimanded by Paul!] . . . Christians are commended for subjecting even the teaching of apostles to the authority and confirmation of Scripture! (Heb. 7:24-25; 10:14; Eph. 2:8-9; Rev. 1:6; I Tim. 2:5; 4:1-5; Gal. 2:11; Acts 17:11)!

The Jews bear unwilling witness to Jesus, and Rome has preserved and carefully transcribed her own condemnation.[8]

The same can be said of the Protestants, formerly a people of the Bible, who have also kept and disseminated it without always believing it.

Conclusion. It is difficult to set down in a few words all the services that the Bible has rendered to humanity, a constantly renewed manifestation of its regenerating power. Vinet has said: "The gospel in the world is freedom's immortal seed." The word "gospel" could be replaced by the word "Scripture," for it is found only in Scripture. It was as inspired by the Bible that the Christians, emerging from the cruel and amoral society of antiquity, were the pioneers in each of the following domains:

the suppression of slavery
the emancipation of woman
compassion for suffering and for human misery
care for the sick, disabled and aged
establishment of hospitals, rest homes and orphanages
the impetus given to the sciences by the suppression of the bonds
   of superstition

the struggle against prostitution, alcoholism and vice
the instruction of children, even of the completely outcast among
   them
youth movements and camps
action against poverty and social injustices
the work of the Red Cross, aid to prisoners and to war victims, etc.

What disciples of the Bible initiated has often been copied or taken over by the state and by political groups when the religious influence has no longer been desired (or when that influence has simply faded out). But there can be no doubt as to the origin. There can plainly be seen the marked difference between Christian countries and non-christian in both standard of living and morality. And even among the first-named a contrast can immediately be noticed, in general, to the advantage of those countries where the people have the Bible, that is, the Protestant lands. Let anyone, for example, compare Northern and Southern Europe, Northern and Southern Ireland, English and French Canada, and Anglo-Saxon and Latin America, etc.[9]

"Blessed is the nation whose God is Jehovah" (Ps. 33:12).

Blessed is the country (if there is one!) which finds its inspiration solely in the Bible!

THE ETERNAL YOUTH OF SCRIPTURE

Being the Book of the eternal God, the Bible is bathed in an atmosphere of eternity. In a sense it is outside of time; and it hovers over the history of our race, our earth and our universe. Revealing the plan of the One who is the Alpha and the Omega, it leads us from eternity to eternity, from that which preceded the great beginning right up to the final consummation of all things.

Since it has never taught anything but the truth, it is the Book for all generations: the experiences of the very earliest ages serve as examples to us and are written for our instruction (I Cor. 10:11). Thus it is that Scripture never grows old. It reveals to us the heart of God and the heart of man in a way which is never outdated. What book of antiquity could endure comparison to it, on this point as on so many other points? All human books rapidly become "dated," so rapidly that textbooks used in one generation are cast aside promptly by the next (and these days are generally kept in use only a few years). Quite the contrary is true of God's Book in its entirety.

Moses edifies us today as does no other book written thirty-five hundred years ago. He brings us to know the sovereign God, who is the Creator and the holy and merciful One. His laws (for example, those of the Decalogue) take their origin from an incomparable and exemplary morality. The social state that he sets before us is superior to that of the most progressive nations and reformers. His precepts on hygiene astonish modern physicians. The worship, rich in imagery, and the priesthood which he depicts serve as the basis for the whole presentation of the gospel of Christ in the epistle to the Hebrews.

The psalmists speak the universal language of the heart—suffering, doubting, calling out for help, communing with God, triumphing and overflowing with joy. During World War I a soldier who came across the Psalms for the first time believed they had just come out and expressed astonishment that none of the newspapers of the day had made any mention of so exceptional and so timely an author!

The prophets seem also to have been writing for our very own age. Such writers as Isaiah, Jeremiah, etc., picture the exact conditions of our world and of believers, all the more strikingly since both their promises and their threats are still in the process of being fulfilled.

The Gospels, filled with the incomparable figure of Christ, have lost nothing of their freshness and purity. Imperishable jewels, they remain forever the most beautiful pages of world literature and those the most widely read.

Both *the Acts* and *the Epistles* serve to perpetually establish and to inspire the church of Jesus Christ.

Finally, *Revelation,* like the writings of the prophets, defies time and astounds every generation by its repeated fulfillments.

This ever living character is affirmed by Scripture itself: "Of old have I known from thy testimonies, that thou hast founded them for ever. Every one of thy righteous ordinances endureth for ever" (Ps. 119:152, 160). "Till heaven and earth pass away, one jot or one tittle shall in no wise pass away from the law, till all things be accomplished. Heaven and earth shall pass away, but my words shall not pass away" (Matt. 5:18; 24:35). "Having been begotten again . . . of incorruptible [seed] through the word of God, which liveth and abideth. . . . For . . . the word of the Lord abideth for ever" (I Peter 1:23-25).

We constantly experience afresh its perennial quality and testify that the Bible ever remains the Word of the Lord, which directly addresses itself to us, here and now.

The *inexhaustible character* of the biblical text is another demonstration of the same fact. A given Scripture passage never has its last word for us. We have read it perhaps dozens and dozens of times, very often with evident profit. Still, under different circumstances, it touches us anew, revealing to us some aspect of the truth up to then unnoticed. Every attentive, believing reader of Scripture is "like unto . . . a householder, who bringeth forth out of his treasure things new and old" (Matt. 13:52). If our heart is right in God's sight, we shall never meditate on the Word without discovering some new revelation in it. And the only way for a preacher to bring a living message, fresh and relevant to the times, is for him constantly to draw from the treasury of the Scriptures those things as new as they are fundamental.

THE UNIVERSALITY OF THE BIBLE

If the Bible is the Book for every epoch, it is also the Book for all men. It literally speaks to all peoples, languages, races and nations; to all ages—from childhood to old age; to all different types of personalities; to all social classes. Has it not had for its human authors the most varied people: shepherds, fishermen, unlettered men, priests, doctors of the law, a medical doctor, intellectuals, kings, statesmen, poets, prophets and historians? Thus it is that Scripture possesses a variety designed to answer to all needs and all tastes. In it is found every sort of writing: historical, juridical, legislative, social, moral, biographical, poetic, sententious, didactic, epistolary and prophetic.

> The lyrics of Greece and Rome are known only to the learned few. We may well ask How is it that the sorrows and joys, the difficulties and doubts, the aspirations and hopes of men, so apart in time and in clime, should find expression in the same songs [the Psalms]. . . . The most cultivated nations bow before it and learn as docile children from its inexhaustible pages; to the rudest tribes light and love are brought from its simple and powerful declarations. . . . While kings and philosophers find wisdom in this inspired volume, it is the companion of the artisan and merchant, the comfort of the widow, and instructor of the unlettered and uneducated. There is no age of man

> when it is not suitable. It gives milk to babes, guidance to the young, strength to men, and consolation to the aged. . . . It is an armory to those who are in battle, a storehouse to those who are lonely . . . a rod and staff to the dying.
>
> We are not surprised that the Bible has been called *the Book*. Sir Walter Scott, during his last illness, asked his son-in-law to read to him out of the Book. "What book?" was the question. And the great man's reply was "There is only one Book, the Bible."[10]

The only work written over a span of fifteen hundred years, the Bible is predestined to adapt itself to the most diverse periods in history. Right from the outset it has been the Book for the ages. It is, moreover, very striking that this most universal of books was produced by a little people set aside from all others, not distinguished at all in the domains of culture, art, philosophy, erudition, power or brilliance of civilization. Greece and Rome, so exceptional from all these points of view, have come far from originating anything like it. And, another remarkable fact, Israel herself has produced absolutely nothing analogous to it. What can we conclude except that the unique and universal character of Scripture is the miraculous product of a uniquely divine inspiration.

It may be suggested that the above declarations are the fruit of imagination and of a preconceived idea. Now this can easily be answered with tangible proofs. The world-wide diffusion of Scripture and the fact that well through the twentieth century it continues to be the top best seller cannot be denied. The entire Bible exists today in 236 languages intelligible to 90 percent of the population of the world. The New Testament has been translated into 289 other languages, spoken by another 5 percent of that same population. Isolated books of Scripture in more than 700 less important languages permit the reaching of another 3 percent of the inhabitants of the globe. The rest of the population—about 2 percent—represent limited groups (in New Guinea and Equatorial Africa and among Latin American Indians, for example), people whose languages have not yet been put into writing, places where there is total illiteracy (Ecumenical Press Service, 1965). To the above statistics 30 to 40 new translations are added every year. In 1962, 50 million Bibles and portions of Holy Scripture were distributed on five continents. A great effort is now under way to triple these figures. In Latin America alone, the distribution had passed 9 million copies in 1961 and 17 million in 1962. As for the gospel on records, the contemporary organization called Gospel Recordings has itself made records in more than three thousand languages and has freely distributed more than 5 million copies of them.

THE SUPERIORITY OF THE BIBLE OVER ALL OTHER RELIGIOUS BOOKS—JEWISH, CHRISTIAN AND PAGAN

Another supernatural character of Scripture stands out when one compares it to no matter what other book. Its real Author is manifestly greater than the human mind, for its message is infinite and eternal.

The Apocryphal books of the Old Testament, sometimes interesting from an historical point of view, are in every way inferior to the canonical writings. We have already cited the very definite opinion of Jerome on this point (p. 172). And Saphir has this to say on the subject: "Who that has tasted the old good wine could mistake for it the diluted and feeble work of man? What is the chaff to the wheat?"[11]

Comparing the sacred text to the sources of Assyrian and Babylonian history, Mr. von Niebuhr remarks:

> The Old Testament stands perfectly alone as an exception from the untruth of patriotism: it never conceals and disguises the calamities of the nation whose history it records. Its truthfulness is the highest in all historical writings—even for him who does not believe in its divine inspiration. At the same time I must also ascribe to it the most minute accuracy.[12]

What a contrast also appears between the Four Gospels and *the Apocryphal accounts of the life of Jesus!* "And how puerile are the miracles which tradition attributes to Him who, in all His doings, glorified and showed forth the Father!"[13] Moreover, John makes it clear that at Cana Jesus wrought His first miracle; thus those He supposedly did during His childhood are excluded (John 2:11).

> And the writings of the apostolic Fathers, beautiful and good as they are, only set forth more brightly the marvelous peculiarity of the inspired apostolic epistles, their inexhaustible depth,

their heavenly simplicity, their wonderful condensation, their transparent clearness, their universality, in short, their divine character.[14]

Neander makes the same remark:

A phenomenon, singular in its kind, is the striking difference between the writings of the apostles and those of the apostolic Fathers, who were so nearly their contemporaries. In other cases transitions are wont to be gradual, but in this instance we observe sudden change . . . a phenomenon which should lead us to acknowledge the fact of a special agency of the divine Spirit in the souls of the apostles and of a new creative element in the first period.[15]

It is, furthermore, most disconcerting to see how quickly the Fathers alienated themselves from Scripture and from the simplicity of the gospel. Two or three centuries after the time of the apostles, they had already initiated some of the deviations which were to distort the church in succeeding centuries. And what can we say of their flagrant errors in the realm of natural laws (see, earlier, chap. 14, subhead "Errors Avoided").

The Koran claims to have been brought from heaven to Muhammad, piece by piece, by the angel Gabriel. Containing a few pious sentences, together with a number of social preoccupations, it bears throughout the marks of a fallible, earthly mind. The mountains are supposed to have been created to keep the earth from moving, to hold it fast as with anchors and cables. Moses' sister Miriam is confused with the mother of Jesus (Sura 19:29). Several times Gabriel brings a special revelation from heaven to justify Muhammad: when he took the wife of his adopted son, when he tried to satisfy all the wives of his harem and when he appropriated as concubines his relatives and such other captives as pleased him (Sura 33:49-52, etc.). The Koran likewise establishes the permanent principle of the holy war and promises the faithful the most carnal of paradises. But the difference between the Koran and the Bible especially shines out in that which the Koran fails to say: the love of God which, in the incarnation, suffers with His creatures; the holiness which requires His punishment of sin; the expiation of transgressions on the cross; the full assurance of pardon; the regeneration which makes man new; and the spirituality and truth of the whole revealed message—all this is what is missing in the book of Muhammad; and by way of contrast, it is the lack of these which all the more provides proof of the divine quality of Scripture.

Neither can *the sacred books of the Hindus* hold up to comparison with the Bible, these Hindu books with their 330 millions of gods, one of the greatest of which, Shiva, is always and everywhere symbolized by the organ of reproduction; the supposition of hundreds of thousands of reincarnations in the form of beast or man, until such time as a nebulous nirvana delivers the individual by bringing an end to his every desire. Once again, in this we find a total absence of a real solution to the problem of sin and misery, of any moving out of the earthly into a pure, liberated life, of an absolute righteousness, and of a blessed and active eternal state in the presence of God.

Here is what we find in Hindu cosmogony: The moon is fifty thousand leagues higher than the sun; it shines with its own light; it animates our body. Night is caused by the sun's setting behind the mountain Someyra, situated in the middle of the earth, and several thousand miles high. Our earth is flat and triangular, composed of seven stages, each with its own degree of beauty, its own inhabitants and its own sea, the first of honey, another of sugar, another of butter, another of wine; in fine, the whole mass is borne on the heads of countless elephants, which, shaking themselves, cause earthquakes in this nether world![16]

For Plato, the world is an intelligent animal. The writings of *the Greek and Roman philosophers,* Aristotle, Seneca, Pliny, Plutarch and Cicero, so remarkable from a great many points of view, abound in declarations, even one of which would suffice to compromise forever our doctrines of inspiration if that error were found in any book of Holy Scripture.[17]

We could continue our comparison for a long time. But let us now limit it to *the divine restraint of the inspired texts.*

The Jews added the two *Talmuds* to Scripture, attributing to them the same divine authority; one of these (the Jerusalem) makes a big in-folio volume; the other (the Babylonian), of twelve in-folio volumes, is the one which scholars study and follow the most assiduously.

The Roman Church, at the Council of Trent, declared that it received "with the same affection and reverence . . . as Holy Scripture

... the traditions concerning faith and practice, that is, the immense repertory of her synodal acts, of her decretals, of her bulls, of her canons, and of the writings of the Holy Fathers."[18]

In that regard, Gaussen says: look at what the Holy Spirit has done in the Bible and admire the heavenly prudence of its inimitable brevity. The whole account of the creation of the world takes only thirty-one verses. The temptation, fall and condemnation of the race is given in twenty-four verses, although many chapters are used to describe the tabernacle and its sacrifices, prefiguring Jesus Christ and His work of redemption. Two chapters suffice to take humanity all the way from the fall to the deluge; then most of Genesis is devoted to the lives of the patriarchs, since they initiate the line that leads to the Messiah. The Ten Commandments and the sublime summary of them (Deut. 6:5; Lev. 19:18) have a good deal more to say about our duty toward God, parents, family, workers, foreigners, goods, life, rest, honor and truth than do all the works of antiquity put together.

Each of the Gospels recounts in 16 to 28 brief chapters—in only 800 lines—the life of Jesus Christ: His birth, youth, teachings, miracles, example, sufferings, death, resurrection and ascension. These facts are set down with such impartiality, reverence for God and man, restraint and truth that we ask again: Is this the way man goes about it to tell anything? Still, the evangelists were "men of like passions," and their hearts burned with love for their Master. How is it then that they could depict with so much calm, restraint, sobriety and apparent impassivity the wretched murder of the One whom they worshiped? And how could they so realistically bring out their own cowardice and carnal spirit, without rationalizing it or adding any further comments?

In *Acts*, Luke retraces in about thirty pages the thirty most beautiful years of Christianity. Again, what admirable restraint! Who but the Holy Spirit could have exhibited this conciseness, this choice of details, this sort of style—devout, brief and richly significant—making use of so few words but teaching so many truths? Add to all this the reserve and voluntary self-effacement of the historian, who can be seen nowhere except in the change of the personal pronoun (the "we" beginning in Acts 16:10). Still, throughout ten whole years Luke shared Paul's journeys and sufferings, from Troas to Jerusalem and Caesarea, and to Rome, from which place Paul cried out: "All forsook me. Only Luke is with me" (II Tim. 4:16, 11).

The thoughts just brought out were suggested by Gaussen; and, with him, we shall quote Origen again: "The sacred volumes breathe the plenitude of the Spirit; and there is nothing either in the prophets, or in law, or in gospel, or in apostle, which does not come down from the fulness of the majesty of God."[19]

CONCLUSION

For a man who can see, the existence of the sun presents no problem; neither do its light, rays and heat; but a blind man, being deprived of direct vision, can doubt everything about the sun if he wants to.

For the believer, the supernatural character of Scripture is more than evident. He knows it is by Scripture that he has come to the light: "Whereas I was blind, now I see!" He met God by means of it, and he has found through Christ pardon, new life and the assurance of eternal salvation. The prophecies have convinced him of the omniscience of the Author of the Book. In the mirror of the Word he has recognized the portrait of his own heart depicted by that One who is able to plumb its depths better than he himself can. Every day, moreover, he continues to experience the power, eternal freshness and universality of Scripture and its superiority over all that is human.

Yes, we cry out with the psalmist: "I delight in thy law. The law of thy mouth is better to me than thousands of gold and silver. My heart standeth in awe of thy words. I rejoice at thy word, as one that findeth great spoil. I have chosen thy precepts" (Ps. 119:70, 72, 161-162, 173).

Unfortunately, all this which to us is irrefutable proof seems not at all to touch the unbeliever. The same is true for him of the plain testimony of creation. "The heavens declare the glory of God; and the firmament showeth his handiwork" (Ps. 19:1). "For the invisible things of him [God] since the creation of the world are clearly seen, being perceived through the things that are made, even his everlasting power and divinity" (Rom. 1:20). Yet the vast majority of men do not glorify the living and true God. Many are the foolish ones who say in their hearts: "There is no God" (Ps. 14:1). Many also are the religious men, even some who claim to be Christians, who challenge God's other witness, the Bible. The reason, in many instances, is that there has been no new birth; and "the natural man receiveth not the things of the Spirit of God: for they are foolishness unto him . . . , because they are spiritually judged" (I Cor. 2:14). The case of Nicodemus shows us that this new birth may indeed be lacking even in the lives of religious leaders and of the "doctors in Israel" (John 3:3-10). Others, who may perhaps have had a better background, find themselves succumbing to the dangers mentioned by Paul: "Take heed lest there shall be any one that maketh spoil of you through his philosophy and vain deceit, after the tradition of men, after the rudiments of the world, and not after Christ" (Col. 2:8). "Guard that which is committed unto thee, turning away from the profane babblings and oppositions of the knowledge which is falsely so called; which some professing have erred concerning the faith" (I Tim. 6:20-21).

Thus we labor under no delusions. The universe is the great book of God for those who will to believe. The Bible is likewise His written Word, to such as receive by faith its testimony of life and power. The supernatural qualities of Scripture enumerated above cannot be, and we do not mean them to be, a rationalistic argument designed to spare our readers from having to exercise faith. On the contrary, we only conclude with Paul, and we repeat: "My speech and my preaching were not in persuasive words of wisdom, but in demonstration of the Spirit and of power: that your faith should not stand in the wisdom of men, but in the power of God" (I Cor. 2:4-5).

23

THE PREEMINENCE OF SCRIPTURE

GOD, THE SOURCE OF ALL AUTHORITY

THE WHOLE UNIVERSE must be in subjection to its sovereign Master, the Creator. He is the ultimate reality, the only source of life, truth and harmony. He is the infallible Legislator, whose spiritual, moral, and physical laws govern the world. "Jehovah is King for ever and ever" (Ps. 10:16). "Unto the King eternal, immortal, invisible, the only God, be honor and glory . . . the blessed and only Potentate, the King of kings, and Lord of lords" (I Tim. 1:17; 6:15).

Like all other creatures, man is dependent on this authority. His fall came about from the fact that he chose to free himself from it, so as to "be as God" and "despise dominion" (Gen. 3:5; II Peter 2:10). His salvation consists in complete submission to the King whom he has rebelled against and in reintegration into the kingdom, where it is the Lord who alone gives the commands and executes them, and who saves the offender.

THE AUTHORITY OF JESUS CHRIST

Christ, as God in the flesh, exerts throughout this world the sovereign rule of His Father. Right from the outset He taught as one having authority and not as the scribes (Mark 1:22).

He does not say as do the prophets: "The word of Jehovah came unto me, saying . . . Thus saith the Lord Jehovah," but rather: "Verily, I say unto you. . . . It was said by them of old time . . . but I say unto you. . . ."

"With authority and power he commandeth the unclean spirits" (Luke 4:36).

He has power (authority, *exousia*) on earth to forgive sins (5:24).

He exercises the same authority over sickness (6:19), death (8:53-55) and nature (Matt. 8:23-26).

God has given Him authority over all flesh, that He should give eternal life (John 17:2).

All judgment has been given to the Son (5:22).

In fact, all things have been given Him by His Father (Matt. 11:27). So He can declare "All authority hath been given unto me in heaven and on earth" (28:18).

Paul joyously exclaims: "In him ye are made full, who is the head of all principality and power" (Col. 2:10).

And John proclaims: "Now is come the salvation, and the power, and the kingdom of our God, and the authority of his Christ" (Rev. 12:10).

But this incontrovertible and absolute authority does not exert itself in any coercive way. Jesus presents Himself as a simple Man with "no beauty that we should desire him," with no royal diadem visible on His brow, and without diploma or priestly ordination (John 7:15), without riches or special social rank. He was even rejected by the chief priests and the elders of His own people, who impatiently demanded of Him: "By what authority doest thou these things? and who gave thee this authority?" (Matt. 21:23).

In fact, His authority is imperceptible except to faith. It results from His profound nature, the power and love which emanate from Him, and the presence of the Father who indwells Him. Devout Israelites that received the testimony of John the Baptist also perceived by what power Jesus acted (vv. 24-27). He spoke; and officers, stupefied, cried out: "Never man so spake" (John 7:46). He chased away demons, and simple souls were "astonished at the majesty of God" (Luke 9:43).

It is true that Christ set forth a number of proofs of His divine prerogatives: His own word, the miracles He did, the testimony from heaven by God the Father and, finally, the Scriptures (John 5:24, 31, 36, 37, 39). But He made this demonstration apart from any delusion or rationalistic intention: only the submissiveness of faith would really accept it. This is why He added: "If any man willeth to do his will [the will of Him who sent Me], he shall know of the teaching [or, the authority], whether it is of God, or whether I speak from myself" (John 7:17).

THE AUTHORITY OF SCRIPTURE

Source and definition. This authority is like that of Jesus Christ; it proceeds from its very nature. It is an immediate consequence of inspiration. If God entirely inspired Scripture (as we have seen that He did), then Scripture is vested with His authority. No other power could either bestow or take away that quality. The Book which repeats thousands of times "Thus saith the Lord!" commands reverence for its Author and obedience to Him. The French writer J. H. Merle d'Aubigné points out:

> The divine authority of the Scriptures and their inspiration are two distinct, but inseparable, truths. The authority of the Scriptures proceeds from their inspiration, and their inspiration establishes their authority; just as the tempering of the metal produces the steel, and the steel results from the tempering. If the authority of the Scriptures falls, their inspiration falls; if, on the contrary, it be the inspiration that is taken from us, the authority likewise vanishes away. The Scripture without inspiration is a cannon from which the charge has been removed.[1]

Someone may perhaps ask: "Isn't this begging the question? Doesn't it amount to reasoning in circles? You affirm that the Bible has authority because it is inspired and because God speaks in it. But this claim comes out of Scripture itself! Is it then inspired because it says it is inspired?" The reply to this objection is found in our earlier chapters, especially the one preceding this. We have been convinced of the divine inspiration of the Bible by its sublime revelation of God, of Jesus Christ and of man, so that we can no longer question it: in the Bible the Lord speaks, not the creature. The prophecies could have been produced only by the omniscient One, and the complete confirmation that Christ gave to Scripture is what has dictated our own attitude toward it. We heard the Word, and we believed (John 5:24; Rom. 10:17). There followed from this a profound experience of regeneration, pardon and new life, which has become our very existence, our true reason for living. And it is the inner witness of the Holy Spirit (Rom. 8:16) which produces this conviction and maintains it. As we have just said, we are fully convinced of this, not by any accumulation of human proofs or intellectual arguments, but by a "demonstration of the Spirit and of power" (I Cor. 2:4-5).

Gaussen tells how, feeling harassed by a thousand doubts, he had sought long in the apologetic writings, but had found no relief and no conviction or satisfaction in anything but the Bible itself.

That word gives testimony to itself, not only by its assertions, but by its effects. . . . It carries in its beams health, life, heat, and light. . . . Read the Bible then. . . . It is the Bible that will convince you. It will tell you whether it came from God. . . . The single reading of a psalm, of a story, of a precept, of a verse, of a word in a verse, will ere long attest the divine inspiration of all the Scriptures to you more powerfully than could have been done by all the most solid reasonings of doctors or of books.[2]

For anyone who by faith accepts the Scriptures as the Word of God, the matter is settled: the authority of the Bible is not to be defended, but affirmed (as in the case of the existence of God and of the excellence of Jesus Christ). C. H. Spurgeon said regarding this subject: "There is no need for you to defend a lion when he is being attacked. All you need to do is to open the gate and let him out!" As Dr. Martyn Lloyd-Jones puts it: It is the preaching and exposition of the Bible that really establish its truth and authority. There is nothing but the Bible, with its doctrine of the fall of man and of sin, that can really explain the whole world situation, as it is today after two major world wars. The same is true regarding the origin of the universe: after so much rationalism and materialistic science, some of our very great scientists are confessing that they have been forced to conclude that there has to be a great Mind, a great Architect behind the universe—the thing which the Bible has always asserted. But Bible critics have hated the doctrine of the fall and of sin. They have maintained that man develops and improves and constantly gets better and better. So it is only reluctantly that these men have come back to the notion of evil and of the ruin of the race. They are now doing it, constrained by the lessons of history, not from any persuasion regarding the authority of the Bible. For our part, it is precisely because of the authority of Scripture that we both believe and teach these things.[3]

Authority of the Scriptures in Israel. The book of the law, the revelation of the divine will, was the very basis of the covenant (Exodus 24:7). The task of the priests and Levites was to teach the law, and they based all their judgments on it (Deut. 17:9-11; 24:8). "For the priest's lips should keep knowledge, and they should seek the law at his mouth; for he is the messenger of Jehovah of hosts" (Mal. 2:7). The authority of the holy Book was exercised over

"every one that trembled at the words of the God of Israel"
(II Chron. 34:19; Ezra 9:4; Neh. 8:9, etc.). The psalmist cried out:
"My flesh trembleth for fear of thee; and I am afraid of thy judgments" (Ps. 119:120). Isaiah solemnly begins his prophecy with
these words: "Hear, O heavens, and give ear, O earth; for Jehovah
hath spoken." Then, observing the lamentable state of Israel, he
exclaimed: "To the law and to the testimony! if they speak not
according to this word, surely there is no morning for them" (1:2;
8:20). And Jeremiah adds: "Cursed be the man that heareth not
the words of this covenant, which I commanded your fathers"
(11:3-4).

The formidable authority of the law makes itself felt in the case
of all who have not been saved by grace and by faith in Christ:
"Cursed is every one who continueth not in all things that are written
in the book of the law, to do them" (Gal. 3:10). All sinners are
"convicted by the law as transgressors. For whosoever shall keep
the whole law, and yet stumble in one point, he is become guilty of
all" (James 2:9-10).

Jesus Christ submissive to the authority of Scripture. We have
already shown (chap 18, subhead "The Consistent Attitude of Christ
Toward Scripture") how Christ took care

> to authenticate the Scriptures without reservation (Matt. 5:17-18)
> to accomplish them down to the very smallest detail (Matt. 26:54;
> Luke 24:44)
> to reply to the adversary with nothing but "It is written" (Matt.
> 4:4-10)
> to set before all His opponents the sacred text: "Have ye not
> read, . . . Is it not for this cause that ye err, that ye know not the
> scriptures, nor the power of God?" (Matt. 12:3; Mark 12:24)
> to repeat, on the cross, the very words of the biblical prophecies
> which He was in the act of fulfilling (John 19:28-30)
> to base His teaching of the disciples, even after His resurrection,
> on all the parts of the Jewish canon (Luke 24:27, 44, 46)
> to announce that the final judgment will be on the basis of the
> Scriptures (John 5:45-47; cf. Rom. 2:12)

What more can we say except that the authority of the written

Word, reinforced by all the authority of the incarnate Word, cannot be broken (John 10:35).

The authority of Scripture in the early church. We have already treated this point in a general way (chap. 19) in our study of the testimony given to the Holy Scriptures by the apostles and by the New Testament. For them, there was no problem. From the moment that it was recognized as fully inspired, its absolute authority could not be questioned for an instant. Entirely submitted to the Scriptures, both the Old Testament and the New, the apostles were to be above all else mouthpieces of the Lord, charged with confirming and finishing the written revelation by presenting Christ to the world and to the church.

Servants of God throughout all the succeeding generations, being neither eyewitnesses of the resurrection nor authors of the sacred books, have been obliged to carry out their role in the church in submission to the revelation. Consequently, their authority has necessarily been different from that of the apostles, a lesser authority, in a sense. Timothy, though called upon to reprove, correct and instruct, was primarily to "preach the word" and to "do the work of an evangelist"—and this "according to sound doctrine" (the words "doctrine," "teaching" and "teacher" are used about thirty times in I and II Tim. and in Titus). It is all of the inspired Scriptures which will make the man of God mature, furnished completely for his ministry (II Tim. 3:16–4:3). Paul also said to Titus that the elder was to hold "to the faithful word" as it had been taught, so as to be able "both to exhort in the sound doctrine and to convict the gainsayers." Then he added: "Speak thou the things which befit sound doctrine. Speak and exhort and reprove with all authority. Let no man despise thee" (Titus 1:9; 2:1, 15). The role of the elder or of the bishop (cf. Acts 20:17, 28) is then to watch over the flock, feeding it with the Word of God, with an authority which rests entirely on Scripture and is guided by it. And if we ourselves carry out the functions of ambassadors for Christ, it is because God has "committed unto us the word of reconciliation," the word which can bind or unbind, giving life to some (those who accept it) and death to others (those who refuse it; II Cor. 5:19-20; 2:14-16).

It is clear that the sovereignty of the Lord is exerted in the church by the authority of the Scriptures in conjunction with that of the Spirit.

A few texts suffice, in fact, to show who gave the commands in the early church. It was by the Holy Spirit that the disciples, baptized and clothed with power, went everywhere as witnesses of Christ (Acts 1:5, 8). By Him, they received the capacity to tell the mighty words of God and to prophesy (2:4, 11, 17-18). The authority divested in them rested on the omnipotent name of Jesus and on the Scriptures, which always supported their testimony. (They would be asked: "By what power, or in what name, have ye done this?" Their reply is found in Acts 3:16, 18; 4:7-12.) They announced the Word of God with assurance because they were filled with the Spirit (4:31, 8). Any ministry, including that of deacons, lays claim to this same fullness (6:3, 5). The Spirit directs His servants (8:29; 10:19), He makes the church grow (9:31), He appoints new workers and sends them out (13:2, 4) and He imposes on them His infallible and strategic directives (16:6-10). At the time of the only "council" mentioned in the New Testament, the elders and the brethren, after comparing the words of the prophets in the Scriptures, both dared to say and could say this: "It seemed good to the Holy Spirit, and to us" (15:15, 23, 28).

Christ is the only Head of the church, and He has not given His priesthood over to anyone else (Eph. 1:22-23; Heb. 7:24-25). So it is He, the Head, who by the Spirit governs His body, gives to each one of His members a supernatural gift with a definite use for it in view, uses the members according to His will and nourishes them with His Word. From this biblical picture it is plain that authority can belong only to the Head: not in any way to the members, or to the body itself (the church), and not to a second head either (which does not exist!). Decrees of a religious community or deductions from the experience of some individual, therefore, could not be made into laws, or there would be usurpation.

PRIORITY FOR THE SCRIPTURES OR THE CHURCH?

For the Roman Church, there is no question here. According to Bellarmine, the authority of the Scriptures is founded on that of the church (*Conciliis*, Lib. II, chap. 12). The apostles, the authors of the New Testament, came out of the hierarchy of the church and were the expression of her authority. (This kind of reasoning cuts both ways, for Mark, Luke and James, and perhaps the author of the epistle to the Hebrews, were not apostles.) Consequently, they say, the church is the guardian of the Scriptures. The Bible can be rightly understood only as interpreted and explained by the clergy (hence, the indispensable notes in Catholic Bibles). Moreover, the church completed the Scriptures to suit herself when she added the Apocryphal books of the Old Testament (at the Council of Trent, in 1546) and when at the same time she decided that tradition, the decisions of the councils and, finally, the decrees of the infallible pope (this dating from 1870) constitute another source of her teaching.

Arguments are not lacking to show, on the contrary, the priority and sovereign authority of the Scriptures.

1. The church obviously did not produce the Old Testament; and we have just seen to what point Christ Himself, the apostles and the first Christians submitted themselves to its authority.

2. The church was raised up by the Word of God, which the apostles preached everywhere and which they preserved at the same time in the New Testament (I Thess. 2:13). Every believer was regenerated by the living, permanent Word of God (I Peter 1:23, 25).

3. A good part of the New Testament is devoted to the way in which the life of the church is to be regulated and maintained. The pastoral epistles, as well as I Corinthians and Galatians (not to mention the Acts and Revelation 2 and 3!) fix the constitution of the church and set themselves the task of correcting certain deviations already apparent during the first century. It is therefore the authority of Scripture which established the church and which made known what the church was really to be. The New Testament then cannot be made dependent on the institution which arose out of its pages.

4. In order to affirm her supremacy, Rome depends in her own way on the words of Christ. But where is she to look for them if not in the Gospels, that is to say, in the Bible?

5. Scripture existed before there were any church Fathers, councils or, of course, popes. It was only at a later time that the different books of the New Testament, written in the first century, were all recognized by the churches. Still, right from the start, their divine

inspiration existed, produced by the Lord, not by the church. In the end the church did nothing but bow before the inspiration of the apostolic writings. Now it is clear that the authority of a book comes from its author rather than from its guardians or its readers. (On the subject of the canon, see again chap. 15.) The epistles of Paul, for example, did not in any way wait for the imprimatur of the church. In the oft-cited text, the apostle praises the Thessalonians for having received his message as being truly the Word of God (I Thess. 2:13). He declares that whoever does not obey what is written is to be excommunicated (II Thess. 3:14). He recommends that his letters be brought to the attention of the brethren and of the churches (I Thess. 5:27; Col. 4:16). He dares to tell the Galatians that if an angel from heaven should contradict this letter, he should be accursed (Gal. 1:8)!

6. They say that, since it formed the canon, the church has authority over the Scriptures. But according to what has just been said, this is no more true than it would be for a judge to have authority over the law which he has received from the hands of a legislator. It is not he who created it. Once convinced of its authority, he limits his role to its defence and to its application. The church, then, is not the guardian but the servant of the Scriptures, not the mother but the daughter, not the author but the reader and interpreter, not the judge but the witness and the defender of the sacred text. If, outside of Scripture, some other source of authority were needed to authenticate it and to give it power over us, would not that other source itself need confirmation, and so on ad infinitum?[4] The same principle holds true in respect to those who are not satisfied with the miraculous birth of Christ. They invented the miraculous conception of Mary (who, however, was shown grace and who called God her Saviour, Luke 1:30, 47) without realizing, as it has been pointed out, that in such a case her grandmother, her great-grandmother and the whole line all the way back would also have needed to be conceived without sin.

7. The Scriptures were produced by men directly inspired by God. It is He, not the church, which has given this inspiration to them; consequently, it is from Him that they get their authority, completely sufficient for our faith to rest upon. Thus Paul declares that the church was built "upon the foundation of the apostles and prophets,

Christ Jesus himself being the chief corner stone" (Eph. 2:20). To be absolutely sure of the apostolic origin of the writings under consideration was the sole preoccupation of those who were agreed as to the constitution of the canon.

8. Any divine authority making itself felt on earth must be worthy of the Lord; that is, it must be stable and infallible. We see such an authority in the theocracy in Israel, the ministry of Jesus as depicted in the Gospels, and the work of the apostles in the drawing up of the New Testament. But Peter himself became reprehensible one day, meriting reproach for hypocrisy and dissimulation (Gal. 2:11-14). As for Paul, he separated from Barnabas and Mark following sharp dissension (Acts 15:37-39). Later, probably because of his poor eyesight, he became mistaken about the identity of the high priest (23:2-5). The pastoral epistles, II Peter, II John, Jude and Revelation 2—3 show how rapidly false prophets and false teachers have, in some cases, usurped authority in the church. This state of things only grew worse as the centuries went by: the church fathers expressed the most contradictory opinions; and absolutely unworthy popes and other religious leaders (the same is true among Protestants also—and this right down to our own day) have been men with no faith at all. Persecutions and monstrous wars have been instigated by ecclesiastical authorities, very many councils have been found to contradict themselves, and dogmas depending on tradition have always gone farther and farther away from the gospel. According to prophecy, the apostasy will come in to hold sway in the so-called religious world, ending up in Babylon, the false church (II Thess. 2:3-12; I Tim. 4:1; II Tim. 4:3-4; Rev. 17).

Foreseeing the disobedience and decadence of Israel, God had had the book of the law placed in the sanctuary as the standard and as the incorruptible witness to the conduct of the people (Deut. 31:24-27). We are convinced that all of the inspired Scripture has been likewise placed in reach of the church, which is continually tempted to slumber, to deviate from the truth and to become unfaithful. As we have already seen, Scripture is always there, not only as a norm, to show up any disobedience, but also as a lighthouse, to point out the right way, an inexhaustible source of life, revival and sanctification.

ATTACKS AGAINST THE AUTHORITY OF SCRIPTURE

The rebellious spirit of man. Created in the image of God and intended to dominate the earth, man possesses an unbelievably independent and ambitious spirit. It was through pride that he fell, through attempting to free himself from the control of the Creator. He was carried away by "the spirit that now worketh in the sons of disobedience" (Eph. 2:2). Above all, he finds it hard to admit his dependence, to recognize the limits of his reason and strength. Any "paternalism" rubs him the wrong way, even when he realizes that it is on the part of God.

All over the world, man makes a tremendous effort to liberate himself from any authority outside of himself. "Why do the nations rage, and the peoples meditate a vain thing? The kings of the earth set themselves, and the rulers take counsel together, against Jehovah, and against his anointed, saying, Let us break their bonds asunder, and cast away their cords from us" (Ps. 2:1-3). This revolt is what produced the cross: "We will not that this man reign over us!" (Luke 19:14). The same rebellious spirit is now striking at the Scriptures, which are hated because of their authority. For the Bible, the Word of God, is the greatest obstacle to what humanity likes to call her "emancipation." The Antichrist is to appear, whom Paul calls "the wicked one," or, actually, "the lawless one" (Greek, *anomos,* II Thess. 2:8). How troublesome the Bible is, reminding the conscience of the indefeasible rights of God and announcing the imminency of the final great assize! The first temptation was a frontal attack against the Word and its authority: "Hath God said?" (Gen. 3:1). Knowing that his time is short, the enemy is now mobilizing all his forces against the indestructible rock of revelation.

Authorities ranged in conflict. Numerous forces vie for authority. Let us consider these.

1. God or man. In all the world there are only two religions: God's, offering redemption by Jesus Christ; and man's, encompassing all the systems based on the inventions and merits of the creature, who wants to save himself by his own efforts. So only two authorities are in opposition: God, Christ and the Bible; and man.

Having already spoken of the first, let us look more closely at the second. It is, in short, a question of a struggle between two sovereignties. God, our Creator and our Saviour, has every right to us. In order to free us and to make us eternally happy, He wants to reign without a rival over our hearts and souls and even over our thoughts. Man fights this claim as much in the realm of religion as in that of reason, science, morality or politics. Humanity constantly succumbs to the temptation to say: "I shall be mistress for ever. . . . I am, and there is none else beside me" (Isa. 47:7-8). Basically, it prefers to adore and serve the creature (itself) rather than the Creator (Rom. 1:25).

With reason made autonomous, science atheistic, morality unregulated, and politics wholly pagan, man, having transformed each of these domains into a new religion—an ideology, to use the modern term—believes he has achieved complete freedom. Far from having escaped all authority, he has simply chosen another one, characterized by its own pontiffs, fanaticism and infallibility. On the plane that concerns us here, the different currents which run counter to the sovereignty of the Word of God all have their source in that same resistance of man to his Creator's will.

2. Authority of the church. In various forms, this tendency tries to push aside, share or diminish the authority of the Scriptures. The pope is proclaimed the only infallible head of the church on earth; the Apocryphal books are added to the canon, to support doctrines not found in it; Scripture is submitted to the authority of the church, and its interpretation depends entirely on the church. The teaching of the church claims to be based on the unanimous opinion of the church fathers, but such unanimity does not exist. Tradition, the decisions of the councils, and the ex cathedra declarations of the pope being put on the same plane as Scripture, the Word of God can be added to at will. The biblical criticism recently authorized by Rome (See the notes in the Jerusalem Bible!) does not have so significant an effect as does criticism among Protestants, for it does not attack the supreme authority of the church.

As for the Orthodox church, also proclaiming herself infallible, she bases her doctrine, not only on Scripture, but also on the decisions of the seven first councils spoken of as ecumenical (already far removed from Scripture in many respects).

3. Authority of religious and critical reason. Beyond expression is the sense of relief with which some theologians have freed them-

selves from the "straitjacket" of an infallible Bible, as they have substituted for it their own reasonings. Professor Brunner says this in the most unmistakable way: "In earlier days this discussion used to be cut short by saying briefly 'It is written'; that is, with the aid of the doctrine of verbal inspiration. Today we can no longer do this, even if we would."[5] "A simple reproduction of 'the' doctrine of the Bible is impossible. . . . Even behind the most primitive forms of Christian teaching, behind the teaching of Jesus and of the apostles, 'sound doctrine' is always something which has to be sought." He maintains that we can no longer identify the Bible as the "Word" of God because the notion of "Word of God" now constitutes a problem in itself.[6]

The Belgian writer S. Van Mierlo explains very well the reason for such an attitude. He says:

> Modern theologians condemn "authoritarian religions" and will not permit any authority outside of man to be imposed on men. But they themselves end up with this kind of religion. For if all Scripture is not inspired by God, if it is in large measure made up of documents of doubtful value, brought together by unknown authors, how is the believer not versed in criticism going to make up his mind? How will he understand where the Bible is simply giving the human opinions of certain august personages? So each man has to consult the theologians to find out what texts he can have confidence in and how he is supposed to regard them. But since these critics often differ among themselves, he will then have to decide on one among them. Thus the selected one will become the voice of authority. So it turns out that while the authority of God is rejected, that of man is accepted.[7]

And what happens when the great theologian chosen as master of a man's thinking changes and even goes so far as to contradict what he has taught; or when he has merely lost his popularity and is replaced by a new authoritarian figure as fallible as himself?

There are those who can see no problem in this. The very character of faith, as they look at the matter, requires liberty, which would no longer be guaranteed if the revelation were to impose on us ready-made facts as authoritative. So then there have to be errors, contradictions, legends and myths in order for us to be certain that a given passage expresses a truth. Thus the "risk of faith" is assured by the method of doubt. The reader will be able to sense by means of his "religious conscience" that which is true in the text; and he can discern by the Holy Spirit whether or not a given text is to become "the word of God" for him (even if, in fact, it contains a mistake or a legend). Such subjectivity, wholly without controls, would leave us with no assurance or certainty whatsoever. Need we say that this "method of doubt" is diametrically opposite to faith? It induces the reader to approach everything with diffidence and to reject whatever does not happen to appeal to him.[8] As Dr. T. Samuel Külling reminds us: "Everything depends on our point of departure: is the book we have to do with divine, or is it simply human? A divine book calls for an attitude of confidence, not one of diffidence."[9]

In his book already alluded to, J. I. Packer expresses himself as follows:

> Now . . . we are in a position to appreciate the fundamental cleavage between so-called "Fundamentalists" and their critics. The latter are, in fact, subjectivists in the matter of authority. Their position is based on an acceptance of the presuppositions and conclusions of ninteenth-century critical Bible study which are radically at variance with the Bible's own claims for itself. On this basis, they think it necessary to say—indeed, to insist—that some scriptural assertions are erroneous. They say we must use our Christian wits to discern between the fallible words of fallible men and the eternal truth of God. But this makes it impossible to regard Scripture as authoritative without qualification: what is now authoritative is not Scripture as it stands, but Scripture as pruned by a certain type of scholarship—in other words, human opinions about Scripture. It is true that these critics pay lip-service to the principle of biblical authority, but their view of the nature of Scripture effectively prevents them from doing so. . . . Their view really amounts to saying that the question of authority is now closed; the supreme authority is undoubtedly Christian reason, which must hunt for the word of God in the Bible by the light of rationalistic critical principles.[10]

D. Martyn Lloyd-Jones, one of the best English theologians, writes:

> We are told that we must accept and believe in the *message* [of the Bible] but that we can ride very loosely to the *facts*. I came across an instance of this the other day. . . . In an article

dealing with a story from the book of Daniel, the writer comments: "We do not think it matters a great deal whether this story is literally true, or a splendid parable for all generations of men." That is typical of this whole attitude. The facts really do not matter very much. What counts is the spiritual message, the teaching. . . .

It is often claimed that this is an essentially new position. But, surely, if you stop to analyze what they say, you must come to the conclusion that basically it is still the same old position. For the questions which immediately arise are these: Who decides what is true? Who decides what is of value? How can you discriminate between the great facts which are true and those that are false? How can you differentiate between the facts and the teaching? How can you separate this essential message of the Bible from the background in which it is presented? Not only so, but there is certainly no such division or distinction recognized in the Scripture itself. . . . There is no hint, no suspicion of a suggestion that parts of it are important and parts are not. . . .

In other words, the modern position amounts to this, that it is man's reason that decides. You and I come to the Bible and we have to make our decisions on this basis of certain standards which are obviously in our own minds. We decide that one portion conforms to the message which we believe, and that another does not. In spite of all the talk about a new situation today, we are still left with the position that man's knowledge and man's understanding are the final arbiters and the final court of appeal. That was precisely the position of the old Liberalism.

However, some would put the case a little differently. They would say that you must recognize as the Word of God that which speaks to you. When something in the Bible speaks to your condition, it is the Word of God; and when it does not, it is not the Word of God. That, of course, is just to put yourselves into a thoroughly subjective position. It still leaves man in control; man is still the authority who decides what is truly the Word of God and what is not.

Another form which the modern attitude sometimes takes is the suggestion that those of us who are Conservative Evangelicals are "Bibliolators," that is, we put the Scriptures in the place of the Lord. Their own authority, these critics tell us, is not the Scriptures, but the Lord Himself. Now this sounds very impressive and very imposing at first, as if they were but stating that for which we ourselves are contending. It sounds as if it were a highly spiritual position until, again, you begin to examine it carefully. The obvious questions to put to those who make such statements are these: "How do you know the Lord? What do you know about the Lord, apart from the Scriptures? Where do you find Him? How do you know that what you seem to have experienced concerning Him is not a figment of your own imagination, or not the product of some abnormal psychological state, or not the work perchance of some occult power or evil spirit?" It sounds all very impressive and imposing when they say "I go directly to the Lord Himself." But we must face the vital question concerning the basis of our knowledge of the Lord, our *certainty* with respect even to His authority, and how we are to come into practical possession of it.[11]

4. Authority of "Science." Sometimes it is the fear of not appearing scientific enough which drives theologians to abandon the authority of Scripture. For many, modern science has become the supreme authority, for fear of which even some evangelicals are being tempted to make totally needless concessions. "Still," continues Dr. Lloyd-Jones (a medical doctor as well as a theologian) :

If you study the history of science, you will have much less respect for its supposed supreme authority than you had when you began. It is nothing but a simple fact of history to say that a hundred years ago and less scientists were teaching dogmatically and with extreme confidence that the thyroid gland, the pituitary gland, and other glands were nothing but vestigial remains. They said that they had no value and no function whatsoever. . . . But today we know that these glands are essential to life. Without arguing in detail about scientific matters, I say that it is not only lacking in faith and unscriptural, but it is ignorant to accord to "Science," "Modern Knowledge," or "Learning" an authority which they really do not possess. Let us be scientifically skeptical with regard to the assertions of "Science." Let us remember that so many of their assertions are mere suppositions and theories which cannot be proved, and which may very well be disproved, as so many have been disproved during the past hundred years.[12]

5. The "inner light." The dissociation of Scripture from the

action and illumination of the Holy Spirit in the heart is yet another danger which we need to reiterate. In the seventeenth century the Quakers thought of the inner light as preeminently important, this being the ultimate witness of the Spirit to the experience of the individual. This attitude practically inclined some to minimizing the role and authority of the Scriptures, and there were even those who went so far as to say that the Scriptures are not necessary. Moreover, an "inspired" declaration of a brother in the assembly was granted the same validity as the sacred text. One can easily see where this line of thought could lead.

We have known people in our own times who have spoken in just about the same way. The excessive preeminence given to the Holy Spirit in their devotions and their preoccupation with gifts, ecstasies, and "prophecies" has tended to neglect of the Scriptures. Why be tied to a Book out of the past when one can communicate every day with the living God? But this is exactly the danger point. Apart from the constant control of the written revelation, we soon find ourselves engulfed in subjectivity; and the believer, even if he has the best intentions, can rapidly sink into deviations, illuminism or exaltation. Let each remind himself of the prohibition of taking anything away from Scripture or adding anything to it (Deut. 4:2; Rev. 22:18-19). Almost every heresy and sect has originated in a supposed revelation or a new experience on the part of its founder, something outside the strictly biblical framework. Once again we must emphasize that the Holy Spirit will always lead, teach and sanctify the child of God in line with and by means of the Word of truth, which He Himself inspired.

6. Risk of confusing illumination and inspiration. When speaking earlier of the illumination needed to understand the Bible (chap. 17), we saw that there are those who confuse this with inspiration. Now infallibility was granted only to the sacred writers as the Lord's representatives in the drawing up of the original manuscripts. When the synagogue or the church granted an equal, or even a greater, authority to the commentators on the Scriptures, they were obviously usurping their rightful place.

Let us cite in more detail what Gaussen writes about the Jews:

> They have considered the rabbins of the successive ages of the Dispersion as endowed with an infallibility which put them on

a level with (if not above) Moses and the prophets. They have, to be sure, attributed a kind of divine inspiration to Holy Scripture; but they have prohibited the explanation of its oracles otherwise than according to their traditions (Talmud, Mishna, Gemara). . . . "My son," says Rabbi Isaac, "learn to pay more attention to the words of the scribes than to the words of the law." "Turn away your children," said Rabbi Eleazar, on his deathbed, to his scholars, who asked him the way of life, "turn away your children from the study of the Bible, and place them at the feet of the wise." "Learn, my son," says the Rabbi Jacob, "that the words of the scribes are more agreeable than those of the prophets."[13]

The Roman Church, as we mentioned earlier, fell into the same confusion. The infallible Council of Trent (first decree, session four) ordered that all the books of the Old and New Testaments be honored, since God is their Author, "and together with them the Traditions relating to faith as well as manners, as having been dictated by the mouth of Jesus Christ or of the Holy Ghost, and preserved in the Catholic Church by continual succession. If anyone receive not the whole of the said books, with all their parts, as holy and canonical . . . or knowingly despises the said traditions, let him be accursed!"[14] Bellarmine, an officially recognized church dogmatician, declared: "The Holy Scriptures do not contain all that is necessary to salvation and are not sufficient. . . . They are obscure. . . . It is not for the people to read the Holy Scriptures. We must receive with obedience of faith many things that are not in the Scriptures."[15] One finds, moreover, in Gaussen extracts from the bulls of Clement XI (Sept. 8, 1713) and of Leo XII (1824) opposing the reading of the Bible in the vernacular. Leo XII complained bitterly of the Bible Societies, "which violate the traditions of the Fathers and the Council of Trent, by circulating the Scriptures in the vernacular tongues of all nations. . . . In order to avert this pest, our predecessors have published several constitutions . . . tending to show how pernicious for the faith and for morals this perfidious institution is."[16]

Although such "infallible" texts have never been rescinded, it can, fortunately, be stated that more recently Catholic priests have encouraged the study of the Bible. It is nonetheless true that it is dangerous at any time to oppose the unique authority of Holy

Scripture. And how many do exactly that for which Jesus repri-manded His contemporaries in the words: "Ye have made void the word of God because of your tradition" (Matt. 15:1-9) !

3. *The danger of bibliolatry.* We come back to this theme, touched upon in chapter 13 (subhead "A belief in inerrancy brings a danger of 'bibliolatry' ") , summing up a few pertinent remarks about it by Adolph Saphir in *Christ and the Scriptures.*

To the one who exalts the authority of the Bible over anything else, the temptation may crowd in to put the Bible, in a way, in the place of God Himself. So bibliolatry would be the tendency to sep-arate the Book from the person of Christ and from the Holy Spirit, and thus to substitute the written text for Him who alone is the light and guide of believers. To transfer to this dead book our faith, reverence and affection would surely come under the category of idolatry.

The example of *the Jews* can help us at this point. They con-sidered Scripture to be the Word of God. They reverenced its very letter, guarding it with scrupulous care and making it the object of indefatigable study. They were zealous defenders of the "oracles of God" and prided themselves on their possession of such a treasure. How was it then that they could not understand the living Word, Jesus Christ, or recognize that He is the exact realization of the por-trait of the Messiah delineated by Moses and the prophets? The Lord Himself explained this: They thought that in the Scriptures they had eternal life, but they did not have the Word of God abiding in them. They reverenced the letter of the sacred text, but they did not recognize Him who is the very substance of it. They believed in a most orthodox way in the authority of Scripture and defended it with great zeal, but they absolutely failed to comprehend its spirit-ual sense. What a tragic and lamentable possibility: to believe in the Bible and yet to reject Christ; to glory in the written Word, and at the same time to cast the Lord out of the sacred city; to hold the Bible in one hand while crucifying Jesus with the other hand!

Is this not bibliolatry? These men had put the Bible in the place of God, who speaks in and by that Book. They thought that instead of a living Lord guiding and influencing them, they now had a Book which contained everything, and that all that was needed was to interpret it correctly. A similar danger could threaten us too if we did not take care to avoid it: that of believing that the Bible contains the truth without really believing the truth which it contains.

The true Israelite looked on the Scriptures as the way that led him to God, the means which He employs to teach, sanctify and comfort; the text-worshiper substitutes the Bible for God so that the Book to him becomes a way of getting along without God. Has not one rabbi put it like this: "God, having given us the law, no longer has the right to interfere by producing new revelations"? Under the pretence of honoring the Bible, such men virtually treated God as though He had ceased to dwell in the midst of His people.

The church herself is in danger of losing sight of the existence of the Holy Spirit, of forgetting that it is on Him alone that she depends, and of putting the Book or her own decrees in the place of the Lord. And now commences man's dominion, by means of manuals, catechisms, commentaries and interpretations. It is trusting to the Spirit's teaching *in* the Book instead of to the Spirit's teaching *by* the Book. Men hope soon to get the teaching all summed up, simplified, reduced to a system and methodized. And then, for all practical purposes, the interpretation of the church and the creed are put above the Bible, which consequently becomes neglected, scarcely opened any more. This is indeed the tendency rooted in man: to substitute shadow for substance, the form for the fullness, rules for life and dead things for the living God; to deify brazen serpents (II Kings 18:4), Bible doctrines (divorced from life) and past experiences.

The easy way is to trust in commentators, interpreters and casuists. One finds the text obscure but the commentary distinct. The text seems severe, but the casuist accommodating. The text is profound and many-faceted, whereas the superficial interpreter is actually an over-simplifier. The text demands inward truth and has in view the operation of a radical cure; tradition has slight, ineffectual means of healing the hurt of the daughter of my people! In time one comes to regard tradition as more precious, more necessary and more practical than the Bible. And this is natural: if one considers the Bible apart from the living God and as a substitute for Him, an exact and detailed interpretation of the code becomes more important than the code itself.[17]

As for ourselves, are we threatened by bibliolatry? Along with believing in the inspiration of the Bible, do we unreservedly submit ourselves to the sovereignty of its Author? Glorying as we do in the Bible, have we taken on us the yoke of its message, as it has come to us straight from the living God? Or, having lost contact with the Spirit, are we possibly continuing to read a text which no longer speaks to us as it did before, one that has actually become, for all practical purposes, a substitute for the Lord's voice? In such a case, has not the written page again become nothing but the letter of the law, to condemn and to kill, since none but the Spirit can give life?

On the other hand, can it be said that the danger of bibliolatry arises out of faith in the inerrancy of Holy Scripture? Absolutely not, for that is an entirely different consideration.

> If the Bible finds its true and vital integration only in the Person of our Lord Jesus Christ, then there can be no bibliolatry in any form. . . . For Scripture, great as it is, is never to be equated with Deity. In all its perfection and truth, it is still a creature, albeit unique among books. According to its own self-witness, it is an instrument of the living God—the sword of the Spirit, the seed incorruptible whereby we are born again, the law of the Lord that converts the soul, the mirror in which we see ourselves in the blazing light of God's truth, the hammer that crushes our hardness of heart. But, great as it is, it is an instrument, an inspired and unique means to an end, not an end in itself. . . . It can never in and of itself be the object of worship any more than God's other book, the book of Nature, can ever be the object of worship.[18]

We have no need to emphasize again (see chap. 13, subhead "Inerrancy produces a paper pope") the accusation sometimes made that those who hold to the absolute inspiration of Scripture have replaced the pope at Rome by a *paper pope*. According to this, some have thus done away with the Lordship of Christ and have made God the prisoner of a book.

Plainly there is no trace of such a hiatus in the Bible. God based all His authority over Israel on the law, as Jesus Christ based His on Scripture and on His Word, shortly to become the New Testament. The Bible remains God's instrument, which in no case could usurp His place. A paper pope would be an inert word, a text lying dormant in the pages of a book. As we have abundantly observed, Scripture always remains living and dynamic; it opens up and communicates to us only if the Holy Spirit illumines and convinces us. When, in accordance with God's command, we submit ourselves to His written revelation, we actually are bowing to His authority as a person. Those who challenge this authority are the ones who are really submitting to another "pope," that is to say, to the fallible reason of man.

FRUITS OF THE AUTHORITY OF SCRIPTURE

Freedom. The unconditional return to the sovereign authority of Scripture was the great objective of the Reformers. Their motto is also ours: Scripture alone and the whole of Scripture. The rediscovery of this set believers free from all the usurpations, superstitions and impoverishments of the earlier centuries. Jesus promised exactly this to all who would accept His clear message: "If ye abide in my word, then are ye truly my disciples; and ye shall know the truth, and the truth shall make you free" (John 8:31-32).

Unity. The authority of Scripture, moreover, assures the spiritual unity of all those submitted to it. For evangelical Christians, this decisive argument prevails: "It is written!" Such stand ready to confess together the whole plain teaching of Scripture, which is considerable. They may differ on secondary matters and on questions of interpretation (Phil. 3:15-16). But they are absolutely assured that they have the same Bible, the same Christ and the same message to deliver to the world. We saw the demonstration of this in our chapter "The Testimony of the Church to the Inspiration of the Bible," as well as in the one dealing with "The Canon." Christianity ceased to present a united front when all kinds of authorities within itself supplanted the dictum of the Scriptures, the infallible Word of God. There is still a great deal more for evangelical believers to do to manifest their fundamental unity. For them also there sounds the clarion call: "To the law and to the testimony!" (Isa. 8:20). Minor differences will no longer stand out so prominently, and the whole body of Christian believers will bring glory to the One who consistently speaks to us in His Word when this motto is really adopted: "Scripture alone, and the whole of Scripture!"

Authority. Without paradox we can say that the believer submitted to the authority of Scripture himself becomes clothed with a part of that same authority. The Bible for him is truly the sword of the Spirit, sharp, two-edged, which he may wield both against himself and against the enemy. Without hesitation or mental reservation he can declare: "It is written! Thus saith the Lord!" With Paul he knows that what he preaches is verily the Word of God (I Thess. 2: 13). Like his Master—because he is delivering its infallible message—he teaches "as having authority, and not as the scribes" (Mark 1:22). Whenever he feels weak and trembling, taking refuge behind the Book, he can maintain: "This Word is not from me, but from God!" In short, he is an effective ambassador because he speaks "as though God were entreating by him" (II Cor. 5:18-20). He dares to declare the whole counsel of God; and he must do so, holding back nothing (Acts 20:27). He knows that his work will not be in vain in the Lord, because the divine Word which he has proclaimed can never return unto Him void (Isa. 55:11).

A free choice. One thing is certain: God, source of all power and sovereignty, does not force us (for the time being) to bow before Him. His revelation does not brainwash us: it does speak to our hearts, calling for the free response of our faith (cf. Acts 17:17). His authority is likewise offered us with no coercion. Now is the hour of divine grace and patience. Blessed are they who, abandoning the slavery of evil and of rebellious imaginations, voluntarily choose liberty in submitting to Christ and to His marvelous Word: "Thanks be to God, that, whereas ye were servants of sin, ye became obedient from the heart to that form of teaching whereunto ye were delivered" (Rom. 6:17)! And Paul adds: "Casting down imaginations, and every high thing that is exalted against the knowledge of God, and bringing every thought into captivity to the obedience of Christ" (II Cor. 10:5).

It is evident, however, that the patience of God is going to come to an end. The hour is approaching when every knee shall bow before Him. A terrible fate is in store for those who would not have Him to reign over them (Luke 19:14, 27). True it is that Christ, who came not to judge the world but to save it, added these words: "He that rejecteth me, and receiveth not my sayings, hath one that judgeth him: the word that I spake, the same shall judge him in the last day" (John 12:48).

CONCLUSION

We could go on indefinitely with the study of this great theme of the written revelation, for we are far from having exhausted it. We must, however, bring it to a close, to give each one time to reflect personally on the truths set forth. It is also time now for each one to take the step that goes on from theory to practice. The God of love, the sovereign Master, the great Judge, indeed longs to reveal Himself. Our part is to remain still, so as to reverently drink in each word which proceeds from His lips; then to obey this word and, finally, to pass on to the waiting world all these glorious truths.

Speak, Lord, thy servants hear!

"Every scripture [is] inspired of God" (II Tim. 3:16).

"Blessed is the man . . . [whose] delight is in the law of Jehovah; . . . on his law doth he meditate day and night. . . . Whatsoever he doeth shall prosper" (Ps. 1:1-3).

"Open thou mine eyes, that I may behold wondrous things out of thy law. Thou teachest me thy statutes. Let my tongue sing of thy word" (Ps. 119:18, 171-172).

"My word . . . that goeth forth out of my mouth . . . shall not return unto me void" (Isa. 55:11).

"Sanctify them in the truth: thy word is truth" (John 17:17).

"Do all things without murmurings and questionings: that ye may become blameless and harmless, children of God without blemish in the midst of a crooked and perverse generation, among whom ye are seen as lights in the world, holding forth the word of life" (Phil. 2:14-16).

FOOTNOTES

PART I

CHAPTER 1

1. G. T. Manley, *The New Bible Handbook*, p. 6.
2. See P. E. Hughes, *Scripture and Myth*, pp. 21-24.
3. Cf. René Pache, *The Future Life*, trans. Helen Needham, pp. 270-74.

PART II

CHAPTER 4

1. Adolphe Monod, *Farewells*, pp. 154-61.
2. Louis Gaussen, *La véritable doctrine de M. Gaussen sur l'inspiration des Ecritures, Trois Lettres*, p. 13.

PART III

CHAPTER 5

1. Erich Sauer, *From Eternity to Eternity*, p. 107.
2. B. B. Warfield, *The Inspiration and Authority of the Bible*, p. 163.
3. Louis Gaussen, *The Inspiration of the Holy Scriptures*, trans. David D. Scott, pp. 116-17.

CHAPTER 6

1. Louis Gaussen, *The Inspiration of the Holy Scriptures*, trans. David D. Scott, p. 280.
2. Ibid., p. 296.
3. Cf. Roland de Pury, *Qu'est-ce que le protestantisme?* pp. 38 ff.
4. Cf. Rudolf Bultmann, *Kerygma and Myth*, trans. Reginald H. Fuller; Bultmann, *The Theology of the New Testament*, trans. Kendrick Grobel; P. E. Hughes, *Scripture and Myth*.
5. Quoted by R. A. Finlayson, cited in Carl F. H. Henry, ed., *Revelation and the Bible*, p. 129.
6. Cf. Gertrud Wasserzug, *Gottes Wort Ist Gottes Wort*, p. 39.
7. Frank E. Gaebelein, *The Meaning of Inspiration*, pp. 9-10.
8. Robert Preus, *The Inspiration of the Scriptures*.
9. James I. Packer, *Fundamentalism and the Word of God*.
10. Ibid., pp. 78 ff.
11. Cf. Preus, pp. 67 ff., 195 ff.
12. B. B. Warfield, *The Inspiration and Authority of the Bible*, pp. 421-22.
13. Louis Gaussen, *La véritable doctrine de M. Gaussen sur l'inspiration des Ecritures, Trois Lettres*, pp. 17, 2-3.
14. Warfield, p. 173.
15. Packer, pp. 178-79.
16. Adolph Saphir, *Christ and the Scriptures*, pp. 74-80.
17. Erich Sauer, *From Eternity to Eternity*, pp. 104-5.
18. Dr. André Lamorte, *La nature de l'inspiration des Ecritures*, pp. 22 ff.
19. Edward J. Young, *Thy Word Is Truth*, p. 15.

CHAPTER 7

1. B. B. Warfield, *The Inspiration and Authority of the Bible*, p. 173.
2. Frank E. Gaebelein, *The Meaning of Inspiration*, p. 9.
3. Louis Gaussen, *The Inspiration of the Holy Scriptures*, trans. David D. Scott, pp. 23-28.
4. Calov, cited in R. Preus, *The Inspiration of the Scriptures*, p. 45.
5. T. C. Hammond, *Inspiration and Authority*, pp. 12-13.
6. Charles Hodge, cited in Edward J. Young, *Thy Word Is Truth*, p. 96.
7. Erich Sauer, *From Eternity to Eternity*, p. 103.
8. Ibid.
9. Ibid., pp. 100-102.

CHAPTER 8

1. Cf. B. B. Warfield, *The Inspiration and Authority of the Bible*, pp. 299-300.
2. Cited in Carl F. H. Henry, ed., *Revelation and the Bible*, p. 140.
3. James I. Packer, *Fundamentalism and the Word of God*, pp. 88-89.
4. Edward J. Young, *Thy Word Is Truth*, pp. 40-41.

CHAPTER 9

1. Adolph Saphir, *Christ and the Scriptures*, pp. 84-85.

CHAPTER 10

1. For the developments of this chapter, we owe much to Roger Nicole's excellent chapter "New Testament Use of the Old Testament," *Revelation and the Bible*, ed. Carl F. H. Henry, pp. 137-51.
2. C. H. Toy, cited in ibid., p. 138.
3. Roger Nicole, "New Testament Use of the Old Testament," *Revelation and the Bible*, ed. Carl F. H. Henry, p. 140.
4. Nicole, pp. 146-48.
5. Cf. Louis Gaussen, *The Inspiration of the Holy Scriptures*, trans. David D. Scott, pp. 161-64.
6. Cf. B. B. Warfield, *The Inspiration and Authority of the Bible*, p. 143.
7. Toy, cited in Nicole, p. 151.
8. R. Rothe, cited in ibid.
9. E. Huehn, cited in ibid.

CHAPTER 13

1. Frank E. Gaebelein, *The Meaning of Inspiration*, passim.
2. Cf. R. A. Finlayson, as cited in *Revelation and the Bible*, ed. Carl F. H. Henry, pp. 223-24.
3. Cf. quotations by Albert Lüscher, *Wenn das Wort nicht mehr soll gelten*, p. 31.
4. Suggested by Gaebelein, pp. 16-22. Translator's note: See also E. R. Thiele, *The Mysterious Numbers of the Hebrew Kings*.
5. See N. B. Stonehouse and Paul Woolley, eds., *The Infallible Word*, pp. 198-99.
6. Cited in Lüscher, p. 64.
7. Ibid., p. 16.
8. J. K. S. Reid, *The Authority of Scripture*, p. 279.
9. S. Van Mierlo, *La révélation divine*, p. 234.
10. Heinrich Vogel, cited in R. A. Finlayson, *Revelation and the Bible*, ed. Carl F. H. Henry, p. 227.
11. Ibid.
12. B. B. Warfield, *The Inspiration and Authority of the Bible*, pp. 179-80.
13. Cited by Finlayson in Henry, p. 232.
14. Cf. Edward J. Young, *Thy Word Is Truth*, p. 104.
15. Ibid., p. 107.
16. Cited in Robert Haldane, *Dieu a parlé*, p. 70.
17. Louis Gaussen, *The Inspiration of the Holy Scriptures*, trans. David D. Scott, pp. 165-66.

18. Ibid., pp. 160-61.
19. James I. Packer, *Fundamentalism and the Word of God*, p. 90.

CHAPTER 14

1. B. B. Warfield, *The Inspiration and Authority of the Bible*, p. 221.
2. François Prévost, *La Vie des Bêtes* (October 1965), 36. This magazine is published under the scientific control of Professor C. Bressou, member of the Paris Institute of Science and honorary director of the Veterinary School at Alfort.
3. Warfield, p. 435.
4. O. T. Allis, *The Five Books of Moses*, pp. 168-72.
5. Suggested in the Supplement to Peake's commentary, as alluded to by S. Van Mierlo, *La révélation divine*, p. 62.
6. Cf. John A. Witmer, "In Defense of the Infallible Word," *The Sunday School Times* CIV (October 27, 1962): 777, 782-83. Translator's note: Note also W. F. Albright, *The Archaeology of Palestine; Recent Discoveries in Bible Lands*.
7. Cf. article on Nineveh in René Pache, *Nouveau Dictionnaire Biblique*, pp. 529-31.
8. Warfield, p. 439.
9. Louis Gaussen, *The Inspiration of the Holy Scriptures*, trans. David D. Scott, p. 215.
10. See William F. Arndt and F. Wilbur Gingrich, eds., *A Greek-English Lexicon of the New Testament*, p. 207; A. Souter, *A Pocket Lexicon to the Greek New Testament*, p. 214.
11. F. F. Bruce, *On the Migration of Abraham*, p. 177.
12. Cf. F. F. Bruce, *The Acts of the Apostles*, p. 162; P. E. Kahle, *The Cairo Geniza*, pp. 143 ff.
13. Louis Gaussen, *The Inspiration of the Holy Scriptures*, trans. David D. Scott, pp. 15-16.
14. Erich Sauer, *From Eternity to Eternity*, p. 106.
15. Gaussen, pp. 254-55.
16. Robert Dick Wilson, cited in S. Van Mierlo, *La révélation divine*, pp. 100-101; see also R. D. Wilson, *A Scientific Investigation of the Old Testament*.
17. Charles Hodge, *Systematic Theology*, I:169.
18. Robert Watts, cited in Warfield, p. 204.
19. Sauer, pp. 122, 127.
20. Albert Lüscher, *Wenn das Wort nicht mehr soll gelten*, pp. 15-16.
21. Robert Dick Wilson, cited in Lüscher, p. 64.
22. J. C. Ryle, quoted by Frank E. Gaebelein, *The Meaning of Inspiration*, p. 25.

CHAPTER 15

1. John Calvin, *Institutes of the Christian Religion*, I:86-91.
2. Cf. Louis Gaussen, *The Canon of the Holy Scriptures*, trans. Edward Kirk, p. 26.
3. Josephus, *Against Apion* I. 8. 861-62.
4. Eusebius, *Evangelical Preparation* VIII. 6.
5. R. H. Pfeiffer, *Introduction to the Old Testament*, cited by Edward J. Young in N. B. Stonehouse and Paul Woolley, eds., *The Infallible Word*, p. 78.
6. Young, in Stonehouse and Woolley, pp. 79-80. For a detailed and convincing study of the Mosaic authorship of the Pentateuch, and its authority, see Oswald T. Allis, *The Five Books of Moses*.
7. See Harold H. Rowley, *The Growth of the Old Testament*, p. 170.
8. For a more detailed description of the Apocryphal books, consult the Bible dictionaries. Translator's note: See also Merrill F. Unger, "Apocrypha," *Introductory Guide to the Old Testament*.
9. Merrill F. Unger, "Apocrypha," *Unger's Bible Dictionary*, pp. 70-71.
10. Tertullian *Prescriptions*, chap. 36; cf. Gaussen, pp. 164-65.
11. Gaussen, p. 412.
12. Ibid., pp. 294-319.
13. Ibid., p. 427.
14. B. B. Warfield, *The Inspiration and Authority of the Bible*, pp. 412-13.
15. Erich Sauer, *From Eternity to Eternity*, p. 133.
16. Gaussen, pp. 431-32.

17. Ibid.
18. Charles Masson, *L'Epitre de St. Paul aux Ephésiens*, p. 228.
19. Charles Masson, *L'Epitre de St. Paul aux Colossiens*, p. 86.
20. Cf. Charles Masson, *Les deux Epitres de St. Paul aux Thessaloniciens*, pp. 9-13.
21. Herman Ridderbos, cited in *Revelation and the Bible*, ed. Carl F. H. Henry, pp. 191-92.

CHAPTER 16

1. Cf. Louis Gaussen, *The Inspiration of the Holy Scriptures*, trans. David D. Scott, pp. 171-72.
2. Suggested by Dr. A. Lamorte, "Manuscrits de la Mer Morte," in René Pache, *Nouveau Dictionnaire Biblique*, pp. 468-71.
3. Cf. R. D. Wilson, *A Scientific Investigation of the Old Testament*, p. 69; "The Textual Criticism of the Old Testament," *The Princeton Theological Review* XXVII (January 1929): 40 ff.
4. Gaussen, p. 169.
5. Wilson, *Scientific Investigation*, pp. 176 ff., 92-97.
6. Cf. Frederic Kenyon, *Our Bible and the Ancient Manuscripts*, p. 264; J. H. Skilton, cited in *The Infallible Word*, ed. N. B. Stonehouse and Paul Woolley, pp. 152 ff.
7. F. F. Bruce, *The Books and the Parchments*, p. 171.
8. Gaussen, p. 168.
9. B. F. Westcott and J. F. A. Hort, *The New Testament in the Original Greek*, p. 2.
10. B. B. Warfield, *An Introduction to the Textual Criticism of the Old Testament*, pp. 12 ff.: "The Greek Testament of Westcott and Hort," *The Presbyterian Review* III (April 1882): 356.
11. Cf. Albert Lüscher, *Wenn das Wort nicht mehr soll gelten*, p. 10.
12. Cf. Gaussen, p. 177.
13. Ibid., pp. 189-90.
14. Ibid., pp. 169-70.
15. Skilton, cited in Stonehouse and Woolley, pp. 160-63.
16. Bengel, cited in Gaussen, pp. 195-96.
17. Kenyon, p. 11.

CHAPTER 17

1. John Calvin, *Institutes of the Christian Religion*, I, 68-73, passim.
2. John Calvin, *Commentary on II Timothy 3:16*, p. 249.
3. Cf. A. Saphir, *Christ and the Scriptures*, pp. 86-87.
4. Erich Sauer, *From Eternity to Eternity*, p. 134.
5. Louis Gaussen, *The Inspiration of the Holy Scriptures*, trans. David D. Scott, pp. 119-23.
6. John Calvin, *Institutes*, I, 57.
7. Gaussen, p. 358.

PART IV

CHAPTER 18

1. See on this subject the excellent work of A. M. Hodgkin, *Christ in All the Scriptures*. Translator's note: See also Norman Geisler, *Christ: The Theme of the Bible*, 1968.
2. Erich Sauer, *From Eternity to Eternity*, p. 131.
3. H. C. G. Moule, cited in Frank E. Gaebelein, *The Meaning of Inspiration*, p. 25.
4. Christopher Wordsworth, *On the Inspiration of Holy Scripture*, p. 51.

CHAPTER 19

1. Frederic Farrar, Otto Pfleiderer, E. Stapfer, cited in B. B. Warfield, *The Inspiration and Authority of the Bible*, pp. 175-76.
2. Friedrich Tholuck, cited in ibid.
3. Richard Rothe, in *Zur Dogmatik*, cited in Warfield, pp. 177-78.
4. Ibid.

CHAPTER 20

1. Emil Brunner, in *Dogmatik* I, cited in Albert Lüscher, *Wenn das Wort nicht mehr soll gelten*, p. 13.
2. Augustine, cited in Philip Schaff, ed., *The Nicene and Post-Nicene Fathers*, III: 28, 353.
3. John Chrysostom, cited in Schaff, XI: 126-27.
4. Athanasius, cited in Schaff, IV: 552.
5. Origen, cited in Robert Haldane, *The Books of the Old and New Testaments Canonical and Inspired*, p. 131.
6. Jerome, cited in Schaff, VI: 101, 122.
7. Louis Gaussen, *The Inspiration of the Holy Scriptures*, trans. David D. Scott, p. 139.
8. Martin Luther, cited in M. Reu, *Luther and the Scriptures*, pp. 28, 24.
9. Martin Luther, cited in Reu, p. 17.
10. Ulrich Zwingli, cited in Jean Rilliet, *Zwingli, Third Man of the Reformation*, trans. Harold Knight, p. 79.
11. John Calvin, *Institutes of the Christian Religion*, I: 81-83.
12. Calvin, III, 173.
13. John Calvin, "Calvin's Reply to Sadoleto," in John Olin, *A Reformation Debate*, pp. 89, 92, 75.
14. Philip Schaff, *The Creeds of Christendom*, III: 360-62.
15. Ibid., p. 489.
16. Ibid., pp. 601-6.
17. Ibid., p. 831.
18. Ibid., pp. 387-88.
19. Cf. Robert Preus, *The Inspiration of the Scriptures*, p. 39.
20. Adolphe Monod, *Farewells*, pp. 92-93, 67.
21. J. H. Merle d'Aubigné, *The Authority of God*, pp. 48-191, passim.
22. Alexandre Vinet, *Vital Christianity, Essays and Discourses*, trans. Robert Turnbull, pp. 99-100.
23. Lewis Sperry Chafer, *Systematic Theology*, I: 61 ff.
24. Donald Grey Barnhouse, *The Invisible War*, pp. 10-11, 14.
25. W. R. Wallace, *If God Didn't Write the Bible, Who Did?*
26. William Culbertson, "The Foundation on Which We Stand," *Moody Monthly* LXVI (April 1966): 27, 48-50.
27. Billy Graham, "In Training for Christ," *Decision* (February 1962), p. 15.
28. James I. Packer, *Fundamentalism and the Word of God*, pp. 174-75.

CHAPTER 21

1. Louis Gaussen, *The Inspiration of the Holy Scriptures*, trans. David D. Scott, pp. 323 ff.
2. William Oesterley and Theodore Robinson, *Introduction to the Books of the Old Testament*, p. 63.
3. Karl Barth, *Church Dogmatics*, I, trans. Thomson and Knight, 528-29.
4. Ibid., p. 531.
5. Ibid., pp. 507-9.
6. Pierre Courthial, "La conception barthienne de l'Ecriture Sainte, examinée du point de vue réformé," *La Revue Réformée* XVII (1966/2): 1-35.
7. Ibid.
8. Barth, p. 502.
9. Courthial.
10. Emil Brunner, *The Theology of Crisis*, p. 41.
11. Emil Brunner, *The Mediator*, trans. Olive Wyon, p. 577.
12. R. A. Finlayson, cited in *Revelation and the Bible*, ed. Carl F. H. Henry, p. 225.
13. Emil Brunner, *Revelation and Reason*, trans. Olive Wyon, p. 290.
14. Courthial.
15. W. Temple, *Nature, Man, and God*, p. 317.
16. D. D. Williams, *What Present-Day Theologians Are Thinking*, pp. 64 ff.
17. Temple, p. 350.
18. R. A. Finlayson, cited in Henry, p. 227.

19. John Murray, cited in *The Infallible Word*, ed. N. B. Stonehouse and Paul Woolley, pp. 41-42.
20. Theodore Engelder, quoted by Finlayson, cited in Henry, p. 228.
21. Edward J. Young, *Thy Word Is Truth*, p. 241.
22. Robert Preus, *The Inspiration of the Scriptures*, pp. 16, 19.
23. James I. Packer, "Contemporary Views of Revelation," *Revelation and the Bible*, ed. Carl F. H. Henry, p. 94.
24. Ibid., pp. 97-98.
25. Cf. D. M. Lloyd-Jones, *Authority*, pp. 34-36.
26. Young, p. 24.
27. Packer, cited in Henry, pp. 99, 102-3.
28. Otto Piper, *God in History*, p. 61.
29. Hans Werner Bartsch, *Kerygma and Myth*.
30. Rudolf Bultmann, cited in P. E. Hughes, *Scripture and Myth*, p. 19.
31. Hughes, p. 27.
32. John A. T. Robinson, *Honest to God*, p. 22.
33. Martin Buber, cited in Robinson, pp. 46-48.
34. Robinson, p. 50.
35. Ibid., pp. 66-70.
36. Ibid., pp. 70 ff.
37. Billy Graham, "Is God Then Dead?" *Decision* (May 1966), pp. 14-15; cf. John I. Paton, "Is God Dead?" *Good News Broadcaster* (February 1966), pp. 3, 5.
38. Gaussen, p. 357.
39. R. A. Finlayson, "Contemporary Ideas of Inspiration," *Revelation and the Bible*, ed. Carl F. H. Henry, pp. 222, 229-30.
40. Jacques Ellul, "Jonas," *Foi et Vie*, No. 2 (March 1952).
41. S. Van Mierlo, *La révélation divine*, pp. 40-43.
42. Emil Brunner, *Eternal Hope*, trans. Harold Knight, p. 127; cf. Hughes, pp. 20-21.
43. A. Bentzen, cited in Henry, p. 342.
44. Finlayson, cited in Henry, p. 234.

PART V

CHAPTER 22

1. Suggested by Adolph Saphir, *Christ and the Scriptures*, pp. 46 ff.
2. Suggested by S. Van Mierlo, *La révélation divine*, p. 209.
3. F. A. Tatford, *Is the Bible Reliable?* p. 12.
4. Cf. Louis Gaussen, *The Inspiration of the Holy Scriptures*, trans. David D. Scott, pp. 345-46.
5. W. H. Fitchett, *Wesley and His Century*, pp. 123-24.
6. Adolphe Monod, *L'inspiration de la Bible prouvée par ses oeuvres*, p. 43.
7. Pascal, *Pensées*, cited in Saphir, p. 52.
8. Saphir, pp. 52-53.
9. Suggested by Frédéric Hoffet, *L'impérialisme protestant*, passim.
10. Saphir, pp. 54-55.
11. Ibid., p. 50.
12. Von Niebuhr, cited in Saphir, pp. 352-53.
13. Saphir, p. 50.
14. Ibid., p. 51.
15. August Neander, *Church History*, cited in Saphir, p. 51.
16. Cf. Gaussen, pp. 253-54.
17. Ibid., pp. 161, 171.
18. Bellarmine, *De Verbo Dei*, cited in ibid., p. 296.
19. Gaussen, pp. 304-5.

CHAPTER 23

1. J. H. Merle d'Aubigné, *The Authority of God*, p. 48.
2. Louis Gaussen, *The Inspiration of the Holy Scriptures*, trans. David D. Scott, p. 340.

3. Cf. Martyn Lloyd-Jones, *Authority*, pp. 41-43.
4. Robert Preus, *The Inspiration of the Scriptures*, pp. 97-99.
5. Emil Brunner, *The Mediator*, p. 323.
6. Emil Brunner, *Dogmatics* I, Prolegomena, trans. Olive Wyon, p. 13.
7. S. Van Mierlo, *La révélation divine*, p. 69.
8. Ibid.; cf. pp. 69-70.
9. T. Samuel Külling, *Bibel und Gemeinde* (October 1965), p. 344.
10. James I. Packer, *Fundamentalism and the Word of God*, pp. 72-73.
11. Lloyd-Jones, pp. 34-36.
12. Ibid., p. 40.
13. Gaussen, pp. 119-20.
14. Cited in ibid., pp. 121-22.
15. Bellarmine, *De Verbo Dei*, vol. II, chap. 19; vol. IV, chap. 3.
16. Gaussen, p. 123.
17. Suggested by Adolph Saphir, *Christ and the Scriptures*, pp. 115-42. Saphir was a Hebrew Christian, a much esteemed Presbyterian pastor in England.
18. F. E. Gaebelein, "The Unity of the Bible," *Revelation and the Bible*, ed. Carl F. H. Henry, p. 401.

BIBLIOGRAPHY

Albright, William F. *The Archaeology of Palestine.* Harmondsworth, England: Penguin, rev. ed., 1960.

———. *Recent Discoveries in Bible Lands.* New York: Funk & Wagnalls, 1956.

Allis, Oswald T. *The Five Books of Moses.* Philadelphia: Presb. & Ref., 1949.

Archer, Gleason L., Jr. *A Survey of Old Testament Introduction.* Chicago: Moody, 1964.

Arndt, William F. and Gingrich, F. Wilbur. *A Greek-English Lexicon of the New Testament.* Chicago: U. of Chicago, 1957.

Barnhouse, Donald Grey. *The Invisible War.* Grand Rapids: Zondervan, 1965.

Barth, Karl. *Church Dogmatics. Vol. I, 2.* Translated by Thomson & Knight. Edinburgh: T. & T. Clark, 1956.

Bartsch, Hans Werner, ed. *Kerygma and Myth.* Translated by Reginald H. Fuller. London: Soc. for Promotion of Chr. Knowledge, 1953.

Bruce, F. F. *The Acts of the Apostles.* London: Tyndale, 1956.

———. *The Books and the Parchments.* London: Pickering & Inglis, 1950.

Brunner, Emil. *Dogmatics.* Vol. I, Prolegomena. Translated by Olive Wyon. London: Lutterworth, n.d.

———. *Eternal Hope.* Translated by Harold Knight. Philadelphia: Westminster, 1954.

———. *The Mediator.* Translated by Olive Wyon. New York: Macmillan, 1934.

———. *Revelation and Reason.* Translated by Olive Wyon. Philadelphia: Westminster, 1946.

———. *The Theology of Crisis.* New York: Scribner, 1929.

Bultmann, Rudolf. *The Theology of the New Testament.* Translated by Kendrick Grobel. New York: Scribner, 1951.

Calvin, John. *Commentary on II Timothy 3:16.* Grand Rapids: Eerdmans, 1948.

———. *Institutes of the Christian Religion.* Vols. I, III. Translated by John Allen. Philadelphia: Presb. Bd. of C. E., 1956.

Chafer, Lewis Sperry. *Systematic Theology*. Vol. I. Dallas: Dallas Sem., 1947.

Courthial, Pierre. "La conception barthienne de l'Ecriture Sainte, examinée du point de vue réformé." *La Revue Réformée*, XVII (1966/2) :1-35.

Culbertson, William. "The Foundation on Which We Stand," *Moody Monthly*, LXVI (April 1966) : pp. 27, 48-50.

Ellul, Jacques. "Jonas," *Foi et Vie*, no. 2 (March 1952).

Fitchett, William H. *Wesley and His Century*. New York: Abingdon, 1917.

Gaebelein, Frank E. *The Meaning of Inspiration*. Chicago: Inter-Varsity, 1950.

Gaussen, Louis. *The Canon of the Holy Scriptures*. Translated by Edward Kirk. Boston: Amer. Tract Soc., 1862.

———. *The Inspiration of the Holy Scriptures*. Translated by David D. Scott. Chicago: Moody, n. d.

———. *La véritable doctrine de M. Gaussen sur l'inspiration des Ecritures, Trois Lettres*. Geneva, Switzerland: Richter, n. d.

Geisler, Norman. *Christ: The Theme of the Bible*. Chicago: Moody, 1968.

Geisler, Norman L. and Nix, William E. *A General Introduction to the Bible*. Chicago: Moody, 1968.

Graham, Billy "In Training for Christ," *Decision*, February 1962, p. 15.

———. "Is God Then Dead?" *Decision*, May 1966, pp. 14-15.

Haldane, Robert. *The Books of the Old and New Testaments Canonical and Inspired*. Boston: Amer. Doctrinal Tract Soc., 1846.

———. *Dieu a parlé*. Marseille: Voix de l'Evangile, n. d.

Hammond, T. C. *Inspiration and Authority*. London: Inter-Varsity, n. d.

Henry, Carl F. H. (ed.) *Revelation and the Bible*. Philadelphia: Presb. & Ref., 1958.

Hodge, Charles. *Systematic Theology*. Vol. I. Grand Rapids: Eerdmans, 1965.

Hodgkin, Alice M. *Christ in All the Scriptures*. London: Holmes, 1909.

Hoffet, Frédéric. *L'impérialisme protestant*. Paris: Flammarion, 1948.

Hughes, P. E. *Scripture and Myth*. London: Tyndale, 1956.

Kahle, P. E. *The Cairo Geniza*. New York: Frederick Praeger, 1947.

Kenyon, Frederic G. *Our Bible and the Ancient Manuscripts*. London: Eyre & Spottiswoode, 1940.

Külling, T. Samuel. *Bibel und Gemeinde*, October 1965, p. 344.

Lamorte, André. *La Bible et le plan de Dieu*. Vevey, Switzerland: Groupes Missionnaires, 1959.

————. *La nature de l'inspiration des Ecritures*. Beatenberg, Switzerland: Bibelschule, 1957.

Lloyd-Jones, D. Martyn. *Authority*. Chicago: Inter-Varsity, 1958.

Lüscher, Albert. *Die letzten Zeiten und das inspirierte Wort*. Langenthal, Germany: Pflug Verlag, 1954.

————. *Wenn das Wort nicht mehr soll gelten*. Langenthal, Germany: Pflug Verlag, 1951.

Manley, G. T., ed. *The New Bible Handbook*. London: Inter-Varsity, 1947.

Marcel, Pierre. "Invites à l'hérésie." *La Revue Réformée* (1964/3), pp. 16-26.

Masson, Charles. *L'Epitre de Saint-Paul aux Colossiens*. Neuchâtel, Switzerland: Delachaux et Niestlé, 1950.

————. *L'Epitre de Saint-Paul aux Ephésiens*. Neuchâtel, Switzerland: Delachaux et Niestlé, 1953.

————. *Les deux Epitres de Saint-Paul aux Thessaloniciens*. Neuchâtel, Switzerland: Delachaux et Niestlé, 1957.

Merle d'Aubigné, J. H. *The Authority of God*. New York: R. Carter, 1851.

Monod, Adolphe. *Farewells*. London: Banner of Truth, 1962.

————. *L'inspiration de la Bible prouvée par ses oeuvres*. Carrières-sous-Poissy, France: La Cause, n. d.

Oesterley, William and Robinson, Theodore. *An Introduction to the Books of the Old Testament*. New York: Macmillan, 1934.

Olin, John. *A Reformation Debate*. New York: Harper, 1966.

Pache, René. *The Future Life*. Translated by Helen Needham. Chicago: Moody, 1962.

————. *Nouveau Dictionnaire Biblique*. Vennes-sur-Lausanne, Switzerland: Editions Emmaüs, 1961.

————. *The Return of Jesus Christ*. Translated by William La Sor. Chicago: Moody, 1955.

Packer, James I. *Fundamentalism and the Word of God*. Grand Rapids: Eerdmans, 1958.

Paton, John I. "Is God Dead?" *Good News Broadcaster*, February 1966, pp. 3-5.

Piper, Otto A. *God in History*. New York: Macmillan, 1939.

Preus, Robert. *The Inspiration of the Scriptures*. London: Oliver & Boyd, 1953.

Pury, Roland de. *Qu'est-ce que le protestantisme?* Paris: Librairie Protestante, 1961.

Reid, J. K. S. *The Authority of Scripture*. New York: Harper, 1957.

Reu, M. *Luther and the Scriptures*. Columbus: Wartburg, 1944.

Rilliet, Jean. *Zwingli, Third Man of the Reformation*. Translated by Harold Knight. Philadelphia: Westminster, 1959.

Robinson, John A. T. *Honest to God*. Philadelphia: Westminster, 1963.

Rowley, Harold H. *The Growth of the Old Testament*. London: Hutchinson, 1950.

Saphir, Adolph. *Christ and the Scriptures*. New York: Gospel Pub., n. d.

Sauer, Erich. *From Eternity to Eternity*. Grand Rapids: Eerdmans, 1954.

Schaff, Philip. *The Creeds of Christendom*. Vol. III. New York: Harper, 1877.

———. *The Nicene and Post-Nicene Fathers*. New York: Scribner, 1893-1903.

Souter, Alexander. *A Pocket Lexicon to the Greek New Testament*. New York: Oxford U., 1916.

Stonehouse, N. B. and Woolley, Paul, eds. *The Infallible Word*. Grand Rapids: Eerdmans, 1953.

Tatford, F. A. *Is the Bible Reliable?* London: Henry E. Walter, n. d.

Temple, William. *Nature, Man, and God*. London: Macmillan, 1960.

Thiele, Edwin Richard. *The Mysterious Numbers of the Hebrew Kings*. Grand Rapids: Eerdmans, 1951.

Unger, Merrill F. *Introductory Guide to the Old Testament*. Grand Rapids: Zondervan, 1951.

Van Mierlo, S. *La révélation divine*. Neuchâtel, Switzerland: Delachaux et Niestlé, 1951.

Vinet, Alexandre. *Vital Christianity, Essays and Discourses*. Translated by Robert Turnbull. Boston: Gould, Kendall & Lincoln, 1845.

Wallace, W. R. *If God Didn't Write the Bible, Who Did?* Chicago: Am. Assoc. for Jewish Evangelism, 1954.

Warfield, B. B. "The Greek Testament of Westcott and Hort," *The Presbyterian Review*, III (April 1882) : 356.

———. *The Inspiration and Authority of the Bible*. Philadelphia: Presb. & Ref., 1964.

———. *An Introduction to the Textual Criticism of the New Testament*. London: Whittaker, 1907.

Wasserzug, Gertrud. *Gottes Wort Ist Gottes Wort*. Beatenberg, Switzerland: Bibelschule, n. d.

Westcott, B. F. and Hort, J. F. A. *The New Testament in the Original Greek*. Cambridge: Macmillan, 1882.

Williams, Daniel D. *What Present-day Theologians Are Thinking*. New York: Harper, 1952.

Wilson, Robert Dick. *Is Higher Criticism Scientific?* Philadelphia: Sunday School Times, 1922.

——. *A Scientific Investigation of the Old Testament.* Philadelphia: Sunday School Times, 1926.

——. "The Textual Criticism of the Old Testament," *Princeton Theological Review* XXVII (January 1929) : 40 ff.

Witmer, John. "In Defense of the Infallible Word," *Sunday School Times* CIV (October 27, 1962) : 777, 782-83.

Wordsworth, Christopher. *On the Inspiration of Holy Scripture.* Philadelphia: Herman Hooker, 1854.

Young, Edward J. *Thy Word Is Truth.* Grand Rapids: Eerdmans, 1957.

SUBJECT INDEX

Albright, W. F., 147
Alexandrian Codex, 180, 191
Allis, O. T., 144
Angel of the Lord, 20
Antichrist, 18
Apocrypha, 171-73
Archer, Gleason, 46
Attitude toward Scripture
  negative, by unsaved, 39
  positive, by saved, 39-40
Authority of Scripture
  attacks against, 313-24
  in early church, 308-9
  fruits of, 324-25
  in Israel, 306-7
  Jesus submissive to, 307
  source of, 304-6

Barnhouse, Donald Grey, 241-42
Barth, Karl, 253, 254-55, 268, 272-73
Bengel, J. A., 75, 198
Bible
  convicts of sin, 286-87
  eternal youth of, 293-94
  is living and active, 285-86
  is offensive armor, 302-3
  regenerates, 287-88
  sanctifies believer, 289-90
  withstands every assault, 291-92
Bible, inspiration of
  affirmed by Bible itself, 81-82
  affirmed by Christ and apostles,
    82-83
  apostles conscious of, when writing,
    84-85
Bible, superiority of
  over apocryphal books, 297-98
  over Hindu books, 299
  over Jewish Talmuds, 299
  over Koran, 298-99
  over tradition, 299-301
Bible, unity of
  assured by plan of salvation, 114-16
  miracle of, 111
  shown by continuance of doctrine,
    116-19

shown by parallelism of Scripture,
  111-13
Bible, universality of, 295-97
Biblical criticism
  appearance of, 250-52
  definition of, 248-50
  modernistic, 252-57
Bibliolatry, 133, 321-24
Bruce, F. F., 138, 153, 192
Brunner, Emil
  on biblical criticism, 255
  on fundamentalism, 131, 135
  on Genesis 1–2, 268
  on "personal encounter," 261
  on resurrection, 151
  on science and faith, 270
  on verbal inspiration, 233, 255, 315
Bultmann, Rudolf, 62-63, 65, 147, 262-
  63, 270, 273

Calvin, John, 60, 120-21, 165-66, 213,
  217, 250-51
Canon
  and Apocrypha, 171-73
  definition of, 159
  determined by inspiration, 159-61
  fruit of divine inspiration, 161-62
  guarded from doctrinal deviations,
    180-81
  Jewish order of books in, 170-71
  of New Testament, 173-78
  not established by authority, 178-81
  of Old Testament, 162-73
  protected against illegitimate books,
    180
  responsible for unity, 184-85
  war on, 181-82
Chafer, Lewis Sperry, 240-41
Christ
  attitude of, toward Scripture, 217-23
  authority of, 303-4
  central theme of Scripture, 215-16
  coming of, a fulfillment of scrip-
    tures, 216-17
  compared with Scriptures, 35-39
  pictured in Scripture, 279-80
  submissive to Scripture, 307

SELECTED SCRIPTURE INDEX